CONTEMPORARY HISTORY IN EUROPE

Contemporary History in Europe

EDITED BY DONALD CAMERON WATT
*Under the auspices of the Institute of Contemporary
History and Wiener Library, London*

INTRODUCTION BY ALAN BULLOCK

London
GEORGE ALLEN AND UNWIN LTD

FIRST PUBLISHED IN 1969

SBN 04 940027 4

PRINTED IN GREAT BRITAIN
in 11 on 12 point Plantin
BY C. TINLING AND CO. LIMITED
LIVERPOOL, LONDON AND PRESCOT

CONTENTS

CONTENTS

ACKNOWLEDGEMENTS

This volume of essays and papers could never have seen the light of day without the spadework put into the organization of the international conference on contemporary history held in London in October 1966, at which so many of them were first presented, by the Director and staff of the Institute of Contemporary History; or the grant for travel provided for that conference by the Ford Foundation. It would never have reached the printer without the meticulous effort put into its sub-editing by Mrs Ann Boas or the organizing ability of Miss Marion Bieber.

The papers here reprinted appear in the form in which they were originally delivered to the conference in October 1966, or printed in the *Journal of Contemporary History*. As a result the bibliographical footnotes do not, as a rule, cover material published since that date.

Our thanks are due to the editor of the *American Historical Review* for permission to reprint the article by Professor Arthur P. Mendel and to Harper & Row, publishers of the Harper Torchbooks edition of the *Journal of Contemporary History*, for permission to reprint the articles by Professor Allan G. Bogue, Dimitrije Djordjević, and Zoltán Horvath.

D. C. Watt

A*

ALAN BULLOCK

Introduction

There is an interesting essay to be written on the reasons for the
changed status and growth, since the war, in the study of contemporary history. Before the war any historian who showed an
interest in what had happened since 1914, even earlier, was looked
at askance by his colleagues and was liable to be accused of the
unprofessional activities of journalism and politics. Now, no
university blanches at the establishment of a centre of twentieth-
century history or shows surprise if some of the best of its history
graduates go on to work in the contemporary field.

If experience in Britain is at all typical, this change has certainly
not taken place because better answers have been found to the
questions which have always troubled historians about writing the
history of their own times: Is it possible to secure access to
reliable sources? How can the historian hope to achieve sufficient
impartiality when studying events which affect him personally?
Most important of all, how can the historian, when he does not
even know what happened next, obtain sufficient distance from
what he is writing about to put the events he describes into an
historical perspective? These questions, as many of the essays in
this volume show, still preoccupy those engaged in the study of
contemporary history, and I doubt if they have got nearer to
answering them to their own satisfaction than Thucydides or
Clarendon did.

No, the explanation must lie in a different direction, in a combination of circumstances powerful enough to overcome these
drawbacks and the doubts and inhibitions they create and to
attract men and women, who could perfectly well have made a
reputation in the study of other periods of history, to work in a
field so full of pitfalls. For no one who wants a quiet scholarly life,
remote from all but academic controversy, or who dreams of
writing a definitive study would choose to work on the history of

the past fifty years. What has this combination of circumstances been?

First, interest. The events through which we have lived since 1914 seem to me to exceed in sheer magnitude, pace, and intensity those of all but a few earlier periods of history. At what other period can one find crowded into the space of fifty years such a succession of events as the two world wars, the Russian Revolution, the Great Depression, the New Deal, the rise and fall of Hitler, the spread of communism, the cold war, the Chinese Revolution, the end of the colonial empires, the emergence of the Asian and African peoples into world history, the discovery of nuclear power, and the first stages in the exploration of space? Judged either by their intrinsic interest or by their impact on human lives, each of these offers an intellectual challenge to anyone eager to search into the causes and sequence of historical change.

Second, a sense of urgency—the conviction that there were facts to be revealed (the facts about the concentration camps, for instance) and lessons to be drawn (such as the price of appeasing the nazis) which it was urgent to bring to the attention of as many people as possible if they were to learn from their own experience and avoid similar disasters in the future.

Third, luck. The capture of the archives of the German Government and the evidence brought to light in the war crimes trials opened up, as never before so soon after the event, the secret history of twelve of the most dramatic years of European history. Far from being denied access to original sources—the most familiar objection to serious study of the recent past—contemporary historians were offered an opportunity rarely enjoyed by the student of any period.

Fourth, experience. The war brought many academics out of their university environment and involved them, whether in the forces, in intelligence or propaganda work, government departments, or in the Resistance, in events which they have later gone back to study and write about. Others have doubled a career in diplomacy (George Kennan, for example) or journalism (Elizabeth Wiskemann and Isaac Deutscher) with the writing of contemporary history or have combined periods of government service with an academic career (Herbert Feis and Arthur Schlesinger, for instance). Contemporary history can never be a professional preserve and it has only been enriched by the constant irruption into it of politicians, from Trotsky to Churchill, and the contribution of writers and teachers with experience outside the academic world.

Fifth, demand. The remarkable increase in the market for well-written history dealing with almost every period of the past is one of the features of post-war publishing, but nowhere has this been more marked than in the demand for accounts of the history of our own time, the events of which have powerfully influenced the lives of all of us. Such considerations may be deplored by those who believe academic pursuits should be sharply separated from the world of popular education, paperbacks, and the mass media, but it is precisely because contemporary history affords a bridge between historical scholarship and the interests and experience of the surrounding world, because it can never be a cloistered pursuit or an intellectual refuge that many of its best practitioners have been attracted to it.

Without pretending that this is at all an exhaustive list, these seem to me to be some of the most important circumstances which combined, after the war, to give a sufficiently powerful impetus to the study of contemporary history to overcome the traditional objections and establish it as a difficult but accepted part of historical studies.

We are now in the second stage of its development, marked by the attempt to develop a more systematic approach by organizing research and building up those aids to the study of contemporary history—graduate training, collections of source material, reference libraries, bibliographies, specialist journals and conferences, the regular communication of work in progress and of information about the accessibility of records—which have long been common in the study of earlier periods. This is particularly hard in a field in which the wealth of new material becoming available all the time (for example, by the lowering of the restricted period for British official records from fifty to thirty years) can easily appear overwhelming, but it is a task which has to be undertaken if training and opportunities for research are to be provided for younger historians who may lack the personal experience of the immediate post-war generation, but who can develop the study of twentieth-century history by establishing a tradition of historical scholarship and by bringing in new fields such as the social and intellectual history of the century which have been comparatively neglected.

The lead has been taken by such institutions as the Munich

Institut für Zeitgeschichte (with a periodical now in its sixteenth year), and by a rapidly increasing number of university centres in Europe and the United States. The difficulty now, indeed, is to keep track of all that is going on outside one's own country and particular field of study. In an effort to improve communications, the Institute of Contemporary History in London organized an international conference in October 1966. Historians from Eastern as well as Western Europe and the United States were invited to attend and to contribute a series of reports on the study of contemporary history in their countries. The result is the present volume.

Anyone familiar with the problems of organizing such a co-operative effort on an international basis will not be surprised at the difficulties which were encountered. Several of the reports were delayed; no report was received from the Soviet Union and the gap has had to be filled by a contribution from an American and a British scholar; as in all co-operative works, differences in approach are apparent as well as in the interpretation of the organizers' requirements. If anyone wishes to say that the product is not so much a book as a collection of working papers, he will be ✓ right. But this is what it was intended to be, and for anyone actively engaged in the study of contemporary history this is precisely its value.

Here for the first time it is possible to see, within the compass of a single volume, but without any attempt to impose a common editorial stamp on them, the variety of approaches and assumptions with which historians in more than a dozen countries are pursuing the study of the twentieth century. At the same time, I know of nowhere else where so much valuable information is gathered together about work in progress, new lines of research, collections of material, institutions, libraries, journals, and much else that the working historian needs to know and often finds surprisingly difficult and time-consuming to discover. Of course it could be improved but what matters is that it has been done for the first time.

With this publication, Mr Laqueur's Institute has made a highly practical contribution to the historical study of the twentieth century and if some means can be found, possibly through the Institute's Journal or through further conferences, to keep the information up to date, the Institute will put contemporary historians still further in its debt.

Biographical Notes on Contributors

JOHN BARNES, Lecturer in Political Science at the London School of Economics and Political Science, is at present working on a biography of Admiral of the Fleet Earl Beatty, whose papers he is editing for the Navy Records Society, and on a biography of Stanley Baldwin (in conjunction with R. K. Middlemas).

KAREL BARTOŠEK, graduated in history and philosophy at the Charles University in Prague. Since 1960 he has worked at the Historical Institute of the Czechoslovak Academy of Sciences. He is co-author of a study of the 1945 Prague rising and of a textbook of twentieth-century history for grammar school students. He is at present writing a history of the Czechoslovak Resistance.

ALLAN G. BOGUE, Professor of American History at the University of Wisconsin, has published *Money at Interest* (1955); *From Prairie to Corn Belt* (1963); and various articles on the economic and social development of the American West. His current research interest involves the application of social science methods to the political and legislative history of mid-nineteenth-century America.

DIMITRIJE DJORDJEVIĆ, senior staff member of the Historical Institute of the Serbian Academy of Sciences and Arts in Belgrade, has published, *inter alia, Serbia's Outlet to the Adriatic Sea and the Ambassadors' Conference in London, 1912* (1958); *Milovan Milovanović*, a biography (1962); *Austro-Serbian Customs War 1906–1911* (1962), all in Serbian; and *Revolutions nationales des peuples balkaniques 1804–1914* (1965).

H. W. VON DER DUNK, who works at the Netherlands Institute of History, will shortly publish a book on Belgian-German relations, 1830–48.

JOHN ERICKSON is Reader in Defence Studies, University of Edinburgh. He is the author of *Panslavism* (1964); *The Soviet High Command* (1962); and editor of *The Military-Technical Revolution* (1966).

HANS HERZFELD, Professor Emeritus of Modern History at the Free University of Berlin, has published *inter alia* a two-volume biography of Johannes von Miguel; *Die moderne Welt* (2 Vols., 1952); *Das Problem des deutschen Heeres 1919–1945* (1952); and *Die Weimarer Republik* (1966).

ZOLTÁN HORVATH, historian, formerly journalist. Publications include *Turn of the Nineteenth Century in Hungary* (1960); *Count Lászlo Teleki* (1964); and *Ungarische Jahrhundertwende* (1966).

LUDWIG JEDLICKA, Director of the Austrian Institute of Contemporary History, Professor of History, University of Vienna and author of, *inter alia*, *Ein Heer im Schatten der Parteien, die militärpolitische Lage Oesterreichs 1918–1938* (1955); and *Der 20 Juli 1944 in Oesterreich* (1966).

LEO KAHN, Principal Archivist at the Foreign Documents Centre of the Imperial War Museum, London, is engaged in preparing a guide to German records (1918–45) in European and American repositories.

HELMUT KRAUSNICK, Director of the Institut für Zeitgeschichte, Munich, editor of the *Vierteljahreshefte für Zeitgeschichte* and author of many publications on German contemporary history.

ARTHUR P. MENDEL, Professor at the University of Michigan, is interested in Russian intellectual history. He is the author of *Dilemmas of Progress in Tsarist Russia* (1961).

CLAUDIO PAVONE is head of the Ufficio Studi e Pubblicazioni of the directorate-general of the Italian State Archives. His studies of the *Risorgimento* and of united Italy have been particularly concerned with the administrative unification of the kingdom and with the Resistance.

RENÉ RÉMOND, Professor at the Paris Institut d'Études Politiques and director of research at the Fondation Nationale des Sciences Politiques, is the author, *inter alia*, of *Lamennais et la démocracie; Les Etats-Unis devant l'opinion française; La Droite en France: de la Ière Restauration à la Ve République*.

JOAQUIN ROMERO-MAURA is a graduate of the Faculty of Law of Barcelona University and is now conducting research into Spanish politics, 1899–1909, at St Antony's College, Oxford.

FRANTISEK RYSZKA, Professor of Contemporary History at the Institute of History of the Polish Academy of Science. His two principal recent works are an inquiry into the state and legal system of the Third Reich and a study of Nazi Germany entitled *Night and Fog*.

ROBERT RHODES JAMES, a Junior Research Fellow of All Souls College, Oxford, and a former Senior Clerk of the House of Commons, has published, *inter alia*, biographies of Lord Randolph Churchill (1959) and Lord Roseberry (1963) and a study of the Gallipoli Campaign (1965).

DAVID SHAPIRO, Senior Lecturer in Government at the University of Essex, has published a *Bibliography of Russian History 1801–1917* (1962), and edited *The Right in France, 1890–1919* (1962).

F. TICHELMAN, Graduate in History of Leyden University 1949–56; since 1964 head of the Afro-Asian Department of the International Institute of Social History, Amsterdam. He specializes in early Indonesian communism and the colonial policy of the Dutch socialist movement.

KRISTER WHALBÄCK has been Research Associate at the Political Science Department in the University of Stockholm since 1965. He is the author of *Einlandsfragen i svensk politik 1937–1940*.

DONALD CAMERON WATT, since 1963 Reader in International History at the University of London, London School of Economics and Political Science; former member of the British team of historians engaged in studying and selecting captured German diplomatic documents; editor of the series 'Survey of International Affairs' of the Royal Institute of International Affairs. He is, *inter alia*, the author of: *Britain Looks to Germany* (1965); *Personalities and Politics; Studies in the formulation of British Foreign Policy in the Twentieth Century* (1965); *Survey of International Affairs 1961* (1966); with K. Bourne (eds.) *Studies in International History* (1967); and numerous articles on contemporary history.

NEVILLE WAITES, Lecturer in French History at the University of Reading, is completing a doctoral thesis on 'Anglo-French relations and the German problem, 1929–1934' and is writing a biography of Aristide Briand to be published in 1970.

STUART WOOLF, Reader in Italian History at the University of Reading and Director of the Centre for the Advanced Study of Italian Society, recently established at Reading, has published, *inter alia*, *Studi sulla nobiltà piemontese nell'epoca dell' assolutismo* (1963) and *Italian Public Enterprise* (1965), and is editor of *European Fascism* (1968).

Britain

ROBERT RHODES JAMES

Soldiers and Biographers

In his diverting account of the curious processes by which, in 1935, he was elected to Parliament as the Junior Burgess for Oxford University, Sir Alan Herbert has described the value of being obliged 'to display all one's political eggs in one basket', for 'one discovers how few the eggs are and of what irregular shapes and sizes'.[1] It is equally salutary for the historian to be compelled to set forth his views on the study of history, and then to contemplate the result. One of the major problems of contemporary life is to find time to *think* amid the helter-skelter of distracting problems and under the ever-increasing burden of routine tasks. And for the historian, no less than for the politician, the civil servant, or the industrialist, a period of pondering the themes of where he is going and why he is going there is both necessary and sobering.

Inevitably, the views of any historian on history and historiography reflect his personal prejudices and academic training. It may be true that English historians often hunt in packs, but the attitudes of most historians tend to be individualistic, and the influences that weighed most heavily in youth usually remain dominant. Thus, when any historian—however sincerely—attempts to discuss historical research and writing he is unconsciously indulging in at least some degree of self-justification. It is, after all, asking a lot to expect anyone to admit, even to himself, that he has been wasting his time. We are all, to some extent or other, prisoners of our individual background, personalities, training, and attitudes.

For the study of history is to the historian a devotional exercise. The historian falls in love with history, and the devotion is lifelong and intense. It is accordingly extremely difficult for him to write with complete dispassion on the subject. However valiantly he may strive to stand apart and deliver a detached judgment, he is emotionally and professionally too deeply involved to do this really successfully. Thus it is that commentaries on history written by historians tend to throw more light on the authors than on the subject. As history, in Geyl's words, is indeed an argument without end, absolute precision is impossible. But it is invaluable, for historian and student, that the former's beliefs should be displayed if only—to refer again to Sir Alan Herbert—to demonstrate to him how few the eggs are, and how irregular in shape and size.

The past year has seen a considerable amount of introspective activity in English historiography, including an entire issue of *The Times Literary Supplement* (7 April 1966) devoted to the subject, and a spirited assault by Professor Barraclough on the 'obsession with causality' and the 'almost neurotic absorption in questions of motivation' that he detects in recent historical work.[2] Such discussions give public expression to feelings of concern about certain tendencies in contemporary historiography. But it is more easy to admit to the existence of these emotions than to specify their causes with exactness. Here, again, we are all prisoners of our own attitudes and prejudices.

Professor Barraclough has re-opened the unending debate on 'objective' and 'interpretative' attitudes towards the study of history. 'By casting doubt on the validity of objective history', he has written, 'and exalting intuition, Dilthey and Rickert permanently weakened the foundation of western historiography.' One does not have to accept Barraclough's entire case in order to agree warmly with many of his comments, and particularly with his condemnation of 'the moral relativism which excuses anything and everything on grounds of time and place, or at the clumsy, heavy-handed verdicts which simply reflect the historian's own moral prejudices'. It is right to be reminded of these superficial and dangerous tendencies, and also of the continuous peril, so often unheeded, of putting forward opinions disguised as facts. But Sir Isaiah Berlin has summarized the opposition to Barraclough's argument when he wrote in 1961 that 'it is the purpose of historians to understand and to explain; they are mistaken only if they think that to explain is *ipso facto* to justify or explain away'.

All history, to quote a phrase of Gibbon, is 'a nice and obscure business', and the formation of 'a consistent and probable narrative' is one of the prime tasks of an historian. How easy to say! And how difficult to achieve! I have much sympathy with a close friend and fellow-historian who observed after a recent discussion on the study and writing of history that 'I sometimes feel that we are all engaged upon a gigantic confidence trick'. Such doubts and apprehensions must assail all historians if they ponder the immensity of the task on which they are engaged; as Tawney once wrote: 'The first feeling of a person who sees a manuscript collection such as that at Holkham must be "If fifty maids with fifty mops—", and a sad consciousness that the mop which he wields is a very feeble one.'

It is customary for historians, when asked to justify their existence and purpose, to declare almost by reflex action that their function is to pursue and elicit Truth. But how? It is on this point that the controversies are aroused. It is urged by some that the historian must eschew judgment—particularly on motives and causes—and confine himself rigorously to the discovery and presentation of facts. This argument is met by the query as to what extent an edifice of facts can by itself provide Truth. And how can Truth be arrived at if motives and causes are ignored? It is when such questions are asked that the statement of Kierkegaard (quoted with approval by Barraclough) that 'history has to do with results; motives and intentions are the business of ethics', becomes so unsatisfying. For this implies that the principal task of the historian is the garnering of facts and the setting forth of results, which can then be left to deliver their own message. This argument seems to be not dissimilar to saying that the task of the archaeologist ends when he has uncovered, retrieved, and factually described an object. It is an argument which diminishes the responsibility of the historian, and makes his task considerably less complex. If the duty of interpretation and of endeavouring to reach full comprehension is removed from the historian, what remains except a mechanic? And to what extent, it is asked, can such an exercise be described as 'a pursuit after Truth'? If an example may be taken from the literary world, Mr Painter's biography of Proust,[3] which is almost entirely interpretative, would not be described as a pursuit after Truth by the exponents of 'objective' history, when it is manifestly clear that the work is precisely that. For it is not Mr Painter's conclusions that would be challenged by the devotees of objective history but his method. Such examples emphasize the complexity of the debate.

For the purpose of illustrating aspects of this general debate in current English historiography, it is relevant to consider recent trends in military history and political biography. These two specialized fields are of particular interest in that each has a considerable attraction to authors from outside the professional academic ranks and each has considerable popularity among the general readership. It is also in these two sectors that the proponents of what might be called 'pure' objective historiography see much to criticize and much to support their argument that the foundations of serious historical study have been undermined.

The tidal wave of books on the subject of the First World War provides one example. For the past ten years this wave has rolled inexorably across the historical hinterland. The first conspicuous feature of this phenomenon is the smallness of the contribution made by professional—by which I mean academically professional —historians.

It would be lamentable if historiography became a closed-shop business, and many notable contributions to our knowledge have been made by so-called amateur historians, but the re-writing of the history of the Great War that has taken place must arouse many qualms. The fact that, until very recently, the British official archives were not available for inspection meant that the majority of these works were merely reassessments (in some cases re-hashes) of existing published material. Furthermore, in some instances these reassessments have been based on an extremely cursory and arbitrary selection of these works. This has not inhibited many of the authors from delivering sweeping judgments on men and events which, taken by themselves, fully merit Barraclough's assault upon 'the chase after causes and motives' as 'high-class entertainment, the historian's version of the "whodunit"'. Many of these works have indeed provided high-class entertainment, and the skill with which the old material has been refurbished for contemporary taste has been considerable—although now and then the final gloss has betrayed the source. In one case, a highly dramatic account of a commander personally decoding 'with the cipher book and the device like a bowstring which was used for decoding cables' the message informing him of his dismissal, turned out to be based upon an allusion in the commander's account to the ancient Turkish method of strangulation! This is not a very serious example. In some instances the distortions were significant; they were based less on incompetence than on an obsession with the dramatic and the picturesque.

For the prime fault in the great majority of these books was one of perspective. In military history it is often extremely difficult to determine the relative significance of events. But it is the most common fault of the journalist-in-history to select the most *interesting*. Every historian is entitled to give his own estimate of the relative importance of events, but in many cases it is plain that the dominant consideration is to interest the reader.

It is curious that military history has a particular attraction for the journalist-in-history. It is not only curious but unfortunate, because the science of military history—and particularly modern military history—is one of exceptional complexity. To establish even the most simple military facts is often extremely difficult. In the first place, contemporary records—if they exist at all—are highly suspect. British War Diaries and naval Reports of Proceedings are usually written under severe difficulties, and even if the officer preparing one had all the facts available to him—which is improbable—it is unlikely that they would be set out with complete dispassion. In a recent discussion on this subject, Admiral Sir Peter Gretton remarked that:

'I hope that historians will take into account the fact that human nature is weak, and although all the facts may be available, very often the main motive behind the Report of Proceedings will be to show the actions of the ship or squadron concerned in the best possible light.'[4]

Personal recollections of participants, at all levels, tend to be unsatisfactory. Official despatches are as trustworthy as the memoirs of generals. The very nature of war means that, very often, the truth of what really happened is known only to the dead. In a war of rapid movement more precision is usually possible, and presents fewer problems than, for example, the Western Front in the First World War. It is a weird experience to attempt to discover military facts from the confused and often contradictory fragments of information that every major battle or campaign throws up. The task is of such difficulty that the historian is often thrown back on what Gibbon called 'a consistent and probable narrative'. But many of the modern generation of journalists-in-history sail blithely through it with supreme self-confidence, scattering praise and blame with untroubled abandon as they proceed.

The fact that professional historians have not contributed greatly towards this extensive re-writing of the history of the Great War can be ascribed in part to the lack of adequate material. But only in part. With a few notable exceptions, the writing of good military history in this country seems to be at a low ebb, and the professional military historians do not, collectively, impress when compared with the sociologists or political historians. It is thus hardly appropriate for the professionals to lament the invasion into the military field of outsiders when their own contribution outside the official histories has been so inadequate. Captain Cyril Falls, in his recent account of Caporetto,[5] and an American, Professor A. J. Marder, in his remarkable work *From the Dreadnought to Scapa Flow*, have made us acutely conscious of the inadequacies of recent military history in this country—and particularly on the First World War. These criticisms are particularly applicable to military biography, which has been somewhat neglected of late by professional military historians. The military historian finds it particularly difficult to accept the concept of history being entirely 'the business of results'; he is deeply interested in *why* certain military events occurred. It is therefore all the more strange that this particular aspect of military history has been so neglected by the professionals. Mr David Chandler's monumental examination of Napoleon's campaigns[6] emphasizes the contribution that can be made by a detailed examination of the methods and techniques of commanders.

Looking at the current scene in military historiography in Britain, one is driven to the conclusion that the 'interpretive' concept has often been carried so far away from serious and profound study that it has given its critics much to fasten upon. But can this failure really justify a wholesale rejection of interpretive history?

The predicament of English political biography is not dissimilar. A reviewer in a recent issue of *The Times Literary Supplement* majestically lamented the low standards of contemporary political biography. In view of the considerable number of serious political biographies that have appeared in the past few years—and which include J. H. Plumb's biography of Walpole,[7] C. W. New's unfinished study of Brougham,[8] and the first volume of Professor Gash's biography of Peel[9]—this condemnation may appear to be both sweeping and ungenerous. Yet it is not difficult to feel sympathy with the anonymous reviewer.

The relevance of biography is often challenged by historians. The historian's complaint against the biographer is that, by isolating a single individual, he puts too strong a light on one tiny detail in a vast canvas and leaves the rest plunged in darkness. This is a valid criticism. It can be said in defence of the biographer that, by this isolation, he often provides the kind of illumination which is the historian's principal task. Biography *en masse* has become wholly accepted since Namier showed the way, but the contribution of the individual biography is still viewed with reserve by many historians. But it can at least be said that if the biographer makes *any* significant contribution to our knowledge of the past he has justified himself. And I have no doubt that, even on this level, the contribution of the biographer can be a very real one. If examples are requested to support this contention, I would cite Miss Perham's admirable biography of Lugard.[10]

The popularity of military history is surpassed only by that of biography, and a certain type of political biography—which I would describe more appositely as biographies of politicians—is no exception. But it is strange that the concept of the 'Victorian' political biography refuses to die. It has been assailed constantly, from Von Ruville (who declared that it was 'a hybrid species, the cultivation of which is of no benefit to science')[11] to Lytton Strachey (who raged against their 'ill-digested masses of material, their slipshod style, their tone of tedious panegyric, their lamentable lack of selection, of detachment, of design')[12] up to the present day. The modern version of the 'Victorian' official political biography is more lively and often better constructed than its predecessor, and in some instances—notably Robert Blake's biography of Bonar Law[13] and Lord Birkenhead's *Halifax*[14]—the results are successful. It is difficult to be equally enthusiastic about the memorials to Lord Waverley,[15] Herbert Samuel,[16] or Aneurin Bevan.[17] And it is evident that Mr Randolph Churchill's biography of his father is to be based firmly on his father's dictum that 'it is not by the soft touches of a picture, but in hard mosaic or tessellated pavement that a man's life and fortunes must be presented in all their reality and romance'.[18]

But the most interesting development in recent years has been the emergence of the 'revising' political biography, in which there is a return to original sources and employment of new material from other sources in order to provide a balanced reassessment of an existing portrait.

Although the official political biographer suffers from restrictions which are usually well understood—not the least of which is the problem, as Rosebery put it, of threading a living crowd[19]—the 'revising' biographer is confronted with problems which are no less complex, although different. These difficulties are greatly increased when an historian undertakes the task. The professional biographer does not experience the qualms that assail the historian when he turns to biography, for the historian is haunted by the presence of the other figures on the canvas. Thus, the historian accordingly tends to write the 'Life and Times' type of biography, almost falling over himself in his eagerness to prove his bona fides to his fellow-historians.

Dominating everything is the problem of the balance between the public and the private life. Put simply—perhaps over-simply— the historian is interested in his subject as an historical figure; the biographer's interest is a personal rather than an historical one. The historian, moreover, often feels under an obligation to tell all, thus in method at least following the 'Victorian' concept of political biography, in which the public man swamps the private one. If biography is indeed, in Gosse's definition,[20] 'the faithful portrait of a soul in its adventures through life', the historian is often an unsatisfactory biographer.

But the reaction away from the Victorian concept can result in an imbalance which is no less serious and is indeed, from the historical point of view, much more serious. The case of Gladstone is relevant. Morley[21] dwelt heavily upon the public life; Sir Philip Magnus-Allcroft[22] concentrated too much on the personal.

A political biographer who is uninterested in his subject's career and historical significance is worthless to the historian, and there have been several instances in revising biographies when it is clear that the authors had no real interest in the very thing that gave their subjects their relevance. A politician must be examined—to adapt Dryden's phrase—*both* in the rooms of State and in his private lodgings where he is 'in his undress'. The revising biographer has the opportunity to do this. But how often is it done?

Unhappily, the standards of accuracy and completeness in some revising biographies have not been as high as they ought to have been. It is depressing to realize that one biographer completely omitted a vital correspondence which he had not troubled to consult, or that another entirely ignored an important and crucial episode, or that a third—although he claimed to have studied original sources—included material which faithfully reproduced not merely the inaccuracies (including misprints) but wholly incorrect deductions (based on an error of dating) of its Victorian predecessor. Incidents such as these help to explain the suspicion with which many historians regard biography.

Political biography requires so many exceptional qualities in the biographer that it is not surprising that so much dissatisfaction exists. The real problem for the serious political biographer is to attempt to keep the balance between an arid Life and Times work and a personal study. There is the problem. The solution is less simply expressed! But at least it must be attempted.

But it is questionable whether academic historians can really be successful political biographers. Politics is a way of life, a manner of existence, a passion and a religion that demands total commitment; the study of history makes comparable demands. The gulf between the political world and academics 'scribbling laboriously by the light of shaded lamps', to quote Sir Harold Nicolson on the Victorian biographers,[23] is vast indeed. There is often in the attitude of the academic to politics an awed fascination, alas not untinged with complacency. The petty compromises, the blows to self-esteem, the necessity for caution, the frustrations and sheer physical strain—all these things that are the daily lot of the politician are unknown to the great majority of academics. And then, the Westminster Square Mile has its rules and its conventions. On some matters it is free-and-easy, on others prudish. By one of those delicious ironies that render life so enjoyable, what is accepted and not accepted at Westminster is almost exactly the opposite of what is approved and frowned upon in the academic world. There is accordingly in many political histories and biographies written by academic historians something just wrong. It is often very difficult to put one's finger on it, but it exists. Sir Ivor Jenning's much-admired works[24] were not greatly thought of in the House of Commons, and one had only to spend a week in the Commons to understand why. Jennings simply was not breathing the same air. But it was very difficult to quote chapter and verse for this emotion. To change metaphors, it was like a tone-deaf scholar of immense erudition, integrity, and sincerity undertaking a biography of Beethoven.

These strictures may appear harsh and unreasonable. The link between historiography and public life is not strong at the present. The academic 'revising' biographers have made some formidable contributions, of which the latest is Mr Blake's biography of Disraeli.[25] Nevertheless, one is conscious of a gap between the academic historians and the reality of politics which in some cases—such as that of Mr Blake—is small, but in others is more considerable and accordingly serious.

As in the case of military history, the domination in serious political biography of professional writers who are not professional historians has given the exponents of 'objective' history much to fasten upon. But, as in the case of the military historian, the political biographer is deeply concerned with causes and motives in history. And, again, documentary information (except perhaps in the case of a Gladstone) cannot tell the full story. The interpretive part of the biographer's task is, accordingly, a crucial one. At present, one feels that many of the academic biographers fail because of a lack of true comprehension of politics, and the professional non-academic biographers are often deficient in the depth of their research and too confident in ascribing motives to their subjects. If it is accepted that the biographer *can* fairly add a new dimension to our understanding of history, then it is essential that the responsibilities he bears are fully understood by himself. It is surely possible for the serious political biographer to justify himself to the point that the adherents of pure objective history are obliged to concede the significance of his contribution. As in the case of recent military history, it is the *manner* in which the task has often been approached that has given the critics of interpretive history an unnecessary amount of ammunition.

But this brings us back to our central dilemma. Is it proper for the military historian or the political biographer to indulge themselves by meddling in matters of causation or motivation? For if this were conceded, how could the right be withheld from the sociologist, the economic historian, or any historian working in any field?

In these two specialized sections one can see the debate on methods and objectives. Both in the 'instant' histories of the First World War, and in the often shallow political biographies that have appeared in recent years, one can see very considerable literary abilities and imaginative qualities being exercised to the detriment of deeper scholarship. In the wider field of historiography one can also see concern among many professional historians at the manner in which, in their estimation, history is being handled, particularly by 'popular' historians. The reaction of professional historians has often been sharp. There is in this something of the resentment against the successful (and often rich) historian, which is unattractive. But the most usual reason is the simpler one, dismay at seeing what seems to the critic to be the mangling of something sacred and precious.

Mr A. J. P. Taylor, however, is a 'popular' historian who defies categorization. His *English History, 1914–1945*[26] was an astounding technical achievement. The narrative control, over more than 600 pages, is remarkable in itself. But on occasions a price has had to be paid in strict accuracy; as this book is likely to be the standard work in schools and universities for a long time, these are much more serious than would otherwise be the case.

But the paths to Truth are many, and the provocative historian is the type of historian we can least afford to denigrate. The attraction and real contribution of Christopher Hill, Eric Hobsbawm, and Taylor lies in the fact that each has a personal and interpretative attitude to history that may jar on the reader—Mr Hobsbawm's Marxism is one of my favourite stimulants—but reveals the mental equipment and wide interests of the author. This seems to me to be a positive contribution to our knowledge of the past; the interpretations may be challenged, but the research that was provoked by this individualism is invaluable. In this sense, the two paths of the objective and interpretative views of history come very close. Hill is respected at Oxford in much the same way that the late Richard Pares was respected. Taylor has done more than any other contemporary historian to make non-historians interested in history. Hobsbawm is a major figure in contemporary historiography, as his *Age of Revolution* and *Labouring Men*[27] have demonstrated.

Each of these three major historians can write. Although it is of course true that ability to communicate learning is not given to everyone, it is unreasonable to view with suspicion those historians who have—and have taken pains to acquire—this capacity. Mr Vincent's recent study of the formation of the Liberal Party[28] and Mr F. S. L. Lyons's *The Fall of Parnell*[29] have reminded us that serious research and serious findings can be presented well. To throw a lump of historical matter at the head of the reader is not particularly flattering to the recipient—whether he be amateur or professional. The peril for the fluent writer lies simply in the fluency itself. When fascination with writing rather than absorption in the study of history itself takes over, the decline is too often swift and lamentable. Here, again, Taylor defies categorization.

When it seems that the writer has taken over from the historian, lo! he turns on his tracks.

So much history is being written now that it would be simple to prove by copious examples either that we are in the midst of a trough or are passing through a glorious period of discovery and excitement. As I said at the outset, the historian is an individual, and his approach, compounded of so many factors and elements, must be individualistic. There is accordingly no pattern in the contemporary scene in English historiography. The true historian will always be a mournful and tragical figure, for he alone knows how feeble and imperfect is his personal contribution. He feels the crushing responsibility of his vocation. Perhaps the one really disquieting aspect of the present situation is the excessive confidence of several historians. In some instances it takes the form of fierce forays on other historians. In others, it consists of definitive assertions supported by a vigorous style and a formidable intellectual artillery. It can be said with justice that the senior members of the British Foreign Office, for all their intellectual power, usually come up with the wrong answer or series of answers. Much the same could be said of some contemporary military historians and political biographers. Perhaps humility and common sense are the most vital qualities in a historian, in whatever field he works, or whichever path he takes to Truth. In historiography, as elsewhere, common sense and humility often seem to be at a discount.

Is it possible to reconcile the debate between the 'interpretive' and 'objective' schools? In the final analysis, each historian's choice will be an individualistic one. But it is at least important to realize that the fact that the interpretive concept has often been carried to such extremes does not, by itself, destroy that concept. These examples emphasize the hazards of the historian's task. And would it not be sad if it were generally accepted that 'history has to do with results' and if historians turned away from what is certainly the most difficult aspect of the strange vocation in which they are engaged?

NOTES

[1] A. P. Herbert, *Independent Member* (London, 1950), pp. 21–30.
[2] Geoffrey Barraclough, 'After the Jubilee', *New Statesman*, 6 May 1966, p. 660.

[3] George Painter, *Marcel Proust*, 2 vols. (London, 1959 and 1965).

[4] *Journal of the Royal United Service Institution*, May 1966, p. 106.

[5] Cyril Falls, *Caporetto* (London, 1965).

[6] David Chandler, *The Campaigns of Napoleon* (London, 1966).

[7] J. H. Plumb, *Sir Robert Walpole*, 2 vols. (London, 1956 and 1961).

[8] C. W. New, *The Life of Henry Brougham to 1830* (Oxford, 1961).

[9] Norman Gash, *Mr Secretary Peel* (London, 1961).

[10] Margery Perham, *Lugard*, 2 vols. (London, 1956 and 1960).

[11] A. von Ruville, *William Pitt, Earl of Chatham* (London, 1907), pp. 355–6.

[12] Lytton Strachey, *Eminent Victorians* (London, 1918), Preface.

[13] Robert Blake, *The Unknown Prime Minister* (London, 1955).

[14] Lord Birkenhead, *Halifax* (London, 1965).

[15] John Wheeler-Bennett, *Lord Waverley* (London, 1962).

[16] John Bowle, *Viscount Samuel* (London, 1957).

[17] Michael Foot, *Aneurin Bevan*, vol. I (London, 1962).

[18] Randolph S. Churchill, *Winston S. Churchill*, vol. I, *Youth, 1874–1900* (London, 1966), p. xxi.

[19] Lord Rosebery, *Lord Randolph Churchill* (London, 1906), p. 3.

[20] Edmund Gosse, 'Biography', *Encyclopaedia Britannica*, vol. III (11th edn., Cambridge, 1910), p. 952.

[21] John Morley, *Gladstone*, 3 vols. (London, 1903).

[22] Philip Magnus, *Gladstone* (London, 1954).

[23] Harold Nicolson, *The Development of English Biography*, Hogarth Lectures on Literature, 1928 (London, 1928).

[24] In particular, *Parliament* (2nd edn., Cambridge, 1952).

[25] Robert Blake, *Disraeli* (London, 1966).

[26] A. J. P. Taylor, *English History, 1914–1945* (Oxford, 1965).

[27] E. J. Hobsbawm, *The Age of Revolution* (London, 1962); *Labouring Men* (London, 1964).

[28] John Vincent, *The Formation of the Liberal Party, 1857–1868* (London, 1966).

[29] F. S. L. Lyons, *The Fall of Parnell* (London, 1960).

JOHN BARNES

Teaching and Research in British Contemporary History*

Interest in contemporary history in this country is considerable. Publishers' lists are full of new works on this century, which find a ready market, and the serious press seems ready to carry not only memoirs and serialized biographies of leading figures of the period, but also articles of some import to the historian. The subject has of course not only an intrinsic fascination to readers who have lived through the period, but also a presumed relevance to the world in which they live. It should be observed, however, that the field is closely confined and can be said almost without exaggeration to consist of our foreign and economic policy failures between the wars and in the 1940s and 1950s. In fact, the concern seems to be with certain narrowly-defined and well-traversed episodes even within these categories. For the remainder, the treatment is general rather than detailed. There is a strong tendency, despite the availability of excellent general works on the period, for there to be a steady stream of additions to their number, based not on an increasing output of detailed monographs examining and reassessing the period, but on a re-hash of certain basic works, a considerable number of which date from the period described. It is with a sense of shock that one reads the claim by the author of a recent and distinguished work on the decline of the Liberal Party to have established only the chronology of its break-up and that for the first time. If this is perhaps a measure of the narrow vision with which the contemporary historian has viewed

* The following publications have been invaluable in the preparation of this paper: George Barlow and Brian Harrison, *History at the Universities* (Historical Association, London, 1966); *Bulletin of the Institute of Historical Research, Theses Supplements*, Nos. 15–27, *Historical Research for University Degrees in the United Kingdom: Theses Completed, 1954–64* and *Theses in Progress, 1966*.

Britain's immediate past, it is a sure indication of myopia that he can condemn in the present the very type of work that he still relies on as the basis for his narrative of the inter-war period.

He may defend himself by making mention of the poverty of our documentary resources. After all, A. J. P. Taylor has committed himself to the view that the period since 1914 'has, as yet, to be studied almost entirely in printed sources'.[1] The effect of this has been greatly exaggerated. Dr Wilson has drawn attention to the press 'as the great untapped source for the writing of recent British political history. Its value for a book of this kind is not easy to exaggerate'.[2] There are few contemporary historians who would disagree, yet it ought to be added that parliamentary papers and debates are even more revealing on most aspects of contemporary history. It is of course true that from public sources it is difficult to describe with any certainty the evolution of policy and events as seen by the government, but it is perfectly possible to evaluate the consequences, necessarily public, of public policy. That for the historian is an equally valid centre of interest. In any case the material for economic, social, legal, and constitutional history is almost all, by its nature, in the public domain. As with their predecessors, both Dr Kenen and Mr Dow[3] have shown it possible to make valuable contributions to knowledge within a few years of the events they describe, yet in all but a few cases economic historians have failed to use both the gain in theory and knowledge to reassess the past, while in the field of social history it remains a regrettable fact that *The Long Week-End* can still be described as 'the best general treatment' of the inter-war period.

But, having said this, it ought also to be observed that Mr Taylor's observation is misleading. Professor Marder, to take but one example, has shown how the privately-owned material of numerous individuals can be made to yield a narrative equal and probably better than any which could be derived from the public records alone. It was Mr Rhodes James who commented at length on the disappointment the Cabinet records were likely to prove to the historian anxious to discuss the evolution of policy. He may not have exaggerated for the post-1945 period, but in the inter-war years the records of Cabinets, ministerial committees and conferences are likely to be revealing, especially when dissensions seem likely to lead to one or more resignations. The departmental archives, as well as revealing much factual material on which policy was based, will provide also the material for innumerable

B

monographs on departmental policies and also on the influence of their ministerial heads—though few were such compulsive minute writers as Lord Avon.

However, the private archives of ministers and others involved in policy-making can be much more revealing. An excellent instance of the use to which such material can be put is found in Mr Ullman's study of British policy towards Russia in the period 1917 to 1921.[4] The first volume derived much of its importance from two documentary collections, the Milner and the Wiseman papers. For the second, the public archives were at last available but it will still owe some if not most of its important material to a private source.

To make an exhaustive list of privately-held papers bearing on contemporary history would involve a much longer paper than this. Dr Wilson, for example, lists twenty-two sources under this heading, some of which, like the Asquith and Lloyd George papers, are well known, even if the latter is not quite so accessible as the Scottish Liberal Federation minutes in Edinburgh University Library. More striking perhaps are the collections, still in private possession, like the Gardiner and the Grigg papers. Any contemporary historian will know and tell you of the delights and frustrations of the chase after papers like these and it is only necessary to remark that, long after the public archives are open, they will still supply the historian with some of his most valuable material.

The following list makes no pretension to completeness and is largely focused on political and service personalities. First there are the collections put together by various public institutions. The British Museum holds several valuable collections: the so-called public papers of A. J. Balfour, of immense value for foreign policy and throwing light on successive Conservative and Coalition governments from the first years of the century to the onset of the great depression; the Arnold Forster papers, of great value for military and foreign affairs; a few of Sydenham's papers; and a whole series of papers, the Campbell Bannerman, John Burns, Herbert Gladstone, Ripon, Scott, and Spender archives, of considerable importance for the history of the Liberal Party and administration. Two other valuable collections here are Lord Cecil's papers, of infinite value for a study of the League of Nations movement and disarmament, but of little value for the periods when he was in office, and the Jellicoe papers which throw much light on the naval side of the First World War.

A second invaluable collection for the study of foreign policy is in the Foreign Office Library; the papers of Grey, Bertie, Carnock, Lansdowne, Lascelles, and Spring Rice. The British Library of Politics and Economic Science has an extensive collection of material among which the papers of the Webbs, the diaries and papers of Hugh Dalton, and the papers of George Lansbury are all particularly valuable to the historian of the Labour movement, while attention should also be drawn to the papers of E. D. Morel of the Union of Democratic Control, to those of Violet Markham with her important contacts in both Britain and the Dominions, and to those of Braithwaite, which are invaluable to historians of the early welfare state. The Cambridge University Library holds four collections of great value for the study of foreign policy, Indian policy, and, of course, for the whole range of domestic policy and Conservative politics in the inter-war period. These are the Baldwin, Crewe, Hardinge, and Hoare papers. The Chamberlain archives are to be found at Birmingham University Library and Neville's diaries and papers will shortly join those of his step-brother and father already lodged there. The Bodleian Library has yet another Prime Minister's papers, those of Asquith, to which they have added the papers of Milner, of two great Liberals, H. A. L. Fisher and Gilbert Murray, and those of Lord Bryce. The National Library of Scotland holds the papers of Haldane and the Liberal Chief Whip, Lord Elibank, in addition to the magnificent collection of Haig material and the Minto papers, of exclusively Indian interest, while the Scottish Record Office holds not only the papers of that confidant of so many inter-war politicians, Lord Lothian, but will soon hold the papers of Steel-Maitland, Baldwin's Minister of Labour between 1924 and 1929. The Beaverbrook Foundation has control of the papers of Lloyd George, Bonar Law, and Beaverbrook himself. There are other individual archives available or at least open to inquiry, of which perhaps the most notable are the Ritchie papers in the National Register of Archives, Keynes's papers in the Marshall Library at Cambridge. Morrison's papers have passed to Nuffield College, where the Cherwell papers are already lodged. Ernest Bevin's will be found in the possession of the Transport and General Workers' Union. The Public Record Office has two collections of military interest, the papers of Roberts and Kitchener, as well as the papers of Bradbury and Sir Otto Niemeyer which are essential to the historian of British finance and financial diplomacy. The India Office Library also has valuable records, including material relating to certain of the Viceroys and the papers of Lord George Hamilton. Perhaps at this point attention should be drawn to the Royal Archives, the TUC archives together with those of other trade unions, a few papers preserved at the Conservative Research Department and the records of the Labour Party, and the collections of military and naval material at Churchill College, Cambridge, Kings College, London, and the National Maritime Museum. All told, it is a formidable total available for the writing of contemporary history.

Equally interesting is the long list of papers that have been made available to contemporary historians either by executors or by families, but which remain in private possession and have to be sought there. Although the papers of the Third Marquess of Salisbury are lodged at Christ Church, Oxford, the papers of his son are lodged at Hatfield and have been sorted. The Churchill archive is at present lodged at East Bergholt and is in full use for the official biography, but it will eventually be made available to historians in the library of Churchill College, Cambridge. Excluding the papers of those still alive, the following far from exhaustive list is indicative of the range of material available: Addison, Alanbrooke, Amery, Beatty, Bevan, Birkenhead, Bridgeman, Buckmaster, Carson, Chilston, Crawford and Balcarres, Cunningham, Curzon, Cushendum, Davidson, Geoffrey Dawson, Derby, Devonshire, Duff Cooper, Elliot, Fisher of Kilverstone, French, Hailsham, Halifax, Hanworth, Hore Belisha, Inskip, Tom Jones, Jowitt, Keyes, Londonderry, MacDonald, McKenna, Masterman, Maugham, Mond, Montagu, Norman, Phipps, Rosebery, Sanders, Sankey, Thomas, Tizard, Trenchard, Vansittart, Wemyss, Wheatley, Henry Wilson, and Winterton. Several collections of interest may have shared the fate of the papers of Bracken and Joseph Ball in being deliberately destroyed, some like those of Sir James Grigg have been attached to other collections, and yet others, like those of the Geddes brothers, Stonehaven, and Sir William Tyrell, do not seem to have survived, except those preserved amongst the public records. But the great majority of the remaining papers are not yet traced and there is little indication as to their fate.

However incomplete this list, and it could certainly be matched and complemented by another at least as long, it clearly shows the irrelevance of Mr Taylor's comment. The documentary resources enumerated here are quite sufficient for a serious approach to be made to writing a definitive history at least for our time. We may add, too, the immense amount of untapped material not only in county and corporation archives but in their published proceedings on topics as important as popular and legislative voting. If one adds to this the demographic data to be found in school and other records, and not just in tax or census returns, the accumulation of private materials and of constituency records, it is quite clear that much could be done to derive from this mass of information clear pictures of social migration, the rise of occupations, of local elites, patterns of political structure and process in their local setting, and the struggle for power in the context of community institutions. Even without the personal material, there is enough behavioural evidence to determine the characteristics of different political movements, of the factions within them and of their political leadership. These patterns, often the basic patterns of political life, could and should be analysed now while the material is still available.

The same must hold true of a rather different class of evidence, at least as valuable, and that which makes contemporary history quite different in kind from any other type of history. There are those who prefer to define it as a period in terms of events or general currents of thought. Professor Barraclough, for example, argues that the opening of the period which is properly called contemporary 'can be placed with some degree of assurance at the end of 1960 or the beginning of 1961'. Most historians find it difficult to accept this and, at least in terms of Britain alone, prefer a date that roughly approximates to the end of the long reign of Queen Victoria.

There are, it is true, many features of the inter-war and post-war period which can trace their roots to that period of 'sowing', as Mr Leonard Woolf termed it, around the turn of the century. It is to this period that we can trace the move from splendid isolation to interdependence, the inauguration of that long love-hate relationship with the French that opened in *détente* but soon as the *entente* became a major influence in our foreign policy; Balfour's foundation of the Committee of Imperial Defence with its ultimate effects both on the machinery of government and on inter-service co-operation; the emergence of rival concepts of Empire, of the tariff reform movement with its effect on British politics for three decades or more, and of the shift of Irish grievances into a move for independence, echoed almost simultaneously in India, twin movements that did much to shape Empire into Commonwealth; the setting up of large industrial combines, the formation of a Labour Party, and the emergence and growth of produce and consumer groups that have reshaped politics into a complex pluralistic pattern; the emergence, too, into political consciousness of new social problems and the development of new policies that were to grow into and shape the welfare state; and finally, over-shadowing all, even if temporarily obscured by the pre-1914 boom in Britain's staple industries, the pattern of structural maladjustment in the economy and overall technological backwardness. It is not difficult to see that these themes have shaped a coherent period and one which is in large measure still our own. And yet it is possible that it is easier to discern these trends and assign them proper significance because so many have worked themselves out or are doing so as we observe them. To a Britain ready to move into Europe and being forced by events to consider transforming a welfare state into a welfare society, patterns seem to be about to shift decisively and this perhaps gives historical perspective. Certainly it is possible already to write about many aspects of this century in straight historical terms without any qualifying adjectives.

To supply a definition of contemporary history, it is preferable to look to the debate over its merits and demerits, the very charges to which it is open. There are three common objections. The first, in terms of source material, is usually concerned that the contemporary historian may derive a false impression of completeness from the immense amount of his material, while in reality significant sources are not open to him. The deficiencies in his evidence do not seem so great on closer examination, nor do they preclude the writing of history. The work of Sir Lewis Namier, for all its faults, is surely evidence of this. 'Ignorance', Lytton Strachey once remarked, 'is the first requisite of the historian, ignorance which simplifies and clarifies, which selects and omits' and there is a good deal of sense in Professor Carr's comment that the historians of earlier periods appear competent 'mainly because they are so ignorant of their subject'. Not until present-day mathematical techniques have made possible some assessment of what proportion of the whole is represented by the surviving evidence from earlier periods will it be possible to assess the extent to which the work of the historian is conjectural, often resting on sources more slender than those available to the insight journalism of the Sunday press.

Inevitably, of course, there is much truth in Butler's mordant remark: 'God cannot alter the past; that is why he is obliged to connive at the existence of historians.' There is a sense indeed, as Professor Butterfield has made clear, in which all histories are little more than interim reports. Each generation has its own particular concerns with a period and each historian his own sense of involvement. Bias then, the obverse of commitment, which is the second charge levelled against contemporary history, is not confined to it. It was the young Marc Bloch's headmaster who told him to beware of bias: 'with the nineteenth century, there is little danger, but when you touch the religious wars you must take great care'.

The third objection seems the most telling, the problem of historical perspective. Professor Oakeshott has reminded us of the dangers of anachronistic thinking by his perceptive distinction between the practical past, 'history for the sake of understanding the present', and the historical past; and yet even here Sir John Neale has fallen under the suspicion of attaching too much attention to Parliament in the context of Elizabethan society. He was led to do so by comparing its position in the Henrician forties with that of a century later and it was in the light of that comparison that the new evidence he discovered became significant. Both the danger and advantages of having in our hands both ends of the guidelines to historical perspective are here evident and we must ask ourselves whether, knowing only what goes before, the contemporary historian can really identify the significant events and trends and assess the nature of their significance.

There are two defences normally offered for the contemporary historian, one rooted in the interim nature of all interpretations and the other in his social duty to supply the responsible account that will otherwise be offered by less reputable writers. But there is a sense in which the account he offers will have a value uniquely its own and will be the essential basis for any subsequent writing on the period. Closeness to events and even commitment can be an advantage and supply an opportunity for insights that might otherwise be denied to subsequent historians. The early accounts of Hitler are by authors torn between the pursuit of objectivity and their personal involvement and they achieve a concentrated insight into the nature of Hitlerism which has enriched the work of their successors but which can scarcely be said to be apparent in the movement's documentation. The contemporary historian, aware of the nuances of his period, can seek the answer to questions which will render unsatisfactory later interpretations which, based on purely intellectual concepts, will offer insights that are rational and stimulating, but in the end quite inadequate to the rich complexity of events they seek to explain.

To understand that this is so, one only needs to remember the lack of understanding shown by younger contemporaries of periods or movements which they neither took part in nor knew. To understand why, it is necessary to observe that their originality was such that younger historians find them impossible to reconstruct unless the generation who lived through them can share their experience by putting in their own version first. Modern documentary materials are invariably, but not inevitably, of a nature which obscures rather than clarifies the essence of a period or a movement with the passage of time. The interpretations of a contemporary historian may be provisional but his insight may serve subsequent generations rather better than having their view shaped by the novelists and the writers of memoirs alone.

A major part of the value of contemporary history derives, too, from the historian's opportunity to interview the men and women involved and to compare the written with the verbal evidence. This ability to treat surviving participants and witnesses as living sources, to be able to question and cross-examine them, and yet be able to reconstruct the period from its most intimate sources, is to my mind what gives contemporary history its unique character and defines with a certain precision the period it covers. In other words the essence of the word 'contemporary' in contemporary history lies in methodology and not in period, in the interaction of living testimony and documentary sources.

There are those who distrust oral history. Strangely enough, in their ranks will be found those who, like Professor Bassett, will analyse information from memoirs, which often represent no more than oral information in written form. This can be unreliable. Morrison, for example, in both his memoirs and his verbal evidence to Sir Harold Nicolson, has been deliberately misleading about his own role in the 1931 crisis and experience would suggest that the oral historian's first task is to assess his subject's reliability for fact, for detail and for atmosphere.

Nevertheless, it is quite clear that more has happened in the past than is recorded or recalled. The historian has to bear in mind President Truman's dictum that 'if everybody could keep a record of his transactions from day to day, it would save a lot of mis-statements in history'. The airliner, the car, and the telephone have done much to obliterate the confidential letter, which used to supply the historian with much of his information, for example about the inner thoughts of his subjects, their private revelations, and the reactions of one man to another. Much now is transacted in conversation that used to find written expression. The picture is not of course quite as black as a simple statement can make it, but the biographer of Baldwin is particularly conscious of these deficiencies in his evidence.

To take another example, there is no documentary source for the decision to issue publicly the Admiralty rejoinder to the Geddes Report in 1922. There are in fact three apparently conflicting claims to the credit, two in biographies and one in memoir form, but on closer examination all three depend upon memory. It is reasonably easy to resolve this conflict of evidence, but the truth could have been established with greater ease and certainty had the surviving participants or witnesses still been alive. This example of course testifies not only to the value of oral evidence but also to some of its pitfalls unless the historian has carefully prepared for his task. Critics of oral history are prone to understate how fragmentary written records are, while the defenders consistently overstate the value of their work and ignore the necessity for thorough research in the primary sources.

There are a number of obvious points for the oral historian to remember, of which the need not to ask leading questions or impose one's own thought patterns on the subject of the interview are perhaps the most important. But the one which is most frequently ignored is the need to prepare carefully by checking all the available documentation and for this purpose this must include evidence of the engagement book and train ticket type. Recollections can never supplant records but they can fill in the gaps in the records if the historian has established where the gaps are.

The contemporary historian, too, must remember that records have a history of their own. Some memoranda are ignored, others widely read and discussed, and the historian without recollections to aid him may not know which is which. In discussions with participants or witnesses there is much to be discovered about the mood, the atmosphere or the emphasis to be given to a decision. Of all these intangibles perhaps the most important to be obtained by the oral historian is, apart from the feel of a person or an issue, an understanding of the unexercised alternatives.

Oral history projects on their own seem to me no substitute for the historian completing his own research. He will often have a better idea of whom he wishes to see and very often this will be the minor character whose recall will be less marred by discretion or the desire to distort and whose memory is frequently better because he has less to remember. One excellent example here is Lord Davidson who, while central to political history only in one office, held a number of posts from which he could intimately observe the political scene at work.

One example from his own career will serve as a final example of the value of oral history and reinforce the claim that much more attention should be paid to it in the field of contemporary history. His was the authorship of the memorandum recommending the claims of Baldwin to the Premiership in 1923. Because of a note appended to it by the King's private secretary, Lord Stamfordham, we know that the outgoing Prime Minister's private secretary, Colonel Waterhouse, stated that it 'practically expressed the views' of his master. Mr Blake has taken this to mean that the document's purpose was deliberately misrepresented, but without evidence as to the dating of Stamfordham's note we cannot be sure that it does not represent a statement made in the course of Waterhouse's second visit to Stamfordham. By persuading Lord Davidson to dictate his recollections of the episode, a number of points came to light, the significance of which were not apparent to him since he had not studied the episode in detail. It became apparent that the memorandum was written at Stamfordham's request and was to be the expression of Davidson's opinion as a peculiarly well-informed back-bencher. Its purpose could not therefore be easily misrepresented and therefore attention must be focused on the second interview as the source of any misrepresentation if any was involved. As in fact we now know, Waterhouse did not misrepresent his master.

It seems to me essential that we should recapture evidence of this sort while it is still available and that this can only be done by interviewing in depth not only the leading personalities of the day but also many of those in their circle or involved in the political and policy-making process in roles that bring them no limelight but make them peculiarly good witnesses for the historian. We have now passed through the stage of near-contemporary accounts and also of general interpretations. The need is for contemporary history to be probed in depth before time has eroded this type of evidence.

There is, however, little evidence to show that research in contemporary history has gained enough impetus to accomplish such a task. Questioning the credulity of word of mouth evidence is something that we have imbibed from our universities and this colours not only many, if not all, students' approach to research, but also leaves with all of them a sense that the historian cannot yet write history about the immediate past.

This shows up quite clearly in the teaching of contemporary history at British universities. Very few university teachers do not expect their students to touch at least upon British history at some point in their career, this despite the attacks made on our island fixation at Cambridge and elsewhere. Again such attention usually includes some teaching of the history of twentieth-century Britain, although it should perhaps be observed that this does not always take place within the history faculty. No less than thirty-two universities make some study of British history in the years after 1900 compulsory for the attainment of one or other of their degrees, usually but not invariably for a single subject history degree. Of these universities, however, both Aberystwyth and Nottingham terminate their British history courses at 1914, while Birmingham's course on 'England and Europe in the Twentieth Century' differs considerably from the remainder of these courses. In general they are of the outline type, often one part of a course covering the whole of British history. The contemporary period is studied as part of a wider period starting in 1500 or 1714 or 1760 or 1780 or 1815. Where a terminal date is established, it is rarely later than 1939, while many of the courses are open-ended and much depends on the practice in each university as to whether and how thoroughly the last few decades are taught. In one at least of our major universities the period is covered in lectures by a nineteenth-century specialist and much of the teaching is in the hands of those even less well qualified to discuss the subject. Without adequate teaching, the existing course set-up can and does lead to a situation where the last fifty or sixty years are in effect neglected, however much the student would like to study them.

With these provisos in mind, the courses can be listed, both Aberystwyth and Nottingham being excluded for the reasons given above.

Aberdeen	British History since 1760.
Bangor	British History 1760–1960.
Belfast	British and Imperial Political and Constitutional History 1714–1939.
	Britain and Ireland 1714–1939.
Birmingham	England and Europe in the Twentieth Century.
Cardiff	British History 1815–1939.
Durham	British History 1783–1939.
	The British Economy in the Twentieth Century.
East Anglia	English Society and Politics 1760–1945.
Edinburgh	British History 1714–1950.
Essex	History of England since 1800.
Exeter	English History 450–1945.
	The British Economy in its International Setting since 1760.
Glasgow	British History from the earliest times to 1945.
	The Economic History of Britain 1750–1950.
Hull	English History 1760 to the present.
Keele	British History from 1558.
Kent	Britain in the Contemporary World.
	Economic and Social History of Britain since 1760.
Lancaster	British History mid-Eighteenth to mid-Twentieth Century. (Not compulsory in single subject history course.)
Leeds	British History since 1688.
	The British Economy 1896–1914.
Leicester	British History 55 BC to 1939.
	English History 1763–1939.
	Economic and Social History to 1950.
Liverpool	British Political and Constitutional History 1760–1945.
London	British History from mid-Eighteenth Century.
Manchester	British History 1815 to the present. (Not compulsory in single subject history course.)
Newcastle	British History 1783–1939.
Oxford	British History 1685–1939.
	British Political and Constitutional History since 1865.
Reading	English History from the Fifth to the Twentieth Century. (Four papers.)
St Andrews	British Political History since 1485.
St Davids	British History 1714–1939.

Sheffield	History of England from 1485 to the present.
	English History 1603–1945.
	Political and Constitutional History of Britain from 1603 to the present.
	English Economic History 1050 to the present.
	Modern British Social History and Social movements.
Southampton	British History 1500–1945.
Swansea	British History 1815–1951.
Trinity College, Dublin	History of Britain 1485–1939.
Warwick	British Political History since 1867. (No compulsory modern British history in single subject course.)

In addition to these compulsory courses, four other universities offer courses as options that are broadly similar to those listed above.

Bristol	British History from 1688.
Cambridge	English History from the mid-Eighteenth Century.
Sussex	British History 1851–1940.
	British History 1896 to the Present Contemporary Britain.
York	Nineteenth and Twentieth Century Western Europe with special reference to Britain.

At first sight this nearly universal coverage of contemporary British history is promising, despite the qualifications made above. However, if we analyse the depth of interest for which the choice of special subjects would seem a clear guide, a very different picture is revealed. Twentieth-century history is not well represented and both Britain and Europe find themselves neglected when it is covered, usually to the advantage of the United States or the Russian Revolution. The list of courses covering British history in its widest sense is not only short but, on closer examination, is to a large extent concerned with the period before the First World War.

(*a*) Courses covering the period until 1918:

| Belfast | Economy and Society in Britain 1875–1914. |
| Bristol | British Social Conditions and Social Policies 1880–1914. |

Exeter	The Condition of England 1889–1914.
Hull	The British Empire 1895–1905.
Lancaster	The Edwardian Age 1901–14.
Southampton	The Industrial Revolution and the British Navy 1815–1918.
Sussex	Poverty as a problem of Social Policy in Great Britain 1885–1914.
Swansea	The Crisis of Liberalism 1884–1905.

(b) Courses covering the period since 1918:

Birmingham	Britain between the Wars 1919–39.
Edinburgh	The War and the Welfare State in Britain 1939–50.
Leeds	British Domestic History 1906–29.
London	Growth of the British Commonwealth 1880–1933.
Newcastle	Britain between the Wars 1919–39.
Southampton	Aspects of British Empire and Commonwealth Reltions since 1880.
Sussex	Economic and Social Policy in Inter-War Britain.

This picture is too harsh, but only slightly so. East Anglia and Kent both have optional subjects in economic and social history, between the wars in the first case and since 1930 in the second, while both Cardiff and Liverpool study inter-war foreign policy. Even so, it is disappointing to find so little work being done at student level on contemporary history proper. It is perhaps not surprising that the research done at post-graduate level reflects the same emphasis on the history of the earlier decades of this century and, in all but a few cases, is being done at a handful of universities. This inevitably means that the stress on regional and local work in political and economic problems which many contemporary historians would like to see is disappointingly absent in most cases.

If one looks at the current research programme of theses of all types, it is clear that the bulk of the work on twentieth-century Britain is being done at Oxford, with particular emphasis on St Antony's and Nuffield, and at London. The latter indeed, even without the thirty or more theses being done at the London School of Economics, which seem to have escaped the net of the Institute of Historical Research, has a clear lead with seventeen theses. Oxford has fourteen in progress. Only seventeen of our universities have theses in progress; of those which have not already been mentioned, Durham, Leeds, Liverpool, and Hull stand out, while seven theses are under way under the collective aegis of the University of Wales. Of the remainder, Cambridge alone stands out by the way it lags behind in this field as in no other.

Easily the most popular topics for research are those connected with the Labour Party and the Labour movement in general. The growth of the party and its organization during the First World War and the immediate post-war years ending with the first Labour government is being analysed in depth,[5] so too are the unemployment and foreign policies of the second Labour government[6] and the attitude of the Labour Party to economic policies, education, and the Common Market. A good deal of useful material is also emerging from a study of its history in Birmingham, in Leeds, in Bristol, in Scotland generally, and, in relation to its social and economic background, in Glasgow. The Independent Labour Party has now been thoroughly discussed in print and work is proceeding on studies of the Commonwealth movement and the Socialist Labour Party of Great Britain. The Webbs too are under study[7] and so also is MacDonald in relation to his constituency. Even in such a well-worked field, where there are already studies of Labour's foreign policy in the 1930s and 1940s, biographies of prominent personalities, and general accounts of the party's history, much remains to be done. In particular, there is room for a fresh study of the Labour opposition in the 1930s; a detailed look at the history of the party's organization and a fresh attempt to tell the story of Labour's post-war administration. Miss Joan Mitchell has already shown how valuable such studies can be.[8]

The trade union movement is also attracting a great deal of attention; one major union, the Electrical Trades Union, is being studied[9] in a field where only a handful of the histories written have more than hagiographical value. Labour relations in a handful of industries are under study and there is also work progressing on the bargaining power of the trade unions generally in the sixty years before 1914. There is no similar work for more recent periods. Again there are detailed studies of the Labour movement in the engineering industry, no less than three theses in progress on the organization and policy of the Durham miners, and particularly valuable research into the operation of the General Strike in particular areas like the West Yorkshire coalfield or North East England.

The comparative insignificance of localized studies, both in this well-tilled field and generally, is particularly disappointing. Dr Jones's study of Wolverhampton Council has shown how satisfactorily such a study can be done, but only in the case of the West Riding Liberals is any attempt being made to study a party other than the Labour Party in its local context in the period after 1918. There is a notable absence of constituency studies on the lines of the pioneer work done for Newcastle-under-Lyme and the area organizations of the major parties retain their total immunity against the historian's art.

The position with regard to electoral history and public opinion is almost equally unsatisfactory. There are studies of the elections of 1906, 1922, and 1929, but, since these are confined closely to the Nuffield pattern, and not even then to the most recent version which does deal with party strategy, many of the most interesting questions about these elections have not been asked, let alone answered. By-elections and local elections, the only accurate guides to opinion before 1938, have been almost totally ignored. Some material in Dr Rowe's thesis on the 1929 election,[10] and Dr Kyba's thorough survey of the by-election in the early 1930s in his 'British Attitudes toward Disarmament and Rearmament 1932–35'[11] are honourable exceptions to this statement. Public opinion in relation to Anglo-American relations between the Easter Rising and the Irish Treaty, to the 1914–18 war, and to the Rhineland before 1925, has received or is receiving attention, while Dr Watkins has dealt in a somewhat pedestrian manner with public opinion and the Spanish Civil War.[12] Again the local context has received little attention and domestic issues have been entirely ignored; even the economy campaign of the early 1920s has escaped the historian. There is one honourable exception on both counts and that is Mr Marsh's study of Birmingham's opinion of protection between 1919 and 1932.[13]

Finally, in looking at the current state of research, one should mention the fact that the economic background of the period has begun to receive attention, although the quality of the work is mixed and far too many of the studies terminate in 1914. The reissue of Duncan Burn's *Economic History of Steel Making 1867–1939*, together with a volume bringing the story up to 1959, and the addition of a semi-official history has reminded us that few industries have received such thorough and distinguished attention. The role of the central monetary authorities has been examined but, with the exception of a handful of studies of nascent government interventions before 1914, government policy has received all too little study. Dr Hancock's study of unemployment policy in the 1920s seems imperceptive[14] and little or no attention has been paid to the transition to a managed economy after 1931. It is fair to say that we know more of government economic policy in the 1950s than we do of the 1930s, but this is only symptomatic of the need to reassess that decade, the rise of the new industries, the rationalization movement, and the effects of protection.[15]

These reflections on the state of current research have already pointed to parts of the subject that have never been covered, as well as to areas wide open for reassessment. There are, however, certain broad areas to which I should like to draw particular attention. The first can be described under the broad heading of biography. I have already described how our sources no longer contain the great series of letters in which Victorian statesmen conducted their business and described their aims. So marked is the pressure of business and so informal much of the conduct of business at the highest level, that there is a general need for the biographical approach as an essential preliminary to the evaluation of other material. Perhaps the recent controversy over the Bethmann-Hollweg memorandum of 9 September 1914 may reinforce this plea by showing that the need for evaluation of a document in personal terms is present in other countries and at other better-documented periods also. As Mr Joll perceptively notes, 'the interpretation of documents necessarily depends on the interpretation of character, for the way in which one reads the documents is determined by one's general view of the nature and motives of the writer . . . and divergent views of a man's character will result in differing interpretations of what he writes'. It is of course true that a historian's view of a man's aims and motives will be based to a large extent on the documents but, as Joll adds, 'it necessarily also influences the way he reads them'. But the case here made is not only that biography should be written but that the work should be undertaken before those privy to the subject's every move, or at least to some of them, succumb to the onset of time, either in memory or in person. One thesis writer has already taken the case of Lord Swinton as his subject[16] but in general there are few sketches of the background, character, attitudes, ideas, and policies of those who have played major parts on the stage and without them it will be increasingly difficult to elucidate the limited (in quality, not extent) documentary resources available. For example, of the fourteen Prime Ministers this century, only two have what may be called satisfactory biographies, Asquith and Bonar Law. Even in the latter case the years 1916–21 deserve rather more attention than Mr Blake was able to give them. There are, however, academic studies of MacDonald[17] and Baldwin[18] in progress, as well as the official Churchill biography, and there is some hope of a fresh study of Lloyd George. Of those who held either the Chancellorship or the Foreign Office, without seeking to be exhaustive, one can point to McKenna, Simon, Hoare, Curzon, Henderson, Kingsley Wood, Dalton, and even Cripps as figures requiring attention. Nor is Halifax's biography satisfactory on his foreign policy. Biographies of Bevin, Morrison, and Austen Chamberlain[19] are also in progress.

It would be tedious to enumerate in detail the biographies of other figures in twentieth-century British history that remain to be written, but there are two classes of men to which I should like to draw attention. The first is that of senior officials involved in policy-making, the second the men who make up the private secretaries' network. To these last may be added the highly influential personalities of royal secretaries. Hankey has found his official biographer,[20] Dr Jones's diaries are being edited,[21] and there is a full biography of Sir John Anderson. But what of such key personalities as Chalmers, Chapman, Bradbury, Sir Warren Fisher, Hopkins, Ismay, and Francis Mowatt? Do they not merit the same treatment as Morant? Among the royal secretaries Stamfordham stands out for study and the private secretaries deserve a rather better fate than the somewhat light appreciation of a few of them by Sir Charles Petrie.[22] We cannot afford to neglect these figures if we are to understand the evolution of policy.

That policy has of course been mainly concerned with the vast expansion of central government and its assumption of a general welfare role. Far too little attention has been paid to its assumption of the management of the British economy and very little more to the way in which it has conducted its management. Nor has the influence of ideas on the economic role of the state received the attention it deserves. The basic narrative of the growth of the welfare state is rather better established. Apart from two general surveys, there have been detailed general histories of both health insurance and unemployment insurance, but, with the solitary exceptions of Beveridge studies[23] and the organization of the National Health Service, the detailed monographs remain to be written. Perhaps the most surprising gap is the absence of any study of the influence of ideas and ideology on the structure of the welfare state as it emerged.

There is a more general point to be made about the literature of political ideas; there has never been any attempt to assess the impact of current political ideas on the political culture or to discover the assumptions on which support for these ideas was given; for example, we have had no discussion of what nationalization meant to potential supporters of the Labour Party in the 1920s while the attractiveness of a doctrine of increased state intervention before the First World War needs to be explained when the only form of state intervention that impacted on the working man was the poor law.

Three other general topics may be briefly enumerated as profitable and necessary fields for study. Firstly the effect of increasing state intervention on grounds of general welfare on the character and organization of the Civil Service is a topic whose importance has perhaps always been recognized, but which has not been tackled by the historian in any detail. Secondly in an age of collectivist politics the interest groups and lobbies of the inter-war period require study and with them the growth in importance of advisory committees. The third, and in many ways the most surprising topic, is the study of the Conservative Party in nearly all its aspects which needs to be studied in the same detailed way in which the Labour Party is being studied.[24]

Two more general points may also be made. There is room for detailed monographs on both the political crises and on the various administrations of the last half century. It is remarkable that, as yet, the Carlton Club meeting has not been written about from original sources, much less the crises in the Conservative Party over the Irish Treaty, in January 1922 or December 1923, to take only a few examples. Equally, the 1924 Labour government is the only one of the inter-war administrations to have had a full length study devoted to it. The second point is in form technical and that is to suggest the study of the genesis and passage of particular statutes as a means of revealing the character of politics and the forces involved in it at any particular time. Mr Barnett is at present proving successfully that this can be done with so recent a statute as the 1957 Rent Act[25] and Mr Ross has already produced a rather unsatisfactory treatment of the Iron and Steel Nationalization Act. There are no comparable earlier studies.

If the picture of the research to be done appears somewhat impressionistic it is a sure measure of how much work remains to be done before the significance of the trends enumerated earlier in this paper can be properly reassessed. But before this can be done, much greater stress will have to be laid on contemporary history in our teaching at universities and schools.

NOTES

[1] A. J. P. Taylor, *English History, 1914–1945* (Oxford, 1965), p. 602.

[2] Trevor Wilson, *The Downfall of the Liberal Party, 1914–1935* (London, 1966), Preface.

[3] P. B. Kenen, *British Monetary Policy and the Balance of Payments 1951–1957* (Cambridge, Mass. and London, 1960), Preface; J. C. R. Dow, *The Management of the British Economy* (Cambridge, 1964), Preface.

[4] R. Ullman, *Intervention and the War* (London, 1961). A second volume will be published in 1968 entitled *Britain and the Russian Civil War, November 1918–February 1920*.

[5] Especially by Mr McKiblin and Mr Whitemore at Oxford.

[6] Notably by Mr Carlton at the London School of Economics and by Mr Skidelsky at Oxford.

[7] By Mr Warner at Cambridge.

[8] Dr Joan Mitchell, *Crisis in Britain, 1951* (London, 1963).

[9] By Mr D. Lewis at Oxford.

[10] Dr E. Rowe, Oxford University B. Litt. Thesis.

[11] London University Ph.D. Thesis, 1967.

[12] Dr K. W. Watkins, *Britain Divided. The effect of the Spanish Civil War on British political opinion* (London, 1963).

[13] J. R. Marsh, *Birmingham Public Opinion and Protection, 1919–32*, Birmingham University M.A. Thesis, 1961.

[14] Dr K. J. Hancock, London University Ph.D. Thesis.

[15] But see Dr Henry W. Richardson, *Economic Recovery in Britain 1932–9* (London, 1967).

[16] Mr A. Earl, Manchester University M.A. Thesis.

[17] By Mr D. Marquand, M.P.

[18] By Mr R. K. Middlemas of the University of Sussex and Mr A. J. L. Barnes of the London School of Economics.

[19] By Mr A. Bullock, Dr B. Donoughue, and Dr G. W. Jones of the London School of Economics and Professor Douglas Johnson of Birmingham University respectively.

[20] In Captain S. W. Roskill, R.N., Churchill College, Cambridge.

[21] By Mr R. K. Middlemas of the University of Sussex.

[22] Sir Charles Petrie, *The Powers behind the Prime Minister* (London, 1958).

[23] An official biography is being written by Miss J. Chambers, Nuffield College, Oxford.

[24] Miss B. Malamant of Yale University is at present studying the Conservative opposition to Neville Chamberlain, and both Dr Ghosh's thesis on *The British Conservative Party and India, 1927–35*, Manchester University Ph.D. Thesis, 1966, and Dr Turner's thesis on *The Conservative Party and Tariff Reform before 1906*, London University Ph.D. Thesis, 1967, deserve special mention.

[25] London University Ph.D. Thesis, 1967.

DONALD CAMERON WATT

Teaching and Research in Contemporary International History in Britain: Opportunities and Openings

To write on the opportunities and openings for research in the field of contemporary international history at a time when the British authorities have just proclaimed their intention of opening the Foreign Office and Cabinet records up to 1937 would seem rather an act of supererogation. In the twenty years of records soon to be released in one fell swoop there is obviously going to be enough material to keep a generation of research students occupied. Within two years all the inner secrets of 1939 will be revealed; within three we may be in a position to know most of the truth about Britain's position in 1940, and whether or not any encouragement was in fact returned to the various peace moves initiated from the European continent in 1940, to give only one example. Scores of theses and monographs are going to have to be written before we shall be able properly to assess the impact of these new materials on our understanding of the history of the 1920s and 1930s. Established scholars, engaged in full-time teaching, are inevitably going to be outpaced by their own graduate students in knowledge and appreciation of the new materials—one can foresee without much difficulty a whole crop of new historical controversies as the next generation of scholars attack and reassess the judgments of their predecessors. By the time this process is at an end there may even be some warranty for doubting whether the whole period can any longer be classed as 'contemporary' history at all; and whether perhaps that adjective would not better be applied to the period after 1945.

This is, at the moment, however, still some time off. For the purpose of this paper and conference I propose to discuss the teaching and conduct of research in contemporary international history in terms of the periods in which work is actually in progress in the universities of Britain. Before embarking on this task however, I feel the nature of 'international history' itself should be defined; for it is a concept not employed as such in more than a handful of British universities—and even in these it has perhaps been more narrowly defined than the nature of the subject necessitates.

Perhaps the best indication of the nature of the approach to history on an international basis is contained in the preamble to the deed establishing the Stevenson Chair of International Relations at the Royal Institute of International Affairs:[1]

Whereas the founder, being desirous of furthering amity and good understanding among all nations, and being persuaded that the study and teaching of history as hitherto practised in this and other countries have not been conducive to this end, that on the contrary in practically all countries the teaching of history and the class books held have had a strong nationalistic bias creating among the peoples from childhood onwards a spirit of antipathy, ill-will and even hatred of other peoples, and being convinced that the teaching of history internationally, and, as far as practicable without bias, would tend to substitute for this spirit a spirit of international co-operation, peace and good-will. . . .

The phrases chosen are perhaps more notable for the idealism which informs them than for the illumination they cast on the real intentions of the founder. But they do make it clear that international history is not national history—and that its teaching and subject matter should be free of nationalistic bias, whether conscious bias expressed in the prejudices and sympathies of the historian or unconscious in the choice of theme or viewpoint. From this it is clear that approaches to the subject matter of international history such as those embodied in courses on, for example, 'Britain and Europe, 1914–1945', 'American Diplomatic History', 'The Foreign Policy of the Third Reich', etc. are not, strictly speaking, courses in international history but in the external aspects of the history of a particular nation. In the UNESCO *Dictionary of the Social Sciences* 'international relations' are defined as follows: 'the contacts of peoples and states across national frontiers'. My own definition of 'international organization' in the same volume however points out that owing to the Latin use of the prefix *inter* with both the accusative case for motion and the ablative for state, the adjective international can apply *both* to activities linking numbers of states and their relationships *and* to the activities of bodies, not themselves states, 'among and parallel to' states, such as, for example, international commercial organizations such as the Royal

Dutch-Shell Oil Company or the Suez Canal Company.[2]

If this definition is accepted international history would seem to be the history of events, relations, and interactions, between and among peoples and states. Domestic history is of interest only in so far as it influences the external behaviour of individual states. And on balance the international historian is more interested in the international consequences rather than the motives informing particular actions by particular governments; since he tends to see such actions as links in a causal chain or quasi-causal series of events on an international rather than a national stage. The writing of international history has tended to concern itself principally with diplomacy, that is with the acts and reports of professional diplomatists and those of their political superiors who were concerned with the formulation of their instructions. It will be one of the contentions of this paper that this approach is perhaps too narrowly conceived.

In the British universities only eleven out of thirty-six give general courses and examinations in what can strictly be called contemporary international history.[3] A better guide to the attention given to contemporary history in these universities can however be obtained if we look at the choice of 'special subjects' offered. In the structure of the British history school the 'special subject' studied from a selection of original sources and materials plays an overwhelmingly important part in guiding the interests of the students and occupying the attention of their teachers. Fourteen out of twenty-six universities at present offer special subjects in the international contemporary field—one more (Liverpool) offers 'British Foreign Policy 1919–1939'.[4] It is to be noted that none of the medieval foundations in England or Scotland, save only Edinburgh, are represented, and that of the latest crop of experimental universities East Anglia, Essex, Kent, Sussex, Warwick, and Lancaster have exchanged such rigorous historical training for the more popular inter-disciplinary approach of the mixed School of Such-and-Such Studies.

It will be seen from this that the teaching of international contemporary history at a specialist level is concentrated *par excellence* in the civic universities, and that there has been an overwhelming concentration—for obvious reasons both of availability of material and of interest—in the decade before the outbreak of the Second World War. The three subjects offered at the London School of Economics are the product of a much more numerous teaching staff engaged in work in the twentieth-century field than is to be found at most other British universities. Reading's second subject is offered only in the mixed degree course entitled 'Modern History and Politics'. Leeds offers its special subject only within a rather similar degree course in 'International History and Politics'.

A third and more rigorous yardstick comes when one examines the work done at the post-graduate level and the development of graduate seminars. The necessarily rather inadequate guides published by the *Bulletin of the Institute of Historical Research* of the University of London on theses for higher degrees completed in the years 1954–64 and theses in progress in the academic year 1965–66[5] show that post-graduate work is and has been overwhelmingly concentrated in the two universities of Oxford and London. Of the twenty-six theses dealing with aspects of international politics after 1920 completed in all the British universities in the decade 1954–64, ten were completed at the University of Oxford, twelve at the University of London, and one each at the universities of Cambridge, Wales (Aberystwyth), Sheffield, and Durham. Of the thirty-six now shown as still in progress, fifteen are registered at the University of London, four at Oxford, seven at the University of Wales (six at Aberystwyth, one at Cardiff), three at Durham, two at Hull, two at Liverpool, and one each at Leeds, Keele, and Cambridge. London's great growth has only occurred after 1956 when a permanent graduate seminar on 'the diplomatic origins of the Second World War' was founded by Professor Medlicott. It is an interesting comment on the length of time that it takes to establish such a seminar that its first Ph.D. candidate only submitted his thesis in 1961, five years later. Only one M.A. candidate, in 1955, has any earlier claim to being a product of Professor Medlicott's creation of a department of international history separate from the department of international relations to which his staff were previously subordinated. The graduate students at Oxford are mainly products of the foundation of St Antony's College in 1951. The grouping at Aberystwyth reflects the tradition of a Chair of International Politics occupied in turn by Sir Alfred Zimmern, Sir Charles Webster, E. H. Carr, and Philip Reynolds.

The subjects chosen for research work by these graduates tend to be concentrated in the 1930s (thirteen out of the twenty-six). Only two are working on subjects after 1945. Two only are concerned with the Peace Conference, three with the early 1920s, and five, three of whom are working on military subjects, have themes covering the whole inter-war period. In terms of the subjects studied there is a very heavy concentration on the Western European powers, Britain, France, and Germany. Only Wales has produced three M.A. students engaged in the study of various aspects of British policy in the Far East. One Oxford Ph.D. on German-Japanese relations has just been completed.[6] Durham has an M.A. candidate registered on 'Yugoslav-Bulgarian relations, 1918–1941' and at London one candidate has just been awarded the Ph.D. for a thesis on 'Attempts to form a neutral bloc in the Balkans, March 1939–March 1940', based mainly, though by no means entirely, on the Italian diplomatic materials.[7] Another, a part-time student, is still slogging through a thesis on 'Fiume 1919'. And one should perhaps mention an excellent Ph.D. thesis recently submitted in the economic history department on the Rumanian government and the international oil industry 1880–1945.[8] Only two students, both at London, are working on aspects of the Soviet role in international politics. Dr Breuning's recently completed Oxford Ph.D. thesis on Germany between East and West dealt naturally with the much discussed theme of German-Soviet relations.

The picture so far painted of current graduate work in Britain in the field of contemporary international history has to be judged both in terms of the linguistic weaknesses of the average British student and the small number of students engaged in graduate research. If one turns to the work of established scholars in the field—where numbers are even more limited—one is at least moving from the realm of subject matter to ideas. Here, at the moment, it would perhaps be true to say that British historians have reached an impasse. In the last decade they have been overwhelmed by the vast mass of detailed material available for limited study of limited sections of the field. Equally they have been frustrated by the slowness with which material has become available to cover the equally glaring gaps in the field. The absence of any documentary material in French foreign policy until two years ago; the absence of any Italian diplomatic documents to cover the period between 1925 and 1939; the continuing existence of the gaps 1922–29 and 1934–38 in the British documentary series; all of this has tended to produce a situation where the historian has been inclined to read the documents, and digest them for his lectures, but rarely to proceed further to the stage of publication.

As a result his students are forced to rely for their secondary reading on works such as Sir John Wheeler-Bennett's *Munich: Prologue to Catastrophe* (London, 1948), which is more than a decade old.[9] The controversy struck up by Mr A. J. P. Taylor's *Origins of the Second World War* (London, 1961), and by Messrs Gilbert and Gott's *The Appeasers* (London, 1963) have only increased the burden on university teachers to use their lectures rather than publications to provide their students with material to balance the controversy.

As a result the concept of international history has tended to focus on diplomatic and military contacts between nations to the exclusion of all others; though there are obviously points to be brought out in the study of the influence of the League of Nations, of the development of regional blocs like the Little Entente, or the Commonwealth, which make the diplomacy of the inter-war years rather different from that of the period before 1914. A second consequence has been to focus attention on the processes which led up to the outbreak of war in Europe in 1939; diplomacy in the Mediterranean, in the Near and Middle East, and in the Far East have been dealt with, if at all, in isolation; and the dilemmas of British and, still more, Soviet policy-makers caught between Japan and Germany cannot properly be elucidated under so compartmentalized an approach. But these are only minor criticisms compared with the distortions apt to be introduced by this concentration on the origins of the war of 1939 itself.

The first distortion that this concentration has introduced arises from the very fact that the war of 1939 opened, for Britain at least, in a manner so conventionally nineteenth-century with an ultimatum and a declaration of war as between nation and nation. Much has, of course, been made of the allegedly novel forms of aggression practised by Hitler against Czechoslovakia and Poland. But by the standards of Louis XIV,[10] let alone Louis Napoleon and Bismarck, Hitler's methods seem remarkably orthodox. Indeed since 1945 historians writing on the origins of the Second World War have consistently stressed this element of nineteenth-century power politics to the exclusion of the ideological elements which bulked so large in much of the contemporary controversy of the 1930s.[11]

Yet if one looks at the way in which the wars of 1939–45 passed so easily into the Cold War, the most striking element is the interaction of ideological and quasi-ideological elements with the more

conventional considerations of power and national interest in the
policies of virtually all of the major powers. It may well be that
future generations of history students will be as much preoccupied with how to disentangle the one set of considerations
from the other as they now are in disentangling religious from
dynastic motives in the study of the history of the Thirty Years
War. Concentration on the question of the origins of the war of
1939 has in fact here introduced a second distortion, in that it has
distracted attention from the growth of political ties, loyalties,
feelings of community and identification which make the old rigid
categories of nation and state often very misleading. During the
late nineteenth and early twentieth centuries there developed a
kind of international community—or rather sets of international
communities—which outlasted the two world wars. These developments, charted up to 1914 by Professor Lyons of Canterbury[12],
add an element of confusion to the international politics of the
1930s which both misled statesmen at the time—contrast for
example the quite unrealistic importance attached by Stimson in
1932 and Roosevelt in 1938 to the role of international opinion,
with Chamberlain's dismissal of the German military-conservative
opposition to Hitler in 1938 as reminiscent of the Jacobites at the
court of Louis XVI—and has muddied the wells of historical
analysis since.

Proceeding from the general to the particular these considerations suggest that there is still much to be done in the comparative
study of resistance movements, on the interpenetration of ideological movements with nationalist political organizations and their
influences on the politics of the powers in the decades of the 1930s
and 1940s. We need for example to test again the hypothesis that
Soviet foreign policy had by 1939 become totally dominated by old-
fashioned considerations of national interest, and that this preoccupation extended into and dominated equally the activities of
the various branches of the international communist movement and
its sympathizers in Europe. Comparative work on the development
of the Popular Front movement between 1935 and 1938, on the
European communist parties during the period of the Nazi-
Soviet Pact, and on the Communist resistance movements after
1941 could well lead us to examine what, by now, have become the
rather too rigid interpretations formed under the influence of the
experience of the Cold War. Similarly there is room for examinations both of the degree of support Hitler's use of anti-communist

slogans earned in Eastern Europe and in France, and the degree to which the nazi appeal to pan-European sentiments found a genuine echo. The intermingling of quasi-ideological and national considerations in American policy-making is much more familiar ground to historians once the Grand Alliance has been truly forged; but, despite Mr Alperowitz's recent and tantalizing twitch of the curtain,[13] there is much we still have to learn about how this intermingling influenced the course of the peace-settlement in Europe in the years 1944–46. Nor, despite the oceans of ink already spilt, do we have any study of Roosevelt's foreign policy in the 1930s that makes any serious effort to relate his actions to their intended effects. Dr David Adams's otherwise excellent Oxford Ph.D. thesis on Roosevelt's foreign policy during his first term[14] follows the example of so much American work on the period in concentrating more on the domestic influences governing the formation of that policy than its effectiveness in attaining its ends or its effects on the policies of the European powers.

A second consequence of this distortion has been to distract attention from the degree to which the existence of the League of Nations and other regional organizations changed the nature of international politics and diplomacy after 1920. Writings on these institutions have been obsessed by their failures rather than their successes. Much has been written of Manchuria and Abyssinia, of the breakdown of the Disarmament Conference, and the failure of the Powers to employ the machinery of the League after 1936. An American scholar, Dr James Barros of Dartmouth, has recently repaired some of these deficiencies with studies of the Corfu Crisis[15] and the Graeco-Bulgarian conflict of 1925.[16] But we still lack studies of the Tacna-Arica dispute, of the League's role in the Turkish dispute with France over the Sanjak of Alexandretta in 1936–37, of the Polish-Lithuanian dispute over Vilna, of the Franco-Spanish dispute in Tangiers, or of League intervention in Liberia, 1932–36. Equally there is a whole field to be explored in the changing nature of diplomacy by conference. At the moment we only have studies of the two principal naval disarmament conferences, Washington in 1921–22[17] and London in 1930,[18] all of these much weighted from the American side. Despite the spate of documentary publications on Locarno in 1925[19] and Lausanne in 1932[20] as yet we lack any adequate studies of either.

For the would-be director of research into problems of international contemporary history now confronts a field divided completely into two by the question of accessibility and availability of documentary material. The problems once faced by the contemporary historian, in that so much of his evidence was of semi-propagandistic provenance, whether in official bluebooks or justificatory memoirs, now only apply to the period after 1945. Research into the history of the inter-war years and the years of the Second World War still has to catch up with and exploit the massive new documentary publications of the Belgian,[21] French, Portuguese,[22] and Hungarian[23] diplomatic documents, as with the increasing publication of Russian records and memoirs.[24] The German diplomatic and military materials still have to be adequately exploited for the light they shed on relations between states in which Germany was not herself directly involved.[25] The series, *Foreign Relations of the United States*, is now nearly complete for the years up to 1945; yet apart from the volumes on Teheran, Malta and Yalta, and Potsdam, the series has been very little used as yet by historians. The immense wealth of Japanese documentation and memoir literature presents obvious special difficulties to the Western international historian; yet it is a pity that recent work by Japanese and Japanese-American scholars writing in English has tended to concentrate on the domestic background to Japanese foreign policy.[26] The present publication of Vatican diplomatic correspondence[27] also opens a rich vein of research into non-national aspects of international politics. The considerable store of Polish[28] and Yugoslav[29] documentation in the west has still to be thoroughly exploited. And though recent Rumanian work on the 1930s is still at the level of primitive Stalinist historiography,[30] there is room for hope that Mr Ceausescu's recent attack on the Soviet Union for concluding the Nazi-Soviet Pact may lead to a more sophisticated publication from or of the Rumanian archives. From the recent work of the Polish historian, Lukas Hirscowicz, on the *Third Reich and the Arab East*[31] it seems there is still a lot of German diplomatic material in the hands of the East German authorities. And the work of East German historians has been growing greatly in sophistication since the crudities of the early 1950s.[32] Recent Czech work has also begun to draw on the Czech diplomatic archives.[33]

For research into the years before 1939, one might envisage five main fields of investigation. The first, already discussed above, is that of conference diplomacy within and beyond the limits of the League of Nations. Differing aspects of this would include the

BRITAIN: CONTEMPORARY INTERNATIONAL HISTORY

development of the Soviet security system on the basis of a network of bilateral non-aggression and non-intervention treaties.[34]
Other themes of equal interest could be found in the later activities
of the Little Entente,[35] of the Balkan Entente, of the Scandinavian
states,[36] of Italy's Rome Protocols, and of the Pan-American conferences, a theme on which there has been curiously little satisfactory work in the United States and none elsewhere. A second
field, also hardly developed outside the rather narrow confines of
German-Soviet relations, is that of military and strategic influences
on the conduct of diplomacy and relations between the armed
forces of different countries.[37]

A third field is that of financial and economic diplomacy. In this
the more it is studied the more important the failure of the international negotiations of 1931-33 to find an international solution
to the breakdown of international trade and finance becomes in
explaining the weaknesses of Britain and France *vis-à-vis* the
aggressive states in the 1930s. From the negotiations over reparations and war debts in 1920-23, through the negotiation of the
Dawes and Young loans, the year of crisis in 1931, the conferences
of Lausanne (1932) and London (1933) to the decline of the 'gold
bloc', the Anglo-French-American stabilization agreement of 1936,
we have only the merest handful of studies, nearly all of American
provenance and based on American evidence.[38] We have some
work on the Chinese silver question in 1934-36, though much
more needs to be done,[39] and only one study of recent origin on
the League of Nations loan to Austria. We have no studies of the
negotiations and discussions of access to raw materials which so
much occupied the League of Nations in 1936-37 or of the question
of Germany's colonial claims,[40] although without these the content
of the Hudson-Wohltat conversations in 1939 are virtually un-
intelligible. The naïve pseudo-Marxist theories on the economic
origins of international conflict which underlay these negotiations,
as they did Secretary of State Cordell Hull's trade agreements
policy, has been commented on in passing by numerous writers.
But we still lack detailed studies of the intellectual and political
climate of opinion from which they sprang.

A fourth field is the role and development of a variety of non-
national entities in developing the kind of contra-national loyalties
from which treason, fifth columnism, 'rather Hitler than Blum',
etc. developed. A number of topics occur to one as worthy of study
in this context. I have already dealt very inadequately with

63

long-range German efforts to influence élite opinion in Britain.[41] And an Oxford D.Phil. thesis is now in progress on the role of the British foreign correspondents in Europe in depicting the onset of nazism as a Europe-wide threat to democracy.[42] There have been a few studies of British opinion and the Jewish question,[43] the rise of nazism,[44] the Spanish Civil War,[45] and appeasement.[46] These have however been static rather than dynamic studies, studies of presentation rather than image. A recent excellent example of what can be done in this field was contained in another London Ph.D. thesis.[47] What one would like to see now would be studies of the role of Willi Münzenberg's and Otto Katz's Paris centre of Comintern anti-fascist propaganda; of the influence of Claud Cockburn's *Week* or Stephen King-Hall's *Newsletters* or of the Friends of Europe's publications.[48] On the other side one would welcome studies of the German and Italian efforts to subvert the French and East European press, of the nazi and Italian radio offensives, of the activities of the *Auslandsorganisation* of the *NSDAP*, the *Volksdeutsche Mittelstelle*, and of Rosenberg's *Aussenpolitisches Amt*.[49] One would equally welcome studies of Japanese encouragement of Indian and Indonesian nationalism.

A slightly different aspect of the same field is that of the intellectual and political influences which led to the migration of nuclear scientists firstly to Germany, then to Cambridge and the United States and produced in this small group, whose influence on the future balance of power was to be without any historical parallel, the climate of opinion which led them to initiate the British and American atomic weapons programmes. A rather different field again would be that of the study of the international disarmament movement and its adversaries in the 1920s, and of other similar lobbies at Geneva. Such studies would have their richly comic element as Robert Ferrell showed fourteen years ago in his study of the origins of the Kellogg pact.[50] But they would also shed a good deal of light on the development of opinion across the boundaries of individual states. Yet another aspect is provided by the quasi-diplomatic activities of international business organizations, from the conflict between the Firestone Rubber Company and the League of Nations over labour conditions in Liberia,[51] through the quasi-nationalism of the 'Big Five' American oil companies in the conflict over the exploitation of Iraqi and Gulf oil in the period 1923–33,[52] to the negotiations of the European steel cartels in 1925–28,[53] a theme so full of reminiscences of British relations with ECSC in the period 1949 onwards.

A fifth field for research in contemporary international history is that of international intellectual influences and the migration of ideas. This has a particular bearing on the question, touched on earlier, of the growth of ties across state frontiers and the development of communities at a supra-national level in this century. Any state considered as a political community today is a network of relationships and connections linking its individual citizens. At times these networks may so follow sub-national, communal divisions that the state is not really the significant political unit; its position as such is usurped by the separate communal groups within it, whether these are organized on 'national-ethnic' lines as in the old Austro-Hungarian empire, on politico-geographical groupings like the southern states of the *ante-bellum* USA, or on religious grounds like the Huguenots in seventeenth-century France or the *millets* of the Ottoman Empire. In such cases, relations between the communal groups may take on some or all of the characteristics we associate with international relations, including that of war.

All this would find fairly general acceptance among historians and social scientists today, though there could well be argument about individual cases. The point I am attempting to make here is that such relationships and connections may equally form themselves above and beyond the limits of the political state. In a very simple and obvious case these links develop between members of similar politico-religious communities in different states, as in the Zionist movement; or as was attempted and theorized about between social democrats in the Second International. They can also develop between states as in the case of the Anglo-American connection or in that of the European movement. And preliminary attempts have been made in the case of Anglo-American relations to measure them, though our limited understanding of their relevance to the consciousness of community in a historical sense makes such attempts often unsatisfactory to the historian.[54] This is in itself a field in which much more research needs to be done. But the field on which I am now attempting to focus attention is not so much this as that of intellectual and cultural movements. A recent pioneering work[55] has called attention to the development between 1880 and 1930 of a literature and of modes of thought on the nature of society on a scale which makes it seem not too

c

far-fetched to talk of there coming into existence 'European' rather than French or German or Italian or Swiss modes of social thought. But there is obviously room for immense developments in this field of what might loosely be called international intellectual history. It is clearly as important, in its own way, for the students of contemporary international history to understand the nature of these contemporary intellectual movements, as to understand the Enlightenment is for the student of international history in the age of the enlightened despots or the theories of the romantics during the era of the revolutions and Napoleon.[56]

Intellectual history is not very much developed in the contemporary field even at a national level, and it may well be that its study at an international level could only be rather vague and imprecise. But there is still a fascinating field for investigation here, in such areas as the influence of Art Nouveau in England and Scotland on the *Sezession* movements in Germany and Austria, the transplantation of the *Bauhaus* movement into the United States, the capture of France and Central Europe by existentialism in the 1940s, the competing influences of Paris, Vienna, Munich, and Berlin in the 1920s and so on, all of which has a bearing on the degree to which the international crisis of 1933–45 in Europe should be seen as a war between nation states, a struggle for mastery in Europe, or as a civil war on a continental scale.

When one turns to the field of history after 1945, the problems of research are very different both in scale and time. Until very recently these years were the province not so much of the historian as of the political scientist. The large bulk of the evidence bears only on the public aspects of international relations. The preliminary task of the historian, the establishment of a narrative of events, is in most cases done.[57] But the material available on the motives and considerations in the minds of the principal actors, the nature and timing of their deliberations and so on is still fragmentary. Archival material is confined to private papers here and in the United States.[58] Official papers are available only in the form of Blue Books, White Papers, etc., or in evidence presented to Senate Committees in the United States.[59] Our main sources are memoirs, which are now beginning to be available to some considerable degree so far as Britain, the United States, Germany, and Austria are concerned. Beyond that one is in the tricky and uncertain field of press reportage and personal testimony,[60] an area where the historian is somewhat more at the mercy of his sources than is professionally comfortable.

It should nevertheless be possible to undertake serious research into international problems involving Britain, the United States, Germany, Austria, and France for the years 1945–56, and, in individual cases, beyond that. Whether the available material is adequate to enable it to be used for training graduate students in the nature and use of historical evidence and in the techniques of its employment and deployment in all but a small handful of cases one may take leave still to doubt. For much more of the historian's reconstruction of motives and intentions must necessarily be imaginative, by inference and analogical argument rather than derivation from direct and reliable evidence, than is so on work in the inter-war years. These are skills that are developed in the process of research, not innate to historical intuition. Work in this field demands a more rigorous self-examination on the historian's part to eliminate bias and to question established myth, and a continuous process of self-reminder of the limited nature of the available evidence and the provisional nature of any conclusions reached, than can be expected of the average graduate student.

That being said, it would seem possible, on the evidence available, to write a reasonably adequate study of the origins and negotiation of the Austrian state treaty; of the European Defence Community and German rearmament; of the cold war in Germany in the years 1945–53; of the diplomacy of the Korean War; of the negotiation of the Marshall Plan and the North Atlantic Alliance; of the Geneva Agreements on South East Asia in 1954; and of the Suez crisis of 1956 and the Lebanese crisis of 1958.[61] The emergence of new powers such as Egypt, India, and China make such studies necessarily much more imperfect where problems are dealt with in which they are involved. But this merely perpetuates a state of affairs which still exists for the inter-war years. The advancing frontier of research is very much limited to European and North American affairs. There is however more than enough territory there to keep us all busy—if not happy.

NOTES

[1] I am grateful to the authorities at the Royal Institute of International Affairs for allowing me to quote from the deed of covenant.

[2] Frederick Hartmann and Hayward Moore, 'International Relations', and D. C. Watt, 'International Organization' in Julius Gould and William L. Kolb, *A Dictionary of the Social Sciences* (London and New York, 1964).

[3] The data on history courses in British universities are taken from George Barlow and Brian Harrison, *History at the Universities* (London, Historical Association, 1966).

Bristol	General Diplomatic History 1815–1939.
Durham	International History 1870–1945.
Leeds	International Relations 1871–1949.
Liverpool	International History 1870–1945.
London School of Economics	International History since 1914. (In the degree of B.Sc. Econ.)
Newcastle	European and International Relations 1878–1939.
Oxford	International Relations 1919–39 *and* International Relations since 1939. (Both in the degree B.A. [Modern Greats].)
Sussex	International Relations since 1900.
Reading	World Politics since 1941.
Sheffield	Europe and the World 1870–1953.
Swansea	General Diplomatic History 1815–1939.

[4] Bristol	The origins of the Pacific War, 1931–1941.
Durham	The Great Powers 1936–1939.
Hull	The origins of the Second World War.
Keele	Diplomatic Prelude to World War II *and* Hitler's Europe.
Leeds	The International Crisis 1929–1939.
London	Peacemaking 1919, the Manchurian Crisis 1931–1933 *and* Anglo-German Naval Diplomacy 1933–1939. (All in B.Sc. Econ.)
Newcastle	The Great Powers 1936–1939.
Nottingham	The origins of World War II.
Reading	The Spanish Civil War *and* Yalta and Potsdam.
Southampton	The Third Reich.
Edinburgh	The Rome-Berlin Axis *and* Destruction of International Society 1925–1939.
Cardiff	Great Britain and the European Crisis 1933–1939.
Swansea	Soviet-German Relations 1919–1939.
St David's, Lampeter	Anglo-German Relations 1933–1939.

[5] *Bulletin of the Institute of Historical Research, Theses Supplements*, Nos. 15–27, *Historical Research for University Degrees in the United Kingdom: Theses Completed, 1954–1964*, and *Theses in Progress, 1966*.

[6] John Chapman, *German-Japanese Military Relations 1936–1945*, Oxford D. Phil. Thesis, 1967.

[7] Frank Marzari, *The Balkans, the Great Powers and the European War 1939–1940*, London Ph.D. Thesis, 1966.

[8] Maurice Pearton, *The Rumanian Oil Industry 1895–1948: A Study in the Relationship between the Rumanian State and Private Capital*, London Ph.D. Thesis, 1966.

[9] Recently reissued with a new introduction. Elizabeth Wiskemann has produced a completely new edition of her excellent *Rome-Berlin Axis* (London, 1967), originally published in 1948.

[10] See for example Mr David Ogg's spirited denunciation of Louis XIV as an aggressor in his *Europe in the Seventeenth Century* (Oxford, 1925).

[11] See D. C. Watt, 'Appeasement. The Rise of a Revisionist School', *Political Quarterly*, 1965.

[12] F. S. Lyons, *Internationalism in Europe, 1815–1914* (Leyden, 1963).

[13] Gar Alperowitz, *Atomic Diplomacy* (London, 1966).

[14] David Adams, *Executive Leadership and the Formulation of a Policy towards Europe during the first Administration of Franklin D. Roosevelt, 1933–1937*, Oxford D.Phil. Thesis, 1962.

[15] James Barros, *The Corfu Incident of 1923, Mussolini and the League of Nations* (Princeton, 1965).

[16] James Barros, 'The Graeco-Bulgarian Conflict of 1925' in Joel Larus (Ed.), *From Collective Security to Preventive Diplomacy* (New York, 1966).

[17] J. Chal Vinson, *The Parchment Peace* (Atlanta, Georgia, 1955). Professor Ernest R. May of Harvard is currently engaged on a new study of the Washington Conference. Attention should also be called to the work of Professor M. G. Fry of Carleton University, Ottawa, in this connection.

[18] Raymond O'Connor, *Perilous Equilibrium* (Topeka, Kansas, 1962).

[19] German Democratic Republic, Ministry of Foreign Affairs, *Lokarno 1925* (Berlin, 1959). See also A. F. Dobrow, *Lokarnskaia Konferentsiia, 1925 g: Dokumenti* (Moscow, 1959).

[20] France, Ministère des Affaires Etrangères, *Documents Diplomatiques Françaises, 1932–1939*. Iᵉ Série, 1932–1935, Tome I (9 Juillet–14 Novembre 1932) (Paris, 1964); *Documents on British Foreign Policy, 1919–1939*, second series, vol. III (London, 1948).

[21] Belgium, Académie royale de Belgique, *Documents Diplomatiques Belges, 1920–1940; La Politique de la Securité extérieure*, Tome I, *1920–1924*; Tome II, *1925–1931*; Tome III, *1932–1936* (Brussels, 1964).

[22] Portugal, Ministério dos Negócias Estrangeiros, *Dez Anos de politica externa* (1936–1947). *A naçao portuguese e a segundo guerra mundial*, Parte I, *O Rearmamento do Exército no quadro pólitica de Alianca Luso-Britânica, 1936–1939*, 2 vols. (Lisbon, 1961–1962).

[23] Hungary, Historical Institute of the Academy of Sciences, *Diplómaciai iratok magyarorszag kulpolitikájahoz 1936–1945*, vol. I (Budapest, 1962); vol. II (Budapest, 1965); vol. IV (Budapest, 1962). Translation of selected documents have been published in *Acta Historica*, Budapest. See Gy. Juhász, 'Beiträge zu Ungarns Aussenpolitik in den Tagen des Ausbruches des Zweiten Weltkrieges, August–September 1939', *Acta Historica*, 1963. M. Adam, 'Documents relatifs à la politique étrangère de la Hongrie dans la période de la crise tchécoslovaque 1938–1939', ibid., 1963, 1964. See also L. Zsigmond, 'Ungarn und das Münchner Abkommen', ibid., 1959; Gy. Juhász, 'La politique de la Hongrie à l'époque

de la drôle de guerre', ibid., 1963; I. Berend and Gy. Ranki, 'German-Hungarian Relations following Hitler's rise to power', ibid., 1964.

[24] See for example, 'Les négotiations militaires entre l'U.R.S.S., la France et la Grande Bretagne, en Août 1939', *Recherches Internationales à la lumière du Marxisme*, N.12, March–April 1959; 'Teheran Conference of the Leaders of the Three Great Powers. Documents', *International Affairs* (Moscow, 1961); 'The Struggle of the U.S.S.R. for Collective Security in Europe during 1933–1935. Documents', ed. M. Andreyeva and L. Vidyesova, ibid., 1963; 'The Crimea and Potsdam Conferences of the Leaders of the Three Great Powers', ibid., 1965, 1966. See also the reminiscences of N. N. Lyubimov and A. N. Erlikh, 'The 1922 Genoa Conference', article in three parts, ibid., 1963; of A. Y. Bogamolov, 'Wartime Diplomatic Missions', ibid., 1961; Admiral N. G. Kuznetsov, 'Before the war', ibid., 1966. Ivan Maiski's memoirs, *Who helped Hitler?* (London, 1965) and *Spanish Notebooks* (London, 1966), are now reported to be under attack in Russia. For an article based on Soviet archival material see A. Stepanov, 'The Historical Experience of Cooperation between the U.S.S.R. and Germany. The 1926 Berlin Treaty', ibid., 1963, August.

[25] I have attempted to show how useful these are for the study of Middle Eastern Diplomacy in the years 1936–39 in my two articles, 'The Foreign Policy of Ibn Saud' and 'The Sa'dabad Pact of July 4, 1937', in *Journal of the Royal Central Asian Society*, 1962 and 1963. They also shed a good deal of light on events in China in the years 1933–37, during which time there was a German military mission engaged in training Chiang Kai-shek's army.

[26] See Akira Iriye, *After Imperialism. The Search for a New Order in the Far East, 1921–1931* (Cambridge, Mass., 1965); Takehiko Yoshihashi, *Conspiracy at Mukden* (New Haven, 1963).

[27] Vatican City, Segretario di Stato, *Actes et documents du Saint Siège relatifs à la seconde guerre mondiale*, vol. I, *Le Saint Siège et la guerre en Europe, Mars 1939–Août 1940* (Vatican City, 1965); vol. II, *Lettres de Pie XII aux Évêques allemands, 1939–1944* (Vatican City, 1966).

[28] These are divided between various *emigré* holdings and the Polish Foreign Ministry archives in Warsaw.

[29] See J. Hoptner, *Jugoslavia in Crisis* (New York, 1962).

[30] See for example B. Balteanu, 'Relatiile Governului S.U.A. cu Regionul Fascist din Romînia (Septembrie 1940–Junie 1942)', *Studi. Revista de Istorie*, 1958; V. A. Varga, 'Attitudinea Governului Romîn Burghezo-Mosieresc fata de tratativele Anglo-Franco-Sovietice din Anul 1939', ibid., 1960; P. Constantinescu-Iasi si I. N. Oprea, 'O Importanta Figura a diplomatiei Europene—Nicolae Titulescu', ibid., 1961. Varga's article, for example, manages to discuss his theme with the use of Rumanian diplomatic archives without ever mentioning the role of the Rumanian minister in London, M. Tilea, in prompting the original British approaches to the Soviet Union.

[31] London, 1966.

[32] Contrast for example Fritz Klein, *Die diplomatischen Beziehungen Deutschlands zur Sowjet Union 1913–1922* (Berlin, 1952), with Alfred

Anderle, *Die deutsche Rapallo-politik: Deutsch-Sowjetische Beziehungen, 1922–1929* (Berlin, 1962).

[33] See, for example, Robert Kraček, 'Německá likvidace demilitarizovaného porýnského pásma 7 Března 1936', *Československy Časopsis Historický*, vol. 11 (1963); Milena Janisová, 'Francouzká zahraniční politika a Československo v obdobi přípcar Mnichova', ibid., English summaries are to be found in *Historical Abstracts* (1964).

[34] See Marlbone W. Graham, 'The Soviet Security System', *International Conciliation*, 1929.

[35] See Piotr Wandycz, *France and her eastern allies, 1922–1925* (Minneapolis, 1962). See also Rudolf Kiszlung, 'Die militärische Vereinbarungen der kleinen Entente, 1929–1937', *Südostforschungen*, 1958–59.

[36] See Nils Ørvik, *Sikkerheits politiker 1920–1939* (Oslo, 1960).

[37] John Chapman's thesis, cited in footnote 6 above, deals in some detail with German-Japanese military relations.

[38] See (i) on reparations, D. B. Gescher, *Die Vereinigten Staaten von Nord-amerika und die Reparationen 1920–1924* (Bonn, 1956); Wolfgang J. Helbich, *Die Reparationen in der Ära Brunings* (Berlin, 1962); (ii) on the economic crisis of 1931–1932, Edward W. Bennett, *Germany and the Diplomacy of the Financial Crisis, 1931* (Harvard, 1962); F. G. Stambrook, 'The German-Austrian Customs Union Project of 1931', *Journal of Central European Studies*, 1961; the same, 'A British Proposal for the Danubian States: the Customs Union Project of 1932', *Slavonic and East European Review*, 1963–4; Andreas Predohl, 'Die Epochenbedeutung der Weltwirtschaftskrise von 1929 bis 1931', *Vierteljahresheft für Zeitgeschichte*, 1953; (iii) Robert H. Ferrell, *American Diplomacy in the Great Depression* (New Haven, 1957); (iv) Jeanette P. Nicholls, 'Roosevelt's Financial Diplomacy in 1933', *American Historical Review*, 1950–51.

[39] See Dorothy Borg, *The United States and the Far Eastern Crisis of 1931–1938* (Cambridge, Mass., 1964); John N. Blum, *From the Morgenthau Diaries, Years of Crisis, 1929–1938* (Boston, 1959).

[40] There is one study of the German colonial movement after 1918, W. W. Schmokel, *Dream of Empire* (New Haven, 1964). The Portuguese diplomatic documents contain a good deal of material on the colonial question in the years 1936–38, as memories of the Anglo-German conversations of 1899 and 1914 on the future of Portugal's African colonies would suggest. See also the very suggestive chapter on British proposals for economic appeasement in 1936–37 in Martin Gilbert, *The Roots of Appeasement* (London, 1966), pp. 150–158.

[41] D. C. Watt, *Personalities and Policies* (London, 1965), Essay 6, 'German influence on British opinion, 1933–1938, and the attempts to counter it'.

[42] An American student, Mr Frank Gannon, is the author.

[43] Andrew Sharf, *The British Press and Jews under Nazi rule* (Oxford, 1964).

[44] Brigitte Granzow, *A Mirror of Nazism* (London, 1964).

[45] K. W. Watkins, *Britain Divided* (London, 1964).

[46] Rudolf Kieser, *Englands Appeasementpolitik und der Aufstieg des*

dritten Reiches im Spiegel der britischen Presse, 1933–1939 (Wintherthur, 1964).

[47] Now published. James V. Compton, *The Swastika and the Eagle: Hitler, the United States and the Origins of World War II* (Boston, Mass., 1967, London, 1968).

[48] See, for example, Arthur Koestler, *The Invisible Writing* (London, 1954); Claud Cockburn, *Crossing the Line* (London, 1959); R. M. Carew Hunt, 'Willi Muenzenberg' in *St. Antony's Papers*, No. IX (London, 1960); Margarete Buber-Neumann, *Von Potsdam nach Moskau* (Stuttgart, 1957). See also on Willi Münzenberg, the two articles of Helmut Gruber, 'Willi Münzenberg. Propagandist for and against the Comintern', *International Review of Social History*, vol. X, 1965; 'Willi Muenzenberg's German Communist Propaganda Empire, 1921–1933', *Journal of Modern History*, vol. XXXVIII, 1966.

[49] Research into these organizations seems virtually to have ceased once Dr L. de Jong demolished the myth of the fifth column in his *The German Fifth Column in the Second World War* (London, 1956). Nevertheless there would be much to be learnt in, for example, a study of the AO's relations with nazi organizations in South America, the Vd.M's activities in Eastern Europe, or the German financial subvention, via the Holländische Buitenlandsbank of *Volksdeutsch* economic activity in Austria, Czechoslovakia, Poland, and the Baltic States from 1926 onwards.

[50] Robert W. Ferrell, *Peace in their Time* (New Haven, 1952).

[51] A subject on which there is copious documentation both published and unpublished in the papers of the State Department, the Foreign Office, and the League of Nations.

[52] See Benjamin Shwadran, *The Middle East, Oil and the Great Powers* (New York, 1959).

[53] A subject on which the German diplomatic archives are certainly and the Foreign Office archives probably full of evidence.

[54] A recent example of this is Bruce M. Russett, *Community and Contention in Britain and America in the Twentieth Century* (Cambridge, Mass., 1963).

[55] H. Stuart Hughes, *Consciousness and Society; the reorientation of European social thought* (London, 1959).

[56] R. R. Palmer, *The Age of the Democratic Revolution* (Princeton, 1959–64).

[57] I cannot forbear to mention here the extreme importance of the volumes of the *Survey of International Affairs*, and its German equivalent *Die Internationale Politik*, as attempts to provide such a narrative from a genuinely international viewpoint.

[58] See D. C. Watt, 'Restrictions on Research. The Fifty-Year Rule and British Foreign Policy', *International Affairs*, London, January 1965, for American private papers available to research. See Essay XIV, D. C. Watt, *Personalities and Policies*, for British sources.

[59] We are promised a publication of *Documents on British Foreign Policy, 1945–1950*, but this is obviously still a long way from fruition, as is the promised extension of Cabinet Office histories into the post-war period.

[60] Two recent examples of how effective such sources can be if properly used are Miriam Camps, *Britain and the European Community, 1955–1962* (Oxford, 1965), and Eli Abel, *The Cuban Missile Crisis* (London, 1966). Terence Robertson, *Crisis 1956* (London, 1965), is a rather more controversial example of the same technique.

[61] The department of politics of the University of Reading is currently launching a research project of a basically historical character into the Lebanese crisis of 1958.

France

RENÉ RÉMOND

Work in Progress

Historical research is never totally independent of the society in which it is carried out. The amount of work done, the directions of its curiosity, its underlying preoccupations, are strongly influenced by the intellectual and material circumstances that govern the historian's work. Contemporary history in France does not escape this determinism, and even the change it has recently undergone provides an illustration of this general proposition.

Barely ten years ago contemporary history, and more particularly that of the years after the First World War, had been practically abandoned by historians to writers who addressed themselves to the general public, and we had good reason to denounce this state of affairs in an article entitled 'Plea for a Neglected Branch of History'.[1] Today the situation has greatly changed and, at any rate in some sectors, glut is taking the place of shortage. Several works on the subject appear every month, or practically every month; some of them are very estimable, and a few actually contribute to revising our knowledge of the period. Looking to the future, the amount of work in progress presages a still more abundant harvest. The history of the most immediate past enjoys such prestige among young historians looking for subjects for their doctoral theses that, to the extent that it is only a passing infatuation not based on considered knowledge of the period and its problems, it almost calls for restraint.

The previous attitude of reserve towards contemporary history was chiefly based on the time-honoured tradition of mistrust of using the historian's tools too close to the event. An intelligible and legitimate loyalty to the principle that each man should stick to his trade lent substance to the view that history was marked off from journalism and contemporary political or occasional writing by the remoteness in time of its subject-matter; history's speciality was the distant past. This attitude was buttressed by an apparently insurmountable practical circumstance, namely the rule that keeps government documents from scrutiny by historians until they are fifty years old. How could proper historical research be undertaken without access to documents? Thus necessity combined with the historian's own views to cause the responsibility for writing about contemporary affairs to be left to the publicists.

The change of heart that has taken place in the last few years owes nothing to a possible modification of the fifty-year rule. Even if it has sometimes been modified in practice, and mild infringements have been permitted in some cases, it still exists, and constitutes an obstacle to research which we shall not attempt to underestimate. But reflection on the purpose of history, its methods and sources, and on the relativity of its results, combined with the enlargement of the field of historical curiosity and the progressive inclusion within its domain of all sorts of previously neglected aspects, have led to a revaluation of the importance of the ban and to the belief that in many cases—all those in which the public archives can supply only supplementary documentation—it is by no means impossible to circumvent the difficulty and undertake genuine historical study without further delay.

A factor that contributed to this change was the increased interest in contemporary history shown by what is usually called the general public. The Second World War, followed by the rapidity and completeness of the process of decolonization, the frequent dramatic turns of current events, the acceleration of the pace of history, all played their part. At the present time the most immediately contemporary history shares with the most ancient history of all, that of civilizations that were believed to have vanished but have been brought to life by recent archaeological discoveries, the favour of a public whose attention is thus concentrated on the two extremes of social development. This elementary curiosity, whether well or ill informed, but greedier for titbits than for going to the heart of the matter, is certainly not in itself sufficient justification for contemporary historical research, but it inclines people in that direction and indirectly favours the change of attitude.

Other factors have worked more powerfully to the same end because they occupy a higher rank in the intellectual scale. In the first place there are the needs of education. As a result of reforms which have brought about big changes in the educational structure and syllabus during the past few years, contemporary history has entered the classroom and the lecture hall. It made its first appearance in the secondary schools but, as one of the principal functions of the universities is the training of secondary school teachers, the universities in their turn had to include all or part of the contemporary period in their teaching and examination syllabus. Thus contemporary history has ceased to be *terra incognita*; academic historians have reconnoitred it and begun to apply to it their analytic methods and their preoccupations. Having become a subject of instruction, it necessarily became an object of research.

Finally, on this matter of research, we must mention the role and policy of a number of institutions whose efforts are directed to the history of the past fifty years, whether out of deliberate choice or because they were founded for the purpose. We shall mention some of the most important of them in connection with books published or work being done under their auspices. In the first place there is the Fondation Nationale des Sciences Politiques, founded in 1945 for the purpose of 'assuring the progress and dissemination of the political, economic, and social sciences in France and abroad'. Its primary purpose was the study of the present; the past, even the immediate past, was not its real business. But the scientific rigour of its work and the quality of its publications greatly contributed to demolishing the prejudice according to which there could be no valid and objective analysis of the immediate past. Moreover, explanation of the present being impossible without knowledge of its antecedents, it was led by the very logic of its work into invading an area that constituted a sort of no-man's-land between history of the past and analysis of the present, and applying to it the methods of political science. The progress of the political scientists, gradually probing further and further backwards in time, has its counterpart in the opposite progress of the historians, gradually working their way closer and closer to the contemporary; the two movements, not concerted but convergent, explain the leap forward in contemporary historical studies.

Other more specialized bodies have actively contributed to the trend, such as the Committee for the History of the Second World War, which has been doing exemplary work for twenty years collecting and preserving documents and material relating to the Resistance; the Institute of Social History, which is devoted to the study of the labour movement, trade unionism, and socialism;

the French Press Institute; the organizations devoted to religious sociology; and others besides.

A whole range of publications exist to publish the work of these various institutions and the results of individual and collective research in general. There are historical reviews, though the part played in them by the completely contemporary is restricted, and juridical reviews. There is the *Revue d'histoire de la deuxième guerre mondiale*, the *Revue française de science politique*, *Le mouvement sociale*, published by the Institute of Social History, and others which it would take too long to enumerate. In addition to these bi-monthlies or quarterlies, there are a number of publications—some of them highly specialized—such as *Esprit de la Résistance*, which is connected with the Committee for the History of the Second World War, as well as others addressed to the general public and devoted wholly or in part to the history of the past fifty years. Let us mention two: the Kiosque series, the original purpose of which was to present events as the press presented them at the time, has helped to demonstrate the importance of the press as a source of information about a period. Its field is not restricted to the twentieth century but, as the major development of the press took place in comparatively recent times, it follows that most of the volumes in the series apply to our own period. The same is true of the Archives series, which fulfils a function in some ways complementary to that of Kiosque by printing unpublished documents found in public and private archives; several volumes that have appeared have enriched our knowledge of the past fifty years.

Thus the curiosity of the man in the street changes in the field of education, and the work of a variety of research institutions combine to stimulate the study of contemporary history, at the same time putting tools and facilities for publication at the disposal of workers in the field. All these things add up to a relatively new situation; and knowledge of the recent past has already begun to feel the benefit, as is shown by the proliferation of publications in the past few years.

The attention of those engaged in these studies is of course not evenly distributed over the period; whether deliberately or by chance, it has tended to concentrate on certain aspects.

Choice of subject depends on various considerations. Partly it follows the line of previous interests, as has been the case with the study of elections or that of the sociology of religion, which were begun before the Second World War. It also reflects the availability of documents; and finally it is subject to the influence of schools and theories. The perpetually changing combination of these various factors, chance or fundamental, explains the unequal development of historical work, which has favoured some sectors and neglected others. The rapid survey of contributions and lacunae that follows illustrates the result of these general factors with concrete examples.

The strides made by political science and the recent revival of political history, which was for a long time eclipsed by economic history, lie at the source of a whole series of works on the political aspect of contemporary history. But even within this category there are great disparities. The study of elections enjoys undisputed primacy; it is of course a speciality of French historiography. The primacy is the result of a priority; the discipline was born with André Siegfried's *Tableau politique de la France de l'Ouest*, published in 1913 and recently republished. This pioneering work remained without posterity for a long time, however; the thread was picked up by François Goguel on the eve of the last war. Since then the study of election phenomena has greatly expanded and has advanced in two different directions. One consists of local monographs tracing how voting has gone, generally within the framework of a department, since the introduction of universal suffrage in 1848 and up to a more or less recent date. The other, originated by the Fondation Nationale des Sciences Politiques, consists of systematic studies of general elections, which have been carried out continuously since 1956. The multiplication of elections in recent years, and in particular the recourse that is had to elections of different types—parliamentary, presidential, referendums—has widened the field for empirical research and theoretical reflection on electoral behaviour. With each year that passes study has become more detailed; thus the comparative analysis of results has been extended from the departmental to the cantonal level, which makes it possible to discover revealing contrasts and significant disparities under the deceptive uniformity of averages. The French school of electoral sociology now possesses a substantial quantity of statistical data, rigorous methods, and a theoretical apparatus. Gaps certainly still exist, but they are being progressively filled. To quote a single example, a work now in course of preparation on electoral abstention dating back to the Second

Republic will contribute new data about a phenomenon that has for too long been neglected but is nevertheless an essential part of political life. As it does not confine itself to description, but aims at explaining both the constants and the variables of its subject-matter both in space and in time, electoral sociology, so far from being self-contained, opens out into other aspects of the French social reality. The strides made in the study of elections have stimulated and nourished all sorts of other research.

Elections, the source of political power and the background of all political life, have been very thoroughly studied, but much less attention has been paid to the exercise of power. This is certainly a gap. There are, however, some signs of the beginnings of re-search into administrative institutions. There is little on the role and work of Parliament, on the Presidency of the Republic, or on the Government. Is the truth that men have masked institutions?

Men? The fact is that it is groups of men rather than individuals who are the subject of study. If the preoccupations of sociologists have indeed penetrated historical research to such an extent that the latter shares the sociological concern for categories and studies the social composition of parliamentary or ministerial personnel (cf. the work of Mattei Dogan)[2] or the supporters of a particular political party, it pays very little attention to individuals. This, indeed, is an inveterate tendency of French historiography. Politi-cal, intellectual, or scientific biography, which is in such repute in other countries and is a field in which striking successes have been scored, is almost completely neglected in France. Thus, most of the statesmen of the twentieth century still await their biographers. Will they have long to wait? Some works have appeared in the past few years: Michel Soulié's *La vie politique d'Edouard Herriot* (Paris, 1962), and Pierre Miquel's *Poincaré* (Paris, 1961). Though not quite in the same field, we may classify with these the first volume of another biography, *Léon Jouhaux, cinquante ans de syndicalisme: Des origines à 1921* (Paris, 1962), by Bernard Georges and Denise Tintant. Other work in progress—some nearly finished, some hardly begun—on Waldeck-Rousseau, Caillaux, and Tardieu are signs that contemporary historiography, retreating from over-estimation of mass action, is preparing to reintegrate the indi-vidual dimension into its view of social development. What J.-B. Duroselle has to say about the role of personality in the *Intro-duction à l'histoire des relations internationales*[3] will be read with interest in this connection.

A study of organizations or parties that set out to channel opinion, win votes, and exert influence on the exercise of power is again considering men in groups rather than as individuals. Though conceived from the point of view of political science rather than history properly so-called—though the fragility of these distinctions is exposed when put to the test—Maurice Duverger's *Les partis politiques* (Paris, 1951), which rapidly became a classic, opened up new perspectives and suggested a whole series of new ideas and methods. Fifteen years have passed without its being followed by a procession of works so numerous that it could reasonably be discounted. The political field is covered very unevenly indeed. The Left is ahead of the Right; a classic phenomenon which is easily explained, the Left having the advantage of being better and more rigidly organized, which makes it easier for the historian to deal with. Jacques Fauvet has written the history of the Communist Party, *Histoire du Parti communiste français*, vol. I, *De la guerre à la guerre, 1917–1939*, vol. II, *Vingt-cinq ans de drames, 1939–1965* (Paris, 1964–65). On the question of its origins Annie Kriegel's *Aux origines du communisme français 1914–1920. Contribution à l'histoire du mouvement ouvrier français*,[4] which stops at the Tours congress, throws doubts on the traditional version and puts forward a new interpretation on the basis of thorough study; this is the beginning of a huge enterprise that will lead to a rewriting of the history of the party.

The history of socialism has inspired two important works in rapid succession: Daniel Ligou's *Histoire du socialisme en France, 1871–1961* (Paris, 1962), and Georges Lefranc's *Le mouvement socialiste sous la Troisième République, 1875–1940* (Paris, 1963). But radicalism still awaits its historian. The death of Jacques Kayser left his great work on the subject[5] at a standstill at the year 1901, when the Radical Party was founded. The size of the gap that is left is indicated by the magnitude of the role played by that party and its leaders in the first forty years of the century, which contrasts with that of the socialist or communist leaders, who were almost continually in opposition and out of power. Nor has there been any study of the parliamentary parties of the classic and moderate Right; there has been nothing on the Democratic Alliance or the Republican Federation. Our own study of the Right, *De la première Restauration à la Vème République*, republished in 1964,[6] took things up to 1962, but is devoted more to its ideology and its variations than to its organizations. However, the organizations referred to generically as the Leagues have been the subject of numerous books during the past few years; as subject of retrospective curiosity they come under the same umbrella as the parties of the extreme Left.

This curious polarization to the two extremes at the expense of the centre, the Radicals, the Christian Democrats, and the Moderates, inevitably falsifies perspectives. Apart from books written for the general public, and the unequal work of J. Plumyène and R. Lasierra, *Les fascismes français, 1923–1963* (Paris, 1962), and of R. J. Tournoux, books are being or have been written, though they are still unpublished, on François Coty, the Croix de Feu, the French Social Party, and Jacques Doriot. Within a short time excellent studies on all the organizations that come within this category will be available. It will then be possible to take the measure of the phenomenon, and to make a proper appreciation of the question of the reality of French fascism to take the place of the often summary judgments expressed on the matter. A still unpublished study of the UNR by Jean Charlot analyses the origin and exercise of power in that organization.

If we pass from the enumeration of subjects to the enumeration of periods, there are a number that stand out. Pride of place goes to the years 1935–38 and the Popular Front. There are several reasons for this: the extent of the strike movement that followed the left-wing victory at the polls, the extent of the labour legislation enacted that changed the condition of the workers, the government's originality—it was the first under socialist leadership that France had known—and the personality of its leader. Finally, the lessons that some people hope to be able to learn from the experience and a subtle mixture of gratitude and nostalgia both help to stimulate interest. Two works opened the way: George Dupeux's election study *Le Front populaire et les élections de 1936* (Paris, 1959), and Louis Bodin's and Jean Touchard's *Front populaire, 1936* (Paris, 1951), which admirably succeed in recreating the atmosphere of 1936 with the aid of newspaper extracts on the Kiosque principle. Subsequent works throw light on one or another aspect of the subject or sum up our knowledge of it, such as George Lefranc's *Histoire du Front populaire* (Paris, 1965) and his *Juin 1936, l'explosion du Front populaire* (Paris, 1966). The *Mouvement social* has just devoted a special number to the subject, and in March 1965 the Fondation Nationale des Sciences Politiques arranged a symposium on 'Léon Blum, Prime Minister, 1936–37';

the occasion was made notable by the number and quality of the participants and the solidity and wealth of their communications, which form the contents of a volume recently published.[7]

Another period that has attracted a great deal of attention is 1939–45, as is explained by the intensity and gravity of those dramatic years. The precursor in the matter was Marc Bloch who, under the impact of the spectacle of military collapse, wrote *L'étrange défaite*,[8] published after his death. The Committee for the History of the Second World War picked up the thread. Almost immediately after the events in question it set about its task of collecting and preserving all documents and evidence relating to the occupation, the deportations, and the Resistance. The work it has done is one of the best examples of what contemporary historians can do to protect the interests of future historians by preventing the disappearance and destruction of their sources. Moreover, the organization does not content itself with merely assembling material; it has promoted studies so abundant that, paradoxically, we are better informed about the history of the clandestine struggle against the invader than we are about other aspects that are wide open to examination. The series entitled *Esprit de la Résistance* is an admirable source for the period.[9] The committee's work offers a practical demonstration that it is not impossible for minds trained in historical method to be objective even about close events which were the theme of passionate controversy. In view of its *a priori* interest in the struggle against the invader, the committee has taken little interest in the other side, the Vichy government and the 'national revolution', or the personality and role of Marshal Pétain. Our knowledge of the years in question suffers from this marked lack of balance. Except for a few unpartisan works, of which Robert Aron's *Histoire de Vichy* (Paris, 1954) is the chief, nearly everything that has appeared on the Vichy regime is vitiated by partisanship or concern for rehabilitation. Let us note in passing that both Robert Aron and the committee have independently set about an attempt to establish accurately the number of victims of the purge and to throw light on a question embroiled and bedevilled by passion or ill-faith, whichever of the two expressions is preferred.

The Fourth Republic, suddenly pushed back into the past by the birth of the Fifth, has already been the subject of several general surveys, such as Jacques Fauvet's *La IVième République* (Paris, 1959), and Georgette Elgey's *La République des illusions*.[10] As the awakening of interest in political science roughly coincided with the origins of the Fourth Republic, we have at our disposal ample studies of the most various aspects of its history.

We have lingered, perhaps unduly, over the political aspects of contemporary history, but this apparent disproportion reflects historical production, which favours the political dimension. So far as number of books is concerned, in spite of the very unequal distribution of subject-matter and the large gaps we have mentioned, economic and social studies are a poor relation. Let us hasten to add that this situation is peculiar to the most immediately contemporary history, because the reverse applies to more distant periods. So far as the latter are concerned, economic history has tended to eclipse political history. Why this unusual situation? There is no doubt that the explanation lies in difficulties of documentation; political facts are more obvious and their implications more tangible, while we are poorly equipped to follow economic developments, and even worse for the study of social groups. Thus in this field the list of gaps is longer than the list of books.

In the field of economics we must mention the work of the Service d'Étude de l'Activité Économique et de la Situation Sociale, a specialized department of the Fondation Nationale des Sciences Politiques. Though its chief concern is following current developments, it by no means ignores the past. At the symposium on Léon Blum its director, Jean-Marcel Jeanneney, presented a weighty communication on the economic policy of the Popular Front government. We must also mention a general work by Alfred Sauvy on the economic history of the inter-war years, the first volume of which, *De l'armistice à la dévaluation de la livre*, appeared in 1965.

We have had no general work on agriculture and the peasants, or on the bourgeoisie and the middle classes, or on the Civil Service. Again it is the world of labour about which we are least ill-informed, because of the almost religious interest traditionally attached to trade unionism; the history of the labour movement is sacred history. There have recently been a number of works in this field: Maurice Labi's *La grande division des travailleurs. Première scission de la CGT, 1914–1921* (Paris, 1964); Antoine Prost's *La CGT à l'époque du Front populaire, 1934–1936. Essai de description numérique* (Paris, 1964); Gérard Adam, *La CFTC, 1940–1958. Histoire politique et idéologique* (Paris, 1964). The Institute of Social History and its organ *Mouvement social*, which among other things have undertaken the publication of a monumental biographical dictionary of the labour movement, are also helping to throw light on that movement and on trade union organizations. But it will be noted that these books give us information only about the organized and militant section of the working class and throw only indirect light on the working conditions, housing, and pay of industrial workers. Antoine Prost is writing a book on ex-servicemen which, we have every reason to suppose, will cover both social history, the study of attitudes and ideas, and that of political forces; a good example of a subject that cuts across several fields too often treated in isolation.

Society as a whole includes numerous special societies, each of which draws its principle of cohesion from a specific profession, supplemented by ways of thinking that have become traditional. By various routes—political developments that put, say, the army or the school question, in the foreground, or the spread of socio-logical interests, or again the increased interest taken by political scientists in pressure groups—historians have come to take an interest in the existence and history of these groups. Three have attracted special attention, the army, the teachers, and the priests. On the first of these Raoul Girardet's pregnant *La société militaire dans la France contemporaine* (Paris, 1952) has been followed by various works, including Vincent Monteil's *Les officiers* (Paris, 1955); Paul-Marie de la Gorce's *La République et son armée* (Paris, 1963);[11] and *La crise militaire française, 1945–1962*, by Raoul Girardet and others (Paris, 1964). There have also been various studies of teachers, their social origin, number, outlook, and in-fluence on political life. As for the priests, it has recently been calculated that books about them appear at an average rate of one a month.

If a balance sheet of the present state of historical research is to pay as much attention to trends that foreshadow the future, even if these are still only taking shape, as to those that are solidly established and have a substantial output to show for it, a special place must be reserved for the study of ideas. A strong current of interest is carrying a number of young historians towards the his-tory of ideas and attitudes, which is inseparable from the study of public opinion. This area of research is divided into two branches. The first is devoted to political ideologies; it keeps contact with the analysis of political parties, since the latter are the expression of the principal ideologies in the field of organized forces, but it also includes within its range of interest a number of phenomena which, though ideological, do not always result in anything so solidly constituted. Jean-Jacques Chevallier's teaching in the Paris law faculty, and that of Jean Touchard at the Institute of Political Studies, and his *Histoire des idées politiques*,[12] have yielded a harvest of books on the political ideas of the past fifty years, as a result of which the study of ideas that inspire ways of behaviour has now reacquired its rights of citizenship in history as properly understood. The other branch is devoted to religion. If one were called on to establish a hierarchy of the various branches of historical work based on their vitality, religious history would occupy a foremost place, side by side with the history of elections and that of the labour movement. This phenomenon owes a great deal to the religious sociology founded a third of a century ago by Gabriel Le Bras, which has made such strides in France that it can be described as another French speciality. The sociologists also have not failed to discover that the explanation of the contemporary phenomena they analyse forces them backwards in time. Simultaneously the notion of the phenomenon of religion as a historical fact has been enlarged and enriched. For too long religious history was restricted to the purely ecclesiastical, but it has gradually widened its scope to include beliefs, feelings, conduct, the whole of the human personality. At the same time sociologists have been going through an opposite development, tracing ways of behaviour and practices back to mental attitudes and systems of ideas. This branch of history, which professional historians for a long time regarded as marginal, existing at the periphery of real history, has ended by being fully integrated into their subject as one of its constituent elements. A number of works have recently appeared or are just being completed on the Sillon (the Catholic social movement founded towards the close of the nineteenth century), the modernist crisis, the Catholic youth movement, the episcopate under the Third Republic, Catholics during the Second World War, the Abbé Lemire, the Christian Democrats, the oecumenical movement, and relations with communism. Some works put forward provisional conclusions and point the way for future research, such as André Latreille's and René Rémond's *Histoire du catholicisme française*, vol. III; *La période contemporaine* (Paris, 1962), and Aline Coutrot's and François G. Dreyfus's *Les forces religieuses dans la société française* (Paris, 1966).

It goes without saying that none of these studies of mental attitudes could have been carried out without a most careful study of the press. Now, the press occupies two positions in relation to contemporary historical research; it is both a source of documentation in regard to other matters and a subject of study itself. As the latter it has been the object of lively interest during the past few years; a research centre, the French Press Institute, the journal *Étude de Presse*, and the Kiosque series are devoted to it. Big projects are in hand which will resume histories interrupted for more than a century. Pending the completion of these, material for future syntheses is being accumulated in the form of numerous monographs on dailies, weeklies, and reviews, generally political or denominational, and at the same time political and religious history is enriched by these studies. All this work is inspired by the methods of analysis developed by Jacques Kayser, who was the great initiator in this field. Let us quote a few titles by way of example: Aline Coutrot's *Un courant de la pensée catholique: l'hebdomadaire 'Sept'* (Paris, 1961); Jean-Pierre Gault's *Histoire d'une fidelité: Témoignage chrétien, 1944–1956* (Paris, 1963); and Françoise Mayeur's *L'Aube. Étude d'un journal d'opinion* (Paris, 1966).

It will perhaps have been noted with surprise that the inventory we have drawn up mentions no work about foreign countries. Does French historiography deliberately ignore all that takes place beyond the frontiers of France? This silence is primarily the consequence of the present writer's own approach in the matter. The intention being to present a view of the present state of research in France, it seemed appropriate to give priority to work in the domestic field. But it must also be admitted that French historians in general take little interest in other countries. However, we must not overlook the revolution in the field of the history of international relations carried out by Pierre Renouvin and continued by Jean-Baptiste Duroselle. They are joint authors of an *Introduction à l'histoire des relations internationales* (Paris, 1964),[13] which states their position and will certainly be a signpost for future work. Much work is being done on the history of colonization (and subsequent decolonization), which occupies an intermediate position between domestic and foreign history; it combines study of the conquest of the territories in question, their life under French administration, and finally the stages in their progress to independence. This field is illuminated by the names of Charles-

André Julien[14] (*Histoire de l'Algérie*), of Jacques Berque,[15] Roger Le Tourneau,[16] and Jean-Louis Miège[17] in connection with North Africa, and of Henri Brunschwig,[18] Robert Cornevin,[19] and Hubert Deschamps[20] in connection with Black Africa. So far from putting an end to work in this field, the independence of the former colonies has given it a new impulse, as is shown by the amount of work in progress.

This rapid survey will perhaps give the reader an impression of heterogeneity. Will he permit us to observe that that is inherent in the nature of the subject? Moreover, it is in conformity with the nature and rhythm of intellectual production. We have not been visiting a finished building, but a busy working site, in parts of which work is well in hand while in others it has barely begun. The important thing is that teams are busy everywhere, animated by a common desire to assure the advance of knowledge and wrest our immediate past from obscurity. The subject of which we have taken a snapshot is in a state of perpetual change and motion, so the closer our portrait is to the reality of the moment the quicker it will become obsolete; but it also shows in broad outline the features of the history of tomorrow.

NOTES

[1] 'Plaidoyer pour une histoire délaissée', *Revue française de science politique*, VII (2), April–June, 1957, pp. 253–70.

[2] cf. Mattei Dogan and J. Narbonne, *Les Françaises face à la politique* (Paris, 1955).

[3] Jean-Baptiste Duroselle and Pierre Renouvin, *Introduction à l'histoire des relations internationales* (Paris, 1964). An English edition, *Introduction to a History of International Relations*, was published in London in 1968.

[4] Annie Kriegel, *Aux origines du communisme français 1914–1920. Contribution à l'histoire du mouvement ouvrier français*, 2 vols. (Paris, 1964).

[5] Jacques Kayser, *Les grandes batailles du radicalisme des origines aux portes du pouvoir 1820–1901* (Paris, 1962).

[6] René Rémond, *La Droite en France. De la première Restauration à la Ve République* (Paris, 1964).

[7] *Léon Blum, chef de gouvernement, 1936–1937*, Collection des Cahiers de la Fondation Nationale des Sciences Politiques (Paris, 1967).

[8] Marc Bloch, *L'étrange défaite* (Paris, 1946). An English translation entitled *Strange defeat; a statement of evidence written in 1940* was published in London in 1949.

Marc Bloch, born in 1886, was appointed Professor of Economic History at the Sorbonne in 1936, and later taught at Clermont Ferrand

and Montpellier. In 1942 he was dismissed by the Vichy regime under the racial laws, and became a leader in the French Resistance. Captured by the Gestapo in March 1944, he was shot in June. His books included *Rois et serfs* (Paris, 1920) and *La société féodale*, 2 vols. (Paris, 1939–40). He was one of the founders, in 1929, of the review *Annales—Economies, Sociétés, Civilisations*.

[9] *Esprit de la Résistance—La Guerre—L'Occupation—La Déportation—La Libération.* The series of volumes under this general title, edited by Henri Michel and Boris Mirkine-Guetzévitch, was published by the Presses Universitaires de France. The first volume appeared in 1954.

[10] Georgette Elgey, *La République des illusions* (Paris, 1965).

[11] An English translation, *The French Army*, was published in London in 1963.

[12] Jean Touchard, *Histoire des idées politiques* (Paris, 1959).

[13] See note 3 above.

[14] Charles-André Julien, *L'histoire de l'Algérie contemporaine*. Vol. I. *La conquête et les débuts de la colonisation (1827–1871)*, (Paris, 1964). See also by the same author *L'Afrique du nord en marche; nationalismes musulmans et souveraineté française* (Paris, 1953).

[15] Jacques Berque, *Les Arabes d'hier à demain* (Paris, 1960). An English translation, *The Arabs, their history and future*, was published in London in 1964.

[16] Roger Le Tourneau, *L'Islam contemporain* (Paris, 1950); also *Évolution politique de l'Afrique du nord musulmane, 1920–1961* (Paris, 1962).

[17] Jean-Louis Miège, *Le Maroc* (Paris, 1952).

[18] Henri Brunschwig, *La Colonisation française du pacte colonial à l'Union française* (Paris, 1949); *Mythes et réalités de l'impérialisme colonial français 1871–1914* (Paris, 1960).

[19] Robert Cornevin, *Le Dahomey* (Paris, 1965).

[20] Hubert Deschamps, *L'Union française* (Paris, 1952); *Histoire de Madagascar* (Paris, 1960).

NEVILLE WAITES

The State of Contemporary History in France*

There should be no need for a paper of this kind. Ideally the historian should, when planning a lecture course, an article, or a book, be able to consult a standard international reference book, periodically kept up to date, in order to find out which historians in other countries have written, or are currently carrying out research, on particular topics. With such a reference work at hand it should very quickly be possible to solve a problem of sources, test a controversial interpretation, or even arrange a joint publication, by writing a letter and receiving a reply in a matter of days. But, while modern communications enable contact to be made across the world within a week, the convention of isolated research accepted by most historians in both Britain and France blinds them to the exciting possibilities of international academic co-operation. To find out what is being done in a particular university or institute today, a personal pilgrimage must be made, as scholars did in the Middle Ages.

Research in blinkered secrecy is wasteful enough for work on

* I should like to thank all those in Paris who made possible this interim study of French research, by kindly sparing time to answer my questions and to recommend sources of information; my gratitude is due particularly to the following: Madame Bourdin and Mlle Poirot-Delpech at the Institut d'Études Politiques, M. Duroselle of the Fondation Nationale des Sciences Politiques and the Fulbright Commission, Marcelle Adler-Bresse at the Bibliothèque de Documentation Internationale Contemporaine, M. Lépissier at the Institut d'Études Slaves, and M. Daillet at the Bureau d'Information des Communautés Européennes, who gave me much information on post-1945 research that is encouraged and often financed by his organization. My thanks are also due to historians at provincial universities in France, who replied helpfully to my enquiries at very short notice.

I need hardly stress that my choice of sources, and judgments based on them, are entirely my own.

periods earlier than the nineteenth century; for topics within the last hundred years, when the rapid development of communications has scattered sources far and wide, individual research is often time-wasting and grossly inaccurate. Only in groups can historians cover the evidence piled up in the twentieth century by the typewriter and duplicator. In an article on the wealth of German source material for research into the Second World War, Marcelle Adler-Bresse concluded that the individual historian could not possibly cope with such wide uncharted waters:

Quelque nostalgie qu'on en puisse concevoir, il faut bien admettre que la recherche individuelle n'a plus de chance de réussite, que l'historien ancien style est voué à l'échec. Pour faire un travail fructueux il faut que le chercheur soit encadré dans un groupe. L'avenir appartient aux instituts scientifiques, aux centres de recherches du type Comité d'Histoire de la deuxième guerre mondiale à Paris et de l'Institut für Zeitgeschichte à Munich, soutenus par l'appui officiel, disposant de toute une équipe de collaborateurs scientifiques. Ces centres, fonctionnant chacun sur le plan national, pourraient prévoir une organisation internationale de recherches, préparant des voyages de prospection, centralisant les résultats acquis, arrangeant des échanges de documents entre les divers pays, cela pour le plus grand bien de l'avancement de l'histoire . . .[1]

The relevance of these words today indicates to what extent she was crying in the wilderness. Since 1961 the situation has become more serious, as source materials have become more abundant and contemporary historians, mostly in glorious isolation, more numerous.

Attempts to remedy the situation have so far done little more than reveal the extent of chaos and inefficiency in the work of contemporary historians. The newly created Institute of Contemporary History, on the national level though without national subsidy, has been attacked for being European-centred and for publishing articles which concentrate on the importance of men, movements, and events in their own time, i.e. historical articles, instead of stressing their legacy to the present and thereby treating them as a background to current affairs. That the institute, with its early growing pains, should have sparked off controversy on these lines is an important service in itself.

On the international level, UNESCO is trying to bring historians together in two ways: firstly by sponsoring the Commission internationale pour une histoire du développement scientifique et culturel de l'humanité, which publishes the *Cahiers d'Histoire Mondiale* three times a year. The commission aims to write objective history, which may explain why its articles concern ancient, medieval, or early modern topics. Among the vice-presidents of the commission, Britain is represented by Sir Julian Huxley and Jacquetta Hawkes. Secondly, UNESCO gives financial support to the Comité International des Sciences Historiques for the organization of international historical conferences, the most recent of which took place in Vienna in the summer of 1965. Here again, twentieth-century history was given a very small place and was certainly not regarded as posing special problems to historians. Such international conferences are useful in enabling delegates to find out what research is being done in other countries; but rather than leave this important function to haphazard verbal exchanges, the French delegation issued a reference book, published by the Centre National de la Recherche Scientifique entitled *La Recherche historique en France de 1940 à 1965*. Historical research in France, though on an individual basis as much as in Britain, is more organized and centrally controlled, in practice, from Paris.

There have always been disputes about where medieval history ends and modern history begins; but it is astonishing to find a far wider divergence of opinion as to what is contemporary history. While we in Britain are uncertain whether the contemporary period should begin in 1890 or in 1914, French official policy is to take it back to the 1789 revolution. Although one can understand the treatment of the history of republican France as a coherent whole, it seems rather arbitrary to classify world history according to the experience of one country. Perhaps the sacrifice in logic is more than compensated by the great respect accorded to contemporary historians in France. In view of the scope of the conference, in this paper contemporary history will be taken to mean the twentieth century.

Although French historians showed a healthy interest in international communication by distributing *La Recherche historique en France de 1940 à 1965* at the Vienna conference, the contents make sad reading for an international historian. A clear analysis by Jean Glénisson of contemporary French historiography, indicates that recent French thought has largely ignored non-French historians. Furthermore, an explanation by Pierre Renouvin of regulations for the acceptance of theses, the essential passports to higher education posts in France, indicates the reason for an inordinate concentration by research students on French domestic affairs in twentieth-century history. The fifty-year rule operates far more stringently in France than in Britain; and, without documentary evidence of government policy or accessible private papers, it is hardly surprising that research topics tend to be concerned with domestic public opinion based on press sources, or the development of industry and agriculture traceable through parliamentary debates, newspapers, and the archives of particular firms. The activities of religious groups are also quite a popular subject for research. Jean Glénisson attributes the association of history with other disciplines, such as sociology, psychology, geography, and economics, to the philosophical influence of Lucien Febvre and Marc Bloch; but so far as research on the twentieth century is concerned, one can see very practical reasons for such tendencies among candidates for the *Doctorat ès Lettres*. And Pierre Renouvin demonstrates clearly how thesis topics determine the nature of French historical research, to an extent far greater than in Britain.

In recent years French historical interest in international relations has been kept alive by a handful of established historians, men like Pierre Renouvin, Jean-Baptiste Duroselle, and Fernand L'Huillier, whose monumental capacity for penetrating research into a wide range of subjects has done much to fill the gaps in French contemporary history. They have benefited from the close relationship between universities and government departments in France in managing to soften the stringencies of the fifty-year rule and to write with some authority on French foreign policy since 1914. Renouvin's work on the causes and course of the First World War is familiar to everyone;[2] he is technically in retirement, of course, but is using any additional spare time for a study of the situation in France in 1917, the time of mutinies and strikes so prejudicial to the French war effort. Duroselle's work on French foreign policy since 1919 is well known already;[3] he has done much, in particular, to stimulate research into Franco-American relations and is currently associated with the Fulbright Commission. His interests today are moving towards the period following the Second World War, to which his book on the Trieste problem, *Le Conflit de Trieste* (Brussels, 1966), and the wide range of research subjects under his supervision, bear witness. L'Huillier, at the University of Strasbourg, apart from his work on Middle Eastern affairs,[4] has done much to clarify the course of Franco-German relations in the twentieth century and is engaged at the moment on a study of the period 1925 to 1933, when high hopes of a Franco-German reconciliation were so bitterly disappointed.

It is important to stress here that French research into non-European contemporary history has expanded quite rapidly. Stuart Schram, an American by origin, but now working for the Fondation Nationale des Sciences Politiques in Paris, has turned his attention from Soviet Russian history to twentieth-century China. [5] He and Hélène Carrère d'Encausse are developing several French research projects on the Chinese Communist revolution. Apart from international sources for this research, there is a valuable collection of rare Chinese newspapers and periodicals in Paris at the École Pratique des Hautes Études, VIᵉ section.

African history will develop more slowly in France, despite the interest in African peoples in their own right, revealed by the numerous theses on problems of colonization and decolonization in progress at universities like Aix and Bordeaux. The important sources in the archives of the Ministère des Colonies have now been moved to the Archives Nationales where they are more accessible. Henri Brunschwig is working with these documents to publish a collection of sources on equatorial Africa, but he is starting in the nineteenth century and, unfortunately, the application of the fifty-year rule means that these archives are closed to historians from 1914.

In spite of the wide range of research in France today on contemporary history, it is clear that there is an unhealthy gulf between established historians such as those mentioned above, who have written so much on French national politics, statesmen, and relations with other countries, and the new generation of historians working on French domestic affairs in this century, with techniques borrowed from sociology, economics, and politics. This recent trend is partly due to the admirable ambition to see history firmly established among the *sciences humaines*; but one senses that twentieth-century international history is a blind spot that is passively accepted in France on the strength of the fifty-year rule,* which could be overcome by energetic use of foreign sources. The field is apparently to be left clear, for the foreseeable future, to the sensationalist writings of journalists and retired soldiers.

The Centre National de la Recherche Scientifique bestrides the whole field of French research, both in science and in letters, like a

* Since this paper was written moves have been made to change this to a thirty-year rule in the near future, which should vastly improve the situation.

colossus. It is true that the regulations for the acceptance of thesis subjects, supervision of candidates, and the presentation of theses are controlled by the *facultés* of each university. Partly for prestige reasons, partly because of the availability of source material, most historical theses are registered in Paris; so that, much to their chagrin, historians teaching in Paris, like Jean-Baptiste Duroselle, find themselves supervising up to fifty theses. The apparent independence of the *facultés* is belied, however, by the financial control of research exercised by the CNRS. If a research student cannot obtain a post in a university as *maître-assistant*, enabling him to write his thesis in his spare time, he is probably dependent on being nominated, after competition with many others, to a post at the CNRS as *attaché de recherche*, which will give him about four years to write the bulk of his thesis. This system is roughly the counterpart of British state studentships, except that, while the CNRS cannot help so many research students, those it can help are supported for a longer period than state students in Britain. A French student must obtain his *Doctorat ès Lettres* before he can join the permanent staff of a university as *maître des conférences* and in this the CNRS plays another important financial role. The thesis must be printed for presentation, according to a Ministry of Education directive of February 1957, and as the cost to the candidate is obviously enormous the CNRS grants a subsidy. In 1957 it agreed to pay 80 per cent of the cost, but budgetary cuts by the French government have reduced the subsidy to about 50 per cent. A student must therefore save a considerable sum of money before presenting his thesis.

There is a limit of 500 pages for the allocation of a subsidy; if the student exceeds the limit he must bear the full cost of printing for the extra pages. Despite this disincentive to verbosity, French professors complain about the excessive size of theses in modern and contemporary history. Roland Mousnier, writing in the *Revue historique*, July–September 1965, quotes examples of theses of 3,000 pages in two or three volumes. He remarks bitterly: '*Comme les candidats renchérissent les uns sur les autres, peut-être sommes-nous en route vers la thèse de 4,000 pages*'.[6] Candidates are often in their forties and are sometimes over fifty. There is a general feeling in French academic circles that reform is needed. At the moment few students get beyond the *doctorat du troisième cycle*, probably a slightly higher standard than the British M.A. thesis, and with that they cannot become a *maître des conférences*.

The number of institutes in France, concerned with particular aspects of contemporary history, is impressive to the visitor. But the term 'institute' can cover a variety of organizations, ranging from hives of activity, like the Institut d'Études Politiques, to small centres collecting specialized documentation, like the Institut d'Études Islamiques, which arranges neither courses nor research projects. The CNRS is working with organizations in higher education and with archives, libraries, and museums, in order to co-ordinate the work of all these specialized institutes, to attach those that are moribund to more active ones, and, by saving money from centralization, to give subsidies to those that are deserving or needy. The Institut d'Études Slaves is a case in point; with more money and staff it could use its library facilities and source materials to much greater advantage. But there is no anticipation in academic circles of immediate improvement, unless government purse strings are loosened.

The most important sources for research in France on contemporary history are locked away. And owing to administrative difficulties some documentary files relating to the years before 1914 are still inaccessible. The files of some ministries are available up to 1920, but not those of the Ministère des Affaires Etrangères. The private papers of ex-ministers and leading civil servants are also subject to the fifty-year rule. Most of the papers are kept in ministry archives until the death of the person concerned, when they all become automatically government property. The study of French foreign policy in the 1930s should soon be released from this severe handicap, however, following the rapid compilation, by Maurice Baumont and Pierre Renouvin, of government documents in *Documents diplomatiques français 1932–1939*.[7] The arrangement of documents in the volumes published so far is of exemplary clarity, with an invaluable subject index and system of cross-reference.

For the study of less important primary sources, newspapers, periodicals, and books on contemporary history, one can use the Bibliothèque Nationale; but most sources are more accessible at the library of the Institut d'Études Politiques or at the Bibliothèque de Documentation Internationale Contemporaine. Like the Royal Institute of International Affairs in London, the BDIC has a remarkable collection of rare sources on the whole of the twentieth century, but the lack of library space makes it necessary to store much material elsewhere.

Generally, the limited number and quality of sources, owing to the fifty-year rule and the inadequate facilities for research due to lack of financial support, are causing considerable anxiety among French historians who are aware of conditions enjoyed by historians in other countries. Commenting wistfully on the magnificent facilities afforded by the Hoover Institution at Stanford University for research into contemporary international history, Jacques Bariéty wrote in the *Revue historique*, July–September 1966:

D'une façon générale, on peut être assuré que par leur esprit d'entreprise et d'organisation, ainsi que par la répartition méthodique des tâches entre eux, les Américains, dans l'histoire des relations internationales à l'époque contemporaine, sont en train de conquérir une place privilégiée.[8]

NOTES

[1] Marcelle Adler-Bresse, 'Les sources allemandes de la deuxième guerre mondiale', *Revue d'Histoire de la deuxième guerre mondiale*, No. 41, January 1961, p. 62.

[2] Pierre Renouvin, *Les origines immédiates de la guerre 28 juin–4 août 1914* (Paris, 1927); *La crise européenne et la Grande Guerre (1904–1918)* (Paris, 1934); *La crise européenne et la guerre mondiale* (Paris, 1948).

[3] Jean-Baptiste Duroselle, *Histoire diplomatique de 1919 à nos jours* (Paris, 1953).

[4] Fernand L'Huillier, *Le Moyen-Orient contemporain, 1945–1958* (Paris, 1959).

[5] Since the date at which this paper was delivered Mr Schram has accepted an appointment in Britain at the School of Oriental and African Studies of London University.

[6] Roland Mousnier, 'Notes sur la thèse principale d'histoire pour le doctorat ès lettres', *Revue historique*, CXXXIV, July–Sept. 1965, p. 123.

[7] *Documents diplomatiques français 1932–1939*, edited by Maurice Baumont and Pierre Renouvin, 1re série (1932–35) vol. I, *9 Juillet–14 Novembre 1932* (Paris, 1964); vol. II, *15 Novembre 1932–17 Mars, 1933* (Paris, 1966). 2e série (1936–39) vol. I, *1er Janvier–31 Mars 1936* (Paris, 1963); vol. II, *1er Avril–18 Juillet 1936* (Paris, 1964); vol. III, *19 Juillet–19 Novembre 1936* (Paris, 1966).

[8] Jacques Bariéty, in a review of Walter C. Clemens, Jr, 'Soviet Disarmament Policy, 1917–1963' in *Revue historique*, CCXXXVI, July–Sept. 1966, p. 279.

Italy

CLAUDIO PAVONE

Trends and Problems

In order to discern the principal lines of development of historical research in Italy in recent years on the twentieth century (and further back as well), and to attempt an assessment of the results achieved, it would be necessary to study the whole of the twenty years since the Second World War. The collapse of fascism made possible a new intellectual vitality, and the seriousness and importance of the accompanying events—military defeat of fascist Italy, victorious anti-fascist Resistance, end of the monarchy and commencement of the republic—provided a stimulus for re-thinking the country's previous history, at least from the Risorgimento onwards. In addition, the principal parties which had led the anti-fascist struggle were at last able to emerge into the light and they were immediately anxious to make their mark, not only upon contemporary Italy but also upon the country's past, which they boldly examined in search of themes to justify their own aspirations. In this way, the examination of conscience—a theme which emerges in various fields of contemporary historiography and which had special reasons for asserting itself in Italy, the cradle of fascism—was tempered, so to speak, and made less painful by post-Resistance optimism.

In a stimulating essay on the weight attached to the theme of continuity in Italian historical writing, an English scholar has recently called attention to the particularly close link between history and politics in Italy.[1] He regards this continuity and this link as surrogate for the non-existent tradition of a unified state. And there is no doubt that the tendencies noted by Woolf were operative in Italian historiography in the post-war period also, and especially in the first years after 1945, when political passions and ideals were at their liveliest and when there still existed, or seemed to exist, unlimited scope for shaping the course which

Italy would follow for a considerable number of years.

This essay helps us to recognize what might be called the end of the 'post-war' phase as the first internal break in the twenty-year period which requires, as we have already said, to be treated as a whole. In the late fifties and early sixties it was recognized in Italy that the more conspicuous after-effects of fascism and the war had been liquidated, that certain traditional social data and problems had been transformed by the economic boom, and that political rivalry, although stimulated by new ruptures and disequilibria, was set on a course, both internal and international, which promised no immediate surprises. This is certainly not the place for a sketch of that development, even on the cultural level; we will confine ourselves to noting a few points which illustrate how this change of atmosphere manifested itself in historiography.

It is worth recalling that immediately after 1945 there recommenced the discussion about the unity of Italian history—an old academic controversy, which was related, however, to the desire to rediscover a national tradition valid for all Italians.[2] But the most recent historiography seems uninterested in following that track. With the decline of the romantic national idea (which had fed the controversy), either as a result of changed world conditions or as a reaction to the fascist degeneration of nationalism, the interest in coming to terms with the past became directed above all to the Risorgimento, and in two fundamental directions. One of them— the more traditional, but refreshed by a new social, political, and scientific interest—focused attention upon the moderate-liberal outcome of the process of national unification; the other initiated a discussion of the relation between Risorgimento and fascism and Risorgimento and Resistance. Naturally, not all the studies— some of them very valuable—published in the late 1950s dealt explicitly with these two problems, but they were implicit in many of them. And this led to a revival of the polemics about 'revisionism' of the Risorgimento—that is to say, about a view of the Risorgimento and of its heritage to united Italy which differs from that of the traditional moderate-liberal historians; and among some of the old, and not so old as well, the question was revived, with a subtle sense of melancholy, of whether it is still legitimate to speak of the 'end of the Risorgimento' since there is a desire, in various quarters and for various motives, to describe the Resistance as the 'second Risorgimento'. But this type of highly ideological debate has begun, in its turn, to die down in recent years. Naturally, however, this does not mean the achievement of a general (and undesirable) uniformity of opinion, but rather a concern to re-convert the traditional theses into hypotheses, to formulate them afresh, and to verify all of them through a more analytical study of the history of united Italy, taking more into account the develop-ment of Italian capitalist structures and bourgeois society as a whole and in relation to other nations.[3]

If we now look at the prevailing currents in post-war historio-graphy we find that here too the beginning of the 1960s marks a change. Immediately after 1945, battle had been joined between idealists and Marxists, and this was what attracted most attention, although there was also a prominent Catholic school (to which we shall return later), and a number of robust and independent lay scholars such as Nino Valeri and Franco Venturi. Idealist history was vigorously attacked by the young Marxist school which em-phasized the importance of economic and social factors, in the name of a dialectic concerned with realities as well as ideas, the latter being treated in close relation with real things. In fact, how-ever, the Marxist historians tackled political history much more enthusiastically than economic and social history; while the Stalin-ist aura which dominated the leading Italian working-class party (the Communist Party) was not propitious for discussion of the fundamental Marxist problems—such as the relation between the economic, the social, and the political—or of its own value as a historical method. As a result, a great many worthy Marxist scholars sought a kind of compensation in meticulous rigour; and since the history of the Italian Communist Party itself could arouse heated political and ideological discussions, this rigour became concentrated upon the point of origin of the Italian working-class and socialist movement.[4]

In the interpretation of contemporary Italian history the young Marxist school opposed the critical theses of Gramsci to those of Croce and Omodeo, who had seen the moderate-liberal outcome of the Risorgimento as the only possible and favourable solution of the Italian problem and as containing all the seeds of further positive development. This controversy produced a lot of good work, but it risked getting into a groove which would prevent its developing fruitfully: on the one hand, the Marxists were over-loaded with ideology (counterpart of their neo-scholastic ob-session); and on the other hand, the historians of Crocean-liberal descent strangely presumed, in their anxiety to defend the respectability of the traditional governing class, to cast all the onus of 'politicalization' upon Marxist historiography while reserving exclusively for themselves the immaculate pastures of scholarship.

In this situation, Rosario Romeo's broadside against Marxist historiography came as a salutary shock:[5] not so much because of his declared cultural-political object, which he went beyond in the course of the polemic, nor yet because all his points were necessarily valid, but rather because of its effects upon the general historical debate. Romeo attacked what appeared to him to be Gramsci's central thesis (this is not the place to discuss how far his interpretation of Gramsci is correct): namely, that the reason for Italy's defective political, economic, and social development lay in the failure to make an agricultural revolution and the failure to establish an alliance, of the Jacobin type, between the progressive Risorgimento bourgeoisie and the land-starved peasants. Ignoring the usual point of the controversy—whether or not such a revolution would have been possible—he reversed the whole tenor of the argument; it was very fortunate, he said, that no such revolution had occurred, because it would have blocked Italy's only road towards her tardy capitalist accumulation—that is to say, the extraction of revenue from agriculture and the Mezzogiorno, and its compulsory diversion into industrial investment and, first of all, into the indispensable infrastructures for the growth and development of industry.

To evaluate the merit of Romeo's treatise would take me beyond the chronological framework of this article. But it can be said that its repercussions have been felt even in the study of twentieth-century Italian history. It induced the Marxists, first of all, to make a profounder study of Gramsci's thought; and then—alongside the internal cultural and political work which they had already initiated but have still not completed (it is unnecessary to recall the twentieth congress of the CPSU and the Hungarian events)—to re-examine the significance of the history of the working-class movement in relation to the general history of society and the state.[6] And further, it induced nearly everybody, Marxists and others, to pay more attention to the problems of 'primitive accumulation' and the point of departure of Italy's economic upsurge, and the special characteristics, up to our day, of Italian capitalism—studying them no longer primarily on the political level but also in their basic structure.[7] Naturally, the general change of intellectual climate, already referred to, contributed decisively to the reception in a more general context of the seeds scattered by Romeo. Indeed, alongside the revival (for many historians, the discovery) of the problems and techniques of long-neglected fields of research in economic development, there has occurred in Italy in recent years a new contact between historiography and the social sciences. Croce, as is well known, condemned sociology as being incapable, unlike the natural sciences, of emerging from the limbo of the pseudo-concept into the realm of the concept; and it is also known that Italian Marxism, in its prevalent Gramscian version, showed little sympathy for that subject, which it suspected of a bourgeois positivist taint. More extensive interchanges with the Anglo-Saxon and French cultures, and also the study of the 'real Italy', making full use of the methods of analysis now available, induced both Marxists and idealists (the Catholics were already more predisposed in this direction) to undertake a certain re-thinking of the relations between history and collateral disciplines. There are still a great many more formulations of programmes and demands for research than there are concrete productions; nor can one be sure whether this tendency, and the whole atmosphere of ideological 'relaxation' of recent years, will develop into a new form of academic ecleticism and immature syntheses, or whether it will give rise to solid and substantial studies.[8]

There is some connection between this new interest in the multiple social levels of the community and the revival of local histories, after 1945, from the ashes of the worn-out tradition of learned studies under the patronage of the old societies and committees of regional history. But whereas the local histories which flourished in the nineteenth and early twentieth centuries were medievally oriented and skipped through more recent decades, and sometimes centuries, in a few hurried final pages,[9] the post-war revival is on other lines; it concerns itself mainly with research on a single locality, province, or region in the period of the Risorgimento and after. The motive of these researches was indeed, as has been said, to examine economic, social and political formations other than those of the state; and it is not by chance that they were specially connected with the study of the workers' and peasants' movements and with the Catholic organizations: that is to say, with phenomena which developed, at least in their first stages, independently of the vertical structure of the unitary state. Thus the study of local history was combined by the Marxists with the question of the relations between the lower and the upper or leading classes, and with the Gramscian theme of a popular-national history; and the Catholics combined it with their researches into all the various manifestations of the Catholic tradition underneath the secular surface of official Italy. Today, these studies, too, have got beyond the stage of initial enthusiasm and are becoming aware of the need for a precise adjustment of 'small-scale' to 'large-scale' history: and here again there is a risk that technical maturity may be paid for by a slackening of intellectual tension.[10]

In Italy, the beginning of the twentieth century coincides with a turning-point of great importance for the life of the country. The reactionary tendency of 1898–1900 having failed, the new liberal impetus began, of which Giovanni Giolitti was to such an extent the most representative politician that the years from 1900 to the outbreak of the First World War are still usually described as the 'Giolittian era'.

Historical studies of this period are among the most copious of the post-war period.[11] They have arrived at conclusions which modify the crude opposition of opinions derived from political polemic, even though more subtle and less easily reconcilable differences of interpretation have emerged. In very rough outline, one may say that no democrat or Marxist would now describe Giolitti as the 'minister for the underworld': Salvemini himself, who had coined the successful slogan, in his later years was to modify his criticisms of Giolitti[12] and in the Marxist camp it was Togliatti himself, the leader of the Communist Party, who began the revision of those judgments which Gramsci had conspicuously borrowed from Salvemini and the anti-Giolittian democrats.[13] On the other hand, Croce's optimism about the Giolittian age in his *History of Italy* has been amply contested in many quarters; and indeed his undeservedly successful medico-bacteriological metaphor (a healthy body but with a predisposition to harbour germs of future disease), which was later used by Chabod,[14] no longer seems adequate to explain the relation between the 1900–1915 period and fascism.

No one today denies the progress achieved in the Giolittian period, both in political liberty and in economic development, within the framework of the greatest reformist experiment so far attempted in Italy. But disagreement begins when an attempt is made to define the limits of this reformism and the causes of its ultimate failure. This discussion raises large questions, and in each of the answers to them there is implied a whole concept of contemporary Italian history. For example, the relations between production, social welfare, and political liberty, and between North and South, between the state and the mass of the people, and between the liberal directing class and the socialists and the Catholics.

It was precisely during the Giolittian period that the Italian economy began to grow; or better, the Giolittian period was grafted on to an economic development which had begun in 1896 and which is considered to be one of the causes of the reactionary trends in 1898–1900. All this is acknowledged today by scholars of varying views, although the controversy between Romeo and Gerschenkron centred on the question of whether there was continuity or an effective change of direction between the economic upsurge and the period 1861–96. Moreover, the limitations and disproportions in economic development, which can hardly be denied, are variously appraised in relation to the problem of the divergence between North and South and of dangerous tendencies in the process of Italian industrialization, due to the fragile democratic structures of a backward country; a country which is obliged to look to the state for establishing the mechanism for economic development and thus creates between a state with a restricted social basis on the one hand and industry on the other, a subtle complicity by which the public power is often degraded to become the direct instrument of the most powerful private interests.[15] Thus Cafagna has felt justified in concluding that 'an unbalanced economic development is, probably, the only kind that history has so far offered, at least for the initial phases of release from stagnation'; but the same author recognizes that the war was destined, contrary to all expectation, to prove itself 'nothing less than a potent breeder of disequilibria'.[16] And Procacci has seen a very close connection between the Italian type of economic development—from which the Giolittian experiment failed to eliminate completely all emulation of the so-called 'Prussian way'—and the war and post-war crises.[17]

On the other hand, that whole bundle of problems—to borrow an expression of Croce's—which is known as 'the Southern question', has been the subject of re-thinking in recent years, as a result of theoretical and historical studies of the economic development and possibilities of reclamation of backward countries,[18] and not merely, we should add, because of a feeling that some of the factual data advanced in Southernist literature have latterly become modified. The Southernist interpretation of the history of united Italy, which was largely derived from Gramsci's thought, regarded the backwardness of the Mezzogiorno as a decisive limiting factor upon any global Italian development that did not include a drastic rupture of the social and political equilibrium established at the unification of Italy; but this interpretation is now considered by many to require adjustment and verification, especially as regards the part really played in the development of the North by the draining away of Southern capital and the formation of a unified national market. It should be added, however, that to see the problem exclusively in terms of economic techniques and productivity does not cover all the significance, past and present, of the backwardness of the Mezzogiorno and the islands for contemporary Italy—whether from the point of view of society, civilization, or politics.[19]

We can now return to the more strictly political problem of Giolittian reform, the problem to which, in conformity with its traditional preferences, Italian historiography continues to devote its main attention. Carocci, in one of the most recent studies of Giolitti, has said that the Piedmontese statesman was more interested in social peace than in economic development; he was above all a minister of the interior with the task of reducing the causes of social tension, by encouraging the restoration of balance between profits and wages when the latter had lagged too far behind. Carocci has also specified that Giolitti's most positive reforming and liberal-progressive move occurred during the earliest years of the new period, almost solely while Giolitti was at the Ministry of the Interior with Zanardelli. The general strike of 1904 and the consequent general election, undertaken to 'punish' the socialists, initiated, according to Carocci, and not only to him, a new conservative trend which Giolitti tried to mediate, thus assuring himself a solid right-centre majority which enabled him to pursue, as far as was possible for a course guaranteed in this way, his programme of reforms. Giolitti's fall at the beginning of 1914 occurred, on this interpretation, when there was no further political manoeuvring space for his attempts at mediation, and also as a result of the contrasting effects of the Libyan war of 1911 (which gave a boost to nationalism), and the concession of almost universal suffrage in 1912 (which drove the conservatives, who feared socialist predominance, into alliance with the Catholics).[20]

But for historians the point which is most significant for today in the Giolittian period is the relation between the Risorgimento liberalism which is the framework of the state, and the socialists and Catholics. At bottom it is the old problem, familiar to the historians of national fascism (Volpe comes especially to mind), of the integration into the state of the popular masses, but envisaged now in such a way that it should not be simply for the sake of the state's power but should provide precise guarantees that the process will be democratic and that there will be no return of corruption and transformism,* and no authoritarian temptations. It is true that within this general perspective, too, opinions differ: on one side it is maintained that the Giolittian reforms were limited by the socialists' excessive reluctance to be integrated within the system (this is the thesis of the moderate-liberal tradition still variously represented in the post-war period); on the other side, the limitation is held to have been caused by the socialists' too great propensity to function as a subordinate element in the existing system (and this, with different shades of emphasis, is the thesis of the whole leftist school of history which still keeps alive the sense of an alternative to the bourgeois power system which has become established in Italy). Among the Catholics, the dilemma is seen as a choice between clerical-moderatism and the democratic version of intransigency.

Two recent books, one on socialism and the other on the Catholic movement, can serve as points of reference for this discussion.[21] Gaetano Arfè has written a thoughtful history of the Italian Socialist Party (for that is his real subject, in spite of the more comprehensive title),[22] devoted to proving that the reformist line personified in Filippo Turati was able to hold to the middle way between 'the abyss of extremism and the quicksand of irredeemable capitulation'. But this defence of Turati's reformism as the only concretely socialist course in the Italy of Giolitti does not exempt the author from a tragic ending to the story, with all his heroes discomfited. We shall return to Arfè's conclusions when we deal with the rise of anti-fascism; but it should be said here that his book provides a sort of inventory of the problems of Italian

* A term originally applied to the middle party formed by Depretis in 1883, drawn from the moderates of both the Right and the Left. Subsequently used to describe the absorption of political opponents.

socialism before the rise of fascism (and also of some which are a post-fascist legacy): relations with other European socialist parties, especially the German and French; relations between party, unions, parliamentary group, industrial workers, and peasants; the problem of alliances with bourgeois democratic movements (especially acute in a scantily developed country like Italy); consequently, the problem of participation in bourgeois governments; significance of the presence in one of the wings of the party or parties which represent the bulk of the working classes of openly collaborationist groups and of anarchist and militantly revolutionary groups; relations between party and intellectuals (in Italy the Socialist Party and, later, the Communist Party have always regarded their authority with the intellectuals as a measure of their own power); and finally, relations between political organization and theoretical Marxism. [23]

Gabriele De Rosa's book, the other mentioned above, [24] also lends itself to some brief reflections on Catholic historiography. To tell the truth, the most candid students of the subject deny the correctness of the expression: Catholic, they say, is a religious term, which cannot properly be applied to historiography. If they mean by this that Catholics have not developed a historical method of their own, they are undoubtedly right, and will certainly continue to be so in the future; though if we consider merit rather than method the question is more open. There are in fact in Italy a Catholic political movement and a Catholic culture (the latter with serious limitations, which the more thoughtful Catholics do not fail to denounce). Catholics are impelled by both the one and the other to study their own history, in rather the same way that Marxists are induced to give preference to working-class and socialist history (and in recent years both parties have begun to perceive the limitations of this tendency). [25] Thus a group of Catholics has been formed to study the history of contemporary Italy, with the direct or indirect motive of justifying the disputed political predominance of Catholics in Italy from 1948 onwards. Lay circles had always shown little interest in the political, social, and organizational problems of Italian Catholics, so Catholic scholars were able to cultivate an almost completely virgin field of research. [26] They have thus been led to ignore the great traditional theme of relations between State and Church, either from a certain distaste for 'summit' questions, or from a reluctance to reopen a question which it is preferred in many political quarters to regard as closed, or at least in abeyance (this also of course involves assessing the Lateran Pacts concluded between the Vatican and Mussolini and included in the republican constitution with the help of the communists). As a result there is less interest in examining fundamental principles and even in the problem of the relations between Church and modern civilization.[27]

The initial stand taken by the new post-war school of Catholic historians asserted the autonomy, both in respect of current secular policies and in respect of their own ecclesiastical hierarchy, of the Catholic movement which found expression after the first war in the Popular Party and after the second in Christian-democracy; and at the same time it looked for the origins of that movement not so much among the liberal Catholics who came to terms with the Italian state which emerged from the Risorgimento, but rather among the Catholic intransigents, the implacable enemies of that state. It interpreted the denial of national unity and the assertion of the Church's temporal claims as a subordinate element in the intransigent attitude, and one which was gradually becoming more moderate; it aimed rather to present this attitude as, above all, a religious and social protest against the secular and bourgeois state, which excluded those popular masses whom the Catholics claimed to represent far more truly than the narrow political class.

Two consequences flowed from these ideas. The first was that it became common usage, among both Catholics and non-Catholics, to speak of a liberal state which had banned from its precincts the workers, the peasants, and the Catholics: an obvious logical fallacy, because it groups together designations derived from totally heterogeneous criteria. But a lucky fallacy, because it corresponded to the opinion, widely diffused in leftist circles of the Resistance and post-Resistance, that the new Italy would be based upon the union of the three mass parties, Communist, Socialist, and Catholic. The second consequence was that a point of fundamental importance was left in obscurity; that of the Catholic attitude towards liberty, and in particular to that modicum of liberty which the state derived from the Risorgimento had at least tried to establish in Italy.[28]

In recent years, however, this line of interpretation has been partly modified, thanks to the influence, it may be conjectured, of the new political line of the left-centre. In his most recent book, referred to above, De Rosa is less schematic and unilateral than in his previous work; his line is more flexible and he takes into account all the political currents of Catholicism, intransigent and otherwise. This leads him to see the Popular Party as the outcome of a complex and subtly varied movement; and don Luigi Sturzo, of anti-moderate and intransigent origins, the founder of the party, who is De Rosa's real hero, becomes linked in theory, as he was once thought to be in fact, with Filippo Meda, who was at the centre of the electoral agreements between Giolittians and Catholics and who had even had a ministry during the war. Sturzo and Meda together drew with them into the new party all those Catholics who were by now reconciled to politics, and first of all the very numerous clerical-moderates. De Rosa, while recognizing the heterogeneous character of a political formation combining men with such different backgrounds, believes nevertheless that the Popular Party possessed a value of its own; thanks to it, the Catholics were no longer like subordinate troops attached to the liberal and 'transformist' majorities; they no longer rejected the state as something alien to their concerns but affirmed their own presence in it 'communally and personally', as something that should partake of Catholic inspiration while independent of the Church, in a democratic and fruitful equilibrium—which, in fact, has been proved by events to be much more precarious than it appears to De Rosa's enthusiasm.

Fonzi, in his turn, in an important recent volume which does not come directly within the scope of this article,[29] has developed an interpretative scheme which attempts to carry the story up to our own day; in his discussion of the Catholics he shifts the emphasis from the claims of the intransigents to the rediscovery of those values of the liberal-Risorgimento state which had hitherto been thought to be congenial only to the clerical-moderates. In other words, Fonzi, like De Rosa, tries to bring together the two currents of post-unification Italian Catholicism; but he places the accent upon the element of co-operation between Catholics and the state and, still more, of their collaboration with those socialists who were also tending towards reformism and co-operation (and hence the exaggerated and symbolic value attributed to the Milanese events of 1895, when both Catholics and socialists were obliged to confront the problem of the state). It is true that the Italian state at the end of the nineteenth century remains for Fonzi something in need of profound renewal; but he now envisages the joint operation of Catholics and socialists in moderately and cautiously reforming the traditional state.

It remains an open question—to conclude our remarks on the

Catholic movement—whether the presence of a party which always, for all the Catholic subtlety of verbal distinction, derives its character and its unity precisely from that designation, will in the long run be a progressive element in the Italian political scene, or a source of further equivocation and confusion.

In dealing with the First World War, Italian historians have traditionally paid little attention to the conflict as a whole, perhaps because they are still more or less consciously influenced by the Salandra government's view of the intervention in 1915 as a mere incident in an 'Italian' war, a view which led Chabod to write that 'Italian policy in 1915 was an 1866 type of policy'.[30] Moreover, it is not so much Italy's war in general that has occupied the historians,[31] but rather the moment of intervention and how the manner in which it was brought about, and the three-and-a-half years of great public hardship which followed, affected the post-war crisis and, in particular, the rise of fascism. In fact, the real subject is always the *débâcle* of the state and of the old liberal governing class; and therefore in what is written about the one clearly victorious war waged by united Italy there is always a note of pessimism and anxious weighing of responsibilities.

The numerous studies published in recent years[32] have thrown clearer light on much of the behaviour of the various political forces in Italy between the Sarajevo assassination and 24 May 1915, when Italy declared war on Austro-Hungary. There is now a sufficient measure of agreement for it to be asserted that the majority of the country was neutralist but that the three main neutralist forces (Giolittians, socialists, Catholics) failed because they were scattered, and paralysed by internal uncertainties and reciprocal mistrust; and that once neutralism had ceased to be absolute and *a priori* (as it was to the end for the socialists), and had become entangled in the question of the compensations to be demanded from Austria under article 7 of the Triple Alliance treaty, it would have been very difficult for Italy to keep out of the war. This picture contains many features which would repay further study. For example, the work of Vigezzi could be followed up. Vigezzi deals with Italian foreign policy on the eve of the Austro-Serbian war (suggesting that, in order to define Italian imperialism more clearly, more attention should be paid to Italy's economic relations with other countries); he has thus contributed to showing that the parties of order still supported the Triple

Alliance at the end of July 1914 and has underlined the affinity between interventionists and neutralists within those parties, and has noted the Salandra government's inadequate appreciation of the interventionists' street demonstrations in May 1915, and, finally, he has recalled, as others have also done, the difference between the democratic and Risorgimento-inspired intervention of Bissolati, Salvemini, and the republicans, and the 'revolutionary' interventionism of some of the anarcho-syndicalists and Mussolini.[33]

The last point has attracted the attention of many scholars because it is related to Mussolini's clamorous repudiation of the Socialist Party in October 1914, in favour of a strictly 'revolutionary' interventionism. The Italian Socialist Party's attitude to the war—absolute hostility up to the moment of intervention and then a withdrawal based on the formula 'Neither support nor sabotage', has been criticized nearly everywhere as a cowardly renunciation; but perhaps Arfè's judgment is more balanced when he says that 'the position of the Italian socialists in Europe was an original one, and it was a moral fact with a religious basis of its own such as political institutions are not able to inspire'.[34] In the first volume of his biography of Mussolini, to which we shall have occasion to return, De Felice suggests that if the Socialist Party had followed the future *duce* into interventionism in 1914–15 it would have seized a precious opportunity of inserting itself into the state and would not have created that gap between itself and the lower and middle bourgeoisie which was later to be filled by the fascist reaction.[35] Manacorda and Valiani have contested this thesis with valid arguments.[36] The former has criticized as illegitimate the identification, implied by De Felice, of the nation with the interventionists, and the latter has reasserted the Socialist Party's coherence and sense of responsibility towards its own pacifist tradition. For the rest, there is not much in common between 'revolutionary war' and the reformist prospect of integration within the state—which are the two trump cards mentioned by De Felice. Moreover, De Felice fails to distinguish clearly enough between the myth of the revolutionary war and the Leninist theory of transforming imperialist war into civil war. He obscures the difference between accepting joint responsibility with the bourgeoisie for a war, with the illusion of being able later on to turn the victory against the bourgeoisie itself, and refusing to participate in imperialist massacre while urging the soldiers to turn their weapons against their own bourgeoisie. Post-war Italy and the origins of fascism form a single historical complex which, as we have already observed, historians are trying to link very closely with the intervention. It is Nino Valeri who has traced most perceptively the continuity and at the same time the development and precipitation of a cultural, psychological, and social atmosphere which was first clearly manifested in the 'radiant days' of May 1915 and then culminated, after passing through the phase of D'Annunzio's Fiume expedition, in the 'march on Rome'.[37]

In the essay referred to above[38] Procacci, for his part, calls attention to the need for discovering also in the structure of state and industry both a continuity with the pre-war situation and the new factors introduced by the war. In a happy phrase he describes a state committed to 'a direction both authoritarian and private-capitalistic', as a result of the interpenetration between its own increased powers and the great protected industry which had developed and concentrated itself during the war.[39]

A preliminary observation is called for here: it is anti-fascism that has produced the critical studies of the history of fascism. That is to say, the fascists have not been able to re-think their own experiences in new terms. Not that there has been any lack of records and of bitter and disillusioned memoirs by ex-hierarchs; but these have mostly been personal outbursts or attempts to pin responsibility on colleagues, or recriminations about the degeneration of fascism with the passing of time. Naturally, this does not mean that the best studies are identified with the militant anti-fascist attitude—on the contrary, the attempt today is to achieve a purely scientific attitude; it means only that this attempt finds its origin and justification in the political and cultural climate created by the Resistance.

We are now seeing the end of the controversy, related to the one mentioned above concerning the end of the Risorgimento, as to whether fascism should be regarded as an anomalous interlude or disease, as Croce would have it, or rather as a 'revelation' and a 'national self-description', according to the well-known interpretations of Giustino Fortunato and Piero Gobetti. The tendency today, above all—though much ground still remains to be covered—is to study fascism in its fundamental character and in relation to the crisis in Italian society, enlarging the picture to include the general retreat of democracy between the two wars and seeking more precise definitions in relation to the fascism of other countries, beginning with nazism. This approach encourages also the reconsideration in new terms of a problem which was at the centre of the fierce political debate which accompanied the birth of the Italian Communist Party in 1921: namely, the reasons why the Italian social revolution so often foretold (by the maximalists) was never even attempted, and whether the chief reason was simply the absence of the subjective condition (that is to say, of a revolutionary party), or whether it was also, or even more, the unripeness of the objective conditions. The fact is that the birth of fascism was a phenomenon closely connected with the deficiencies of socialism (and later of communism), although it is true that there has been a tendency among moderates to harp too exclusively upon this connection and to leave in obscurity the much more direct responsibility of the bourgeoisie and the dominating liberal class. The most recent studies (we cannot enter into more detail) are in sufficient agreement as regards Giolitti when he was returned to power after the war with the most coherent plan for political stabilization evolved by traditional liberalism, but found himself unprepared for the explosive emergence of the two mass parties, the Socialist and the Popular Party; they attribute to him not so much the intention of consciously encouraging fascism but rather of making use of it to bring the socialists to reason (in other words to co-operate, as subordinates, with the bourgeoisie), after which the fascists in their turn, having been in this way accommodated within the constitution, would cease to disturb the normality of the system. To analyse why this plan failed would involve entering into the merits of social and political relations in Italy after the war.

The most recent book to attempt a synthesized account of the birth and development of fascism is the first volume, which we have already mentioned, of Renzo De Felice's biography of Mussolini. Aiming at a difficult balance between general historical perspective and the adventures of his stormy protagonist, the author has made extensive use, for the first time, of public and private archives. He has not achieved equally convincing results throughout the book. What convinces least is precisely the term 'revolutionary' as applied to a character like Mussolini, who, although authentically subversive, never possessed the moral fibre or the intellectual dedication to justify the description of revolutionary, or even socialist (Arfè's portrait of Mussolini as maximalist is much more convincing).[40] And it is singular that an author

who frequently endorses the traditional judgment of the maximalists as pseudo-revolutionaries should want to make an exception
precisely of their noisiest and most volatile leader. But by giving
credit to the thesis of a revolutionary war, De Felice does tend to
establish that Mussolini's action was still revolutionary after he
became an interventionist, at least until Caporetto; and some of the
most persuasive pages of the book are those in which he describes
the turn to the right, in the nationalist sense, by which the country,
and Mussolini with it, reacted to that defeat. From that moment
he dates the opening of a new and ever more reactionary cycle of
Mussolini's life—a cycle which closed with the speech of 3 January
1925, which initiated the process of definitely imposing fascism
upon the state. It is during that phase that the problem arises of
the early fascism and its 'leftist' character, which was to be
polemically denied and asserted in many debates as fascism developed. De Felice inclines to allow that description of the earliest
fascism, though he makes clear that the movement founded by
Mussolini in 1919 was both ambiguous and opportunist. It was
between October and November 1920 that Mussolini—whose
tortuous and tactically subtle course is ably traced by De Felice—
definitely chose to move rightwards, coming to an agreement with
Giolitti at the expense of D'Annunzio, who was still at Fiume. It
was certainly a crucial moment—and De Felice rightly emphasizes
it—when fascism, severely defeated in the 1919 elections and un-
decided in face of the Fiume adventure, succeeded in becoming a
political force of national importance, and at the same time came
up against the agrarian reaction which had flared up particularly
in the lower Po valley. De Felice has not succeeded, within the
framework of this first volume, in giving sufficient prominence to
the effect of the economic crisis of the autumn of 1920 upon the
new orientation of opinion in the country and upon the new
impetus of fascism.[41]

Historians have hitherto paid much more attention to the origins
of fascism, including its relation to the myth of the 'mutilated
victory' (meaning that the sacrifices made in the war were insufficiently compensated by the peace treaties) than to the twenty-year
story of fascism in power.[42] But this limitation is beginning to be
abandoned, both in projected works and in some already completed. Thus distinctions are beginning to be made between groups
and tendencies within fascism;[43] the relation between fascism and
nationalism is being clarified;[44] the juridical ideas of fascism are

being studied (these too in relation to its nationalist background),[45] and also, as a result of the general revival of interest in institutional history, the organization of the fascist state.[46] Foreign policy during the first ten years of fascism has been recounted afresh by Di Nolfo;[47] and the story of fascist economics, and more particularly its economic policy, is now being centred primarily upon the initial free trade period, the 'quota 90' lira (i.e. the 1927 deflation), the repercussions in Italy of the 1929 world crisis, the foundation in 1933 of the Institute for Industrial Reconstruction (IRI), and corporativism and autarky.[48]

The ideological significance of fascism has traditionally been one of the main themes for study, on account of its close relation to anti-fascist policy and struggles.[49] There have been attempts at a comprehensive definition of the fascist phenomenon on an Italian and on a European scale, and condemnations and rehabilitations of Italian humanity and culture during the twenty years, and public confessions of personal anguish, and examinations of conscience, both of the individual and the generation; and no historian as yet has quite unravelled this confusion of memoirs and intellectual and literary material.[50] But one may hope that by doing so more and more light will be thrown not only upon fascism and militant anti-fascism but also upon those Italians who, although fascist at one stage of their lives, later became in various ways and in variously significant senses anti-fascist.[51]

The coming to power of fascism and its consolidation after the murder of the socialist deputy Matteotti (1924), and the ineffective parliamentary reply of the secession to the Aventine, represent a new turning for the anti-fascist parties also; the hard lesson of facts compelled them to an indispensable examination of conscience and to a first attempt to reshape their programmes. Arfè concludes his pessimistically tormented socialist history by indicating, first in Matteotti and then in younger and intellectually livelier groups (for example, those associated with the review *Quarto Stato*), the growth of a new anti-fascist consciousness desiring to transcend old controversies and sterile bandying of reproaches. And the conclusion of De Rosa's history of the Popular Party likens don Sturzo and Francesco Luigi Ferrari in their exile to such men as Péguy and Bernanos, 'longing for a profoundly Christian freedom'.[52] But in truth the story of anti-fascism still offers much scope for research: the exiles, the clandestine organizations in

Italy, the thousand threads linking the centres on both sides of the Alps and also linking, sometimes polemically, the old and new generations.[53]

In this story the Italian Communist Party has a special place, thanks to its membership of the Third International and also to the very circumstances of its birth, accompanied by controversies which are still alive today. Thus Arfè, advancing a theory dear to Pietro Nenni, has written that the Livorno schism from which the Communist Party was born in 1921, during the full fascist offensive, 'marks the beginning of decline for the Socialist Party and the Italian working-class movement':[54] a theory which the communists, obviously, have always vigorously contested, although Spriano has recently inclined to a more balanced view.[55] It seems needful to distinguish in this dispute between a short-term judgment, concerned with effective defence against the tide of fascism, and a long-term judgment which must necessarily take into account everything that the Communist Party has represented in Italian history in the following decades.

The communists, as already mentioned, have only recently begun to take a historical interest in the experiences of their party; and it was Togliatti himself who led the way, with a deliberately 'detached' (and documented) essay on the original, left-wing, leading group led by Amadeo Bordiga and the new group attached to Antonio Gramsci.[56] And Gramsci himself, who has had such a wide influence on Italian culture since the war, is now beginning to be studied without either polemical or hagiographical motives. Thus the purely ideological interpretations are giving way to biography and to the attempt to reconstruct the whole mental and political evolution of this complex personality, from his libertarian anti-Jacobin phase—to give an example of one of the most controversial themes—to his conception, as expressed in the *Quaderni del carcere* of the party, as the 'modern *Prince*'.[57] Nor of course is there any lack of criticisms from the Left of Gramsci's role in the Italian working-class movement.[58]

With the Second World War as a whole Italian historiography has been very little concerned.[59] It has preferred to concentrate its attention upon the Resistance in Italy and the immediately preceding events, such as the collapse of fascism (25 July 1943) and the armistice which followed on 8 September.[60]

At a Conference at Genoa in 1959 Roberto Battaglia attempted to divide the historiography of the Resistance into periods and to trace the process by which it emerged from the field of memoirs and journalism.[61] He tried also to place historically the origin of his own *Storia della Resistenza italiana* which is still today the most important comprehensive account, in an edition thoroughly revised by the author and published after his lamented death.[62] In the new edition Battaglia attempted further to articulate his story, so as to profit from recent research and stimulate a more profound study of the material, while retaining the overall unity and the bold approach which make the chief value of his work.

The two great dangers threatening Resistance historiography are, first, hagiography (the sentimentality of sectarian party spirit) and, second, the reaction to it, which is a frigid academicism. The first danger is certainly the greater; it always lies in wait upon anniversary celebrations, etc. The second arises from a tendency which is not in itself harmful, so long as it does not take the place of critical discussion.[63] For example, the National Institute for the History of the Liberation Movement in Italy, under the presidency of Ferruccio Parri, has always concerned itself as much with the collection and editing of sources as with the publication of essays and monographs.[64] Further, it is also a question of different generations: alongside the participants, who seek to reassess critically the events in which they participated, there are more and more younger scholars seeking with open minds a knowledge of the recent past based upon reliable data.

This factual approach has also stimulated a remarkable growth, though of varying quality, of local histories and studies devoted to particular situations or social groups. This tendency, however, also implies a recognition of the pluralistic character of the resistance movement, with its many rank-and-file initiatives, which alone make it possible to understand the positions adopted by the leaders at the centre and to judge their relevance to various concrete situations.[65] On the other hand, the need to set the Resistance within an objective situation more extensive than itself has led to the study of its relations with the Allies, as distinct from a certain *odi et amo* which reflects, on the Italian scale, some of the weightiest military, political, and social questions of the Second World War.[66] But no historian has yet undertaken to organize the memoirs and other material relating to the 'Kingdom of the South' (i.e. that part of Italy, south of the front line of 1943–44, where the royalist government of Badoglio survived); whereas we have two good studies, one by an English and one by an Italian scholar, of the neo-fascist government of the North (the 'Repubblica Sociale Italiana' or 'Republic of Salò'), and of the regime of the German occupation.[67]

As regards questions of fundamental interpretation, they are to a great extent open and indeed there has been a clarification of terms in recent years. This was inspired by the intention, widely expressed but not always acted on, of advancing positively beyond the first phase of study, in which the tendency was to accept as criteria of judgment not only the ideals operative during the Resistance but also the political positions of the various parties since 1945. Take, for example, the debate on whether the Resistance was or was not 'betrayed': obviously, those historians who are close to the political forces which have dominated Italy for the last twenty years (Christian Democrats and their allies) incline to the view that the Resistance was fulfilled and there is nothing to complain about, whereas those who are excluded from power have not always resisted the temptation to deplore a betrayed and repudiated Resistance. We are thinking particularly of certain currents in the dissolved Party of Action, because the communists are a special case; their position tends to safeguard the continuity of party policy during and after the Resistance. It seems clear that historians should try to resolve this dilemma, which easily becomes charged with emotion, submitting the results of the Resistance to an unprejudiced examination, in relation to the forces and ideals which contributed to form it and with an eye also to what Italy has been like in the years that followed. This problem is linked to another, which is that of the 'unity' of the Resistance. This was a political ideal proclaimed by many (and with particular force by the communists), in various different senses, during the struggle, and it can no longer be taken as an adequate criterion. On the contrary, the present concern is to restore to every sector of anti-fascism and of the Resistance its exact likeness, with indifference to the risk of discovering that those events were lived through by men who cherished many different aims as well as those which they held in common. And one could give more examples: Resistance for re-establishment or Resistance for revolution? Was it primarily patriotic or primarily social? to what extent was it a new phenomenon compared to pre-1943 anti-fascism? Was it spontaneous or the product of party organization? Was it political or religious?

Much of the best writing on Resistance is now concerned with these and kindred questions;[68] for example, there is research on such specific points as the nature and functions of the committees of national liberation (whether these committees were *ad hoc* instruments in the struggle, or whether they were organs which might have become the nucleus of a new institutional system).[69]

And this problem leads on to a considetation of the present Italian constitution and the character of the parliamentary regime since the war—questions which have been of interest hitherto mainly to jurists, publicists, and politicians.[70]

In the first decades after 1866 the emergence, out of hagiography and journalism, of serious historical study of the Risorgimento was a slow development; if we compare with it the growth after the Second World War of historical studies of united Italy up to and including the Resistance, the comparison must be largely in favour of the later period as it has developed in recent years. Greater critical awareness, more accuracy in formulating many of the old problems and in defining new ones, and an insistence upon scrupulous documentation—these factors have all acquired more importance and have helped to increase the maturity of Italian historiography in many respects.

It is thanks to this tendency that the practice of publishing recent documentary sources is, at last, beginning to be favoured in Italy. Thus systematic textual criticism, which before the war had scarcely begun to touch the field of the Risorgimento, has been fully applied to the history of united Italy, assisted by the Marxist neo-scholasticism already mentioned. The great series of *Italian Diplomatic Documents*, produced by a commission at the Foreign Ministry—a novelty for Italy—will be carried up to 1943,[71] and other projects are in the care of institutes and publishing houses.[72] The state archives are encouraged by law to make ever more intensive use of documentary sources, and permission has recently (since 1963) been granted for free consultation of all documents more than fifty years old; it is also granted with increasing frequency for those of more recent years, especially up to 1925.

In addition to documentary sources we must note also a lively interest in the study of journalistic and cultural sources. We can do no more than mention the impetus given by Garin to studies of nineteenth-century Italian culture, and the faintly Alexandrian vogue of anthologies of magazines and newspapers, usually prefaced by lengthy critical essays. This indicates also an awakening

interest in the study of public opinion, of the channels in which it
is formed, of its degrees of representativeness, and of its influence
on the decisions of the governing class.[73]

In the end, however, there emerge from the brief survey we have
made some deficiencies in contemporary historiography which are
not negligible and which show that in this—as in so many other
branches of Italian culture—there are still traces of the provincial
isolation imposed by a centuries-old tradition. Pre-fascist Italy
only succeeded, and with great difficulty, in making a dent in this
tradition; it was refurbished with vulgar emphasis by fascism;
and it has been attacked again, but not yet entirely overcome, in
the post-fascist period.

The chronological limit within which this study has had to be
confined is itself an indication of one of the worst lacunae in the
present situation: the lack of studies dealing with the most recent
years. Italian historiography today stops at 1945, or at the latest
1948, and even this *terminus ad quem* was not fixed without discussion and controversy. In partial contradiction of itself, Crocean
historicism had set arbitrary bounds, like Pillars of Hercules, between the remote and the recent past: only the former could be a
subject of calm and peaceful study, while the latter was inevitably
abandoned to the tumult of passion and the active will. This point
of view later became embodied in academic attitudes and prejudices; it coincided with a political timidity which was shared by
almost all sectors, though for different reasons. It could be said
rather paradoxically that Italian historiography, being tied up in
this way by politics, became embarrassed to exhibit its bondage
too openly and therefore shrank from dealing with themes which
might make its situation too obvious. This becomes all the clearer
when we reflect that since the war there have been far more studies
of contemporary history (the nineteenth and twentieth centuries)
than of all the other centuries together; so the enthusiasm of
Italian historians now flows in a rather narrow chronological
channel, close to the present day, though not very close. And yet
we may add, as regards the *terminus ad quem*, that the list of
diploma theses in history published by the *Bulletin of the Society
of Italian Historians* reveals a satisfactory trend among the younger
students towards the study of recent events. Moreover, it can be
foreseen that an impetus in the same direction will be derived
from the fortunate diffusion among Italian universities of those
chairs of contemporary history which are at present only a timid

overture, to say nothing of the teaching requirements of the renovated secondary schools.

A second major deficiency of Italian historiography (which is not confined to contemporary history) is its scanty attention to the world beyond Italy. Here again one may refer to the country's long political and cultural isolation which has resulted in the 'inadequate organization for historical research abroad' and the 'modest institutions for Italy's international relations and responsibilities'.[74] Although there are outstanding exceptions,[75] it must be recognized that much ground still remains to be made up; but as regards organization, things are slowly improving. The quality of diploma theses confirms this improvement, but much still depends upon Italy's academic structure, which is inadequate for the needs of a modern country and many sectors of which, in many aspects, call for substantial reforms. For example, the almost total dearth in Italy of the international harvest of works on the 'third world' is certainly a result of the inferior professional level which usually obtained in the chairs of 'colonial history and politics', recently transformed into less archaic chairs of 'history and institutions of African and Asian countries'.[76]

Italians, as the reader will have deduced from the titles we have discussed, are not fond of writing histories that cover long periods; they prefer monographs which permit of more refined and subtle, and sometimes slightly esoteric, effects of light and shade. Thus it is that the only comprehensive history of united Italy to have appeared since the war is the work of an Englishman.[77] And the work of a scholar who has undertaken a full-scale history of modern Italy, to be carried up to the present day, has so far covered, in its first four volumes, only the period 1700–1860.[78]

This phenomenon can be related to the lack of any tradition of learned essays addressed to a numerous cultured public; and it is discreditable, especially to historians of the Left, that nobody since Croce has dared to write general histories of Europe and Italy together.[79] In fact in Italy there exists hardly anything between the learned, and academically profitable, monograph, and the historical romance of the kind that used to be written by Oriani or Borgese. Nor, in a different field, have recent discussions such as those aroused in France, for example, by Braudel on *la longue durée* called forth any fruitful response in Italy.

If we now turn to the other extreme of historical writing, the biographical, we again find a traditional deficiency in Italy, confirmed by the Marxist prejudice in favour of studying social structures and the Crocean-idealist principle of identifying personality with the works produced by it. It is understandable that Fausto Nicolini, a scholar particularly close to Croce, felt obliged in the biography he devoted to his master to make the distinction between 'true biography', which coincides with the subject's philosophical, poetic, or political works, and 'biography in the narrow sense', which studies how the subject 'conducted and realized the business of living which conditioned his special activity'. But Valeri himself, from whom I have quoted the above comment on Nicolini's position, has been one of the leaders of the renewed interest in biography.

Salvemini in his day, and from his 'concrete' point of view, had urged Italians to study things and men at close hand, in the hope that this would restrain them in the end from metaphysical wanderings. But today the partial return to biography can also be attributed to the objection of the idealists themselves to the providentialist view which obscures individuality (Chabod, for example, exhibits a certain perplexity of this kind), and also, and above all, to historians like Venturi and Valeri—of whom the one, in the history of Illuminism and of the eighteenth century, and the other, in the history of the nineteenth century, have deliberately centred their study on the 'biographical method' and the zest for reconstructing character.[80]

What discussions of methodology have formed the background and contributed to a more or less clear notion of the lacunae in the works we have been discussing in these pages ? A reasoned reply to such a question is outside the purpose of this article, and in any case it could not be confined to works dealing with the twentieth century.

We shall not be far wrong, however, in saying that Italian historians in recent years have failed to discuss adequately the basic premisses of their activity. They have preferred to tackle concrete tasks of interpretation of Italian history, in particular from the Risorgimento onwards. There have been some discussions of principle and method, however—and especially between idealists and Marxists—which have revived some important problems: for example, the legitimacy of the historical 'if', the existence in history of the forces defeated in the struggle to control the state, the kind of sources to be used in studying the lower strata of the population, and the duty of recognizing the ineluctable reality of the *fait accompli* while not limiting the historian's role to this recognition. But there has been little discussion of the place of history within the general scheme of the sciences, or even of whether it is legitimate to call history a science, or of the ensuing fundamental questions of method, such as the relation between interpretative hypothesis and document, or narrative and analysis, and the question of formalizing the historians' language. In other words, Italian historians, with due exceptions, do not seem to have been sufficiently concerned with those discussions which we associate with the names of Bloch, Febvre, Braudel, and Labrousse in France, and Carr, Butterfield, Gardiner, Dray, and Stuart Hughes in the Anglo-Saxon countries.

The fact is that although the common historiographical background has given Italian historical writing a remarkable maturity and homogeneity in many fields, it has not given sufficient stimulus, either to idealists or Marxists, to question the background itself and to confront it with traditions of historiography derived from different cultural contexts. The result has been that the discussion of methodology and principle has been advanced more by philosophers than by historians.[81] It was the philosophers who first felt, alongside the influence of Marxism (and the Marxism of the philosophers did not altogether coincide with that of the historians) the influence of existentialism, phenomenology, and neo-logical-positivism, thus initiating a notable revivification of Italian thought, with repercussions also upon the meaning of history. And this has led to a progressive separation between the most lively philosophical thought and historical thought—a paradoxical outcome for a historiography which, in both its idealist and its Marxist department, had formed the ambitious project of resolving philosophy into history.

NOTES

[1] S. J. Woolf, 'Risorgimento e fascismo: il senso della continuità nella storiografia italiana', *Belfagor*, vol. XX, 1965, pp. 71–91.

[2] E. Sestan, 'Per la storia di un'idea storiografica: l'idea di una unità della storia italiana', *Rivista storica italiana*, vol. LXII, 1950, pp. 180–198. Salvatorelli returned briefly to this question in 1954 to repeat one of his earlier theses; see L. Salvatorelli, *Spiriti e figure del Risorgimento* (Florence, 1961), pp. 30–5.

[3] A kind of catalogue of many of these questions, relating not only to the Risorgimento but also to the post-Risorgimento period, cleverly argued from the point of view of liberal historiography, is provided in the collection of lectures given by Walter Maturi at the University of Turin; W. Maturi, *Interpretazioni del Risorgimento* (Turin, 1962). For the problems emphasized above, see, among many works of different tendencies; L. Cafagna, 'Intorno al revisionismo risorgimentale', *Società*, vol. XII, 1956, pp. 1015–35; C. Pavone, 'Le idee della Resistenza: antifascisti e fascisti di fronte alla tradizione del Risorgimento', *Passato e Presente*, No. 7, Jan.–Feb. 1959, pp. 850–918; *Problemi dell'unità d'Italia*, (*Atti del II convegno di studi gramsciani*) (Rome, 1962); A. Garosci, 'Primo e secondo Risorgimento', *Rivista storica italiana*, vol. LXXIV, 1962, pp. 27–51; F. Rodano, 'Risorgimento e democrazia', *La rivista trimestrale*, vol. I, 1962, pp. 63–130; the report of R. Moscati, 'Vecchie e nuove forze politiche di fronte allo Stato unitario', and the subsequent discussion in *Atti del XL Congresso di storia del Risorgimento italiano* (Rome, 1963), pp. 231–59; R. Romeo, *Dal Piemonte sabaudo all'Italia liberale* (Turin, 1963); F. Fonzi, *Il giudizio sul Risorgimento di un cattolico antifascista, Francesco Luigi Ferrari*, in *I cattolici e il Risorgimento* (Rome, 1963); the posthumous collection of essays by R. Battaglia, to which the editor, E. Ragionieri, has given the title of *Risorgimento e Resistenza* (Rome, 1964). See also the very recent discussion on 'The end of the Risorgimento': R. Moscati, 'La tradizione del Risorgimento e la presente realtà italiana', *Elsinore*, vol. I, No. 1, December 1963, pp. 57–63; R. Romeo, 'Il significato storico della tradizione risorgimentale', ibid., vol. I, No. 2, Jan. 1964, pp. 63–7; R. Moscati, 'Uno stato senza parametri', ibid., vol. I, No. 3, Feb. 1964, pp. 76–9; C. Casucci, 'Il Risorgimento è una tradizione finita?', *Il Mulino*, vol. XIII, 1964, pp. 1168–71; L. Castelnuovo, 'Il tema del Risorgimento', ibid., vol. XIV, 1965, pp. 1173–77; E. Ragionieri, 'Fine del Risorgimento? Alcune considerazioni nel centenario dell'unità d'Italia', *Studi storici*, vol. V, 1964, pp. 3–40.

[4] At the centre of this movement was the review, *Movimento Operaio*, of which Franco Della Peruta was the moving spirit, and the Istituto Feltrinelli of Milan. Among the many initiatives in the field was that undertaken by the *Bibliografia della stampa periodica operaia e socialista italiana (1860–1926)*, directed by Della Peruta. So far the only volumes to have appeared are those devoted to Milan edited by Della Peruta, and to Messina, edited by Gino Cerrito (Milan, 1956 and 1961). A similar initiative, though on a more restricted scale, was undertaken by the *Ente per la storia del socialismo e del movimento operaio italiano* (Modigliani Foundation), which has published two parts of a first volume of a *Bibliografia del socialismo e del movimento operaio italiano*, devoted to *I Periodici* (Rome-Turin, 1956).

[5] R. Romeo, 'La Storiografia politica marxista', *Nord e Sud*, No. 21, August 1956, pp. 5–37; No. 22, September 1956, pp. 16–44. This essay and Romeo's reply to his critics, in which he broadens the scope of his argument considerably, are republished in R. Romeo, *Risorgimento e capitalismo* (Bari, 1959).

[6] See, for example, the discussion started in the final numbers of *Movimento Operaio* by the editor Armando Saitta. (The review ended in 1956.) See also F. Diaz, 'La storiografia di indirizzo marxista in Italia negli ultimi quindici anni', *Rivista critica di storia della filosofia*, vol. XVI, 1961, pp. 331–53.

[7] See, for example, a volume more directly connected with the debate started by Romeo; *La formazione dell'Italia industriale. Discussioni e ricerche*, ed. Alberto Caracciolo (Bari, 1963), with an introductory essay by the editor, and papers by A. Gerschenkron, R. Romeo, L. Dal Pane, A. S. Eckaus, L. Cafagna, D. Tosi.

[8] An echo of the attempt to define in a new way the problem of historical research is to be found in the recent discussions on the establishment of faculties or departments of historical sciences which have been taking place principally under the auspices of the Società degli storici italiani.

[9] This lamentable tradition is perpetuated in some recent monumental histories of Italian cities. See, for instance, the final volume, vol. XVI, of the *Storia di Milano* (Fondazione Treccani degli Alfieri, Milan, 1962), and of the history of Mantua: *Mantova. La Storia*, vol. III. *Da Guglielmo III duca alla fine della seconda guerra mondiale* (Mantua, Istituto Carlo D'Arco, 1963).

[10] It is not possible to list here even the principal works on the subject. We must limit ourselves to a few works of major importance because of their general character: R. Molinelli, *Le classi sociali in una città delle Marche dopo il 1860* (Jesi, 1951); in his review of this volume in *Movimento Operaio* (Nos. 15–16, March-April 1961, p. 605) Salvemini cited it as an example of the renewed interest in the history of united Italy; R. Romeo, 'Storia regionale e storia nazionale', *Cultura moderna*, No. 6, December 1952, pp. 36–9, then in *Antologia di critica storica*, edited by A. Saitta, vol. III, *Problemi della civiltà contemporanea* (Bari, 1958), pp. 344–50; E. Ragionieri, *Un comune socialista: Sesto Fiorentino* (Rome, 1953); M. Stanghellini and U. Tintori, *Storia del movimento cattolico lucchese* (Rome, 1958); in the preface to this volume Fonzi invites students of the Catholic movement to welcome on their part the appeal made by Ragionieri to students of socialism, given that 'in the cities change takes place more slowly and is less obvious, while being more substantial and more lasting', ibid., p. 12; see also the *Presentazione* of C. Violante and T. Pedio, *Storia della storiografia lucana* (Bari, 1964); E. Santarelli, *Le Marche dall'Unità al fascismo* (Rome, 1964).

[11] The most important essay of the immediate post-war period was written by Salvatorelli in 1950 for the *Rivista storica italiana*. It has now been republished together with other writings on Giolittian themes; see L. Salvatorelli, *Miti e storia* (Turin, 1964), pp. 417–73.

[12] See, for example, his introduction to A. W. Salomone, *Italian Democracy in the making. The political scene in the Giolittian era 1900–1914* (Philadelphia, 1945), in Italian, *L'età giolittiana* (Turin, 1949).

[13] P. Togliatti, *Discorso su Giolitti* (Rome, 1950).

[14] See B. Croce, *Nuove pagine sparse*, vol. I (Naples, 1948), p. 332; also F. Chabod, 'Croce storico', *Rivista storica italiana*, vol. LXIV, 1952,

pp. 516–21. The literature on Croce is very abundant. A fairly adequate bibliography is that of E. Cione (Milan, 1956).

[15] For discussions on Italian economic development see the volume cited in note 7 above. See also the reconstruction attempted by Romeo in his *Breve storia della grande industria italiana* (Bologna, first edn. 1961, second edn., revised and expanded, 1963), as well as his preface to the Italian edition of S. B. Clough, *Storia dell'economia italiana dal 1861 ad oggi* (Bologna, 1965). See also B. Caizzi, *Storia dell'industria italiana dal XVIII secolo ai giorni nostri* (Turin, 1965).

[16] L. Cafagna, 'L'industrializzazione italiana. La formazione di una "base industriale" fra il 1896 e il 1914', *Studi storici*, vol. II, 1961, pp. 690–724.

[17] G. Procacci, 'Appunti in tema di crisi dello Stato liberale e di origini del fascismo', *Studi storici*, vol. VI, 1965, pp. 221–37.

[18] See, for example, the stimulating attempt at a thesis offered not by a historian but by a professed economist: P. Saraceno, 'La mancata unificazione economica italiana a cento anni dalla unificazione politica', in *L'economia italiana dal 1861 al 1961. Studi del primo centenario dell'unità d'Italia* (Milan, 1961), pp. 692–715. The whole volume should be consulted.

[19] Among the final expositions of the Southern polemical school should be noted M. L. Salvadori, *Il mito del buon governo. La questione meridionale da Cavour a Gramsci* (Turin, 1960). See also the anthologies from opposite viewpoints, *Il Sud nella storia d'Italia*, edited by R. Villari, and *Il Nord nella storia d'Italia*, edited by L. Cafagna (Bari, 1961, 1962). The very idea of an anthology on the North is to be seen in connection with the climate of neo-capitalist euphoria of the years of the Italian 'economic miracle'.

[20] See G. Carocci, *Giolitti e l'età giolittiana* (Turin, 1961). On 1904: G. Procacci, 'Lo sciopero generale del 1904', *Rivista storica del socialismo*, No. 17, Sept.–Dec. 1962, pp. 401–38. The war in Libya has not yet attracted any Italian scholars of the new generation. Nor have the electoral reform and the subsequent elections of October 1913 been the subject of any specific study, although they have been dealt with in many books on the period of Giolitti.

[21] The first of the books referred to is G. Arfè, *Storia del socialismo italiano (1892–1926)* (Turin, 1965). A good synthetic reconstruction of socialism in the Giolittian era is that of L. Valiani, 'Il partito socialista italiano dal 1900 al 1918', *Rivista storica italiana*, vol. LXXV, 1963, pp. 269–326; a paper given to a conference at Florence in January 1963, published with those of G. Bosio, C. Francovich, P. Masini, G. Manacorda, G. Arfè, and F. Catalano in *Il movimento operaio e socialista in Italia. Bilancio storiografico e problemi storici* (Milan, 1965). The most complete monographical research on this very sensitive zone of the Italian working-class movement in the first part of this century is that contained in the three volumes of P. Spriano: *Socialismo e classe operaia a Torino dal 1892 al 1913* (Turin, 1958); *Torino operaia nella grande guerra (1914–1918)*, (id., 1960); *L'occupazione delle fabbriche* (id., 1964).

[22] Arfè's book lacks an analysis of the social forces on whose support

the party was based. There is also a little, but this is very good, on this subject in the two good essays of G. Procacci: 'La classe operaia italiana agli inizi del secolo XX', *Studi storici*, vol. III, 1962, pp. 3–76; 'Geografia e struttura del movimento contadino della Valle Padana nel suo periodo formativo (1901–1906)', ibid., vol. V, 1964, pp. 120–41.

[23] At the beginning of Italian socialism, the anarchic phase linked with the Bakunist wing of the First International had to be mastered. It left a legacy in the important debate between the empiricist and positivist, Turati, and the greatest Italian Marxist philosopher before Gramsci, Antonio Labriola. Communist historiography, apart from some wavering, inclines towards Labriola; Arfè is all for Turati. For a renewal of the discussion with various interventions, see *Studi storici*, vol. VI, 1965, Nos. 2, 3, 4; on the anarchist tradition, revived in the first years of the new century by the Sorelian syndicalists, see E. Santarelli, *Il socialismo anarchico in Italia* (Milan, 1959); at the other extreme, F. Manzotti, *Il socialismo riformista in Italia* (Florence, 1965); on the major episodes of a revolutionary nature in the immediately pre-war years, L. Lotti, *La settimana rossa* (Florence, 1965).

[24] G. De Rosa, *Storia del movimento cattolico in Italia*, vol. I. *Dalla Restaurazione all'età giolittiana*, vol. II. *Il Partito popolare italiano* (Bari, 1966). The two volumes are a reworking, with the variations noted above, of the *Storia politica dell'Azione cattolica in Italia* (covering the period 1874–1919), 2 vols. (Bari, 1953–54), and of the *Storia del partito popolare* (id., 1958). Note also the work published by De Rosa as editor of the *Rivista di politica e storia* and of the historical collections published by Edizioni di storia e letteratura of Rome and by Marcelliana of Brescia.

[25] For the Marxists see note 6 above.

[26] This they did almost alone. The only monograph written by a layman (a communist), and that is old-fashioned, is G. Candeloro's *Il movimento cattolico in Italia* (Rome, 1953). See also G. Spadolini, *Giolitti e i Cattolici (1901–1914)* (Florence, 1960).

[27] The best exception is P. Scoppola, *Crisi modernista e rinnovamento cattolico in Italia* (Bologna, 1961), who laments the scant attention paid after the war to the bonds which unite political manifestations with the religious and cultural background. Since the classical work of A. C. Jemolo, *Chiesa e stato in Italia negli ultimi cento anni* (Turin, first edn. 1948, second edn. 1963), which is like the swan song of liberal Catholicism, the only essay is that of F. Fonzi, 'Stato e Chiesa', in *Nuove Questioni di storia del Risorgimento*, op. cit., pp. 325–88. For a strictly Italian view of the characters and work of the two Popes of this period see the proceedings of two conferences: *Aspetti della cultura cattolica nell'età di Leone XIII* (Rome, 1961) and *Benedetto XV, i cattolici e la prima guerra mondiale* (Rome, 1963), edited by Giuseppe Rossini, who edits for the same publishing house a *Collana di storia del movimento cattolico*.

[28] In this case too we must limit ourselves to a few essential bibliographical references. An early exponent of the theme outlined above is F. Fonzi, *I cattolici e la società italiana dopo l'Unità* (Rome, first edn. 1953, second edn., with a note in reply to various critics, 1960). The theme was taken to an extreme and translated into political terms by

De Rosa in his *Storia politica dell'Azione cattolica*, cited in 'I partiti politici dopo la Resistenza' in the miscellany *Dieci anni dopo, 1945-1955* (Bari, 1955), pp. 113-207. A work more concerned with the motive of liberty and the problems of relations between politics and religion is that of P. Scoppola, *Dal neoguelfismo alla democrazia cristiana* (Rome, 1957).

[29] F. Fonzi, *Crispi e lo 'Stato di Milano'* (Milan, 1965).

[30] Isolated but remote exceptions are: L. Albertini, *Le origini della guerra del 1914*, 3 vols. (Milan, 1942-43), published posthumously; M. Toscano, *Pagine di storia diplomatica contemporanea*, vol. I. *Origini e vicende della prima guerra mondiale* (Milan, 1963), the writings collected in this volume stem from the years 1936-49. The phrase of Chabod's, quoted here, comes from his 'Considerazioni sulla politica estera dell'Italia dal 1870 al 1915' in the collection of essays by various authors *Orientamenti per la storia d'Italia nel Risorgimento* (Bari, 1952), p. 48.

[31] The most recent synthesis of Italy's participation in the war is that of P. Pieri, *L'Italia nella prima guerra mondiale (1915-1918)* (Turin, 1965), revising and enlarging his contribution to the *Storia d'Italia* edited by L. Valeri (see note 79).

[32] See also L. Valiani, *Le origini della guerra del 1914 e dell'intervento italiano nelle ricerche e nelle pubblicazioni dell'ultimo ventennio*, a (cyclostyled) report to the Italo-Soviet historical conference held in Rome, 28-30 May 1966; M. Fatica, 'Bilancio di contributi recenti sulle origini e i fini dell'intervento italiano nelle prima guerra mondiale', *Critica storica*, vol. V, 1966, pp. 407-30. See also *Atti del XLI Congresso di storia del Risorgimento italiano*, held at Trento in 1963 on the theme 'Italy in the First World War' (Rome, Istituto per la storia del Risorgimento italiano, 1965).

[33] See R. Vigezzi, 'La neutralità italiana del luglio-agosto 1914 e il problema dell'Austria-Ungheria', *Clio*, vol. I, 1965, pp. 54-97; *I problemi della neutralità e della guerra nel carteggio Salandra-Sonnino (1914-1917)* (Milan, 1962); 'Le radiose giornate del maggio 1915 nei rapporti dei prefetti', *Nuova rivista storica*, vol. XLIII, 1959, and vol. XLIV, 1960. A first volume in which Vigezzi reviews and develops his researches is about to appear. The many studies by C. de Biase are inspired by an almost hagiographical re-evaluation of the conservative Premier, Salandra, who led Italy into the war. These are now gathered into one volume, *L'Italia dalla neutralità all'intervento nella prima guerra mondiale* (Modena, 1965).

[34] C. Arfè, op. cit., p. 219.

[35] R. De Felice, *Mussolini il rivoluzionario (1883-1920)* (Turin, 1965), pp. 262-63.

[36] Manacorda in the review which appeared in *Studi storici*, vol. VI, 1965, pp. 369-76, and Valiani in the work cited in note 21. Valiani also wrote an excellent essay on *Il partito socialista italiano nel periodo della neutralità 1914-1915* (Milan, 1963), republished from the *Annali*, vol. V, 1962, of the Istituto Feltrinelli.

[37] N. Valeri, *Da Giolitti a Mussolini. Momenti della crisi del liberalismo* (Florence, 1956) and *D'Annunzio davanti al Fascismo* (Florence, 1963). See also on Fiume P. Alatri, *Nitti, D'Annunzio e la questione adriatica*

(*1919–1920*) (Milan, 1959); R. De Felice, *Sindacalismo rivoluzionario e fiumanesimo nel carteggio De Ambris-D'Annunzio* (*1919–1922*) (Brescia, 1966); one should also note, on the rise of fascism, the essays of P. Alatri collected in the volume *Le Origini del fascismo* (Rome, 1956), and the classic work of A. Tasca, *Nascita e avvento del fascismo*, recently reprinted with an introduction by De Felice (Bari, 1966). For an example of this tendency applied in the field of local history (though not very satisfactorily) to fascism, see M. Vaini, *Le origini del fascismo a Mantova* (*1914–1922*) (Rome, 1961).

[38] See note 17.

[39] The theme of the war-time economy of Italy is dealt with in A. Monticone, *Nitti e la grande guerra* (*1914–1918*) (Milan, 1961).

[40] See G. Arfè, op. cit., pp. 169–75.

[41] For the importance of the economic crisis see F. Catalano, *Potere economico e fascismo. La crisi del dopoguerra, 1919–1921* (Milan, 1964). See also G. Manacorda's essay cited in note 36.

[42] The most complete treatment of the subject is that of L. Salvatorelli and G. Mira, *Storia d'Italia nel periodo fascista* (Turin, 1956). The series of lectures given at the Sorbonne by Chabod and published after his death have had a considerable success in Italy: F. Chabod, *L'Italia contemporanea* (*1918–1948*) (Turin, 1961). A brief synthesis is that of G. Carocci, *Storia del fascismo* (3rd edn., Milan, 1963).

[43] See, for example: R. De Felice, 'Giovanni Preziosi e le origini del fascismo (1917–1931)', in *Rivista storica del socialismo*, No. 17, Sept.–Dec. 1962, pp. 493–555; A. Aquarone, 'Aspirazioni tecnocratiche del primo fascismo', in *Nord e Sud*, vol. I, No. 52, April 1964, pp. 109–28. One should also note De Felice's *Storia degli ebrei italiani sotto il fascismo* (Turin, 1962).

[44] F. Gaeta, *Nazionalismo italiano* (Naples, 1965), and also the anthology cited in note 14.

[45] P. Ungari, *Alfredo Rocco e l'ideologia giuridica del fascismo* (Brescia, 1963).

[46] A. Aquarone, *L'organizzazione dello Stato totalitario* (Turin, 1965.)

[47] E. Di Nolfo, *Mussolini e la politica estera italiana* (*1919–1933*) (Padua, 1960). Di Nolfo follows the broad lines traced by G. Salvemini, *Mussolini diplomatico* (Bari, 1952), examining it and integrating into it the evidence provided by the publication of the Italian diplomatic documents. The war in Ethiopia has only just begun to emerge from the fog of apologetics and silence: see A. Del Boca, *La guerra d'Abissinia, 1935–1941* (Milan, 1965).

[48] We can only limit ourselves to the general works cited in notes 15 and 18. See also the new and more fully documented edition of E. Rossi, *Padroni del vapore e fascismo* (Bari, 1966).

[49] See also the useful collection of essays from various authors, more in the nature of an ideological and moral testimony than historiographical, edited by Costanzo Casucci, *Il fascismo. Antologia di scritti critici* (Bologna, 1961).

[50] In recent years, courses of public lectures on the history of Italy in the fascist years held in the theatres of the principal cities have had a

considerable success. They have made possible the collection of testimonies and of attempts at interpretation of real usefulness even though of unequal value. See the volumes which collect together the lectures held in Rome, Turin, and Milan: *Lezioni sull'antifascismo* (Bari, 1960); *Fascismo e antifascismo (1918–1948)*, 2 vols. (Milan, 1962); *Trent'anni di storia italiana (1915–1945)* (Turin, 1961).

[51] See a comment by Casucci, who generalizes and speaks quite simply of an 'Italy' which becomes first fascist and then democratic (op. cit., p. 430).

[52] See in G. Arfè, op. cit., the final chapter 'Matteotti e l'etica dell'antifascismo'; and G. De Rosa, op. cit., p. 557.

[53] On the exiles see the somewhat out-of-date work of A. Garosci, *Storia dei fuorusciti* (Bari, 1953). On the socialists in exile, G. Arfè, *Storia dell'Avanti!*, vol. II, *1926–1940* (Milan-Rome, 1958). On Piero Gobetti and his spiritual legacy there is a considerable literature. On the activity in Italy of the 'Centro socialista interno', inspired by a profound spirit of reform, see S. Merli, 'La ricostruzione del movimento socialista in Italia e la lotta contro il fascismo dal 1934 alla seconda guerra mondiale', in *Annali dell'Istituto Feltrinelli*, vol. V, 1962, pp. 541–846. On the ex-populists, who now have no representative organization, and on the record of the Christian Democrats the best contribution is that of an American scholar, R. Webster, *The Cross and the Fasces. Christian Democracy and Fascism in Italy* (Stanford, 1960); Italian edition, *La Croce e i Fasci. Cattolici e fascismo in Italia* (Milan, 1964). The fullest and most comprehensive history of anti-fascism is also that of an American, C. F. Delzell, *Mussolini's enemies. The Italian Anti-Fascist Resistance* (Princeton, 1961); Italian edition, *I nemici di Mussolini* (Turin, 1966).

[54] G. Arfè, op. cit., p. 304.

[55] P. Spriano, *L'occupazione delle fabbriche*, op. cit., p. 155.

[56] See P. Togliatti, *La formazione del gruppo dirigente del partito comunista italiano nel 1923–1924* (Rome, 1962). A *Storia della sinistra comunista*, printed anonymously in the edition 'Il programma comunista' of the International Communist Party, was begun by a publication centre, ascribed to Bordiga; the first volume, which goes to the end of 1919, was published in Milan in 1964. As a symptom of the development of interest in the history of the Third International, the crucial framework within which to understand the evolution of the Italian Communist Party, we should note *La rivoluzione permanente e il socialismo in un paese solo: scritti di Bucharin, Stalin, Trotskij, Zinoviev*, with an introductory essay by G. Procacci (Rome, 1963).

[57] See S. F. Romano, *Antonio Gramsci* (Turin, 1965), which, however, by a rather over-brusque inversion of the usual approach, ends to all intents and purposes in 1921, and G. Fiori, *Vita di Antonio Gramsci* (Bari, 1966). Also: R. De Felice, 'Studi e problemi attorno alla figura e l'opera di Antonio Gramsci', in *Clio*, vol. I, 1965, pp. 424–60; L. Paggi, 'Studi e interpretazioni recenti di Gramsci', in *Critica marxista*, vol. IV, No. 3, May-June 1966, pp. 151–81.

[58] For a history of literature deliberately presented as political history see A. Asor Rosa, *Scrittori e popolo. Saggi sulla letteratura populista in*

Italia (Rome, 1965), where Gramsci's guiding concept, '*nazionale-popolare*', is critically treated. To illustrate, in a more general way, a historiographical tendency which could be defined as that of the 'New Left', although it is still being developed, see S. Merli, 'Relazione programmatica della direzione della rivista', in *Rivista storica del socialismo*, No. 25-26, May-Dec. 1965, pp. 270–88.

[59] Two works of a general character are: G. Gigli, *La seconda guerra mondiale* (Bari, 1964) and R. Battaglia, *La seconda guerra mondiale* (5th edn., Rome, 1966). See also the many studies of diplomatic history by Mario Toscano.

[60] On these two last themes there has been a flood of memoirs both accusatory and exculpatory by generals and politicians, among which one cannot really make a distinction. A useful guide is the report of P. Pieri, 'La storiografia italiana relativa al 25 luglio e all'8 settembre', in *Atti del Convegno nazionale sulla Resistenza*, published in *Rassegna del Lazio*, special number, Rome, 1965, pp. 15–28.

[61] R. Battaglia, 'La storiografia della Resistenza', in *Il Movimento di Liberazione in Italia*, No. 57, Oct.–Dec. 1959, pp. 80–131, reprinted in idem. *Risorgimento e Resistenza*, op. cit., pp. 175–225.

[62] First edition (Turin, 1953); new edition (Turin, 1964). Other general studies are: M. Salvadori, *Storia della Resistenza italiana* (Venice, 1955); R. Carli Ballola, *Storia della Resistenza* (Milan-Rome, 1957); 2nd edition revised with the title *La Resistenza armata (1943–1945)* (Milan, 1965). Of Battaglia it has been said that he experienced the Resistance as a fighter of the *Partito d'Azione* and that he wrote its history as a communist. Salvadori is an exile and an ex-member of the British SOE. Carli Ballola was a socialist. On the Catholic side one should note the work of Mario Bendiscioli.

[63] Among the major preliminary attempts at the publication of sources are *La Resistenza in Italia. 25 luglio 1943–25 aprile 1945*, bibliographical essay edited by L. Conti (Milan, 1961); G. Pansa, *La Resistenza in Piemonte. Guida bibliografica 1943–1963* (Turin, 1965); *Il Movimento di Liberazione a Ravenna*, catalogue of documents held by the Istituto storico della Resistenza di Ravenna, edited by L. Casali, 2 vols. (Ravenna, 1963–65).

[64] The Institute began in July 1949 the publication of a review, *Il Movimento di Liberazione in Italia*, now in its 82nd number.

[65] Again we can only cite a few examples: C. Francovich, *La Resistenza a Firenze* (Florence, 1961); E. Piscitelli, *Storia della resistenza romana* (Bari, 1965). On the liberated zones, F. Vuga, *La zona libera di Carnia e l'occupazione cosacca (luglio–ottobre 1944)* (Udine, 1961); A. Bravo, *La repubblica partigiana dell'Alto Monferato* (Turin, 1964); E. Gorrieri, *La Repubblica di Montefiorino* (Bologna, 1966). On a very particular regional situation: M. Pacor, *Confine orientale. Questione nazionale e Resistenza nel Friuli-Venezia Giulia* (Milan, 1964). On the history of the armed guerrilla formations: M. Giovana, *Storia di una formazione partigiana* (in the Cuneo district) (Turin, 1964). On a sector of the working class: R. Luraghi, *Il movimento operaio torinese durante la Resistenza* (Turin, 1958). On the part played by Italians in the resistance movements

in other countries: A. Bartolini, *Storia della Resistenza italiana all'estero* (Padua, 1965).

⁶⁶ The most comprehensive monograph is that of an American: N. Kogan, *Italy and the Allies* (Cambridge, Mass., 1961); Italian edition, *L'Italia e gli Alleati* (Milan, 1963). An examination which attempted both a synthetic and an analytic approach was presented to the Second International Congress on the History of the European Resistance in Milan in 1961 by F. Parri and F. Venturi, 'La Resistenza italiana e gli Alleati', in *La Resistenza europea e gli Alleati* (Milan, 1962), pp. 237–80. A selection of documents with a full commentary is that edited by P. Secchia and F. Frassati, *La Resistenza e gli Alleati* (Milan, 1962).

⁶⁷ F. W. Deakin, *The brutal Friendship. Mussolini, Hitler and the fall of Italian Fascism* (London, 1962); Italian edition, *Storia della Repubblica di Salò* (Turin, 1963). The other work mentioned is E. Collotti, *L'amministrazione tedesca dell'Italia occupata, 1943–1945* (Milan, 1963). The two volumes have in common the extensive use of the German and Italian documents captured by the Allies in 1945.

⁶⁸ See, lastly, the report of S. Cotta, 'Lineamenti di storia della Resistenza italiana nel periodo dell'occupazione', in *Rassegna del Lazio*, op. cit., pp. 28–45. Cotta has the merit of critically restating many problems; but in his anxiety to put forward a moderate and more elevated interpretation of the Resistance he has involved himself over-hurriedly in a new attempt at defining the problems which is both wrong and over-simplified. A lively discussion on Cotta's essay is still in progress in various centres.

⁶⁹ There is an abundant political literature on the Committees of National Liberation. On the historiographical level there is F. Catalano, *Storia del CLNAI* (Comitato di liberazione nazionale Alta Italia) (Bari, 1956). See also on the CLN and the Resistance in general the interesting volume by G. Quazza, *La Resistenza italiana. Appunti e documenti* (Turin, 1966).

⁷⁰ See the final chapter 'La fondazione della Repubblica' of G. Carocci, *Il Parlamento nella storia d'Italia. Antologia storica della classe politica* (Bari, 1964).

⁷¹ Thirteen volumes have appeared so far covering the years 1914–40.

⁷² See the anthology *Testi e documenti di storia moderna e contemporanea*, published by the Istituto Feltrinelli.

⁷³ Note the *Cronache della filosofia italiana (1900–1943)* (Bari, 1st edition 1955) and *La Cultura italiana fra '800 e '900. Studi e ricerchi* (Bari, 1962). For the anthologies, see for example the *Collana di periodici italiani e stranieri* begun by the publishing house Feltrinelli and *La cultura italiana del Novecento attraverso le riviste* published by Einaudi. Recently the firm Cappelli began, under the editorship of Renzo De Felice, a series of anthologies of newspapers; so far they have published the volumes on the *Corriere della Sera (1919–1943)*, edited by P. Melograni, and on the *Stampa nazionalista*, edited by F. Gaeta (Bologna, 1965). The publisher Laterza, on the initiative of the Istituto nazionale per la storia del movimento di liberazione in Italia, has prepared a collection of essays on some of the Italian daily newspapers: *1919–1925. Dopoguerra e fascismo. Politica e stampa in Italia*, editor B. Vigezzi (Bari, 1965).

[74] These two explanations were advanced by Romeo in his report to a conference of Italian and Soviet historians in Moscow in October 1964; see *I Quaderni di Rassegna sovietica*, vol. I (Rome, 1965), p. 110. (See also *Clio*, vol. I, 1965, p. 408.)

[75] See V. Zilli, *La rivoluzione russa del 1905*. Vol. I. *La formazione dei partiti politici (1881–1904)* (Naples, 1963); L. Valiani, 'La dissoluzione dell'Austria-Ungheria', in *Rivista storica italiana*, vol. LXXIII, 1961, pp. 265–320; vol. LXXIV, 1962, pp. 52–92, 250–85; vol. LXXVI, 1964, pp. 601–70; A. Garosci, *Gli intellettuali e la guerra di Spagna* (Turin, 1959); E. Collotti, *La Germania Nazista* (Turin, 1962). It should be added that the best historical reviews are devoting more and more space to non-Italian subjects and making greater use of foreign authors.

[76] For the opposite argument to that developed here—that is for the interest shown by foreign historians in contemporary Italy—see the rapid survey by R. Romeo, 'L'Italia unita nella storiografia internazionale del secondo dopoguerra', in *Nord e Sud*, Nos. 66–67, June–July 1965, pp. 178–88.

[77] D. Mack Smith, *Italy. A modern history* (Ann Arbor, 1959); Italian edition, *Storia d'Italia dal 1861 al 1958* (5th edn., Bari, 1961). The book has had a considerable success with the general public, less with the academic world.

[78] G. Candeloro, *Storia dell'Italia moderna*, vols. I–IV (Milan, 1956–64).

[79] Only one important general history, written in collaboration, has been compiled since the war, the *Storia d'Italia*, co-ordinated by Nino Valeri. His volume IV *Da Cavour alla prima guerra mondiale* (Turin, 1960) contains essays by F. Cataluccio, L. Valiani, L. Bortone, P. Pieri; volume V (1960) *Dalle crisi del primo dopoguerra alla fondazione della repubblica* is entirely the work of F. Catalano, who has developed his own work (Milan, 1962) expanding the proportion devoted to the years of the Second World War and extending the final date to 1948. A second revised edition of the entire *History* has now appeared (1966). Useful but patchy collections of essays by various authors containing very full bibliographies are *Nuove questioni di storia del Risorgimento e dell'Unità d'Italia* and *Questioni di storia contemporanea* the latest editions of which were issued respectively in 1961 and 1952–55 (Milan). The four volumes devoted to contemporary history, edited by Ettore Rota, have some essays on non-Italian themes.

[80] See the anthology *La vita sociale della nuova Italia*, edited by Nino Valeri for the publishers UTET in Turin. This involves a series of biographies, the first volume of which covers from Nicolini to Croce. The *Dizionario biografico degli italiani*, edited by the Istituto dell'Enciclopedia italiana in Rome has reached vol. VII (to the name Bellotto). After bitter polemics it has been extended to cover men in the twentieth century

[81] See for example the volume in which Delio Cantimori, the most important academic historian to embrace Marxism, gathered together many of his essays of methodological value, D. Cantimori, *Studi di storia* (Turin, 1959). In the review of this by G. Manacorda (in *Studi storici*, vol. I, 1959–60, pp. 158–68) a discussion was opened, though it did not advance very far, on the position of the historian in the intellectual scene

and on his ethics. The *Rivista storica italiana* in 1961, on the initiative of
A. Momigliano and Pietro Rossi, opened a discussion on historicism in
contemporary thought, in which a number of Soviet historians inter-
vened. The review *Clio*, to give another example, began the publication of
bibliographical information under the rubric 'theory and history of historiography'. For a polemical review of some of these problems in the form
of a history of institutions, see I. Zanni Rosiello, 'Sull' unificazione
amministrativa: a proposito di alcuni studi recenti', *Rassegna degli Archivi
di Stato*, vol. XXV, 1965, pp. 83–106.

S. J. WOOLF

Research into Contemporary History in Italy

The writing of contemporary history belongs to a long-standing tradition in Italy. The works of Guicciardini and Machiavelli, as well as those of many lesser historians of the period, offer a good case for arguing that in its origins modern historiography consisted in large part of contemporary history. In twentieth-century Italy, particularly since the end of the Second World War, an analogous concern with contemporary history is easily perceptible. The most cursory glance at publishers' lists, periodical publications, or the *National Historical Bibliography* of recent years is sufficient to indicate the degree of interest. A disproportion between the number of works published on modern and contemporary history compared to those on earlier periods is, of course, characteristic of most Western historiography today. But the flood of translations of foreign works on mainly recent history reflects a presumably accurate assessment by commercial publishers of the interest of a growing reading public. It also reflects one of the major limitations of Italian historiography in the contemporary field: an absolute predominance of research on national history, resulting in an almost total absence of Italian participation in discussions of the major, non-Italian historical themes of the twentieth century.

No survey of the organization and nature of research in contemporary history in Italy can fail to enquire into the reasons for this widespread interest and this limitation of Italian historical production. It is commonplace to explain the interest in recent history of the younger generations in terms of the cataclysmic effects of political events in this century and the rapidity of scientific and technological development. These explanations are no less valid for Italy than for other countries. But to a foreigner, this somewhat generic desire to understand and explain the instability of the post-war world seems to run deeper in Italy than in most countries. The reasons are undoubtedly complex, but two deserve to be singled out because they have left a deep mark on Italian historiography. In the first place, the overthrow of fascism led to a certain sense of guilt that a dictatorial regime could acquire and maintain power so easily and for so long a period. It might have been expected that this feeling would die down with the passing of the years. But a growing dissatisfaction with the real or imaginary inadequacies of the post-war republican state, often linked to the inheritance of fascism, has continued to act as a potent stimulant of historical research. It has led to a critical re-examination of the history of Italy, and in particular of the century since unification, in order to discover the origins and explain the apparent survival of certain characteristics of Italian political life, as well as to teach the younger generations what the fascist period bequeathed to Italian society.

The second explanation which can be offered for the widespread concern with recent history is the close interdependence of history and politics traditional to Italian intellectual life. At least since the early nineteenth century history has been regarded as much an instrument of political struggle as an object of research. Both fascism and the mass parties which emerged from the anti-fascist resistance movement left a strong imprint on the character of Italian historiography through their desire to identify themselves with what each regarded as the 'true' line of Italian historical development. In recent years, as the political struggle has become less disruptive and as many traditional problems are changing face under the impact of a more rapid economic development, con-temporary history is emerging from its subordination to the immediate contingencies of politics and is becoming the object of more detached research. Such is the impression of a considerable number of works of high quality on the Giolittian period, fascism, and the resistance movement. But it is enough to look at the numerous politico-cultural journals to realize the strength of the tie between history and politics which still remains. If sometimes dangerous in this field of difficult objectivity, such a tie has offered an interpretive stimulus to the writing of contemporary history which has often raised its tone.

These reasons, as much as any structural weaknesses in the organization of historical research, help to explain the almost exclusive concentration of Italian historiography on national history to the exclusion of research on foreign history or major international themes, sometimes even at the risk of ignoring the dimensions or distorting the perspectives of research into Italian history. There are certainly (and always have been) exceptions to this generalization, such as Grendi's work on the Fabians, Zilli's large-scale study of the Russian revolution of 1905, Valiani's researches into the dissolution of the Austro-Hungarian empire, Toscano's studies of European diplomacy, Garosci's works on the Spanish civil war, Collotti's study of Nazi Germany.[1] But these remain isolated examples which hardly bear comparison to the contributions to non-national contemporary history made by historians of other countries.

Various explanations have been offered of this disproportionate concentration of effort. In a recent survey of post-war Italian historiography, Professor Romeo pointed to the unsuitability of the Italian structural organization to encourage research abroad, and suggested that the lack of studies might reflect Italy's reduced international responsibilities.[2] This explanation, while extremely plausible for the period until the First World War, seems less valid since 1945. For, although in practical terms Italian influence on world politics is limited, the growth of international organizations, particularly in Europe, has inevitably led to a far closer and more continuous contact with foreign cultures and traditions. It is rather in the long-term intellectual and structural effects of the cultural isolation imposed by twenty years of fascism, and in the not unnatural concern to explain the major catastrophe which befell Italy (whether for moral or ideological reasons), that the present writer would look for an answer.

In the last few years the position has undoubtedly improved. The most interesting historical journals, such as the *Rivista Storica Italiana*, *Studi Storici*, the *Nuova Rivista Storica*, the *Rivista Storica del Socialismo*, dedicate a large proportion of their space to non-Italian subjects. The lists of B.A. theses in history point to a growing interest in foreign history. Major international themes, such as communism, fascism, or the relationship of economic to political development, are attracting increasing attention. But as yet this interest has not resulted in a significant stream of Italian works on foreign history. Its most visible feature is the remarkably rapid translation of foreign books on contemporary history. It remains, however, limited to the European and Western world, ignoring almost entirely recent African, Asian, and Latin American history.[3] The one exception to this is the work produced by the Istituto per il Medio e l'Estremo Oriente at Rome, which, however, appears to have had little impact or influence on the general characteristics of Italian contemporary historiography.

Until the last few years, the organization of historical research in Italy can hardly be said to have assisted research in contemporary history. Indeed the quantity, and in good part high quality, of work in this field bears witness to the intensity of interest and determination of particularly the younger generation of historians to go outside the institutional structure.

No 'institute of contemporary history' exists in Italy. This is not surprising given the general lack of historical research institutes and of facilities for graduate research. What is perhaps more surprising at first sight is that, until about five years ago, the existence of contemporary history was not officially recognized. The teaching of contemporary history, in so far as it existed within the academic structure, depended upon the predilections of individual professors of history, in the same way as—at a more elementary level—it depended on the interest and sense of responsibility of schoolteachers to continue their courses beyond the official closing-date of 1918. Until recent years, probably the major part of what formal teaching of contemporary history was done within the universities took place in faculties of law and political science and (to a lesser degree) of economics, rather than in faculties of letters, and tended to be limited to specific fields, such as colonial or economic history, international politics (*storia dei trattati politici*), or the history of institutions. In consequence, while a proportion of students who took degrees in law or economics may have acquired a knowledge of one or another aspect of contemporary history, those who 'majored' in history in the faculty of letters were for the most part paradoxically left without any formal training in recent history.

In the last decade, growing insistence on the part of the general public that the post-war generation be taught the history of the fascist period in schools, and an increasing awareness of the consistent interest of students and young research-workers in contemporary history, has led to considerable discussion of the problems involved and some initial improvements. If the major advances have been made outside the universities, this may well be due not so much to any unwillingness on the part of professional historians, as to the difficulties of introducing significant improvements in any single sector in the absence of a large-scale reform of the entire university system.

The teaching of history is divided among four faculties: letters, *magistero*, law, and economics,[4] although in practice it is only possible to 'major' in history in the faculty of letters. Within letters and *magistero* (a faculty offering a university degree in the humanities, foreign languages, and pedagogy to schoolteachers) the chairs of history have traditionally been divided between ancient, medieval, modern, and *risorgimento* history. As no rigid closing-dates exist, it has always been possible for the *risorgimento* professor to teach contemporary history.[5] The teaching of political science in most faculties of law explains the existence of history courses wholly separate from those of the faculties of letters and *magistero*. The history courses in faculties or institutes of political science tended to be on recent periods, but were limited by a framework centred on political and economic doctrines and politics. Students could follow courses on the post-1945 period, international politics, the theory of communism, and colonial history. The most serious teaching of contemporary history has resulted from the courses held by professors of the history of treaties. But most of the other courses tend to be regarded as subsidiary, and taught with little preparation, at an extremely low level. The recent transformation of chairs of 'colonial history and politics' into chairs in 'the history and institutions of Afro-Asiatic countries' was symptomatic of the general situation in faculties of law. But outside the field of 'political science', it has proved almost impossible to modernize such obligatory courses in the faculty of law as the history of law, because of the deep-rooted tendency to regard such academic subjects as limited to the classical or medieval period. Only in the history of institutions are there serious indications of a willingness to accept the last century as a period worthy of study. Little need be said about the faculty of economics and commerce. As its title suggests, it has always been regarded as a professional training-school for business and industry. In consequence, the teaching of economic history—of which recent and contemporary history could only form a part—has been subordinated as a subject of little apparent practical application and hence as unimportant. On the other hand, there are undoubted signs of the indirect influence of economics on the study of contemporary history.

In the last few years, certain improvements in the academic

structure have had an immediate beneficial effect on the teaching of contemporary history. The subject was first officially recognized some five years ago by the institution of a new category of *libere docenze* (equivalent to the German *Privatdozent*) in contemporary history. There are now nearly twenty historians with that title, giving supplementary courses in the universities. The creation of a series of subsidiary chairs without security of tenure (*incarichi*), general to all faculties, has led to a far more regular provision of the teaching of contemporary history in the faculties of letters, *magistero*, and law. Three full chairs of contemporary history were created in the early 1960s (although two have subsequently lapsed), and it seems almost certain that at least three more will be created in the next few years.

More important than these innovations is the proposed reform of the teaching of political science through the creation of new, separate faculties of political science. Chairs of constitutional history, the history of political institutions, and the history of parties are envisaged, and it seems not improbable that more chairs of contemporary history will be created. The very nature of the subjects taught in the new faculty (politics, economics, political and economic doctrines, international politics, sociology, history) shows a decisive shift of emphasis towards studies on contemporary affairs. In this framework contemporary history possesses the possibility of acting as a catalyst.

These are the first modest signs of an acceptance and encouragement of contemporary history in official academic circles. As yet they are not comparable to the major initiatives which have been taken in the United States, Great Britain, and other countries. Two major obstacles to the teaching of history—and hence of contemporary history—remain within the university structure. In the first place, there is little evidence that the discussions and proposals (mainly deriving from the Society of Italian Historians) for the creation of a separate faculty, or at least a department, of historical sciences with a degree in history will have any concrete outcome. In consequence, the teaching of history at the undergraduate level remains fragmented and subordinated to the more general requirements of each separate faculty, with limited possibilities of expansion.

In the second place, with one notable exception which will be described below, no graduate institutes of history exist in Italy. Although it has become easier in recent years for history graduands to continue their studies because a greater number of scholarships are available and other facilities have been added, there is still no provision of graduate training courses in the methodology of history.

The only exception to this lack of graduate schools is the Institute of Historical Studies 'Benedetto Croce' (Istituto Italiano per gli Studi Storici) at Naples, created in 1947, before the philosopher's death. The institute, which possesses Croce's library, has always held seminars on contemporary history, and in recent years courses on (mainly Italian) contemporary history have been offered with a certain regularity. Both Italian and foreign students follow these courses at the same time as pursuing their own researches, and there are indications of a growing interest among them in contemporary history.

It is necessary to look outside the universities for the major initiatives in this field. It would not be unfair to say that virtually all the most important projects of research which have resulted in series of specialized publications have come from outside the strictly academic structure. Indeed even in the didactic field in recent years an important initiative has emerged from outside the 'profession' in the form of public courses on the history of fascism and the resistance movement, held in numerous cities and sometimes resulting in publications.[6]

Already in the fascist period the existence of a private Institute for International Political Studies (ISPI), directed by Volpe, offered a *point d'appui* for studies in contemporary history, of which a certain proportion escaped serious ideological or propagandistic distortions. In the last twenty years the Rivista di Studi Politici Internazionali has acted to some extent as a focal point for the study of international relations, sponsoring publications beside its journal. But since the war, no single institute has had the same centralizing effect as ISPI. A few officially recognized institutes are concerned either wholly or in part with contemporary history. The Central Giunta for Historical Studies (Giunta Centrale per gli Studi Storici)—which, despite its title, does not act as a centralizing body, but merely provides a common framework for the presidents of the various institutes—publishes the *National Historical Bibliography*, which, of course, covers the field of contemporary history. The Institute of Modern and Contemporary History (Istituto Storico per l'Età Moderna e Contemporanea) was created through the division in 1926 of the former Italian Historical

Institute into separate medieval and modern sections. But, despite its 'contemporary' label, it still tends to concern itself primarily with the publication of diplomatic documents of the nineteenth century and of papers of nineteenth-century statesmen such as Ricasoli. In fact, the Institute for the History of the Risorgimento (Istituto per la Storia del Risorgimento), which published the *Rassegna Storica del Risorgimento*, has shown a greater interest in the twentieth century, particularly in the period up to the First World War. But only one officially recognized institute exists dedicated to the study of the twentieth century. The Institute for the History of the Liberation Movement in Italy (Istituto Nazionale per il Movimento di Liberazione in Italia), founded immediately after the war, concerns itself (as its name indicates) with a specific field, but has taken care not to limit itself to the actual chronology of the resistance movement and is showing increasing interest in the entire fascist period. The head institute in Milan, which is linked to separate institutes in the main cities of Northern and Central Italy and in Naples, not only collects and conserves documentation and testimonies on the resistance movement, but publishes an important journal, *Il Movimento di Liberazione in Italia*, and sponsors other publications. The existence of these institutes helps to explain the considerable interest and high quality of so many of the publications on the Resistance. Indeed, Italian historiography on contemporary history shows a wholly understandable but almost disproportionate concentration on the resistance movement compared to the many other problems of the period.

No other institute concerned with contemporary history has anything approaching the History of the Liberation Movement's official character. The most important initiative in Italy since the war in probably any section of the study of contemporary history was the creation of the Istituto Giangiacomo Feltrinelli in Milan, founded and financed by the publisher Feltrinelli in the 1950s, as a specialized library. Concentrating on the history of socialism and the working-class movement not only in Italy but throughout Europe, the institute acquired within a decade one of the major collections in Europe. It acted as a focal point in Italy for studies on left-wing movements, gathering together a group of brilliant young historians and compensating in part for the gaps in the university system. It began a series of publications of documents and research papers on contemporary history, besides providing a bibliography of the periodical press of the Italian socialist and working-class movement. Although of unequal value, this work possessed the undoubted merit of shifting the horizon of left-wing studies from a predominantly Italian to a European scene. These weightier publications and projects of group research, many of which appeared in the impressive *Annali* of the institute, were backed up by the publication of the important and lively journal, *Movimento Operaio* (1949–56).[7] Unfortunately, through the arbitrary decision of the proprietor, the staff of the institute was dismissed and the library closed in the mid-1960s. Whatever the reasons behind the decision, it appears all the more unjustified in view of the fact that the institute had been able to acquire certain important private archives and collections on the understanding (at least implicit) that they would be available to the public. It is uncertain what the future of the institute will be, but official measures have been taken to avoid its sale outside Italy. In 1966 the institute showed renewed signs of activity, initiating the reprint of Italian Communist Party documents. It is to be hoped that the library will be maintained intact and opened to the public again.

The Istituto Gramsci, founded by the Italian Communist Party in Rome, is an institute which has interests in the same field although it enjoys smaller financial resources and is limited in its scope by more definite political commitments. It possesses a unique collection of PCI publications and documents, of particular value for the early years of the party, the period of illegality and resistance to fascism. This collection is made easily available to serious research-workers. The institute itself has no publications, but it has sponsored a number of conferences on problems of Italian contemporary history some of which have attracted contributions by foreign marxist historians.[8]

Two other initiatives in the field of left-wing movements deserve mention. The first is the publication since 1956 of a bibliography of Italian socialist and left-wing movements (ESMOI), which has so far come out in three volumes. The second is the publication by two former members of the Feltrinelli Institute of *Rivista Storica del Socialismo*, a new journal which has now reached its twenty-seventh number and established itself as a successor to *Movimento Operaio*. Although reservations can be made about the journal's political commitment, which to the present writer has vitiated the scientific value of some of its contributions, there can be little doubt about the importance of this publication.[9]

The creation in 1966 of a new institute in Turin, the Fondazione Einaudi, may well herald a major breakthrough in the field of contemporary history. The institute possesses Luigi Einaudi's library which reflects this scholar-statesman's wide-ranging interests. It offers scholarships and more permanent research posts in history and the social sciences, and concerns itself mainly with the questions of unitary Italy, and in particular the history of the ruling classes and the historical evolution of Italian economic development. The institute's intention of encouraging collaboration between historians and social scientists augurs well for the future.

Finally, mention should be made of three small institutes. The Centro Studi Piero Gobetti was founded in Turin in 1961, and named in memory of a young intransigent anti-fascist publicist, who died in 1926 following a fascist assault. Centred around his remarkable library, it is of importance for the study of the origins of fascism and indeed of the first quarter of twentieth-century Italian history. The centre holds conferences and publishes a cyclostyled journal with a considerable amount of useful information. But its main function has been to act as an effective stimulant in encouraging students to write their B.A. theses on the origins of fascism and the resistance movement.

The second institute—the Centro di Documentazione Ebraica Contemporanea in Milan—was also founded a few years ago. It possesses an interesting collection of documents and publications on contemporary Jewish matters, and especially on antisemitism, and publishes a valuable series of *quaderni*.

Finally, the Istituto Luigi Sturzo in Rome has been responsible for publishing the *Opera Omnia* of the creator of the Popular (now Christian Democrat) Party, don Sturzo. The first volumes appeared in 1954.

The liberality and breadth of mind of the authorities responsible for the direction of the State Archives needs to be underlined, if only because it stands in strong contrast to the attitude of many other countries. Although the official limit for the free consultation of documents is fifty years, permission is easily granted to scholars with serious intent up to about 1930, and in specific cases even up to 1943. As the Archivio Centrale dello Stato in Rome contains the police archives, part of the archives of the Fascist Party, those of the private secretariat of Mussolini, besides the private papers of leading statesmen, such as Giolitti, the importance of this concession needs no emphasis. Access to the archives of individual ministries which retain their own collections—Foreign Affairs and Defence—require specific permission. In the case of the archive most frequently used—that of the Foreign Ministry—there are few obstacles to consultation up to 1930. It is difficult to tell what would occur at the other ministries (which are legally bound to hand over their archives to the Archivio Centrale after forty years), as it would appear that as yet nobody has attempted to explore them.

Two ministries—following a practice common to many countries—have taken the initiative of publishing large-scale selections of their own documents. The major collection is that of diplomatic documents published by a commission attached to the Foreign Ministry. The series is intended to cover the entire period from 1900 to 1943, and has so far produced thirteen volumes covering various years between 1914 and 1940. The historical sections of the Ministry of Defence have published a considerable number of volumes on the Italian army and navy in the two world wars. The inventories and catalogues published by the State Archives have so far barely touched the nineteenth century. But the series will include a catalogue of the archive of the anti-fascist movement, *Giustizia e Libertà*.

The interest in contemporary history shown by commercial publishers has already been mentioned. All the major publishing houses have participated, and some (especially Einaudi, Feltrinelli, Laterza, and now Editori Riuniti) have paid considerable attention to foreign, as well as Italian, contemporary history. Symptomatic of this general interest is the space given to the twentieth century in the only serious overall history of Italy to be published for some decades. A cursory glance at publishers' lists is enough to indicate a preference for some rather than other aspects of contemporary history. The national and international history of socialism and communism has attracted considerable attention. This is not surprising given the existence of the Feltrinelli and Gramsci institutes, an important communist publishing house (Editori Riuniti), and a politically and intellectually powerful left-wing movement. The Catholic publishing house Cinque Lune, and a few other publishers, such as the Morcelliana of Brescia, have tried (though with little success) to counterbalance this emphasis by a series of volumes on the Catholic movement and party in Italy. The collapse of liberal Italy, the origins of fascism, and the resistance movement have all naturally given rise to numerous publications.

Einaudi and Feltrinelli began to publish anthologies of important politico-cultural journals, while Capelli and Laterza have recently started to publish anthologies of Italian newspapers, reflecting a traditional concern for the history of intellectuals, which is now perhaps beginning to develop into an interest in the formation of public opinion. The launching of a new series of biographies to illustrate the 'social life of the new Italy' by UTET (of which nine volumes have so far been published, including biographies of Gramsci, Croce, the Olivetti family, etc.) may be indicative of a new development in a historiographical tradition somewhat hostile to biographies. A certain interest in the historiography (though not the methodology) of contemporary history—typical of all Italian historiography—can be seen in the publication of a series of 'Questions of contemporary history' by Marzorati, and in the final volume of an 'anthology of historical critiques' published by Laterza.[10]

In contrast to this positive picture, one should note the reluctance of certain semi-official publishing initiatives to pay adequate attention to the twentieth century. Only after bitter discussions was it agreed to advance the closing date of the Italian National Biography (*Dizionario Biografico degli Italiani*) from 1799 to the present day. The final volumes of the large-scale official histories of Milan and Mantua reflect a notable degree of insensitivity towards the writing of local or regional history in the contemporary period.[11]

One final observation deserves to be made. Research in all fields in Italy is dominated by the universities. In a country where serious bottlenecks exist in the university system at the graduate level, the existence of the various institutes has had the positive effect of offering a small but significant stream of young historians the possibility of continuing their researches in the contemporary field. But for these extra-academic initiatives, the study of the twentieth century might well have been dominated by self-justificatory memoirs on the one hand and by politically motivated occasional pieces on the other. Nevertheless, these institutes cannot act as an effective substitute for an outdated university system, while it is far from clear that the university institutes are prepared to give recognition to, and collaborate with, these 'irregular' extra-academic initiatives. In the last few years the Italian National Council of Research (CNR) has begun to subsidize research in the human and social sciences. The funds thus made available have undoubtedly assisted research in history, including the contemporary field. But it is to be wondered whether the ultimate effect will not be that of strengthening the power of university professors still further by channelling the greater part of the funds through the universities.

Signor Pavone has dealt in some detail with the main directions of Italian research and writing on the contemporary history of Italy. In other fields, however, so far little more than lip-service would appear to be paid to the need for a broader approach. Even in works on foreign policy (with some few exceptions, such as the studies of Toscano, Vedovato, or Mosca), comparatively little attention has been given to foreign diplomatic documents. Italian fascism has been studied in isolation, with little attempt to compare its structural characteristics to those of other countries, or to place the study of the phenomenon in the perspective of the more general crisis of the Western democracies. No historian has tried to define the physiognomy of the pre-fascist liberal state by reference to other similar or contrasting parliamentary regimes, such as those of France, Spain, England or Germany.

There has been a similar insensitivity towards utilizing the concepts and instruments of the social sciences. The years of fascism undoubtedly hindered the development of the social sciences, although Benedetto Croce and the post-war Marxists must also share the blame for discouraging sociological studies. The very isolation of Italian historiography until recent years has often left it unaware of the developments of foreign historiography in this direction. The most striking example can be seen in the field of economic history. Until the publication in the late 1950s of a now famous polemic between Romeo and Gerschenkron on the primitive accumulation of capital in Italy,[12] it would not be unfair to say that few scholars concerned with the economic history of the contemporary period thought it necessary to understand and apply concepts of modern economic theory. There is still an excessive concentration of interest on the political aspects of Italian economic development and economic policies.[13] There have been even fewer attempts to apply the concepts and methods of sociology and political science. Sociologists have initiated researches into the post-war magistracy and political parties. Historians could profitably apply some of their techniques to such fields as parliamentary elections and composition in the pre-fascist period, the public administration under fascism, the magistracy before and during fascism. A greater readiness to absorb some of the methods of political science would benefit studies on political parties, trade unions, and industrial confederations.

These deficiencies have long existed in Italian historiography, and there are definite indications of a willingness to overcome them. In other fields, such as the writing of large-scale histories of long periods or of works on the immediate past (particularly important for Italy, since the problems of the post-1945 period are so closely related to the inheritance of fascism and the ideals and aims of the resistance movement), there is little evidence that Italian historians wish to follow trends of 'Anglo-Saxon' or French historiography. Certain recent biographies may well be indicative of an attempt to experiment with a methodology hitherto alien to the national tradition.

In general, it would not be unfair to say that Italian historiography of the contemporary period has shown itself at its best in its traditional fields of interest, which it has developed with skill and sophistication. In the writing of political history Italian historians have avoided the dangers of retreating into pure narrative and have concentrated on the analysis of problems and reconstruction of situations. A consequence of this has been a preference for minute, detailed research which lends itself more easily to this approach than large-scale histories. But it remains the history of politics or political parties, of the existing or potential ruling classes. There is still relatively little interest in the social forces underlying the parties or the long-term economic movements which often condition politics.[14] Intellectual or cultural history has always represented one of the strong points of Italian historiography. Despite the revision of the Crocean approach to history, which has proceeded apace since the war, there has remained a marked preference for the history of ideas. Too often this type of history tends to be considered as a self-contained field of study, possessing little relationship to the real world. But at its best, when the texture of intellectual, social, economic, and political history is ably woven, there can be little doubt about the depth it adds to historical interpretation.

For a foreign historian to make proposals about improving the range or quality of the work of Italian historians is a highly delicate matter. However, for the purpose of the present conference it is necessary to offer some brief conclusive suggestions.

There can be little doubt that the regular teaching of contemporary history within the universities could provide the necessary rigorous training. But to achieve this end various requirements must be borne in mind. In the first place, regular courses would have to be held on the more general problems of contemporary international history and, as far as possible, on the history of the major countries, as well as on the methodology and techniques of contemporary history. In the second place, adequate provision would have to be made for the continuance of studies by graduate students, encouraging them to spend a period of their initial training years abroad.

The value of individual research institutes outside the university structure cannot be under-estimated. To some extent they already serve to co-ordinate research by virtue of the nature of their specialized interests. These could be fruitfully developed by collaboration with institutes with similar interests in other countries.

There has been a certain reluctance on the part of Italian historians to undertake group projects of research. But in the contemporary field where the mass of documentation is so overwhelming, group research is a necessity if historians are not to continue writing on the same problems, where the basic spadework has been done by previous generations of historians or where the evidence can most easily be interpreted. The problem seems particularly acute for Italy, where regional and local structures and rivalries have left so deep an imprint. It is an approach which has possibly more validity for economic, social, religious, or institutional history than for political history, and it implies a readiness to learn from the social sciences.

Group research could be useful not only to the study of the contemporary history of Italy. International collaborative ventures of individuals, groups, or institutes could open up new paths of research and new perspectives which have hitherto been obscured by the isolation of research in individual countries. It is not difficult to point to examples: comparative studies of fascism, of the crises of Western democracies, of public attitudes towards the various types of political systems, of the character and collapse of Western imperialism, of working-class movements, of the political organization of Catholicism, of the nature and effects of the world economic crisis of 1929, of the problems of reconversion to peace following the two world wars, of initiatives and support for supranational organizations. The difficulty remains that of initiating and co-ordinating such research.

Naturally these suggestions for group research are not intended as a substitute for or limitation on individual research, which has shown itself to be so predominant a characteristic of Italian historiography and of such high quality. They are merely put forward as proposals for an additional method of research, which could assist in filling some of the lacunae of research in contemporary history.

NOTES

[1] E. Grendi, *Il movimento operaio inglese e i fabiani* (Milan, 1964); V. Zilli, *La rivoluzione russa del 1905. I. La formazione dei partiti politici (1881–1904)* (Naples, 1963); L. Valiani, 'La dissoluzione dell'Austro-Ungheria', *Rivista Storica Italiana*, 1961, 1962, 1964; M. Toscano, *Pagine di storia diplomatica contemporanea* (Milan, 1963); A. Garosci, *Gli intellettuali e la guerra di Spagna* (Turin, 1959); E. Collotti, *La Germania nazista* (Turin, 1962).

[2] R. Romeo, 'Gli studi italiani di storia contemporanea (1815–1915) nel secondo dopoguerra', *I Quaderni di Rassegna Sovietica*, I, 1965, p. 110.

[3] Among the very few exceptions, one can point to E. Collotti Pischel, *La rivoluzione ininterrotta* (Turin, 1962), on the Chinese revolution, and R. Rainero, *La democrazia in Africa* (Milan, 1962). The latter volume forms part of (to my knowledge) the only series dedicated to the extra-European world: 'Terzo Mondo', published by *Comunità*, with little success.

[4] Besides these four faculties, faculties of political science existed in a few universities, such as Florence, Rome, Perugia, and Padua, where history courses were taught. But in general political science formed part of the faculty of law.

[5] Indeed, as the choice of courses is wholly dependent upon the professor, it is theoretically possible for any of the history professors to offer a course in contemporary history.

[6] *Lezioni sull'antifascismo* (Bari, 1960); *Trent'anni di storia italiana (1915–1945)* (Turin, 1961); *Fascismo e antifascismo (1918–1948)* (Milan, 1962).

[7] 'Testi e documenti di storia moderna e contemporanea'. 'Bibliografia della stampa periodica operaia e socialista italiana (1860–1926)': 1956 (Milan), 1961 (Messina). The *Annali dell'Istituto Giangiacomo Feltrinelli* began in 1958.

[8] *Problemi dell'Unità d'Italia* (Rome, 1962); *Tendenze del capitalismo italiano*, 2 vols. (Rome, 1962).

[9] Another journal—*Movimento Operaio e Socialista*—now in its twelfth year, has expanded from local Ligurian history to more general themes in recent years.

[10] The general history referred to is the *Storia d'Italia*, co-ordinated by Nino Valeri, published in 5 vols. by UTET of Turin (2nd ed. 1965):

vol. 4 covers from Cavour to the First World War, and vol. 5 (by
F. Catalano) from 1918 to 1948. The latest initiative in communist history
is the reprint of PCI documents and newspapers by Feltrinelli, who has
now expanded these reprints to other parties, entitling the series: 'Movi-
menti e partiti politici in Italia dal 1900 alla caduta del fascismo'. Cinque
Lune publishes a series: 'Collana di storia del movimento cattolico'. The
Einaudi series of anthologies is called: 'La cultura italiana del Novecento
attraverso le reviste'; that of Feltrinelli: 'Collana di periodici italiani e
stranieri'; Capelli has published anthologies of the *Corriere della Sera*
(*1919–1943*), ed. P. Melograni, and the *Stampa nazionalista*, ed. F. Gaeta
(Bologna, 1965). The Laterza volume is called: *1919–1925. Dopoguerra e
fascismo. Politica e stampa in Italia*, ed. B. Vigezzi (Bari, 1965). For the
historiography of contemporary history: *Questioni di storia contemporanea*,
ed. E. Rota, 4 vols. (Marzorati, Milan, 1952–55); *Antologia di critica
storica*, ed. A. Saitta, vol. III. *Problemi della civiltà contemporanea* (Bari,
1958).

[11] *Storia di Milano*, ed. Fondazione Treccani degli Alfieri, vol. XVI
(Milan, 1962); *Mantova. La Storia*. Vol. III, *Da Guglielmo terzo duca alla
fine della seconda guerra mondiale* (Mantua, 1963).

[12] R. Romeo, *Risorgimento e capitalismo* (Bari, 1959); A. Gerschenkron,
articles in the *Journal of Economic History*, 1955, and the *Rivista Storica
Italiana*, 1960, republished in *Economic Backwardness in Historical
Perspective* (Harvard, 1962).

[13] Although a considerable quantity of material has been published on
detailed aspects of Italian industry, as well as two recent general histories
of Italian industry, R. Romeo, *Breve storia della grande industria in Italia*
(Bologna, 1963); B. Caizzi, *Storia dell'industria italiana* (Turin, 1965), the
only overall history of Italian economic development is that of an
American scholar, S. B. Clough, *Economic History of Italy* (New York,
1964). Virtually nothing exists on long-term economic movements, or on
agricultural history.

[14] For an exception to this statement, see the articles by G. Procacci on
the origins of the working-class and peasant movements at the beginning
of the twentieth century in *Studi Storici*, 1962, 1964.

Germany

HANS HERZFELD

After the Catastrophe

Even in the classical German historiography of the nineteenth century, with its characteristic concentration on the state, on political issues, and on the history of ideas, contemporary history (which we regard as the invention of our own times) was by no means unknown. Ranke, who drew a sharp dividing line between history and politics, gave warning of the dangers inherent in a preoccupation with politics, which threatened to prejudice the objectiveness and hence the reputation of the historian. But he himself did not avoid them altogether, as can be seen in his history of the Serbian revolution,[1] while the writing of political history as practised by the partisans of a greater or smaller Germany, whose leading representatives vigorously criticized Ranke's restraint—Dahlmann and Droysen, Sybel and Treitschke—restricted their research into early and modern history quite deliberately and intentionally to themes where their findings could be evaluated and applied to the political problems of their own times. The sum total of Bismarckian historiography, too, of the generation following the establishment of the German Empire, down to Erich Marcks[2] and Arnold Oskar Meyer[3] on the one hand and Johannes Ziekursch[4] and Arthur Rosenberg[5] on the other, represents—in an admiring, apologetic, or critical manner—a great debate on the character and significance of the Bismarckian Empire, one which affected and influenced the course of current events down to the end of the Weimar Republic.

The same is true to an even greater extent of the great debate, following the peace treaties of 1919, on the origins of the First World War and the war-guilt question, in which the historians also took part, with all the personal involvement of the generation immediately concerned. Formal respect was still paid to Ranke's warning against the dangers of contemporary history, with regard both to its method and content—dangers threatening the very existence of the historian—but this warning, while it could not check the basic historical impulse which seeks to integrate the present into the whole of past history, did serve to inhibit uncritical and careless interpretations of the recent past.

It was in Germany, too, that the great debate on the nature of historicism, as the characteristic *Weltanschauung* influencing modern modes of thought since the end of the eighteenth century, was waged with particular intensity, long before Friedrich Meinecke's momentous study, *Die Entstehung des Historismus* (1936), on which he had worked for decades, presented the most impressive treatment of the question. Although the place of contemporary history had by no means been finally recognized, and scepticism and reserve reigned supreme on the surface, the developments which established its necessity were irresistibly gaining ground, whatever the difficulties presented by the acutely political character of its most prominent themes.

The kind of research in contemporary history undertaken in Germany since the end of the Second World War has been determined by the completeness of the country's collapse, which put in question the entire concept of German history as previously held by the majority of historians, and confronted them with the task of 'mastering' the past in a fresh light, in order to give to a nation which seemed for a moment to be deprived of any history a new and clear understanding of the continuity and discontinuity of past and present.

In 1946 Alfred Weber suggested that, in order to avert the threat of 'nihilism', historical concepts as formulated in the past would have to be discarded. In the same year Friedrich Meinecke brought out his slender volume on *Die deutsche Katastrophe*[6] which he had written, without using any resources except the accumulated fruits of a lifetime of critical concern with historical problems, during the final convulsions of the war. To this day it remains one of the most outstanding achievements in the field of contemporary history in virtue of the masterly balance he maintains between criticism of Prussian and German history and loyalty to those moral values which he was still able to accept. But even for Meinecke, the break with the German power-state of the past appeared so final that he began to seek the future of Germany in the form of a German 'Switzerland', a Germany whose reconstruction would be based entirely on spiritual foundations, on the concepts of Goethe-Societies. Renewal, he thought, would come only through the personal example of men of good will. It was not until 1948 that, amid the stresses of the Berlin blockade, and sooner than had been expected, when the outlines of a new German state entity—divided, it is true—began to take shape, Gerhard Ritter brought out his book on *Die deutsche Frage: Betrachtungen über die geschichtliche Eigenart des deutschen Staatsdenkens*. The revised edition of 1962 appeared—rather significantly—under the more complex title *Das deutsche Problem: Grundfragen deutschen Staatslebens gestern und heute*.[7] In this book a leading German historian, who had himself been a member of the anti-Hitler resistance movement, openly faced all the accusations drawn up by those for whom modern German history as a whole, from Luther via Frederick the Great and Bismarck to Hitler, is nothing but a fatal chain-reaction of events leading to the abyss of 1945. Its worth is recognized, although many of its particular arguments are widely contested; it is in any case deserving of praise for facing all the controversial issues which lie at the centre of the preoccupation of Germans with their present. Only Hans Rothfels' book, *Die deutsche Opposition gegen Hitler*,[8] which first appeared in the United States in 1948, can rank as its equal in providing a stimulus to the incipient controversy.

Given the pressing impatience with which, both in Germany and abroad, definitive works by professional German historians on the large themes of national-socialism and Hitler's career were prematurely demanded, it should be recalled that Alan Bullock's work, *A Study in Tyranny*,[9] was not for that matter published before 1952 either. It is true of the first five years after 1948 that, even when the zonal barriers, with their crippling and isolating effect, were removed, the state of the German archives and the inadequacy of the source materials then available, presented almost insurmountable difficulties to the pursuit of any large-scale historical investigation into these most burning problems. This is clearly seen in the early stages of the development of the Munich Institute of Contemporary History, which was founded in 1947. The mere range and abundance of extremely valuable source publications on German history since the First World War, overwhelming even for the specialist, shows that there was no lack of willingness to tackle the delicate problems of the course of events leading to the collapse. But it was precisely in order to make the attempt at such a comprehensive synthesis that the preliminary tools had first to be fashioned by patient labour, and, like all genuine historical research at all times, the study and presentation of these complex problems required the courage to assume considerable risks.

It is no mere coincidence that the courage to make this experiment was shown at the Berlin Institute of Political Science, where Karl Dietrich Bracher brought out his weighty and still unmatched book, *Die Auflösung der Weimarer Republik*, in 1955.[10] From the start the historical investigations carried out at the Berlin Institute were closely linked with and open to suggestions from the departments of politics and sociology, disciplines which by their very nature are more oriented towards an analysis of the present, more given to generalization, in contrast to the more particularizing formulation of problems typical of old-style historiography. This marked a decisive step towards meeting the specific requirements of contemporary history which underlie its study in the United States above all, but also to some extent in France and England. Bracher's and Sauer's book, completed in no more than five years, and the equally massive study of the national-socialist seizure of power in 1933 and 1934, by Bracher, Wolfgang Sauer, and Gerhard Schulz, three representatives of the younger generation of historians, published in 1960,[11] not only provide evidence that the ground for contemporary history as a scholarly discipline in its own right had been well and truly laid; they also have formative importance for its further expansion. In contrast to those who are tempted to evade the search for the roots of the victory of national-socialism, and to isolate the history of the crisis years from 1929 to 1933, Bracher (although he placed great emphasis on the actual chain of events leading up to 30 January 1933) strongly underlines the question: how far are the roots of the catastrophe to be sought in the more deep-lying and distant of the peculiarities of the German social structure. His introduction gives critical attention to the impact of the '*Eigenweg*', the peculiarities of modern German history since the French Revolution. Even though some detailed aspects of his position still give rise to controversy, his systematic examination of the history of the Weimar Republic from 1919 to 1933, in the attempt to find out whether it was not from the first weighted down and finally fatally over-burdened by the strength of the German tradition in the officer corps, the Civil Service, the economy, and society as a whole, all of which made it impossible for the democratic forms of government taken over from the victorious West to take root and develop in Germany—this endeavour has had the most fruitful results. At the same time Bracher remained enough of a historian to reject a simple determinist explanation of events until he reaches the last phase of Hitler's rise to power, and to insist on the abiding element of the possibility of free choice, a freedom which defies the purely rational.

With these works as pace-makers, the pre-history and history of national-socialism has remained, at least quantitatively, the overwhelmingly predominant preoccupation of German historical writing, in which the participation of the younger generation of historians is still a marked feature. The Munich Institute of Contemporary History, after a hesitant start, has come to occupy a central position in research; its library and archives in particular have been of great and growing service to international historical research. Although drawn in more and more as experts and authorities for the denazification and war-crimes trials, it has been able to expand the scope of its research to include the period since 1945. The *Vierteljahrshefte für Zeitgeschichte* published by the Institute under the direction of Hans Rothfels, has become one of the leading international periodicals in the field. Although the Institute is mainly concerned with the analysis of the source material, it cannot be said that the work sponsored by the Institute has tried to avoid the more controversial issues of the present, which at one time were dealt with more quickly and more thoroughly abroad. Thus, for example, the two-volume study, *Anatomie des SS-Staates*,[12] based on the extensive evidence of four specialists, probably represents the most thorough treatment of such burning questions as the ultimate responsibility for the giving and obeying of orders in the SS; the running of concentration camps, the execution of the *Kommissarbefehl*, and the extermination of the Jews.

The first exploratory large-scale works on the particularly difficult and much disputed problem of the position and attitude of the sciences and the universities in the Third Reich (as exemplified by the Institut für Geschichte des Judentums under Walter Frank), and of the role of law and its administration under national-socialist rule, are now being published or are in an advanced state of preparation. It is one of the merits of this research centre and its devoted and diligent staff and contributors, that it provided a base from which a number of German historians were able immediately and critically to repudiate the strange theories advanced by A. J. P. Taylor and David Hoggan on the origins of the Second World War,[13] so that their books had no more than a limited and short-lived success.

In addition to this main stream of research, we must note the intensive work on the history of the Second World War, particularly its military aspects. For these studies we have now a broad and solid foundation of source material, provided by the publication of critical editions of the War Diaries of the Supreme Command of the armed forces,[14] of Hitler's instructions for the conduct of the war and his comments on the reports submitted by the staff at the situation conferences, first analysed by Felix Gilbert,[15] Halder's diaries,[16] and Hitler's table talk, edited with a critical commentary by Henry Picker.[17] Andreas Hillgruber's penetrating treatment of the decisive phase of the war, from the defeat of France to Hitler's attack on the Soviet Union, *Hitlers Strategie. Politik und Kriegsführung, 1939–1941*, published in 1965,[18] demonstrates the value of these sources as a contribution to the history of the war as a whole.

With these studies of the catastrophe of the recent past and the situation of Germany today as its starting point, German contemporary history has increasingly turned its attention to the problem of continuity in history, to seeking out the strands which will give German history an intelligible pattern. The part played by militarism in German history, since the Hohenzollerns of the eighteenth century, a question first investigated in Wheeler-Bennett's *Nemesis of Power*,[19] and one that has again become topical because of the rearmament of the German Federal Republic, was from the first recognized as a question deserving thorough study. It is presented in a massive synthesis in Gerhard Ritter's *Staatskunst und Kriegshandwerk*, of which three volumes have appeared so far. These three volumes—a fourth has just been published—which display an astonishing mastery of an enormous range of themes, reach the climax of the First World War.[20] Ritter's extremely personal judgments have brought him into conflict with Fritz Fischer, whose *Griff nach der Weltmacht*, first published in 1961,[21] has drawn the two into the centre of an impassioned controversy—not entirely free from a personal acrimony that is not without effect on the subject under discussion—which has already lasted more than five years, and whose end is not yet in sight.

It should be emphasized that it is precisely Gerhard Ritter who has condemned the exaggerated importance attached to military matters in recent German history from the time of Bismarck, with special emphasis on Tirpitz's naval building programme, the Schlieffen plan, the July 1914 crisis, and, above all, in his treatment of the Hindenburg-Ludendorff ascendancy during the 1914–18 War. The position he takes on these questions shows how unbendingly Ritter has been guided by the obligation of the historian to present the whole truth, however unpalatable, and invalidates the reproach that his work is only an apologia for the past. Fischer's spectacular thesis of an all-pervading imperialist aspiration to world power—not necessarily an aspiration to world hegemony—which, he says, dominated the thinking of all the politically decisive elements in the country from the Wilhelmine era, and most particularly the thinking of the government on the eve of and during the First World War, has been transformed into the argument of a single thread running through virtually the entire nation. Fischer argues that the government (not excluding Bethmann-Hollweg) used the opportunity of the July 1914 crisis to launch a preventive war, and that throughout the war, from the September 1914 war-aims programme until the summer of 1918, its actions were determined by a boundless annexationist drive. The great debate around this thesis, which in any case, because of its high degree of over-simplification, yields a formula for the origins of the German catastrophe of the twentieth century which contradicts all historical experience, is still in its early stages, and will presumably remain in the foreground of general interest for a long time. But a full clarification of the problem requires a more comprehensive, more detailed and far-reaching examination of the individual phases of the story, if rigid positions are to be avoided, positions taken up once and for all, in which, moreover, questions such as the interconnections between economy and politics have so far received little attention, being treated only in the most general terms.

This alone indicates the necessity to overcome certain limitations characteristic of the older German school of historical research. These undoubtedly derive from its predominant interest in the state and in strictly political issues, and from its undisputable bias in favour of the primacy of foreign over internal affairs, supposedly formulated by Ranke and Bismarck. On the other hand, there is today an extremely marked interest in constitutional and party history; study of the development of the modern party system, and the problem of the transformation of the old parties, which consisted largely of people of rank, into modern mass parties, has been greatly encouraged by similar English and French investigations. This was already clearly seen in such pioneering works as Gerhard A. Ritter's *Die Arbeiterbewegung im wilhelminischen Reich*[22] (1959) which, like the books by Peter Gay and Carl E. Schorske,[23] two American scholars, is an exemplary examination of the development of the German Social-Democratic Party from 1880 to 1914 into a popular mass party. At about the same time the Commission for the History of Parliamentarism and Political Parties, whose performance is comparable in scope and achievement to that of the Munich Institute of Contemporary History, began its valuable work. Steadily modernizing and reassessing its methods, it has up to now commissioned about thirty volumes on party development, from the time of Bismarck's establishment of the Empire to the new parties formed since 1945. The volumes of documents on the history of the First World War and the November revolution (*Der interfraktionelle Ausschuss 1917–18*, 2 vols., 1959; *Die Regierung des Prinzen Max von Baden*, 1962), edited by Erich Matthias and Rudolf Morsey, who are also responsible for the substantial collective work, *Des Ende der Parteien* (1960),[24] portraying the dissolution of the parties in 1933, are not the least valuable of its achievements. Thomas Nipperdey's book, *Die Organisation der deutschen Partien vor 1918* (1961),[25] can perhaps be taken as a measure of what has been accomplished in this field of research. It gives a comprehensive and methodical account, along the lines pursued above all by McKenzie in England,[26] of the process of modernization of the old party system, paying marked attention to the social aspects of its history.

Even though these works on parties, which lie in the field of contemporary history, could fall back on similar undetarkings in the Weimar period, the reserve of the professional German historians with regard to social and economic history, notwithstanding the tradition established by Gustav Schmoller[27] and the powerful impulse given by Max Weber,[28] and to a lesser degree by Werner Sombart,[29] increased rather than diminished. The sturdy bridges built in the nineteenth century between the specifically economic and the historical orientation of research were, with one exception only, almost entirely ignored. The exception was in the field of *Land* and local history, with, for most of the time at least, a marked emphasis on the Middle Ages. Largely through the work of Otto

Brunner[30] and Walter Schlesinger,[31] the varied problems and methods involved were presented with a fullness that was decidedly superior to that shown in modern and contemporary historiography. In these latter, there was some danger of falling behind the work being done in other countries in everything concerned with the broad economic and social historical basis of political developments. Today the attention devoted to filling these gaps has become most marked, although its fruits cannot be harvested until an adequate number of historians has been trained to make full use of the methods and approaches of sociology and economics, and to apply them meaningfully to the specific requirements of history. Largely as a result of the efforts of the Deutsche Forschungsgemeinschaft, the need has been clearly perceived to promote, as a matter of pressing urgency, concrete research in the field both of general German history and of local and regional history, in order to trace the course and impact of the vast processes of industrialization in the nineteenth and twentieth centuries, if lost ground is to be made up. When this work has been done, the conditions will have been created for the incorporation of these aspects into the compass of the general historical process, on a scale comparable with that of the *New Cambridge Modern History* and the parallel collective work put out by Cambridge on modern economic history.

The study of the problems relating to German Jewry is a special task being given increasing attention by contemporary German historical research. For a long time the study of the catastrophe and the developments leading up to it were dealt with mainly by non-German historians, the majority of whom, however, came originally from Germany, like Eva Reichmann, Hannah Arendt, and Adolf Leschnitzer.[32] Apart from the final tragedy, necessitating a detailed inquiry into the roots of anti-semitism—as conducted by the Wiener Library and the Leo Baeck Institute in London—the issue leaves the German historian with a number of ancillary problems. It is his task to study the emergence of the all-important German-Jewish symbiosis in the nineteenth century and its impact on Germany's economic, political, and cultural life; to analyse and assess these phenomena scientifically; to make the source material available, and to attempt to formulate his findings, as Horckheimer and Adorno[33] of Frankfurt University have done, and more recently the Historical Commission in Berlin. The examination of these problems is attracting the attention of a growing number of historical institutes all over Germany.

The burning question remains, however, whether, after fifteen years of endeavour and undeniably hard work, the outlines of a new concept of history have begun to emerge among German scholars. Methodical scientific historical reasearch as practised—in the modern sense of the word—for about one hundred years, is almost by definition a discipline which must take a long time to assimilate the process of change. This is true even in the case of a Germany that has experienced three major and violent upheavals: 1918, 1933, and 1945. It cannot be denied that the impact of revolution in the twentieth century on academic work has been disconcerting. Nazi rule particularly had claimed an incalculable toll of highly qualified historians, of whom only a few, like Hans Rothfels and Dietrich Gerhard, have returned to Germany. Gerhardt Masur's portrayal of the cultural crisis of the nineteenth century in *Prophets of Yesterday. Studies in European Culture, 1890–1914* (1961)[34] is so significantly relevant precisely because, though it is rooted in Friedrich Meinecke's history of ideas, it also reflects the truly international and supra-national insights which he acquired as a result of his emigration. The great number of young American historians of German name and extraction who seem to form the spearhead of research into modern German history, provide further evidence of the losses sustained by two consecutive generations of German historians. Nevertheless fundamental problems are being tackled on a broad front by a large number of ambitious and gifted young historians. If their work fails to dispel foreign doubts as to the flexibility of the German approach to history, it may at least serve to restrict them to the realm of ascertainable fact. Pride of place is accorded to the reappraisal of the 'nation-state' concept, which for too long played an exaggerated part in German thinking. Basing his conclusions on his impressive Bismarckian researches, Hans Rothfels pointed out— even before 1933—that the Founder's relation to the nation-state was more complex than his unquestioning admirers were prepared to admit. Starting in Königsberg with the analysis of the problems of the German East, Rothfels blazed a highly personal trail that broke through the barriers erected by a view of history exclusively based on national developments, as his admirable *Zeitgeschichtliche Betrachtungen* (1959)[35] prove. Theodor Schieder, in his short but exceedingly important essay, *Das deutsche Kaiserreich von*

1871 als Nationalstaat (1961),[36] investigated critically and yet not without sympathy the entire problem of Germany's national identity and self-awareness, as manifested, for example, in the treatment meted out to the national minorities within the Kaiser's Empire, or in such artificially inflated national symbols as the annual Sedan-day celebrations. Studies by his pupils, such as Ulrich Wehler's *Sozialdemokratie und Nationalstaat* (1962),[37] dealing with the position of the Social-Democratic Party in a strongly nationalistic state from the time of Karl Marx to the outbreak of the First World War, demonstrate the powerful impact of a nationalistic climate on the outlook of a working-class party which saw itself as an internationalist and revolutionary movement. Schieder's collected papers, *Staat und Gesellschaft in unserer Zeit*[38] (1958), containing essays on various aspects of nineteenth- and twentieth-century events, exploring such topics as the much debated question of the 'non-consummated German revolution', the structure and development of Germany's political parties, the failure of German middle-class liberalism, the problems of state power in an industrialized age, indicate that contemporary issues are certainly being discussed and analyzed by German historians.

Schieder's essays *Über den Typus in der Geschichtswissenshaft*,[39] as well as his short *Einführung in die Geschichtswissenshaft* (1965),[40] reveal some further significant departures in German historical thinking. These not only stress the importance of economic and social history, but also re-examine, perhaps not quite so radically as the *nouvelle école* in France, the influence of the personal element on the chain of events. Although unwilling to deny completely the contribution of the individual to history, despite its recent exaggeration, German historians are nevertheless ready to examine the role of the general underlying forces in history, without however adopting the moralizing overtones in the work of Ranke, and particularly of his pupils. Similar changes have taken place in other fields. After Hans Rothfels, in his *Zeitgeschichtliche Betrachtungen*, had critically examined the problems of the primacy of foreign policy, *Realpolitik*, and the influence of social and economic structures, Karl Dietrich Bracher, in his *Deutschland zwischen Demokratie und Diktatur* (1964),[41] embarked within a framework of international relations and political science on a detailed analysis of the relationship between domestic and foreign affairs, which led him to assume mutually reinforcing impulses between these two fields of force, conclusions that definitely demolish the rigid positions taken up in the nineteenth century.

Certain shortcomings in the research on contemporary history in Germany today are still discernible. Whereas up to 1933 foreign and diplomatic history had attracted too much interest and absorbed too much energy, the reverse might be said to be true today. The great debate over the 'wrong turnings' taken by German historians has for the last decade restricted all work almost exclusively to problems of German history, and to the revision of the German concept of history. Meanwhile the discussion of other topics, such as international relations, has been sadly neglected. This means that problems have now to be tackled which since 1945 have shown themselves to be relevant to our strife-torn present and to all the unresolved problems of the future. Hans Rothfels contends that contemporary history starts in 1917, with the Russian Revolution and the American intervention in Europe, when our planet truly became one world. But in Germany the discussion of the broader world political developments since 1945 has been very limited so far. Although historians are increasingly willing to respond to stimuli from related disciplines, they remain somewhat reluctant to venture into fields which do not lend themselves to detached scholarly investigation and the state of whose source material remains somewhat problematical.

But even here a breakthrough has occurred, if only because the problem of the division of Germany cannot be entirely disregarded by the inquirer into the German past. This, of course, focuses attention on the question where exactly in this borderland between past, present and future, the line must be drawn beyond which the scholarly historian cannot legitimately venture. In conclusion, however, it can be stated that the pursuit of German contemporary history after the catastrophe of the Second World War has become a considerably livelier and more searching discipline than it was after the First World War.

NOTES

[1] Leopold von Ranke, *Die Serbische Revolution. Aus serbischen Papieren und Mittheilungen* (Hamburg, 1829).

[2] Erich Marcks, *Otto von Bismarck. Ein Lebenbild* (Stuttgart and Berlin, 1919); *Bismarck, eine Biographie, 1815–1851* (Stuttgart, 1951); also, *Aufstieg des Reiches*, 3 vols. (Stuttgart, 1936).

[3] Arnold Oskar Meyer, *Bismarcks Kampf mit Österreich am Bundestag zu Frankfurt (1851 bis 1859)* (Berlin and Leipzig, 1927); *Bismarcks Glaube im Spiegel der 'Losungen und der Lehrtexte'* (Munich, 1933); *Bismarck, der Mensch und der Staatsmann* (Stuttgart, 1944).

[4] Johannes Ziekursch, *Politische Geschichte des neuen Deutschen Kaiserreiches*, 3 vols. (Frankfurt/M. 1925–30).

[5] Arthur Rosenberg, *Die Entstehung der deutschen Republik 1817–1918* (Berlin, 1928); *Geschichte der deutschen Republik* (Karlsbad, 1935), English translation, *History of the German Republic* (London, 1936); *Entstehung und Geschichte der Weimarer Republik* (Frankfurt/M., 1961).

[6] Friedrich Meinecke, *Die deutsche Katastrophe: Betrachtungen und Erinnerungen* (Zürich and Wiesbaden, 1946). The English translation entitled *The German Catastrophe, reflections and recollections* was published in Boston in 1950.

[7] Gerhard Ritter, *Europa und die deutsche Frage* (Munich, 1948). Revised edition *Das deutsche Problem: Grundfragen deutschen Staatslebens gestern und heute* (Munich, 1962).

[8] Hans Rothfels, *Die deutsche Opposition gegen Hitler* (Hinsdale, Illinois, 1948). An English translation entitled *The German Opposition to Hitler. An assessment* . . . was published in London in 1961.

[9] Alan Bullock, *Hitler: A Study in Tyranny* (London, 1952; revised edition 1964).

[10] Karl Dietrich Bracher, *Die Auflösung der Weimarer Republik. Eine Studie zum Problem des Machtzerfalls in der Demokratie* (Stuttgart/Düsseldorf, 1955).

[11] Karl Dietrich Bracher, Wolfgang Sauer, and Gerhard Schulz, *Die nationalsozialistische Machtergreifung. Studien zu Errichtung des totalitären Herrschaftssystems in Deutschland 1933–34* (Cologne, 1960).

[12] *Anatomie des SS-Staates*. Vol. I. Hans Bucheim, *Die SS—das Herrschaftsinstrument: Befehl und Gehorsam.* Vol. II. Martin Broszat, Hans-Adolf Jacobsen, and Helmut Krausnick, *Konzentrationslager. Kommissarbefehl. Judenverfolgung.* (Olten, 1965).

[13] A. J. P. Taylor, *The Origins of the Second World War* (London, 1961). David L. Hoggan, *Der erzwungene Krieg. Die Ursachen und Urheber des Zweiten Weltkriegs* (Tübingen, 1961).

[14] *Kriegstagebuch der Oberkommando der Wehrmacht (Wehrmachtsführungsstab) 1940–45*, ed. by Helmut Greiner and Percy Ernst Schramm, 4 vols. (Frankfurt/M., 1961–65).

[15] Felix Gilbert, *Hitler directs his War* (New York, 1950).

[16] *Kriegstagebuch. Tägliche Aufzeichnungen des Chefs des Generalstabes des Heeres 1939–1942.* Three vols. ed. by Hans-Adolf Jacobsen. Vol. I, *Vom Polenfeldzug bis zum Ende der Westoffensive (14.8.1939–30.6.1940)*; vol. II, *Von der Geplanten Landung in England bis zum Beginn des Ostfeldzuges (1.7.1940–21.6.1941)*; vol. III, *Der Russlandfeldzug bis zum Marsch auf Stalingrad (22.6.1941–24.9.1942)* (Stuttgart, 1962, 1963, 1964).

[17] *Hitlers Tischgespräche im Führerhauptquartier 1941–42*, ed. by Henry Picker (Bonn, 1951); 2nd edn. ed. by Percy E. Schramm (Stuttgart, 1965).

[18] Andreas Hillgruber, *Hitlers Strategie, Politik und Kriegsführung, 1939–1941* (Frankfurt/M., 1965).

[19] John W. Wheeler-Bennett, *Nemesis of Power. The German Army in Politics 1918–1945* (London, 1953).

[20] Gerhard Ritter, *Staatskunst und Kriegshandwerk. Das Problem des 'Militarismus' in Deutschland.* Vol. I, *Die altpreussische Tradition (1740–1890)*; vol. II, *Die Hauptmächte Europas und das Wilhelminische Reich (1890–1914)*; vol. III, *Die Tragödie der Staatskunst. Bethmann Hollweg als Kriegskanzler (1914–1917)* (Munich, 1954–60); vol. IV, *Die Herrschaft des deutschen Militarismus und die Katastrophe von 1918* (Munich, 1968).

[21] Fritz Fischer, *Griff nach der Weltmacht. Die Kriegszielpolitik des Kaiserlichen Deutschland* (Düsseldorf, 1961; 2nd edn., Düsseldorf, 1964). An English translation, *Germany's Aims in the First World War*, was published in London in 1967.

[22] Gerhard A. Ritter, *Die Arbeiterbewegung im Wilhelminischen Reich. Die Sozialdemokratische Partei und die freien Gewerkschaften 1890–1900* (Berlin, 1959).

[23] Peter Gay, *The dilemma of democratic Socialism; Eduard Bernstein's challenge to Marx* (New York, 1962). Carl E. Schorske, *German Social Democracy, 1905–1917. The Development of the Great Schism* (Massachusetts, 1955).

[24] Erich Matthias and Rudolf Morsey, *Das Ende der Parteien 1933* (Düsseldorf, 1960).

[25] Thomas Nipperdey, *Die Organisation der deutschen Parteien vor 1918* (Düsseldorf, 1961).

[26] Robert McKenzie, *British Political Parties: the distribution of power within the Conservative and Labour parties* (London, 1955; revised edn., 1963).

[27] Gustav Schmoller, 1838-1917, political economist, was Professor of Political Science at Halle (1864), Strasbourg (1872), and Berlin (1882). He was a member of the Prussian Staatsrat (1884), the Prussian Academy of Sciences (1887), and the Prussian Upper House (1899). Among his major works is *Grundriss der allgemeinen Volkswirtschaftslehre*, 2 vols. (1900–04).

[28] Max Weber, 1864–1920, political economist and sociologist, was a student of legal and economic history, later turning to sociology; noted for his work on the relation between the spirit of capitalism and Protestant ethics. He was professor at Berlin (1893), Freiburg (1894), Heidelberg (1897), and Munich (1919). Among his chief works are *Wirtschaft und Gesellschaft* (1921-2), *Gesammelte Politische Schriften* (1921), *Religionssoziologie*, 3 vols. (1920–23), *Gesammelte Aufsätze zur Sozial- und Wirtschaftsgeschichte* (Tübingen 1924).

[29] Werner Sombart, 1863–1941, political economist, was one of the founders of modern social science; at first a supporter of Marxism he later reacted against it, although he was not a believer in National Socialism. He was professor at Breslau (1890) and Berlin (1914). Among his major works are *Sozialismus und soziale Bewegung* (1911), *Der modern-Kapitalismus* (3 vols., 1903–08, 1919, 1928), *Die Juden und das Wirtschaftleben* (1911), *Deutscher Sozialismus* (1934).

[30] cf. Otto Brunner, *Land und Herrschaft. Grundfragen der territorialen Verfassungsgeschichte Südostdeutschlands im Mittelalter* (Baden, Vienna, 1939); *Adeliges Landleben und europäischen Geist* (Salzburg, 1949); *Neue Wege der Sozialgeschichte; Vorträge und Aufsätze* (Göttingen, 1956); *Feudalismus. Ein Beitrag zur Begriffsgeschichte* (Mainz, 1959).

[31] cf. Walter Schlesinger, *Die Enstehung der Landesherrschaft* (Dresden, 1941); *Kirchengeschichte Sachsens im Mittelalter*, 2 vols. (Cologne, Graz, 1962); *Beiträge zur deutschen Verfassungsgeschichte des Mittelalters*, 2 vols. (Göttingen, 1963).

[32] Eva Reichmann, *Hostages of Civilisation, the social sources of national socialist anti-semitism* (London, 1950); *Die Flucht in den Hass. Die Ursachen der deutschen Judenkatastrophe* (Frankfurt/M., 1956). Hannah Arendt, *The Origins of Totalitarianism* (New York, 1955), translated as *Elemente und Ursprünge totaler Herrschaft* (Frankfurt/M., 1955); *Eichmann in Jerusalem. A report on the banality of evil* (New York, London, 1963), translated as *Eichmann in Jerusalem. Ein Bericht von der Banalität des Bösen* (Munich, 1964). Adolf Leschnitzer, *Saul und David: die Problematik der deutsch-jüdischen Lebensgemeinschaft* (Heidelberg, 1954), translated as *The Magic Background of Modern Anti-Semitism. An analysis of the German-Jewish Relationship* (New York, 1956). Also 'Antisemitismus' in *Wörterbuch der Soziologie*, ed. by W. Bernsdorf and F. Bülow (Stuttgart, 1955).

[33] Theodor W. Adorno and Max Horkheimer, *Dialektik der Aufklärung. Philosophische Fragmente* (Amsterdam, 1947); *Reden und Vorträge* (Frankfurt/M., 1962). Max Horkheiner, 'Über die deutschen Juden', *Germania Judaica* (Cologne, 1961).

[34] Gerhard Masur, *Prophets of Yesterday* (New York, 1961).

[35] Hans Rothfels, *Zeitgeschichtliche Betrachtungen*: Vorträge und Aufsätze (Göttingen, 1959).

[36] Theodor Schieder, *Das deutsche Kaiserreich von 1871 als Nationalstaat* (Cologne, 1961).

[37] Ulrich Wehler, *Deutsche Sozialdemokratie und Nationalstaat in Deutschland von Karl Marx bis zum Ausbruch des Ersten Weltkrieges* (Würzburg, 1962).

[38] Theodor Schieder, *Staat und Gesellschaft im Wandel unserer Zeit. Studien zur Geschichte* (Munich, 1958).

[39] Theodor Schieder, from *Staat und Gesellschaft*, see above.

[40] Theodor Schieder, *Geschichte als Wissenschaft. Eine Einführung.* (Munich, Vienna, 1965).

[41] Karl Dietrich Bracher, *Deutschland zwischen Demokratie und Diktatur. Beiträge zur neueren Politik und Geschichte* (Berne, 1964).

HELMUT KRAUSNICK

Research and Research Institutes in Germany

Mr S. J. Woolf's interesting and, in my view, very accurate report of the state of research into contemporary history in Italy has a number of close parallels with research in Germany. In Germany, in at least as great measure as in Italy, the impact of a political and moral catastrophe, bringing with it the desire for understanding and reorientation, provided a powerful stimulus to research into contemporary history and confronted it with special tasks and duties. That the German historian, especially in his literary activities, encountered many difficulties in the present state of things in his attempt to meet these obligations—as a result of his lack of perspective on the events he was dealing with—is obvious. Contemporary history necessarily arouses very personal reactions, attitudes, and antipathies among those who lived through the events with which contemporary history deals, especially when it deals with a part with which they have not yet come to terms or a period the tide of whose events is still in full flood. The difficulty of research was, moreover, enhanced by the open desire of German statesmen after 1945 to educate the general public on the subject of the origins and record of nazism, in order to further the development of democracy among the German people: that is to say, they wanted to use historical science primarily and directly as a means of political instruction. These politicians' expectations were, however, irreconcilable with the nature of the scholarly institutions which they desired to set up; they were in principle also irreconcilable with the requirements of a genuine and solidly-based political education itself. Such a process cannot be based on summary and short-lived analyses analogous to those of the daily press. Only when it was possible, by reliably-produced scientific research, to free the picture of our past both from the fog of national socialist propaganda and mythology and from the dubious additional twilight into which it had fallen in the cross-examinations and distorted visions of the Nuremberg trials, could genuine insights be discovered and convincing education be provided.

Thus the first practical task of German research into contemporary history after 1945 was to discover and describe what had actually happened, to bring matters into the open and illuminate those areas of reality which the national socialist regime had obscured or made the subject of propaganda. This meant of necessity that research was concentrated on specific cases, limited questions and processes in the narrow field of purely political events which could be investigated and clarified by means of documents. By now much work has been done in this direction: as far as facts go, our knowledge of the national socialist period rests on secure foundations thanks largely to the efforts of German research into contemporary history. Beyond this, however, German scholars have a second more important and more difficult obligation, namely that of answering the question of the causes of national socialism and thus explaining, without excusing, what actually happened. This obligation led German researchers very soon to regard their work from two principal points of view: (i) the national socialist era must in no way be, as it were, bracketed outside German history as a kind of short-term absurdity but must be ordered within the continuity of German history; (ii) while doing full justice to specifically German preconditions for the rise of national socialism, account must also be taken of the influence of the general international tendencies of the period of sociological and psychological changes in the modern mass society. The relentless analysis of German contemporary history of the exclusion of all humanity from policy, as practised by national socialism, must in the end also call into question the merits of a neutral 'historicism', which threatened to turn 'tout comprendre' into 'tout pardonner'.

Apart from one or two exceptions it is not the case in Germany, as, according to Mr Woolf, it is in Italy, that university historians have avoided research into contemporary history or adopted a reserved attitude towards it. Such research has undoubtedly established itself as an academic discipline within the framework of historical science as a whole. Lectures and seminars on contemporary history take place in practically every institution of higher learning in the Federal Republic, though this is not necessarily always reflected in the designations of professorial chairs.

However, at Tübingen, Darmstadt, Hamburg, and Bonn there are professorial chairs whose titles proclaim them to be wholly or partly concerned with contemporary history. As in Italy, the progress of this subject has been assisted by the development of political science: one field in which the two disciplines are especially useful to each other is the study of political parties.

As in Italy, German political memoirs of the recent past began by dealing to a disproportionate extent with themes of persecution and the Resistance. To some extent this was also true of German writings on contemporary history. This preoccupation with the Resistance was by no means wholly due to a desire to refute the thesis of the collective guilt of all Germans, that is to show that the identification of the German people with national socialism is unjustified, as this was increasingly propagated abroad for understandable reasons during the Second World War, a process which no one observed with greater anxiety than the members of the German Opposition. The concern of German research into contemporary history with the Resistance against Hitler was much more directed to act as part of the political education of the German people by the establishment of democratic precedents and democratic examples.

Among the younger generation of German contemporary historians, the main effort today is directed to establishing accurate standards of differentiation; the inclination is to regard the representatives of the Opposition according to their then domestic attitude and origins very critically and to scrutinize the plans of the 'bourgeois-conservative' Opposition for the future constitution of Germany with particular suspicion. In my view, this is to overrate the practical importance of their plans: for if the attempt to overthrow Hitler had succeeded, the course of subsequent events would have assumed its own momentum as a result of the various political factors involved, for example the trade unions, and theoretical plans would have been more or less superseded.

I will now enumerate the principal German research institutes concerned primarily with contemporary history, indicating in each case their main field of activity. Apart from the Institute for Contemporary History at Munich, to which I shall return, there is, firstly, the Research Institute for the History of National Socialism at Hamburg: it works on a predominantly regional basis and is at present concerned with the history of the Nazi Party before 1933. The Commission for the History of Parliamentarism and Political

Parties, in Bonn, concentrates on the transition from constitutionalism to the parliamentary system of the Weimar Constitution, on the parties and political organizations in the Weimar Republic and in the post-war period. Also in Hamburg is the Commission of the Evangelical Church in Germany for the History of the Dispute between Church and State in the National-Socialist Period. The Commission on Contemporary History of the Catholic Academy in Bavaria is mainly concerned with the attitude of the Catholic Church towards nazism. The Office for Research into Contemporary Military History at Freiburg im Breisgau primarily studies the military history of the Second World War, collaborating on occasion with the Centre for Military Research. The Research Centre of the Friedrich Ebert Foundation at Bonn studies *inter alia* the history of the German Social Democratic Party, the workers' resistance to national socialism, and the beginnings of German administration and politics after 1945. The Research Institute of the German Association for Foreign Policy at Bonn deals with German foreign policy and international policies after 1949. The Theodor Heuss Archiv at Stuttgart is mainly concerned with German history since 1945. The Johann Gottfried Herder Institute at Marburg concentrates on the history of Eastern Germany up to and including the post-war expulsions. The Collegium Carolinum at Munich is a research centre for the history of Bohemia and Moravia, including the twentieth century. Research centres concerned with the history and persecution of German Jewry are the Institute for the History of German Jewry at Hamburg and the Germania Judaica Library at Cologne, as well as regional institutes in Baden-Württemberg and Hesse.

The Institute for Contemporary History at Munich has the special responsibility, though it claims no monopoly in this field, of promoting the development of free research into contemporary historical problems, irrespective of day-to-day contingencies. For this purpose it draws on its own library and archives and also on the Federal Archives and those of the Länder. Although the main centre of its work is the national-socialist period from 1933 to 1945, it is also concerned with the prehistory of national socialism in the broadest sense and has increasingly turned its attention to related phenomena such as, for example, fascist movements outside Germany which form part of the general character of the period. In connection with its original area of obligation, research into national socialism, the Institute has for some time been making available, by means of a card-index system used for the Nuremberg trial records and since perfected, microfilmed German documents released by the Americans for research purposes. In addition to the Contemporary History Quarterly (*Vierteljahrshefte für Zeitgeschichte*) published since 1953, which has over 4,000 subscribers, the Institute is also responsible for the publication of the series *Schriftenreihe der Vierteljahrshefte für Zeitgeschichte*[1] in which manuscripts of medium lengths are published every six months or so.

NOTE

[1] The *Schriftenreihe der Vierteljahrshefte für Zeitgeschichte* include the following titles:

1. *Das Tagebuch von Joseph Goebbels 1925–26*, ed. by Helmut Heiber.
2. Martin Broszat, *Nationalsozialistische Polenpolitik 1939–1945*.
3. Hermann Pünder, *Politik in der Reichskanzlei*.
4. Lothar Gruchmann, *Nationalsozialistische Grossraumordnung*.
5. C. F. Latour, *Südtirol und die Achse Berlin-Rom*.
6. Rudolf Heberle, *Landbevölkerung und Nationalsozialismus*.
7. Enno Georg, *Die wirtschaftlichen Unternehmen der SS*.
8. Ladislaus Hory and Martin Broszat, *Der kroatische Ustascha-Staat 1941–1945*.
9. Rolf Geissler, *Dekadenz und Heroismus*.
10. *Komintern und Faschismus*, ed. by Theo Pirker.
11. *José Antonio Primo de Rivera*, selection of speeches and writings with commentary by Bernd Nellessen.
12. Alan S. Milward, *Die deutsche Kriegswirtschaft 1939–1945*.
13. Hans Mommsen, *Beamtentum im Dritten Reich*.
14. and 15. Babette Gross, *Willi Münzenberg. Eine politische Biographie*.
16. Dieter Petzina, *Autarkiepolitik im Dritten Reich, der nationalsozialistische Vierjahresplan*.

The Netherlands

H. W. VON DER DUNK

The Shock of 1940

Conditions for the study of contemporary history in the Netherlands have been not very favourable for a long time. To explain
this phenomenon we have to deal with various circumstances,
partly historical, partly psychological, partly simply practical.
History has lost, at least in Europe, a great deal of the nationalistic
character which inspired historians in the nineteenth and in the
early twentieth century, and which helped originate many of their
most impressive achievements. But still it is natural that the history
of one's own country should hold a central position in the field of
historical research, if only because documents and other essential
sources of the national past are most easily available.

Now the Netherlands as a small country has played in our
century only the role of spectator of the great events and upheavals
which have changed the face of the earth. Of course, it underwent
these changes, as did the other countries, but it did so without
being able to play a leading or even a considerable part in them.
World politics were not influenced by The Hague as they were in
the seventeenth century—Holland's 'golden age'. To discover the
essential phases of modern history, to look into the kitchen where
the most important meals have been prepared, the historian would
not go to the Dutch archives. There only the reactions of a small
people can be found. So it is quite natural that those countries
which played first fiddle in dramatic events should produce the
historians to undertake the research work. As history can never be
written in an ivory tower, interest and enthusiasm for a special
period depends on the possibilities of studying that period, and
these possibilities in their turn depend on the importance of the
country concerned.

There is also the point that Dutch historians, partly as a consequence of the age of nationalism, have always been fascinated by

the glorious periods of their past: the great revolt against Spain in the sixteenth century; the splendour and vigour of the Republic during the seventeenth century. The major part of their work was and still is devoted to these ages which saw the birth and highest prosperity of their nation. The eighteenth century, era of the definitive decline of the old Republic, for a long time roused relatively little interest, because it lacks these attractions. But in recent years a slight change in this respect can be noticed. And even the nineteenth century, which brought to the Netherlands the present monarchy, the constitution, and the birth of a modern society (as elsewhere in Western Europe), seems unable to arouse overwhelming enthusiasm among Clio's servants. In fact it has come off hardly better than its predecessor. The reluctance to open some essential archives to free research may partly explain this. To give one example: we are still waiting for a real political biography of the greatest statesman of the nineteenth century, the father of the constitution of 1848, Thorbecke. The publication of his papers is still going on, but is far from complete. And where the country's history in the last century still presents some blank spaces of uncharted territory (although the multitude of monographs and the confident tone of some of our textbooks may suggest the opposite), it is less surprising to find little disposition to study the history of the present one.

But we have to examine this attitude more closely. Why this reserve in exploring the most recent past, a reserve which was noticeable before the Second World War and formed a psychological obstacle to the study of contemporary history? Why the reluctance to open some of the most important archives? There appears to be some connection with certain specific features of Dutch tradition and history. The old Republic and the later Kingdom of the Netherlands were small, but marked by vigorous controversies, political and religious, which led to a series of heated party struggles. It would be going too far to give here even a rough sketch of these conflicts. But as an example we may take the antagonism between the Orangist party and the so-called States party, especially dominant in the province of Holland. This controversy actually lasted throughout the seventeenth and eighteenth centuries.[1] In the nineteenth century we find some traces of the old feud again in a new antagonism between the Christian groups and parties on the one hand and the liberal-rationalist groups on the other. The first wished to base the state and its politics on the

Bible and on Calvinist dogma (the Catholics, who first joined the Liberals to free themselves from the discrimination to which they had long been subject, later formed an alliance with the Protestant parties). The second, who were the heirs of the Enlightenment and in some respects of the principles of the French Revolution, wanted a secularized neutral state. And on both sides we can find a lot of further differences and variations, which in their turn gave rise to the formation of new party groupings. So the nation was split into the confessional and the anti-confessional camp in the first place, and into a number of minor divisions in the second. These divisions marked not only political, but also religious and social bodies, often without much contact with each other. This phenomenon, which we call *verzuiling* (denominational segregation of the nation), finds its reflection even today in the existence of five broadcasting systems.[2]

Vigorous domestic controversies of an ideological character are not typical of the Netherlands alone. What is typically Dutch (or Protestant?) is perhaps the tendency to split these ideological blocs further, and the fact that this took place in a small area with a small population, where everybody knows everybody else. Equally typical for the Dutch situation was the extremely long period of peace and neutrality, lasting from the Napoleonic wars till the Second World War (with a short interruption in the 1830s: the Belgian revolution and separation). Without this period of peace the domestic controversies could not have played the part they did. The presence of these hardened ideological and social blocs in a small territory has not favoured or stimulated free research into the recent past. Moreover, divided though the nation was into small factions, the long period of peace created one belief and one state of mind common to all of them: belief in neutrality as a political virtue. This was the result not only of the prolonged stability of the country, but also of the secondary role which the Netherlands had come to play in Europe since the Peace of Utrecht, and of the old, deep-rooted precept that trade, the source of the nation's wealth, required peace. The maxim that wars will always have disadvantageous effects often dominated politics as far back as the late seventeenth century.[3] A few years ago a lecture given in Oxford about Dutch research on the Second World War was opened with the remark: 'The Dutch hate war, and in the last two centuries they have waged it but seldom.'[4] I am afraid this statement, although correct in the strict sense of the word, may give the impression that the Dutch were moved above all by humanitarian or ethical considerations. Of course, such motives counted, even in politics, but the Dutch dislike of becoming involved in war arose from their consciousness that they were too weak to play a decisive part in it, and with good reason feared its devastating effect on their prosperity. The First World War, which spared the country, intensified this belief in neutrality.[5] Living on a (more or less) wealthy and peaceful island, Dutch scholars were unlikely to be attracted by the study of their own chaotic times.

There were of course exceptions, to be found, understandably enough, largely at that end of the political and social spectrum which displayed the most outspoken opposition to society. In the Netherlands, as elsewhere, the socialists were in opposition to state and monarchy. After the First World War the majority of the Dutch Socialist Party (SDAP) did not go as far as some radical leaders in advocating revolution and the proclamation of a republic, themes very much in the air at the time, and indeed, during the later 1930s the party even became reconciled with the monarchy. The danger of fascism contributed to this reconciliation with a state which both believed in and guaranteed democracy. Nevertheless it is in the socialist camp, or among its sympathizers, that we find in the inter-war years a marked inclination to study the history of the recent past. This past of course became identified with the struggle of the Socialist Party and the working classes, and a great deal of what was written in those years must be regarded as political or party literature rather than as scholarly work.[6]

As a result of the Second World War this whole period of neutrality and high-minded non-engagement, which had hampered the study of contemporary history, came to an abrupt end. The blow which struck Belgium in 1914 came for the Dutch in May 1940. And it came with much greater force, as nazi aggression surpassed the agression of Imperial Germany in brutality and power, and as the mentality of neutralism was more deeply rooted in the Dutch than in the Belgian people. The five years of German occupation were an ice-cold mental shower which obliterated many of the country's earlier features. After 1945 it was impossible for Dutch politicians to think again in pre-war terms of neutrality. Security now had to be found in engagement and in alliances.[7] Resistance to the German occupiers had largely dissolved the old controversies and ideological blocs, although it did not destroy them completely, and after the liberation much of the expected thorough renovation of the nation proved to be an illusion.

I have dwelt at such length on the background of the Dutch scene and on certain of its historical and psychological features because historians, too, are children of their time and environment. The Second World War marked a turning point for Dutch historians too, and so the record of what has been and is being done in the field of twentieth-century history is not such a sad one as might perhaps have been deduced from what has been said up to now. Since 1945 there has been increasing activity and interest in this field, and we can already cite numerous publications, some of them of great value not for Dutch historiography alone.

To give due credit to pre-war achievements, mention must first of all be made of the foundation of the International Institute of Social History in Amsterdam in 1935 by the late Professor N. W. Posthumus. Posthumus was a pioneer in the Netherlands in the field of economic history, a discipline which was still looked upon by the professionals before the war as the stepchild of political and cultural history. Posthumus, an able organizer, had in 1914 established the Netherlands Economic History Archives in The Hague, and the Economic History Library in Amsterdam. In the 1930s he laid ever greater emphasis on the study of social history. The formation of the institute was one of his most important contributions to Dutch historical science. It has become possibly the leading institute in Europe in the field of social history.[8] To mention only some of the collections he and his colleagues succeeded in acquiring over the years: the Marx-Engels archives, the Axelrod archives, the important Kautsky archives, and the archives of the German Social-Democratic Party (SPD) before 1914. There are also, among many others, collections about Trotsky and Bebel. For English social history the Kashnor collection is of great value. And then of course a multitude of Dutch socialist archives and pamphlets can be found, as for instance those of Troelstra, the great leader of Dutch socialism, and of such prominent men as Saks, Wibaut, Vliegen, and Schaper.[9] The work of collection was carried on by Posthumus's successor, the late Professor A. J. C. Rüter. The institute's journal, the *International Review of Social History*, appears in English three times a year.[10] The emphasis of the institute's work has been laid up to now on the collection and cataloguing of the material, an enormous undertaking in itself which will still take years. But historians who in the future may wish to study the history of socialism in Europe will find there a most admirable and indispensable centre of documentation.

Another foundation which should be mentioned is the well-known State Institute for War Documentation, established in Amsterdam after the liberation with the purpose of investigating the history of the Netherlands in the Second World War. This is in some ways a unique enterprise, bearing witness to the change of climate and historical interest which was the consequence of the war. It was the Dutch government-in-exile in London which took the initiative, but in the occupied country itself thoughts were turning in the same direction. The institute soon became the centre of all research into the occupation. A library of tens of thousands of books, pamphlets, newspapers, diaries and other manuscripts, written during the war, has been built up (about 2,000 linear feet). The records of the *Reichskommisariat* (the German occupying authorities, directed by Seyss-Inquart) form of course an essential part of the collections. Statements have been taken by members of the institute from leading German officials and from numerous Dutchmen: fascists, collaborators, men of the resistance movement, and bystanders who became involved in these matters. The policies of the German authorities, the part played by the Dutch nazis, the so-called NSB men (Nationaal-Socialistische Beweging), and by the Dutch officials who went on functioning under German rule, all this belongs to the field of research. Although its purpose and activities are strictly scholarly, the institute has often been put to practical use, as in some of the recent war-criminal trials in Germany and Austria, where important information could be furnished by members of the institute. *Progress Reports* (in English) are published to record its activities. But the collection of materials is only one side of the work which is being done. A series of publications throws light on different aspects of the occupation. For instance, there is a special study of the underground press,[11] and another about the part played by the Dutch railways during the war.[12] This may at first sight seem a curious subject, but it involved some rather delicate questions in connection with the problem of collaboration. It is generally known that the Dutch railwaymen, on the instructions of the government-in-exile, started a general strike in September 1944. When the battle of Arnhem was lost, many thousands of them had to go underground, with all the dangerous consequences. This strike, lasting till the end of the war, acquired something of a halo in the consciousness of the population, as did the whole resistance movement. But it is also a fact, which the author of this study was able to demonstrate, that before the strike the Dutch railwaymen had kept things going and thereby helped the Germans, without any sympathy it is true, and even without any clear insight into the consequences of their actions. The deportation of the Jews from their ghetto in Amsterdam to the camp in Westerbork, whence they were deported to the gas chambers in Eastern Europe, was executed after all on Dutch railways and with the technical co-operation of the Dutch personnel. I mention this not to suggest that the Dutch railwaymen should be blamed for indirect collaboration in the vilest enterprise of our century. Indeed, the circumstances were far too complex to justify the lighthearted use of such emotional words as 'collaboration'. It is given only as an example of the tricky problems involved in such a seemingly harmless subject as the story of the railways. Rüter had to conclude that the heroic strike in 1944–45 was only one side of the coin, and he got into serious trouble with the management of the railways, who wished to keep the image spotless. (The study had to be submitted to the management because the work was written at the request of a state institute and the railways in the Netherlands have a semi-public character.) After a dispute which lasted five years, Rüter got his way.[13] Other people in civil or public service during the occupation, as for instance the ordinary police, were often faced with the same difficulties as the railways and on the whole did not show up better.

This raises a general problem of contemporary history, which often concerns persons who are still alive, and ideas and images which still have force and may even still have a valuable function. It was quite natural that the Dutch, shocked by the rigour of the later years of the occupation and by the horrors they had to witness, should be inclined to identify themselves with the actually rather small group of genuinely active resisters. They also tended to simplify the contrast between the people and the invader, and to overlook the variety of attitudes among the inhabitants, especially during the first years when the outcome of the war had not yet become clear and the nazis still showed some moderation in their conduct. The overwhelming majority of the nation certainly hated nazism and hoped for an allied victory, but many of them in practice could not escape co-operation with the enemy. So historical research cannot avoid, in this respect, destroying some cherished ideas. Rüter was not the only one who had to face this problem.

The institute has also published a detailed study of the large strike in Amsterdam in February 1941, which was called in protest against the first *razzias*, the round-ups of Jews on a large scale.[14] This strike can in a way be considered as the beginning of the organized underground movement. Other studies deal with the organization which supplied funds to this movement; with the strikes in April and May 1943; with the big round-up in Rotterdam on 10 and 11 November 1944.[15] One work, dealing with leather supplies, gives valuable information on the German bureaucracy in the Netherlands and how the apparatus worked in practice—information which few, perhaps, would expect to find in a book about leather.[16] Attention should also be drawn to the voluminous work of Professor J. Presser, of Amsterdam, on the extermination of the Dutch Jews. This came out in 1965; no other work published in the Netherlands since the war has made such a deep impression on the general public. It became a bestseller. This is due partly to the subject matter, but partly certainly to the author. I do not myself altogether agree with Presser's method and conception, or with his treatment of all the problems involved; but his work gives a moving account of this atrocity.[17] Before its publication we had had the useful work of A. Herzberg about the Jewish tragedy in Holland.[18]

Much useful research work about the war has been done also outside the Institute for War Documentation. L. de Jong (director of the Institute) published a thesis on the German fifth column, and contributed a survey of the Second World War to the large *History of the Netherlands*.[19] Two more recent publications examine the general question of fascism in the Netherlands, which was represented not only by the official fascist movement, the NSB, which joined the occupiers from the first and disappeared with them.[20] Also of great importance for this period is the work of the Commission of Investigation established by the Lower House of Parliament. The Dutch ministers in exile during the war submitted to the commission an account of their policy and activities, and a large number of other persons gave evidence. The results have been published in nineteen large volumes.[21] Important documentary sources are also to be found in the big trials, held shortly after the war, of Mussert, the leader of the NSB, Rauter, the *Höhere SS-und Polizeiführer* (the German commander of the police and ss), and General Christiansen, senior commander of the Wehrmacht.[22]

The military aspects of the war (the part played by the Dutch was a rather modest one) is in the hands of the Sections for Military History of the army and navy staffs. Civilian historians in Holland have seldom shown a strong passion for purely military matters, with the possible exception of the glorious naval history of the seventeenth century. One carefully detailed publication is *The Struggle on Netherlands Territory during the Second World War*.[23] Some of the resistance groups have collected material on their own activities, *Oppression and Resistance*, and there is a valuable book about the opposition of the Protestant church.[24]

War hit the Netherlands not only in Europe. The Dutch Indies were overrun by Japan, and the Institute for War Documentation has a special section to deal with these territories. Here the documentation and research are on the whole far more complicated and laborious than in the case of the homeland, and the results are correspondingly meagre.

Without listing other studies, enough has been said to show that a good deal has already been done about the war and the occupation, and that we now have a pretty detailed and comprehensive picture of this period. Some gaps still remain to be filled, of course, and certainly judgment about the events, persons, and institutions will change as they recede into the distance and the emotions connected with them subside.

But contemporary history is not quite identical with the history of the Second World War. It is true that up to now a great deal of the attention and time of Dutch scholars has been spent on this single though complex event, which jolted the nation out of its neutrality. That is understandable and even defensible. But there is a growing awareness of other urgent historical questions of the twentieth century, equally worthy of study. There is, for instance, the colonial problem. The Netherlands, one of the oldest and richest colonial empires, witnessed the loss of the Dutch Indies after the war. The majority of the nation certainly saw this loss without much pleasure, and without much knowledge or understanding of the changes which had taken place during the war in the Far East. The 'Indonesian question' is a somewhat sensitive spot in the consciousness of a large part of the nation, and this, I think, explains the fact that on this dramatic episode—actually the only one after the war when the Netherlands really stood in the spotlight of world politics—there exists no satisfying literature. As the United Nations, and especially the United States, also played a part in the affair (and a rather decisive part), we should be careful not to blame the Dutch alone for this gap. But certainly the subject presents an extensive field, especially for Dutch research. The roots lie in the pre-war period, when Indonesian nationalism was born, and that is where study has to begin. A start has already been made by the publication of documents about Dutch rule from 1900 to 1942.[25] The first volumes justify the expectation that we will get a solid basis for further research work. We shall no doubt find among those historians who undertake it some who will emphasize what was done by the Dutch for the Indonesian people, and others who will emphasize what should have been done.

I have dealt so far with what is being done in the field of traditional political history, indicating some representative investigations and publications. There is however a growing realization among Dutch (as other) historians that the writing of history is something more than the presentation of facts and the interpretation of events, that we have to get down to an understanding of the general forces and conceptions which often lie behind the great events of our age, that the aim of historical science is not to 'write a story', but to get a better insight into the historical roots of society. It lies beyond my task here to deal with the development of such essential related sciences as sociology and political science in the Netherlands, but many studies in the field of contemporary history do in fact lie between these disciplines and history.[26] A multitude of articles and smaller studies about the Dutch political system could be listed here which belong to history as well as to political science.[27] There are studies of Parliament and the political parties,[28] of democracy today,[29] and of such major general movements of our age as socialism and communism.[30] The cold war also attracted attention.[31] There is even a new branch, a mixture of history and political science developed from the special study of war-time phenomena: the so-called 'Polemologie'. Founder of this science is Professor B. V. A. Röling of Groningen, who has undertaken a general analysis of these phenomena in an attempt to find the general laws (who knows!) which might have played their part and to establish the possibility of avoiding future conflicts.[32] I need hardly add that Röling's ideas are still rather warmly contested in the small world of Dutch scholarship.

It would therefore certainly be wrong to suggest that contemporary history in the Netherlands today is hypnotized by the last war and the German occupation, as the rabbit by the serpent. Increasing co-operation with political science and sociology will bring new impulses and put new questions to the historian. On the whole it can be said that, especially among the younger generation at the universities, interest in the recent past, in fascism, communism, and socialism, is growing and may one day rival the traditional interest in the country's 'golden age' or in the rebellion of the sixteenth century. Today we have caught up a bit on the backlog which existed before the war in this field. It is therefore to be hoped and expected that the establishment of separate chairs for contemporary history at all the Dutch universities (where this field nowadays is still often treated as an annex of modern history) will not be postponed till the twentieth century itself has become part of the good old days.

NOTES

[1] An excellent introduction to these questions is the short work, written for the English public, by G. J. Renier, *The Dutch Nation* (London, 1944).

[2] See B. W. Schaper, 'Religious Groups and Political Parties in Contemporary Holland', in *Britain and the Netherlands*, 2 vols., eds. J. S. Bromley and E. H. Kossmann (London, 1960, Groningen, 1964).

[3] This question is dealt with by J. C. Boogman, 'Enkele aspecten van het Nederlandse natite-besef in historisch perspectief', *Oost-West*, vol. 5, No. 3, and *Die holländische Tradition in der niederländischen Geschichte*, Westfälische Forschungen, vol. 15, 1962.

[4] A. E. Cohen, 'Netherlands Research on the Second World War', *Britain and the Netherlands*, vol. I, p. 231.

[5] See on Dutch foreign policy, C. Smit, *Hoogtij der Neutraliteitspolitiek 1899–1919* (Leiden, 1959). Smit also edited *Bescheiden betreffende de buiterlandse politiek van Nederland* (The Hague, 1961–2), a semi-official collection of documents on foreign policy, which so far goes up to 1917.

[6] For example H. P. G. Quack, *De Socialisten* (Amsterdam, 1899–1901); W. van Ravesteyn, *Het Socialisme aan den vooravond van den Weredoorlog* (Amsterdam, 1939). Much information is also to be found in the memoirs of several socialist leaders, as Troelstra, *Gedenkschriften* (Amsterdam, 1939); F. M. Wibaut, *Levensbouw* (Amsterdam, 1936), J. H. Schaper, *Een halve eeuw van strijd* (The Hague, 1933), and J. W. Albard, *Een kwart eeuw parlementaire werkzaamheid* (1938).

[7] See on Dutch foreign policy after the war the study by S. I. P. van Campen, *The Quest for Security: some aspects of Netherlands foreign policy 1945–50* (The Hague, 1958).

[8] A short survey of Posthumus and his work is given by A. J. C. Rüter in: *Bulletin of the International Institute of Social History*, 1953, No. 1 (Leiden, 1953).

[9] Saks, pseudonym for Pieter Wiedijk (1867–1938), was a Marxist pamphleteer and editor of *De Nieuwe Tijd* 1902–13. See F. de Jong, *J. Saks* (Amsterdam, 1954). Florentius Marius Wibaut (1859–1936) was a pioneer of socialist municipal policy in Holland. Willem Vliegen (1862–1947) belonged to the reformist wing, advocating reconciliation with the state. Johan Schaper (1868–1934) was a socialist MP.

[10] *International Review of Social History* (Van Gorcum-Assen). This review publishes articles by historians of various countries on social subjects and also documents of the Institute. A detailed bibliography covers recent publications on social questions all over the world.

[11] L. E. Winkel, *De ondergrondse pers 1940–1945* (Amsterdam, 1960).

[12] A. J. C. Rüter, *Rijden en Staken* (Amsterdam, 1960).

[13] See Th. J. G. Locher, 'Rüter The Historian', *International Review of Social History*, 1965, No. 3.

[14] B. A. Sijes, *De Februaristaking* (1954).

[15] P. Sanders, *Het National Steunfonds* (1960); P. J. Bouman, *De April-Meistakingen van 1943* (1950); B. A. Sijes, *De razzia van Rotterdam* (1951).

[16] A. J. van der Leeuw, *Huiden en leder, 1939–1945* (1954).

[17] J. Presser, *Ondergang, de vervolging en verdelging van het Nederlandse Jodendom 1940–1942*, 2 vols. (The Hague, 1965). While the Dutch press at first reacted with admiration and praise, the professionals followed with more critical comment. Cf. the long review by I. Schöffer in: *Tijdschrift voor Geschiedenis*, 1966, No. 1, and my own review: 'Die Verfolgung des hollandischen Judentums', in *Neue Politische Literatur*, 1966, No. 4 (Frankfurt/M. 1966). An extremely sharp critique was published by J. Meyer in the Dutch review for history teachers *Kleio*, January 1966.

[18] A. Herzberg, *Kroniek van de Jodenvervolging* (Amsterdam, 1949–54).

[19] L. de Jong, *De Duitse vijfde colonne in de tweede wereldoorlog* (1953); revised ed. in English: *The German Fifth Column in the Second World War* (London, 1956); *Algemene Geschiedenis der Nederlanden*, XII, p. 376 et seq.

[20] G. A. Kooy, *Het échec van een 'volkse' beweging. Nazificatie en denazificatie in Nederland 1931–1945* (Assem, 1964); L. M. H. Joosten, *Katholieken en fascisme in Nederland 1920–1940* (Hilversum, 1964). An interesting historiographical study is the thesis by I. Schöffer, *Het nationaal-socialistische beeld van de geschiedenis der Nederlanden* (Arnhem-Amsterdam, 1957).

[21] *Enquètecommissie regeringsbeleid 1940–1945* (The Hague, 1949–56).

[22] *Het proces Mussert* (The Hague, 1948); *Het proces Rauter* (The Hague, 1952); *Het Proces Christiansen* (The Hague, 1950), all edited by the State Institute for War Documentation in its documents series.

[23] *De strijd op Nederlands grondgebied tijdens de Wereldoorlog II.* 11 vols. (1952–). Another study in this field is J. J. C. P. Wilson, *Vijf Oorlogsdagen en hun twintigjarige voorgeschiedenis* (Assen, 1960).

[24] *Onderdrukking en verzet*, 4 vols. (The Hague, 1946); H. C. Touw,

Het verzet der Kerk, 2 vols. (The Hague, 1946). This, like other works brought out shortly after the war, now needs some correction.

[25] S. J. Van der Wal, ed. *Bronnenpublicatie betreffende de geschiedenis van Nederlands-Indië 1900–1942* (Groningen, 1963–64). Another source publication is to be brought out by the State Institute for War Documentation: *Nederlandsch-Indië onder Japanse bezetting*. Studies dealing with the pre-war period are: J. M. Pluvier, *Overzicht van de ontwikkeling der nationalistische beweging in Indonesia 1930–1942* (The Hague, 1953), and the publication edited by H. Baudet, I. J. Brugmans a.o. *Balans van beleid. Terugblik op de laatste halve eeuw van Nederlands-Indië* (Assen, 1961). On the war period see: *Nederlandsch-Indië onder Japanse bezetting*, ed. I. J. Brugmans. For the post-war period see C. Smit, *De liquidatie van een Imperium* (Amsterdam, 1962). This list could be continued, but on the whole the subject is still rather neglected.

[26] The book by G. A. Kooy (see note 20) is a sociological case-study. The author presents a detailed analysis of nazism in one special place, the little town of Winterswijk, which he hopes will be useful as a kind of model and example of the operation of nazifying and denazifying factors in society.

[27] The political science review *Acta politica* presents a survey of what has been done since the war in the field of contemporary history and political science in Holland (*Acta politica*, 1966, vol. I, Nos. 1–4). Here we may mention: A. van Braan, *Ambtenaren en bureaucratie in Nederland* (Zeist, 1957); F. van Heek a.o., *Sociale stijging en daling in Nederland* (Leiden, 1958); H. A. Brasz, *Ontwikkelingen in het Nederlandse communalisme* (Assen, 1960); E. van Raalte, *De ontwikkeling van het minister-presidentschap in Nederland, Belgie, Frankrijk, Engeland an enige andere landen* (Leiden, 1954); G. J. Lammers, *De kroon en de kabinetsformatie* (Ymuiden, 1952).

[28] A. Hoogerwerf, *Ontwikkelingen in de Nederlandse politieke partijen* (The Hague, 1961); S. W. Couwenberg, *Het Nederlandse partijstelsel in toekomstig perspectief* (The Hague, 1960); J. Barents and J. J. de Jong, *Partis politiques et classes sociales aux Pays-Bas* (Table Ronde de l'Association française de science politique 1955); E. van Raalte, *Het Nederlandse parlement* (The Hague, 1958); J. Th. Rume, *De eerste Kamer der Staten Generaal* (Nijmegen, 1957); W. Drees, *De vorming van het regeringsbeleid* (Assen, 1965). Drees is the well-known socialist who after the war presided as Prime Minister over more cabinets than any other Dutch politician.

[29] J. Barents, *Democracy, an unagonized reappraisal* (The Hague, 1958); H. J. Pos, L. van der Horst a.o. *Democratie, Achtergronden en mogelijkheden* (Amsterdam, 1946); J. L. Heldring a.o., *Democratie in debat* (Meppel, 1964); B. W. Schaper, 'Democratie in West en Oost' (*Oost-West*, 1963, No. 2).

[30] W. Banning a.o., *Liberalisme en Socialisme* (Amsterdam, 1956); J. de Kadt and G. Ruygers, *De grondslagen van het socialisme* (Amsterdam, 1947); W. van Ravesteyn, *De Wording van het communisme in Nederland 1907–1925* (Amsterdam, 1948).

[31] B. H. M. Vlekke, *Tweespalt der Wereldrijken* (Haarlem, 1953);

CONTEMPORARY HISTORY IN EUROPE

B. M. I. Delfgauw, R. C. Kwant a.o., *Aspecten van de koude oorlog* (Assen, 1964); I. A. Diepenhorst, *Het vraagstuk van de oorlog* (Groningen, 1953); idem, *Kernoorlog en kernbeslissingen* (Utrecht, 1965).

[32] B. V. A. Röling, *De wetenschap van oorlog en vrede* (Groningen, 1961); idem, 'National and international peace research', *International Social Science Journal*, 1965.

Spain

JOAQUIN ROMERO-MAURA

The Civil War and After

The Civil War of 1936–39, which split Spain right down the middle, gave rise to bitter post-mortem speculations among Spanish historians. The attempt to fix responsibility for the disaster reflected not only their own political and emotional involvement, but also their adherence to the traditional mode of interpreting history in purely political terms.

At the end of the war those historians who had been liberals or further to the left, and who had maintained their position during the war itself, were either in exile or at least out of the running. Thus the greater part of recent Spanish historiography is the work of a group which may be broadly described as that of 'establishment historians', conservatives of all kinds and men adhering to the traditional view of history. But the last few years have seen the rise of a small group of young and promising historians who may, in very general terms, be described as being on the left wing.

For their part, the victors set out to have history written in conformity with their own interests and proclaimed ideology. Official versions of Spanish history were published which are still in use today. Until 1966, when the censorship was abolished, an extremely vigilant body of political censors scrutinized all manuscripts; but the effect of this on the work of the professional historian should not be exaggerated. Extremely sensitive to unacceptable trends in the press and in books likely to reach a wide public, the censorship was not excessively demanding when it came to scholarly publications. Unless they dealt with the Civil War period or certain other subjects that were taboo, writings aimed at the specialist were usually passed with few deletions. More crippling than the censor's scissors has been the tight control of source material.

Historical research and writing has been more severely handicapped since the Civil War by the political climate than by direct political interference. It was perhaps only natural that during the war and in the years immediately following passions should have been so strong as to blind the historian. 'If in this book you hope to find eclectic opinions in a conciliatory and amiable vein, ambiguous formulas of exquisite tolerance, harmonious solutions . . . do not bother to read on', a historian wrote in 1938.[1] This has been the prevailing attitude.

With the passage of time, the tone grew somewhat less strident, but passions did not cool. 'The following pages are written for those who are deaf, those who are forgetful, who ignore the truth and cling to a liberal conception of the monarchy, wherein the King is but an "august zero"', wrote Galindo Herrero in the introduction to his useful *Los partidos monárquicos bajo la Segunda República*.[2]

It would obviously be a mistake to blame the deficiencies of those whom we have called 'establishment historians' entirely on political partisanship. An extreme version of historical events may still be accurate. A strong ideological bias may even play a positive part by focusing the historian's attention on new fields of research. But in Spain, though patriotic fervour has produced floods of patriotic prose, it has not given rise, for the period concerned, to studies on such subjects as Spanish foreign policy or the Spanish domination of Morocco; militarism has not fostered research into military history; militant Catholicism has not produced a single major work on the Church in modern Spain. Moreover, not only Diego Sevilla Andrés himself, biographer of Maura and Canalejas, but many of his colleagues as well, would profit from heeding his own admonition, that 'we should not expect [Maura] to reason and react as though the 18th of July [1936] had caught him in the flower of youth or in the years of his prime'.[3]

Inclination, habit, and ideology seem to incline the conservative historian to adopt the traditional view of history and to investigate political history at the expense of institutional, social, and economic studies. Of this particular school, there are some outstanding representatives, notably Melchor Fernández Almagro, the Duke of Maura, and Jesús Pabón. The works of these three set the background for any political study of contemporary Spain, and they have been widely plundered by lesser Spanish historians. Almagro, who died in 1966, was the author of several books on the whole contemporary period. He published only one major work after the war, his comprehensive *Historia política de la España contemporánea*.[4] Gabriel Maura, too, who died in 1963, published no more than one major book on contemporary history after the Civil War: *Por qué cayó Alfonso XIII* (1948).[5] Jesús Pabón, professor of Spanish contemporary history at the University of Madrid, is best known for his scholarly biography of Cambó.[6]

Maura and Fernández Almagro were men of the past, accepting francoism merely as an alternative to the disorders or the leftism of the Republic in its decline. Their dislike of the stridencies of the system and their hankering after 'better times' made them, and Jesús Pabón, look backwards with nostalgia—an attitude which, though it may be politically impractical, has no doubt preserved in all three their sense of history and historical perspective. They are not altogether free of the prevailing passions, but they never lose their sense of historical purpose and of what is relevant. It is surely no coincidence that they are also the only historians of this group who write well, something which the student of modern Spanish history learns to appreciate.

What of the other historians adhering more or less closely to the traditional view of history? It is unlikely that anyone acquainted with their output would deny that there is something crude, something that can only inadequately be defined as mediocrity, in the writings of many post-Civil War historians, an element absent from the work of their predecessors. It is not a matter of superficiality and inaccuracy—in fact, many of them are much more reliable and have behind them many more hours of work than certain historians of yesterday, such as Lema, Fabié, or Romanones. What one comes to question is not so much the seriousness of their work, but rather their purpose in producing it. Though many of their books are useful, sometimes very useful indeed, they are distinctly patchy, even garbled. Perhaps the explanation of their incoherence is that it derives from the peculiarity of the present Spanish situation, of which they are part.

The Civil War taught all Spaniards—victors and vanquished alike—a sad lesson, which was quickly learnt and which made them forget all previous experience: the lesson that violence can pay, and pay well. The rulers of today, and those who benefit from their rule, know that without it they could never have dreamed of such an era of privilege and domination; those on the losing side can only reflect on what might have been, had they prevailed in the conflict. This basic preoccupation becomes immediately apparent whenever the origins of the Republic are discussed, and the part played by the Republican conservatives, as well as the rights and wrongs of the last king's attitude in the last few days of his reign. Some, like the Marquess of Luca de Tena, heartily approve of the king's decision to depart without offering resistance: 'His attitude [in 1931] paved the way for the Movement which brought salvation, and which began five years later. We won the Civil War in 1939; in 1931 we would have lost.'[7] Others, like Gonzalo Fernández de la Mora, who may be considered a *maître à penser* of today's ruling class, defend a different point of view, though their motivation is the same: 'If the moderates had not joined forces with the anarchists and separatists, would the Spanish people have accepted a change of regime [in 1931]? And if such a change had come about nonetheless, would not the defensive reaction of 1936 have set in much sooner?'[8]

These are the themes commonly debated in Spain and, not unnaturally, among Spanish historians. This kind of perspective has affected their attitude towards the entire contemporary period and given rise to the widely accepted idea of the 'two Spains', a confused expression which carries a strong connotation of intransigence. In García Escudero's words: '. . . there was no such thing as a "Spain of the middle way", so that one had to opt for one or another of the two *real* Spains'.[9] Putting it more bluntly: if force can preserve privilege, there is no reason why privileges should be surrendered. This is no discovery of Spanish philosophers. But unfortunately in Spain the formula has been seen to work, and the results are a constant reminder to the advocates of more sophisticated procedures.

Not unnaturally, the supporters of the regime have tried to justify its origins by a new outlook, a new political philosophy. But all their attempts to prove that the system is, from the strictly political point of view, anything but the personal rule of one man, have ended in failure. The bankruptcy of its ideology, of the official Falangist doctrine, has long been apparent, and all have come to sense that the newness, the originality of the system resides exclusively in the leader's person. However, because of a strange blend of fear and vested interest, of the lack of any other experience, or in deference to past sacrifices and exploits, only a few on the side of the victors are yet prepared to admit this. Even those who are not Falangists themselves or members of the apparatus, tend to share the intolerance characteristic of those who triumphed. Their high-handed treatment of political opponents and of those merely out of sympathy with the regime, their disdainful attitude towards their betters of yesterday, rest on the assumption that they have created something new and durable, that they hold the truth, the magic formula.

The underlying idea could not be simpler: political problems are an unnecessary appendix to politicians. If society is properly ruled, political problems vanish, only social and economic problems remain. If a government will only carry out its daily routine efficiently, the urge to engage in politics will die out, and politicians will turn to other, more useful and less lucrative, occupations. Unhappily, this dream of the enlightened despot makes the historian and his job as obsolete as politics and politicians, and government a matter of piecemeal social engineering. This particular brand of pragmatism is in itself inhibiting enough for the historian who likes to believe in the usefulness of historical studies.

Equally paralysing is the obscure impression that many of the proclaimed rights, of which so many take advantage, are nothing but abuses—a feeling which generates, close below the surface, a vague but palpable dread of the future. The all-pervading presence of an arbitrary and, by its nature, temporary regime, has led to constant compromise at all levels. The carnival has been taken for granted so long that most Spaniards shy away from the thought of Ash Wednesday, which will inevitably put an end to a game without rules and without reference to the past or indeed the future. Those historians who are acclimatized to such conditions and have no other point of reference, find themselves without a part to play. Nobody will listen to them, and Caesar least of all, so that even the dubious refuge of history *ad usum principis* is closed to them. They are thus reduced to the status of apologists of the regime, champions of patriotic intransigence, gossip-mongers or tellers of parables. Almost invariably they take a moral stand, and their writing usually meanders along some hidden, sentimental course, lending it a touch of the bizarre. There are innumerable examples to choose from. M. García Venero, author of many interesting works on diverse aspects of contemporary Spanish history, declares at one point that he wants to 'make patent once again [his] limpid historiographic morality, which follows a single and august watchword: Spain'.[10] In the introduction to his biography of Canalejas, and mindful of the latter's anti-clericalism, Diego Sevilla Andrés quotes St Ignatius (*Exercicios*, 22) to justify his own attitude of 'compassionate understanding' towards his subject.

For all these reasons, it is extremely difficult to discern actual trends in the investigations of this group of historians. When Gabriel Maura wrote *Por qué cayó Alfonso XIII*, he had in mind the possible 'exemplary value of History'. And Pabón assures us that he was prompted to study the figure of Cambó in the hope that he might contribute to the understanding of the Catalan problem. But in the case of most of their colleagues, it is far from clear how they came to choose their particular subjects. Since the historian is considered to be of little value to Spanish society as it is at present, there is no demand for the investigation of specific aspects of history. But this complete freedom of choice, instead of making historians more 'objective', seems only to have made them more arbitrary.

Biography has claimed much of their attention, not surprisingly, perhaps, in view of the circumstances already discussed. Though a bibliographical catalogue would be out of place here, the biographies of General Prim and of Prat de la Riba, by R. Olivar Bertrand, may be singled out in addition to those mentioned earlier, as well as those of Santiago Alba and Melquiades Alvarez by García Venero.

The Republic is usually treated as a separate period, and so is the Civil War. On the first of these, there is only one relatively impartial study, that of J. Plá,[11] which is useful but limited to the strictly political aspects. The official version, as it were, of the Republican period is that of J. Arrarás.[12] Much has been written on the Civil War, but most books on this trickiest of subjects are not only biased, but grandiloquent and uninformative. M. Aznar's military history of the conflict is probably the coolest one.[13] The best compendium of the Republic and Civil War period by a Spanish author may be the account by C. Seco Serrano.[14] Apart from Galindo Herrero's interesting but slight study of the monarchist parties under the Second Republic, there is no serious book by any member of this school of historians on any party or organized movement for the whole contemporary period.[15]

Intellectual history has attracted more interest. But if we except Vicente Cacho's work on the Institución Libre, Maria Dolores Gómez Molleda's recent and most valuable book on regenerationism,[16] and some minor studies, mainly on Costa, we are left with nothing but literary criticism and a mass of literature devoted to the discussion of 'the Spanish Problem' which does little to remedy the present poverty of Spanish work in the field under consideration, and serves only to swell the already inflated volume of Spanish essayism.[17]

In recent years a violent reaction against the traditional view of history has set in among some of the younger historians. One man, at first almost alone, did more in this context than anyone could have expected—J. Vicens Vives, who died all too soon in 1960. He left a body of works[18] which constitute a major and indispensable source for anyone interested in the economic and social history of contemporary Spain. He also left a number of young and enthusiastic disciples.

Of the dominant school of historians, Vicens Vives spoke bitterly: 'Many seem to think that the nineteenth century was merely one long struggle between dogma and godlessness, absolutism and liberalism,' he wrote in his book on nineteenth-century Catalonia. 'The majority of today's historians still believe these things and write of them in a way that defies understanding: their view of Spain, and of Catalonia along with Spain, is monstrous and incomprehensible gibberish'.[19] He himself was interested in a different kind of history: 'History is life as such, in all its complex diversity.' He brought tables and graphs into history books, and from his chair of Economic History at the Faculty of Economics of Barcelona University he gave new life and greater vigour to social and economic studies.

It is hard to say to what extent the presence and encouragement of Vicens Vives has been responsible for the fact that a group studying political, social, and economic history from this different point of view has sprung up precisely in Barcelona. No doubt the very fact that Barcelona is an important industrial and financial centre has helped to encourage interest in the economic and social problems of the past. Indeed, this environment has produced a number of valuable monographic studies, providing factual data without any consistent attempt at interpretation.[20] An additional factor which may account for the prevalence of a social and economic interpretation of history and the emphasis on social and economic studies may reside in the natural reaction against the system on the part of the Catalan intelligentsia and in the strength of left-wing opposition in Barcelona.

Among the younger historians of the 'Barcelona group', most

of whom were disciples of Vicens Vives, some are breaking new ground in fields that have previously been pretty much unexplored. But the volume of their published work is still slight, so that one cannot yet say much about them. Of those already in print, the book on the First International in Spain by J. Termes is of particular interest and certainly the most ambitious. A short essay on syndicalism in Barcelona (1915–23) by A. Balcells, and a slender volume on the Barcelona Stock Exchange by J. Fontana and V. Villacampa are also useful. For the light it sheds on the demographic aspects of the period under discussion. J. Nadal's recent book is fundamental. Those interested in the First Republic will find A. Jutglar's volume on Pi y Margall helpful.[21]

Unfortunately, a number of young historians seem to be afflicted with an irresistible urge to publish quickly. At the root of this there lies no doubt a conscious effort and desire to propagate the 'new' outlook on history, and of course each publication does add to the sum of information; but it does also mean that the author is held back from delving more deeply into his subject, which is usually abandoned as soon as the initial study is in print. Furthermore, this attitude has prompted one or another member of this school to devote much of his time to the writing of general books, based largely on the work of Vicens Vives rather than on original research.

Superficiality is sometimes unconsciously encouraged by the publishers specializing in Catalan-language publications. They are understandably eager to bring out as many books on Catalan history as they can, and are constantly in need of acceptable originals. (Incidentally, a working knowledge of the Catalan language is fast becoming indispensable to anyone interested in contemporary Spanish history.)

Not unnaturally, the 'new' view of history was something of a revelation, and not a few of its adepts are aware of their role as innovators,[22] a frame of mind which in certain cases leads them to disdain political history altogether, to explain everything in purely economic terms, to apply the concept of social class highhandedly, and to indulge in sweeping generalizations. But then the past history of Spain is not of a kind to encourage those who think that religion and authoritarian politics do not always go hand in hand, that reformism is not necessarily a betrayal of the working class, or that the bourgeoisie is sometimes capable of acting in accordance with purposes which do not necessarily favour nothing but its own material interests. As in the case of those whom we have called 'establishment historians', the intransigence of some of the younger historians is no doubt the direct result of the strained political situation of Spain and the collective experience of the last thirty years.

If the tendencies and schools of thought to be observed among Spanish historians are basically the result of such political considerations, the low standard of so much contemporary material, irrespective of tendency, is more likely to be due to the discouraging conditions in which the Spanish historian has to work.

In the first place, the general and almost complete lack of means is a formidable handicap. Like most of his colleagues in other countries, the Spanish historian cannot expect to make a living from his books. Yet there are practically no grants or scholarships available to support the young historian. University chairs are few and only full professors can hope to support themselves adequately on their salary alone—though a recent reform has at least raised the salary of lecturers above subsistence level. The historians who are neither professors nor lecturers nor have private means, that is to say the overwhelming majority, have to earn their living in some other way, so that they must consider themselves fortunate if they are able to give three or four hours of the day to their historical work. Characteristically, two of the best books published in recent years were produced by non-professional historians.[23]

Another handicap is the deplorable state of affairs in regard to sources. Official archives are generally very difficult to get at, if not totally inaccessible, since the military archives covering the whole contemporary period are closed and the same applies to Police and Guardia Civil archives as well as to most of the papers of all the Ministries.

Printed sources present a number of problems. Authors who do not quote their sources, and books without indexes or any kind of bibliography, are all too common. Furthermore, in the absence of bibliographical studies, particularly on social and economic matters,[24] the student does not know where to look for references to authors and titles on the period he is investigating. Even for books which may turn out to be fundamental, he is thus reduced to haphazard browsing and must hope to come across them by chance, in some second-hand bookshop or in a library catalogue he is consulting for some other purpose. To make things even more complicated, in all important Spanish libraries many books, mainly on social topics, have for political reasons been withdrawn from the shelves and even from the catalogue; and, needless to say, most of the works published since 1939 outside Spain by exiled historians are not to be found in any of these libraries. Besides, most Spanish libraries are sadly incomplete, due to a secular lack of interest as well as to lack of funds. While speaking of libraries, it is worth mentioning that most of them have very short and impractical opening hours, a fact which is particularly galling to those whom circumstances oblige to be part-time historians only. As for newspaper libraries, those of Madrid and Barcelona are very good and fortunately survived the hazards of the Civil War.

When it comes to private papers, a number of problems have to be taken into account. Those still in existence remain in private hands, and their owners are often reluctant to let the historian see them. Vicens Vives spoke of the 'collective cowardice' of Catalan industrialists, who refused him access to their family archives. This is the attitude of practically all those who possess private papers, and must be attributed in part to an obvious lack of understanding of what the historian's job is. But those who fear personal attack or libel are not altogether fanciful. In the impassioned atmosphere which pervades Spanish society, such abuses have been far from rare, and blatant calumny has been used, for example, in attempts to implicate people in responsibility for the Civil War. Politicians and statesmen of yesterday are still the subject of acrimonious argument, and many would delight in the discovery that a puritan conservative was a secret drunkard or that a violently egalitarian demagogue had a duchess for his mistress. Nevertheless, the precautions taken by most owners of private papers are altogether excessive. The most distressing point by far, in regard to private archives, is that many of them, and most of the major ones, were destroyed in the course of the Civil War.

While we are on the subject of sources, it may be of interest to mention that the last decade or so has brought with it the publication of a number of memoirs (e.g. A. Hurtado, Gaziel, Ametlla, C. Soldevila, M. Maura) and volumes of correspondence (Torres i Bages and Maragall, Galdós) which have in some degree helped to ease the task of the historian. Another positive development of recent years is the incipient tendency to reprint some old publications of value, complete works and documents of various kinds, though in most cases the editing leaves much to be desired. Admittedly, a considerable proportion of the best books on contemporary Spanish history have been published outside Spain, by exiled Spanish historians and foreign scholars. But it is only fair to say that for all the reasons, both emotional and practical, which this brief survey has tried to analyse, the historian working in Spain has long had the cards stacked against him.

NOTES

[1] J. Navasal y Mendiri, *La hora de España* (Burgos [?], 1938), p. 1; see also J. Arrarás (ed.), *Memorias Intimas de Azaña* (Madrid, 1939), p. 6; R. Oyarzun, *Historia del Carlismo* (3rd edn., Madrid, 1965). Appendix (1940), pp. 451–8.

[2] Santiago Galindo Herrero, *Los partidos monárquicos bajo la Segunda República* (2nd, revised edn., Madrid, 1956). For similar attitudes see J. M. García Escudero, *De Cánovas a la República* (2nd edn., Madrid, 1953), p. 12; A. Pérez y Gómez, *Don Juan de la Cierva, Ministro de Alfonson XIII (1864–1938)* (Murcia, 1965), p. 15.

[3] *Antonio Maura, o la Revolución desda arriba* (Barcelona, 1954), p. 29.

[4] Two vols. (Madrid, 1956). During the Republic he produced a *Historia del Reinado de Alfonso XIII* (Madrid, 1933), and after the war a biography of Cánovas (Madrid, 1951).

[5] Maura also wrote a history of the Regency of Maria Cristina (Madrid, 1928), and one of the Primo de Rivera dictatorship (Madrid, 1930).

[6] *Francisco Cambó (1876–1918)*, vol. I (Barcelona, 1952); vol. II has not yet been published.

[7] T. Luca de Tena, Introd. to J. Cortés Cavanillas, *Alfonso XIII, vida, confesiones y muerte* (Madrid, 1956).

[8] G. Fernández de la Mora, in a review of M. Maura's *Asi Cayó Alfonso XIII* in *ABC*, 23 January 1966.

[9] García Escudero, op. cit., p. 12.

[10] *Antonio Maura 1907–1909* (Madrid, 1953), p. 168. For similar statements see also his *Historia del Nacionalismo Catalán* (Madrid, 1944).

[11] J. Plá, *Historia de la Segunda República*, 4 vols. (Barcelona, 1940); by the same author, a useful biography of Cambó, *Francisco Cambó, Materials per una història d'aquests ultims anys*, 3 vols. (Barcelona, 1928).

[12] J. Arrarás, *La Segunda República*, 2 vols. (Madrid, 1956–64); by the same author *Franco* (Burgos, 1938).

[13] M. Aznar, *Historia militar de la guerra de España* (Madrid, 1940).

[14] *Historia de España*, vol. IV—*Epoca Contemporánea (1931–1960)* (Barcelona, 1958). The author is professor of Contemporary History at Barcelona University and inclined to favour social studies.

[15] Though some would consider the works of Comín Colomer on the Spanish Communist Party (2 vols., Madrid, 1965) and on anarchism

(2 vols., Madrid, s.d.) historical writing; their only merit is that as a member of the police the author has seen some normally inaccessible documents.

[16] V. Cacho, *La Institución Libre de Enseñanza*, vol. I: 1860–1881 (Madrid, 1962); M. D. G. Molleda, *Los reformadores de la España Contemporánea* (Madrid, 1966).

[17] Of these books, the best known is Laín Entralgo's *España como problema* (2 vols., Madrid, 1956). For another standard interpretation, see R. Calvo Serer, *España sin problema* (Madrid, 1949). The collection compiled by Calvo Serer, and published by Rialp, contains a good selection of this kind of literature.

[18] His main work on the contemporary period is included in: *Historia Económica de España* (Barcelona, 1959), written in collaboration with J. Nadal; *Historia social y económica de España América* (ed.) 5 vols. (Barcelona, 1957–9), and his slender but valuable *Aproximación a la historia de España* (Barcelona, 1952).

[19] *Cataluña en el siglo XIX* (Madrid, 1961), pp. 309–10. The Catalan version appeared in 1958, as the first part of *Industrials i Politics del Segle XIX*, by Vicens Vives and M. Llorens.

[20] Among the most useful: P. Voltes, *La Banca barcelonesa de 1840 a 1920* (Barcelona, 1963); Fr Cabana, *La Banca a Catalunya* (Barcelona, 1965); J. L. Martín Rodríguez and J. M. Ollé, *Orígenes de la industria eléctrica barcelonesa* (Barcelona, 1961); A. del Castillo and M. Riu, *La Maquinista terrestre y marítima* (Barcelona, 1955); Oriol Bohigas, *Barcelona entre el Pla Cerdá i el barraquisme* (Barcelona, 1963).

[21] J. Termes, *El movimiento obrero en España—La Primera Internacional (1864–1881)*, (Barcelona, 1965); A. Balcells, *El sindicalisme a Barcelona (1915–1923)*, (Barcelona, 1965, published in Spanish 1965); J. Fontana and V. Villacampa, *La Bolsa de Barcelona de 1851 á 1930* (Barcelona, 1961); J. Nadal, *La Población española en los siglos XVI a XX* (Barcelona, 1966). Nadal, the closest collaborator of Vicens Vives, is lecturer on Economic History at Barcelona University; A. Jutglar, *Federalismo y Revolución—Las ideas sociales de Pi y Margall* (Barcelona, 1966).

[22] Cf. A. Jutglar, *L'era industrial a Espanya* (Barcelona, 1962), p. 12.

[23] C. Martí (a priest), *Los orígenes del anarquismo en Barcelona* (Barcelona, 1959), and J. Benet (a lawyer), *Margall i la Setmana Tràgica* (Barcelona, 1963, Spanish translation, 1965).

[24] A group of historians (J. Termes, A. Balcells, and others) is working on a bibliography of social history for Spain in the nineteenth and twentieth centuries, under the direction of Giralt Raventós, Professor at Valencia University, who is the author of many basic articles on viticulture and the *'problema rabassaire'* in Catalonia.

Sweden

KRISTER WAHLBÄCK

Secrecy and Neutrality

On 17 June 1940 Mr Björn Prytz, the Swedish Minister in London, had a conversation with the Under-Secretary of State for Foreign Affairs, Mr R. A. (now Lord) Butler. According to Mr Prytz's report to Stockholm, Mr Butler assured him that no opportunity would be missed to reach a compromise peace with Germany if reasonable conditions could be obtained.

As is well known, this incident was fully disclosed only when, on his own initiative, Mr Prytz made his report known to the Swedish public in September 1965, a quarter of a century after the event.[1] The possible significance of this piece of evidence will of course not be discussed in this context. The episode has been cited only because it provides, in at least two respects, an appropriate starting point for a survey of recent Swedish research on the diplomatic aspects of contemporary history.

In the first place, it brings up the question of the extent to which a small power's diplomatic source material may contain relevant information even on great issues in which it was not directly involved. This will of course largely depend on sheer chance, and on the abilities of individual diplomatic representatives; there are, however, some indications that a non-aligned position of the Swedish kind may often provide brighter prospects for comprehensive information than might be expected from a consideration of its power potential. Some recent diplomatic memoirs seem to bear this out,[2] although we will know nothing for certain until we are given access to the archives.

This brings us to the second and more important point: the rules on secrecy surrounding Swedish official source material on relations with foreign states. The fifty-year rule is still in force, although a Royal Commission in a preliminary report has proposed that it be cut down to thirty years. In practice, exceptions are made by government decision for the inter-war period, and sometimes even later, provided that still delicate subjects—such as relations with Soviet Russia—are not involved. The Swedish government seems to pay more attention to the susceptibilities of foreign powers than most states today; this is the reason why, for example, the Prytz report has not yet been published officially, although some members of the wartime government had taken the liberty to refer to it in their memoirs ten years before Prytz made its contents known. It should be noted in this context that Swedish legislation is rather liberal towards disclosures of these kinds, at least if they do not involve the full publication of documents or if it can reasonably be said that they do not endanger the security of the country. Much information on Swedish policy in the Second World War has been made available in memoirs; a former social-democratic Minister of Finance, Ernst Wigforss, published his *Minnen III: 1932–1949* (Stockholm, 1954); Gustaf Andersson, Liberal Party leader from 1934 to 1944, published, a year later, *Från bondeåtget till samlingsregeringen*, and C. A. Ehrensvärd, a prominent army officer for more than twenty years (1935–57), is the author of *I rikets tjänst* (Stockholm, 1965). On the other hand, a self-imposed discretion operates to such effect that as yet not even the slightest inside account is to be found of any major Swedish foreign policy decision after 1945.

Thus Swedish rules and practices in this field appear on the whole to be rather restrictive compared to the situation in most other countries. This may partly be explained by the natural circumspection of a small power, partly also by the unusual continuity of Swedish foreign policy, at least since the democratic break-through at the end of the First World War. This continuity —which incidentally also extends to the narrow circle of leading decision-makers[3]—is often stressed by official spokesmen and is obviously considered as an asset. Thus evidence on measures that may cast the slightest doubt on the strict adherence to traditional neutrality and non-alignment, or that would generally be judged unwise by today's standards, tend to be considered more embarrassing here than in the other Nordic countries, where basic security policies have been modified since the last war. Even Sweden's policy in the Second World War falls more often than not within the scope of this tradition; signs of repudiation in the immediate post-war years disappeared fairly quickly.

In these circumstances, it is hardly surprising that so little has been written on recent Swedish foreign policy, even in the last few years. There are no official histories, on the British model, of, for example, the Second World War, not even its military aspects. The only exceptions are two small publications by the Ministry of Foreign Affairs provoked by public controversies: *1945 års svenska hjälpexpedition till Tyskland* (The Swedish Relief Expedition to Germany in 1945), and *Förhandlingarna 1945 om svensk intervention i Norge och Danmark* (The Negotiations on Swedish Armed Intervention in Norway and Denmark in 1945), both published in the series *Aktstycken utgivna av Kungl. Utrikesdepartementet*. The annual *Aktuellt och historiskt*, published by the research section of the Staff College in Stockholm, has however presented some studies in this field. Diplomatic documents have been published only on some issues arising in 1940.[4] On private initiative, a collection of German documents was published in 1960 as a kind of supplement to the official 'White Books' on the transit issue in *Historisk Tidskrift* (The Swedish Historical Review), by Ulf Brandell and Åke Thulstrup. Of quite another character is of course the annual publication of the Ministry of Foreign Affairs, *Utrikesfrågor: Offentliga dokument m.m. rörande viktigare svenska utrikespolitiska frågor* (Foreign Affairs: Public Documents, etc. Concerning some important questions of Swedish foreign policy). A project for a large composite work by prominent historians on the history of Swedish foreign policy was launched in 1945 on the initiative of the then Minister of Foreign Affairs, Mr Chr. Günther, and was completed in 1961. Three of the volumes, written with full access to the archives of the Ministry, cover the years from 1872 to 1939; for the inter-war period, only a preliminary outline of some important issues was aimed at.[5] Swedish post-war foreign policy has been analysed only on the basis of official declarations and public debates.[6] In general, Swedish historians interested in contemporary diplomatic history have either resigned themselves to following the fifty-year rule closely,[7] or in a few cases have chosen subjects from other countries where source material is more easily available.[8]

It would however be unfair to ascribe this state of affairs to the secrecy rules alone. Established traditions within the discipline have also played their part. There are no separate departments or chairs of modern history in Sweden, except for one in Gothenburg, recently established. The centre of interest has traditionally been the Middle Ages or the great-power era rather than the last fifty years. The demands for a sufficient perspective in time and for source material without glaring gaps seem to have retained their power in Sweden longer than in many other countries. All this has no doubt been rapidly changing in the last few years, but so far the change has hardly left its mark on published studies.

The void left by the historians has in part been filled by other disciplines. Thus, to take a random example, it is no coincidence that the only works on Swedish foreign policy in the Second World War to be published in recent years were written by political scientists, less preoccupied with the unavoidable incompleteness of their sources.[9] The standard work on Swedish trade policy in the Second World War was written by a diplomatist who was himself engaged in shaping that policy: Gunnar Hägglöf, *Svensk krigshandelspolitik under andra världskriget* (Stockholm, 1958).

This is even more true if we turn from the diplomatic to the domestic sphere of contemporary history, which has for a long time been the almost exclusive domain of the political scientists. This has incidentally had an important influence on the development of political science in Sweden; the American trend towards theory and generalization has been slow to penetrate a discipline so largely engaged in conducting research by traditional methods. Only two major works can as yet be assigned to this new trend: Hans F. Petersson, *Power and International Order: An Analytical Study of Four Schools of Thought and their Approaches to the War, the Peace, and a Post-War System 1914–1919* (Lund, 1964), and Björn Molin, *Tjänstepensionfrågan: En studie i svensk partipolitik* (The Supplementary Pensions Question: A Study in Swedish Party Politics), published in 1965.

The different aspects of contemporary domestic politics have been rather unevenly covered. The functioning of the parliamentary system was earlier studied in a number of works, although from a rather narrow perspective, concentrating on the procedures and events marking a change of government, etc. Six major works, largely covering the period 1900–36, were published in 1941–57 in the series edited by the political science association in Uppsala, *Skrifter utgivna av Statsvetenskapliga föreningen i Uppsala*. The biographic sector, by contrast, is almost totally neglected; only two or three first-rank politicians in this century have been portrayed in works of reasonably scholarly standard. Ivar Anderson's study of Arvid Lindman, who was Conservative Prime Minister

1906–11 and 1928–30, and Leif Kihlberg's two-volume biography of Karl Staaff, Liberal Prime Minister 1911–14: Knut Petersson has written a life of Alfred Petersson, who was Minister of Agriculture 1905–09, 1911–14, and 1917–20.

Political parties are not given much attention either; in particular, their internal structure and the distribution of power within them is left almost wholly blank. There is a short survey by Agne Gustafsson of party congresses and the influence of the membership in *Modern demokrati* (ed. Pär-Erik Back, Lund, 1963). An up-to-date concise analysis of the Swedish party system is presented in Pär-Erik Back, 'Partiväsendet', in the composite work *Samhälle och riksdag*, vol. II (Stockholm, 1966). The conflict between the Conservative Party and its youth organization on the attitude to adopt towards nazism is dealt with in Erik Wärenstam, *Sveriges nationella ungdomsförbund och högern 1928–1934* (Stockholm, 1965). There is only one study of the motives and interaction of the parties in a major political issue, in the study of the pensions question by Björn Molin. Interest groups have been more thoroughly analysed, both in general works and in monographs on, for example, individual trade unions.[10] Research on the press and the mass media has yielded works on specific newspapers rather than studies of their political influence in general.[11] Swedish election statistics offer unique opportunities for analysis of voting behaviour, and extensive opinion polls have provided additional insight, presented in some recent studies.[12] The functioning and recruitment of the Swedish Riksdag has been analysed in a recent composite work, *Samhälle och riksdag* (Society and Parliament), 4 vols. (Stockholm, 1966).

One conspicuous feature of Swedish research in contemporary history is its parochialism. The very few studies on the foreign policy of other states have been referred to above. The domestic politics of foreign countries have not been studied to any greater extent; only three major works have been published in recent years: Jurij Borys, *The Russian Communist Party and the Sovietization of Ukraine* (Stockholm, 1960); Olle Nyman, *Der Westdeutsche Föderalismus: Studien zum Bonner Grundgesetz* (Uppsala, 1960); Göran Lindahl, *Uruguay's New Path: A Study in Politics during the First Colegiado, 1919–1933* (Stockholm, 1962).

International relations is not a separate discipline in Sweden. The Institute for International Affairs in Stockholm, an independent centre for information and research in the field, has expanded its research section rapidly in the last few years. Most of its publications are, however, still centred on national security and defence problems.[13] Since 1965, a periodical issued by the Institute, *Strategisk Bulletin*, deals with the same kind of problems. It should be noted that the Norwegian journal, *Internasjonal Politikk*, has published a number of studies, sometimes by Swedish scholars, on Scandinavia in international politics, for example the articles in the 1965 volume by Barbara Haskel and Ingemar Dörfer on the Scandinavian defence pact negotiations in 1948-49. The impending establishment of an institutional framework, on a joint Nordic basis, for research in international relations may impart an important stimulus to Swedish research in other parts of the subject as well.[14] A Nordic Committee for the Study of International Politics was set up in 1959. Since 1965 it has published the semi-annual journal, *Co-operation and Conflict; Nordic Studies in International Politics*, providing both information on recent developments in the Nordic countries and a forum for Nordic scholars in the discipline, irrespective of their fields of specialization. The behavioural approach to politics, applying methods from sociology and psychology, has made little impact on Swedish research in contemporary history as yet; the founding in 1966 of an international institute for peace and conflict research in Stockholm may be expected to bring a change.[15]

It is not a particularly bright picture of Swedish research activity in contemporary history that emerges from the preceding pages. The comparatively slender output may to some extent reflect no more than the crippling effects of rapid expansion in university education, which has required that most resources be concentrated on teaching rather than research. However that may be, the very fact has left its mark on this short survey in another respect too. There has been no mention of important and controversial issues, or of competing interpretations of contemporary Swedish society, its political system, and its role in international affairs. The absence of any disagreements worth mentioning is rather natural in a situation where the published research offers only isolated islands of knowledge. It is however also due to the nature of the subject matter; the politics of a small, prosperous, and peaceful country, marked by increasing community of values and lack of dramatic events, do not stimulate any kind of basic disagreements among its analysts either.

As to methodology, the interesting point seems to lie in the future rather than in the immediate past. Among political scientists the traditional descriptive-analytical method inherited from historians has rapidly grown out of date in recent years, although practical needs will certainly ensure its continued existence along with the new methods of varying sophistication inspired by the work being done in the United States. It remains to be seen whether there will be any parallel trend towards generalization within the historical disciplines as well.

NOTES

[1] *The Times*, 9 September 1965. A complete account in *Dagens Nyheter*, 8 September 1965.

[2] Vilhelm Assarsson, *I skuggan av Stalin* (In the Shadow of Stalin: Moscow memoirs 1940–43) (Stockholm, 1963); Erik Boheman, *På vakt: Kabinettssekreterare under andra världskriget* (On Duty: Foreign Under-Secretary in World War II) (Stockholm, 1964); Sven Allard, *Ryskt utspel i Wien* (Stockholm, 1965); German transl. *Diplomat in Wien: Erlebnisse, Begegnungen und Gedanken um den Österreichischem Staatsvertrag* (Cologne, 1965).

[3] E.g. Östen Unden was Foreign Minister 1924–26 and 1945–62, Chairman of the *Riksdag* Committee on Foreign Affairs 1937–45, and Member 1962–65; Rickard Sandler was Foreign Minister 1932–39 and Chairman of the Committee on Foreign Affairs 1945–64; and Erik Boheman was head of the Political Division of the Foreign Ministry 1928–31, Permanent Under-Secretary 1937–45, and Vice-Chairman of the Committee on Foreign Affairs 1959–64.

[4] *Förspelet till det tyska angreppet på Danmark och Norge 1940* (The Prelude to the German Attack on Norway and Sweden in 1940) (Stockholm, 1947); *Transiteringsfrågor och därmed sammanhängande spörsmål april–juni 1940* (Transit Issues and Corresponding Questions, April–June 1940) (Stockholm, 1947); *Transiteringsfrågan juni–december 1940* (The Transit Issue, June–December 1940) (Stockholm, 1947) and *Frågor i samband med norska regeringens vistelse utanför Norge 1940–43* (Questions Arising from the Norwegian Government's Exile, 1940–43) (Stockholm, 1948), all published by the Ministry of Foreign Affairs in the series *Aktstycken utgivna av Kungl. Utrikesdepartementet.*

[5] *Den svenska utrikespolitikens historia*, vol. III: 4, 1872–1914 (Stockholm, 1958), by Folke Lindberg; vol. IV, 1914–19 (Stockholm, 1951), by Torsten Gihl; vol. V, 1919–39 (Stockholm, 1959), by Erik Lönnroth. An expanded part of Lindberg's work has been published in English: *Scandinavia in Great Power Politics 1905–1908* (Stockholm, 1958).

[6] Nils Andrén and Åke Landqvist, *Svensk utrikespolitik efter 1945* (Swedish Foreign Policy since 1945) (Stockholm, 1965), and Elis Håstad, *Den svenska utrikesdebatten om FN och alliansfriheten* (The Swedish

Debate on the UN and Non-Alignment) (Stockholm, 1955). A concise account is given in Lennart Hirschfeldt and others, *Svensk utrikespolitik under 1900-talet* (Swedish Foreign Policy in the Twentieth Century) (Stockholm, 1958).

[7] Wilhelm M. Carlgren, *Neutralität oder Allianz: Deutschlands Beziehungen zu Schweden in den Anfangsjahren des ersten Weltkrieges* (Stockholm, 1962); Jörgen Weibull, *Införunionsupplösningem 1905: Konsulatfrågan* (Prelude to the Dissolution of the Union in 1905: The Swedish-Norwegian Negotiations on the Consulate Issue) (Stockholm, 1962); Torsten Burgman, *Svesnk opinion och diplomati under rysk-japanska kriget 1904–1905* (Public Opinion and Diplomacy in Sweden during the Russo-Japanese War, 1904–05) (Stockholm, 1965).

[8] Wilhelm M. Carlgren, *Isvolsky und Aehrenthal vor der bosnischen Annexionskrise* (Uppsala, 1955); Karl E. Birnbaum, *Peace Moves and U-Boat Warfare: A Study of Imperial Germany's Policy towards the United States April 18, 1916–January 9, 1917* (Stockholm, 1958); Carl-Axel Gemzell, *Raeder, Hitler und Skandinavien: Der Kampf um einen maritimen Operationsplan* (Lund, 1965).

[9] Åke Thulstrup, *Med lock och pock: Tyska försök att påverka svensk opinion 1933–1945* (German Attempts to Influence Swedish Public Opinion, 1933–45) (Stockholm, 1962); Krister Wahlbäck, *Finlandsfrågan i svensk politik 1937–1945* (The Finland Issue in Swedish Politics, 1937–45) (Stockholm, 1964); Krister Wahlbäck and Göran Boberg (ed.), *Sveriges sak är vår: Svensk utrikespolitik 1939–1945 i dokument* (Some Documents on Swedish Foreign Policy, 1939–45) (Stockholm, 1966).

[10] Nils Elvander, *Intresseorganisationerna i dagens Sverige* (Stockholm, 1966); Lars Foyer, *Former för Kontakt och samverkan mellan staten och organisationerna* (Forms of Contact and Co-operation between the State and the Interest Organizations) (Stockholm, 1961); Olof Ruin, *Kooperativa förbundet 1899–1929: En organisationsstudie* (Lund, 1960); Ingemar Lindblad, *Svenska kommunalarbetarförbundet 1910–1960* (Swedish Municipal Workers' Union, 1910–1960) (Gothenburg, 1960); Hans Wieslander, *I nedrustningens tecken: Intressen och aktiviteter kring fösvarsfrågan 1918–1925* (Towards Disarmament: Interests and Activities Surrounding the Defence Issue, 1918–1925) (Lund, 1966); Hans Meijer, *Kommitté-politik och kommittéarbete* (Political Role and Forms of Work of the Royal Commissions) (Lund, 1956).

[11] Ivar Anderson, *Svenska Dagbladets historia* (Stockholm, 1960); Leif Kihlberg, *Dagens Nyheter och demokratins genombrott*, 2 vols. (Stockholm, 1960); Jarl Torbacke, *Journalistik på osäkra villkor: Den liberala Afton-Tidningen och dess föregångare* (The Liberal Newspaper Afton-Tidningen and Its Predecessors) (Stockholm, 1966); Jörgen Westerståhl and C. G. Jansson, *Politisk press: Studier till belysning av dagspressens politiska roll i Sverige* (The Political Press: Studies Illustrating the Political Role of the Daily Press in Sweden) (Gothenburg, 1958), is an exception.

[12] Bo Särlvik, *Opinionsbildningen vid folkomröstningen 1957* (The Formation of Public Opinion in the 1957 Referendum on the Supplementary Pensions Question) (Stockholm, 1959); idem, 'Politisk rörlighet och stabilitet i valmanskåren' (Change and Stability in the Swedish Elec-

torate), *Statsvetenskaplig Tidskrift* (The Swedish Political Science Review), 1964; idem, 'Skiljelinjer i valmanskåren' (Cleavages in the Swedish Electorate), *Statsvetenskaplig Tidskrift*, 1965; Bo Andersson, 'Some Problems of Change in the Swedish Electorate', *Acta Sociologica*, 1962; Rune Sjödén, *Sveriges första TV-val: En studie i radions och televisionens roll som propagandamedier under 1960 års valkampanj* (Sweden's First TV Election: A Study of the Role of Radio and Television as Propaganda Media in the 1960 campaign) (Stockholm, 1962).

[13] E.g. Per Ahlmark and Hans-Åke Dehjne, *Den svenska atomvapendebatten* (The Swedish Debate on Nuclear Weapons) (Stockholm, 1965); Rolf Björnerstedt (ed.), *Svenska kärnvapenproblem* (Swedish Problems of Nuclear Arms) (Stockholm, 1965).

[14] The proposed organization is outlined in an expert report, published in the Nordic Council series of joint Nordic investigations, 1965:4, *Forskning af International politik* (Research on International Politics).

[15] The programme for the Institute is given in the report of a Royal Commission, 'Internationellt fredsforsknings—institut i Sverige' (An International Peace Research Institute in Sweden), published in the series *Statens offentliga utredningar*, 1966:5.

Czechoslovakia

KAREL BARTOŠEK

The State of Historiography

The bibliography compiled for the purposes of this essay lists about 700 titles, all published within the last five years, and ranging from solid monographs to slender pamphlets. To these must be added the hundreds of articles contributed to scientific, cultural, and political journals. Clearly, in the present brief survey only the truly fundamental problems of this abundant historiography can be examined. But first, a few remarks about what may be called the 'objective conditions' in which Czechoslovak historians are studying the twentieth century.

To begin with the social climate: the Czechs and the Slovaks, the two nations that make up present-day Czechoslovakia, have always been small nations (combined, the country has 15 million inhabitants). Although a commonplace, it is well to remember that the Slovaks and the Czechs have not had long historical experience as an independent state: the Slovaks had no independent political existence for 1,000 years (from the tenth century), and the Czechs for 300 years in the modern period (from the seventeenth century). This is probably the source of their 'history complex', and the explanation of the paramount position given to reflections on the past in a period when these entities were forming as modern nations. Not only in the nineteenth, but also in the twentieth century, historical reasoning was given pride of place in Czech politics and national ideology, as seen in the work of the founder of modern Czech politics, the historian František Palacky, or in the person of the most striking figure in Czech national life at the end of the nineteenth and the beginning of the twentieth century—Thomas Garrigue Masaryk. The preoccupation with history (providing historical justification for national and state existence) was given an even greater impetus by the birth of an independent state and the national exhilaration which accompanied its establishment, the subsequent German occupation and the new threat of Germanization—all within a span of less than thirty years. The same pattern can be traced in Slovakia, where the process of forming into a modern nation continued into the twentieth century.

The first thing to understand, therefore, is the objective reason for the leading place given to the study of history in Czechoslovakia. This was not a peripheral area of national life. It was neither remote nor self-contained; on the contrary, it reached into the fields of politics, ideology, and culture. And the reverse has also been true—politics, ideology, and culture have influenced the formation of historical thought. This has had not only its positive aspects, but also some negative ones.

The new regime established in Czechoslovakia in the years 1944–48, with the victory of the people's democratic revolution, did not weaken the position of historiography in national life. Every revolution must justify itself by history, and perhaps even more so after it has triumphed. It introduces a new point of view, a new outlook on the past, and it discovers new aspects of that past. In endeavours to instil its own concept of history into the social consciousness, and for this purpose makes use of all the means at its disposal. It is often one-sided and demands an *apologia* for its present acts and measures. This is not the first time that there has been this 'revolutionary violation' of history.

The material conditions for research into twentieth-century history are in general very encouraging. In the main research institutes—the Historical Institute of the Czechoslovak Academy of Sciences in Prague and in Bratislava, the Institute for the History of the Communist Party in the same two cities, the Military Historical Institute, and the Academy's Institute for the History of European Socialist Countries, both in Prague—more than half the research workers concentrate on the history of the twentieth century. In addition, the entire staff of the Prague Institute for International Politics and Economics, and several workers in other institutes, are engaged in this field. At the main faculties of colleges and universities there are specialized research departments for twentieth-century history and many research workers are employed on this in regional museums and in state archives. The number of people employed by the state or state institutions to devote themselves primarily to work in this field can be put at 300 to 400.

There are scholarly journals dealing mainly with the twentieth century: *Příspěvky k dějinám KSČ* (Contributions to the History of the Communist Party of Czechoslovakia—circulation 7,000), *Historie a vojenství* (History and Military Science—circulation 2,000), and *Slovanský přehled* (Slavonic Review—circulation 2,600). Furthermore, there are contributions on recent history in all scientific historical journals. In addition, the various institutes publish non-periodic collections of studies. There is no specialized publishing house in Czechoslovakia for the history of the twentieth century, but most of them assign a prominent place to this literature. As elsewhere, the publication of 'dry' scientific monographs often entails a financial loss; the state has made grants for these publications, mainly to the publishing house of the Czechoslovak Academy of Sciences, *Academia*. In recent years there has been a notable increase in the publishing activity of regional publishing houses; their publications are actually often of more than regional interest and since 1964 have exceeded the number published by the central institutions.

Extensive archives are at the disposal of historians of the twentieth century: these are to be found in the state administration, the security offices, the army, diplomatic sources, banks, industrial organizations, political parties, and in private possession. Almost all the material covering the period up to 1938 is freely accessible. Most of the archives for the period 1938–45 are at the historians' disposal, as well as a large number for the post-war years. Studies on the post-1945 period have been based on the archives of the government, the Central Committee of the Communist Party, and a number of ministries.[1] A number of collections of documents on recent history published in the last few years are not intended to serve propaganda purposes alone (as was often the case in the 1950s); they also try to give objective information on the given problem.[2] The new political climate of the 1960s has also released a stream of memoirs which are an important supplementary source for historical work.[3]

This does not mean that everything is in order in regard to the material conditions for research. Czechoslovak historians rightly complain that the libraries with foreign literature are poorly equipped, that the documentary and bibliographical services are inadequate, that some archives dealing with the post-Munich period are inaccessible, that some have not been kept in proper order, and so on. But it is probably true that there are few countries in the world where the historian of the twentieth century has such abundant archive sources open to him.

Of course, material conditions are not everything. Historiography is not without its tensions and conflicts in the present social climate. The writing of history is tied up with politics and ideology and 'interferes' in them—and historians are not always praised for their struggle for truth. Recent years have, however, brought important changes; people are realizing more and more the need for historical writing as a source of knowledge that enriches a country and generates new and creative ideas. There still persists, however, the old idea of historiography, which restricts this social science to its use as an 'instrument of education' or of vulgar apologetics. It is true that the number of problems that are tabu for publication has been greatly reduced, but some still remain. It would nevertheless be a mistake to describe the conflicts in historiography and social consciousness as occurring between 'official' and 'unofficial' views only. This can be seen by glancing through any issue of *Příspěvky k dějinám KSČ*. It is published by an 'official' party institute, but the large number of very unconventional articles in it proves that this schematic interpretation is unwarranted. The conflicts are manifold, as for example among direct participants in the events at issue, leaders of the resistance to fascism, many of whom were unjustly condemned in the 1950s and then rehabilitated a few years ago. They are not always inclined to embrace fraternally the historians who are seriously seeking the truth about these events.

The historians are a numerous and heterogeneous lot—they differ in intellectual capacity, in character, and in their conception of the historian's task. Despite all differences among them, I believe that today they are a fundamentally diligent and well-balanced group. Czechoslovak historians of the twentieth century have gone through an intellectual shock since 1956—some of them immediately and some belatedly. Their writings have been critical of their own previous schematic conceptions and they are making good resolutions about the responsibility of a scholar and his moral character. The result has been the rejection of 'marxism' in its Stalinist version; today authentic marxism is conceived as the dynamic for an historian's work, and as the free way to find out the truth. I do not wish to say that free and frank thinking is taken for granted; even in the community of Czechoslovak historians there are some conservatives; but the change that has taken place in the last few years, the intellectual protagonists of this change, and 'public opinion' among historians would scarcely permit a return to the old schematic and over-simplified approach, although the latter has some powerful defenders.[4]

To understand the state of affairs in the field examined here it should be noted that the basic core of research workers are people between the ages of thirty and forty, who are, for the most part, untainted by careerism. In their callow youth they wholeheartedly believed everything that revolutionary practice and theory presented to them; then they suffered a painful shock. But the shock had a salutary effect, and it has created a situation in which nihilism does not dominate (although it is not wholly absent), but there is a genuine desire to seek and to comprehend the truth. The source of this new revolt against myths and illusions is probably to be sought in the affinities felt by this generation with the democratic spirit of the pre-war Czechoslovak intelligentsia and its fine tradition of avant-garde intellectual life.

I do not wish to give an idealized picture of the state of affairs. As I said, it is not free of conflict; the 'academic' may sometimes clash with the committed, 'rebellious' concept of historiography. But such ills are to be found in every intellectual milieu, and there is also the conflict between the desire to have a safe job and the desire to follow one's own convictions. But it seems to me—and dozens of recent discussions substantiate my belief—that the prevailing intellectual climate is one in which questions are freely asked and criticisms freely made.

Among the subjects on which attention is mainly concentrated, the 'Czech question', in the broad sense of the word, comes first. The trauma of our country's history derives in large part from the relationship between Czechs and Germans, and it would be surprising if this relationship were not central to the historians also.

Studies have been undertaken on the fall of the Austro-Hungarian monarchy and the birth of an independent Czechoslovakia in 1918. These follow on from the studies made at the end of the 1950s, but they differ in their serious and scholarly attitude from the wave of propaganda literature of the preceding years. Although they continue to pay attention to the social-revolutionary movement, Czechoslovak historians have begun to make deeper studies, including the international aspects of this problem.[5] German-Czech relations are a particularly important theme for the period between the two wars, and in this respect Czechoslovak historical writing is often highly polemical, answering the extensive revanchist literature that appears in West Germany. Despite their passionate involvement (not always conducive to sober scholarship), Czech historians have turned out serious and well documented studies on the relations between Czechs and Germans in the pre-Munich republic.[6]

But the outstanding theme in the analysis of the 'Czech question' was and remains the period 1938–45, the time of the nazi occupation, of the anti-fascist struggle, and the origin of the people's democratic regime. Most of the literature on twentieth-century history in Czechoslovakia deals with the period between the Munich agreement and the events of May 1945. These books are the most popular, with editions often ten times as large as those on other subjects.[7] The great appeal of this theme in the last few years cannot be fully explained by its historical significance alone, by the fact that these years were a crossroads of history for Czechoslovakia. The magnitude of this appeal has been increased by political developments since 1962; in these years a number of unjustly condemned resistance fighters have been rehabilitated. Books have recently appeared on themes that had been ignored since 1949, while the old themes have been examined in a new light, and with greater understanding for the subtle and complex historical truth.[8]

In 1964–65 dozens of titles appeared marking the twentieth anniversary of the liberation. They represent all genres of historical studies, from reportage and the classical monograph to comprehensive attempts at synthesis.[9] A large group of historians are collaborating on a synthesis of the history of the national-liberation struggle during the Second World War, which is to be in three parts. Although Czechoslovak historians have had experience of team work (at the turn of the 1950s they produced a collective work on the history of Czechoslovakia, and another on the history of the Communist Party), the present project has contributed much that is new. Collective work here has meant not just the sum of individual monographs, as was usually the case before, but genuine creative collaboration among nearly 300 people throughout the republic. Discussions on different problems have been systematically organized and a document centre for research has been set up which is preparing several volumes of documents from the archives for this period. In the course of a few years it has become an important intellectual workshop, not limiting itself to the period 1938–45 (one of the methodological principles of this collective is to set the period of occupation and resistance against the background of the whole of Czechoslovak and European history in the twentieth century). The style of work of this collective is exemplified in the volume published in 1965.[10] This deals frankly with the objective and methodological problems of the trilogy, the gaps in research, and the hypotheses underlying the work—all of it designed to provoke a creative discussion and confrontation. It has been translated into German, French, and Russian, and copies were sent to specialized institutes and distinguished experts in Europe for criticism.

The second dominant theme of Czechoslovak historiography could in one sense be included in the first. It is another vital nationality problem, the Slovak question, which is necessarily linked with the Czech question. When we speak of recent developments in Czechoslovak historiography, research on the Slovak problem is rightly put in the front rank. The reasons for this lie, again, in the development of Slovak society, in the growth of national consciousness (and self-confidence); more directly in the political rehabilitation of thousands of communists and democrats whose activities created the most significant national and revolutionary tradition of the Slovaks—the Slovak National Rising in 1944. In this work the historians were largely responsible for the initiative. The new feature of the present situation is that it is not only Czech historians who are contributing to the analysis of the Slovak question; for the first time in history an extensive national Slovak school of history with its own institutes, journals, and publishing houses took part, with the typical dynamism of youth setting out on a new venture. In the last three years several dozen books have been published in Slovakia, dealing primarily with the Rising and the rehabilitated group of Slovak intellectuals around the journal *DAV*.[11] The main purpose of these publications is not 'to turn old theses inside out'[12] (even though there has been such a tendency). They endeavour to give a genuine scientific analysis, which is not averse to indulging in the complexities and paradoxes of history.

A comprehensive analysis of the relations of Czechs and Slovaks has become a cardinal theme of Czechoslovak historiography. It is no longer so one-sided as it was in the not-so-distant past: there have appeared the first attempts to analyse Czech nationalism in regard to the Slovaks. This is significant not only for the correct approach to historiography, but also from the standpoint of political practice, which has hitherto recognized only Slovak nationalism.

The third theme on which Czechoslovak historiography is concentrating is the economic and social development of the country and the social-revolutionary struggle. This is a logical result of the general Marxist orientation of historiography. In the 1950s hundreds of studies appeared on this topic, assembling a large number of facts. The new feature characteristic of work on these questions in recent years would seem to be, in addition to the studies that fill in areas formerly left blank, the attempt to achieve a broader synthesis of economic developments, and of some aspects or forms of the social revolutionary struggle.[13] There has been, in particular, a great increase in the number of works dealing with the history of different Czechoslovak factories. In 1960–64 alone, 150 titles were published on this topic, and dozens have been added since.

The fourth and last theme I should like to mention is the history of the working-class and communist movement. This, too, continues the work done in the 1950s and the reasons are clear: they lie in the nature of the present regime. The more recent work, however, is on a much higher level than in the preceding period. *Přehled dějin KSČ*, published in 1961, was not an 'official text', in which every statement and conclusion had to be treated as sacred, thus condemning historians—as did Stalin's *History of the CPSU*—to the role of ruminants chewing over 'truths' that had been uttered once and for all. After its publication, systematic analytical work continued, and soon the 1961 text was criticized as being in some respects inadequate or outdated. The most noteworthy aspect here is not the greater number of titles, the increase in factual knowledge (primarily in regard to regional history), but the new concepts and attitudes in regard to several sectors of the working-class movement.[14] Much of this work—dealing chiefly with the 1930s and the period after 1945—has appeared only in periodicals, but their small size does not lessen their value. They display a greater sensitivity to the intricacies and turning points in the development of the communist movement, particularly in the analysis of the forces and tendencies striving to find a Czechoslovak path to socialism. In recent years there have appeared a number of studies in journals and books on the history of the

Communist International, a true critical analysis of which is essential for any serious research into the history of the Czechoslovak working-class movement.[15]

This outline of the four 'great themes' does not, of course, exhaust the list of works now being produced by Czechoslovak historians. It seemed of greater interest to single out the main features rather than give a bibliographical list of the entire output.

A few words about some of the problems of theme and method in Czechoslovak historiography today.

In the first place, there is the danger of a national, provincial, limited outlook—an old problem of Czechoslovak intellectual life, and particularly noticeable in the years after the First World War. The evaluation of phenomena only from the standpoint, and within the framework, of their own nation, the inability to make a genuine comparison, an uncritical and subservient adulation of the national entity—these are characteristics which Czechoslovak historians have unfortunately not yet entirely overcome. Although there has been some change in this respect in the last few years, not all historical writing has applied the principle that German nationalism cannot be answered by Czech nationalism, just as Czech nationalism should not be countered by Slovak nationalism.

This danger does, however, seem to be retreating to the periphery of the historical field. The latest studies on the expulsion of the German minority from Czechoslovakia in 1945–47 take a genuinely historical, non-moralizing approach; the authors declare that the expulsion was necessary in the concrete historical situation, but at the same time it is spoken of as a 'shocking solution' and a 'tragic consequence' of previous events for which German chauvinism and nazism bear the main responsibility; at the same time this does not excuse the anti-German chauvinism among the Czechs and Slovaks. The very fact that Czechoslovak historians now recognize this danger of provincialism and speak of it openly is an encouraging indication that it is probably only temporary. One way to overcome it lies in the work on world history which is at the present time the main long-term task of the Historical Institute of the Czechoslovak Academy of Sciences and of research workers in other places. Another way is the independent analysis of the history of the Soviet Union, on which scarcely any work has been done up to now.[16] And, finally, one cannot fail to see the beneficial effect of the more abundant international contacts of Czechoslovak historians in recent years.

Another important problem in the work of Czechoslovak historians is to conquer the fatalistic social-economic determinism which often led to over-simplified explanations of complex historical phenomena, a misunderstanding of the role of chance, a neglect of other possible alternatives in historical development. In the present discussions on ways to overcome this fatalistic determinism there is no question of abandoning the Marxist concept of the laws of history and the role of class interests and class struggles in modern society. It is a different problem.

Historical writing here has clearly been influenced by Gramsci's humanist concept of Marxism and by the broad 'anthropological current' in contemporary Marxist thinking. There is frequent discussion of Marx's idea, as developed by Gramsci, that people are not only spectators but are actors on the stage of history. The most progressive historians are endeavouring to make concrete historical analyses of each phenomenon and to emphasize the possibility of human choice and decision in history. In the best works we see an attempt to 'psychologize' historiography; after a twenty-year pause, studies of the Czech national character are again appearing. A while ago this was rigorously stigmatized as 'un-Marxist'. In short, the historians are trying to present history as truly the history of man and not the history of general categories.

The third problem may be called the 'totality of history'. Until now the historians have usually restricted their studies largely to political or social-economic development, thereby impoverishing the history of man. But signs of change can now be seen; the collective of authors preparing the history of the Resistance is trying to realize the new conception of history which will include analyses of culture and its social role (not merely the 'cultural peaks' but also 'mass culture'); an analysis of public opinion, not limited to the active currents consciously influencing history, but also of the autonomous thinking of the man in the street; analyses of everyday happenings; and attempts to make use of the findings of modern sociology in analysing such matters as the attitude of the citizens to the institutions of an industrial society.

Included in this attempt to grapple with the problem of 'total history' are the endeavours to raise the theoretical level of historical writing. In Czechoslovakia the tendency which the French call '*l'histoire événementielle*' has been very widespread. This chronicle style of listing facts often shows a highly academic and dignified countenance. Undoubtedly there are historians who choose this method because they genuinely fear a 'new schematicism'. But no really great history can be written unless it attempts large generalizations; we find numberless examples of this. And great ideas do not usually arise from small themes. Unfortunately, an analysis of the 'great themes' is a rather rare phenomenon in Czechoslovak writing on the twentieth century. Books that investigate a particular phenomenon over the course of a century scarcely exist in Czechoslovakia; we are still awaiting works which cover the revolution of 1918, or the revolution of 1945, in all their aspects. While we pay our respects to the dozens of minor monographic studies, the lack of great themes is undoubtedly a weakness.

Perhaps this is too sketchy an account of the state of affairs, but it may convey some idea of the situation. I do not wish to give a wrong impression of its strenths or its weaknesses. It seems to me that historiography is now going through an encouraging and dynamic period and that, despite all its weaknesses, it will be able to take its rightful place in culture and society: in order that it may aid in the endeavours to liberate man by making the contributions that a science of mankind's past can make.

NOTES

[1] Cf. J. Navrátil and J. Domaňsky, *Boj KSČ o lidovou armádu* (The Struggle of the Communist Party for a People's Army), based on army archives—except for espionage and counter-espionage material—for the years 1945–48; or the monograph by K. Kaplan, *Utávření generální linie vystavby socialismu v Československu* (Shaping the General Line for Building Socialism in Czechoslovakia), about the years 1948–49, making abundant use of the documents in the Communist Party archives.

[2] *Chtěli jsme bojovat* (We Wanted to Fight—documents on the struggle of the Communist Party and the people for the defence of Czechoslovakia in 1938), vol. I, 426 pp., vol. II, 452 pp. (Prague, 1963); V. Král, *Die deutschen in der Tschechoslowakei (1933–47)*, 664 pp. (Prague, 1964); *Cesta ke Květnu* (The Path to the May Events—the birth of people's democracy in Czechoslovakia), compiled by M. Klimeš, P. Lesjuk, I. Malá, and V. Prečan, 2 vols., 796 pp. (Prague, 1965); *Boj o směr vyvoje československého státu* (Struggle for the Development of the Czechoslovak State—October 1918 to July 1919), vol. I, documents in the series of academic editions *Prameny k ohlasu Velké Říjnové socialistické revoluce a vzniku ČSR* (Sources on the Response to the Great October Socialist

Revolution and the Origin of Czechoslovakia), 432 pp. (Prague, 1965);
Č. Amort, *Heydrichiáda*, 320 pp. (Prague, 1965); V. Prečan, *Slovenské
narodné povstanie* (Slovak National Rising—documents), 1,220 pp.
(Bratislava, 1965).

[3] Among the most interesting are: Gustav Husák, *Svedectvo o Slovens-
kom narodnom povstaní* (Testimony on the Slovak National Rising),
618 pp. (Bratislava, 1964); R. Vetiška, *Skok do tmy* (Leap into the Dark),
dealing with the anti-fascist struggle and appearing in an edition of
51,900; P. Reiman, *Ve dvacátych letech* (In the Twenties), 555 pp.
(Prague, 1966).

[4] For example, the reply of ten historians to an article by V. Král,
published in February 1966, in which he tried to resurrect the incorrect
theses about the Slovak National Uprising in 1944 that were widespread
in political practice and in journalism in the 1950s.

[5] Cf. Z. Kárník, *Za československou republiku rad* (For the Czechoslovak
Republic of Soviets—about the national committees and Czech councils
in the Czech lands, 1917–20), 276 pp. (Prague, 1963); and Koloman Gajan,
Německy imperialismus a československo-německé vztahy v letech 1918–21
(German Imperialism and Czechoslovak-German Relations in 1918–21),
283 pp. (Prague, 1962).

[6] Cf. the volume of articles, *Německá otázka a Československo* (The
German Question and Czechoslovakia), 291 pp. (Bratislava, 1962);
J. César-B. Černý, *Politika německych burožazních stran v Československu
v letech 1918–1938* (Policy of German Bourgeois Parties in Czechoslo-
vakia 1918–38), vol. I, 1918–29, 512 pp., vol. II, 1930–38, 584 pp.
(Prague, 1962).

[7] For example, T. Brod and E. Čejka, *Na západní frontě* (On the
Western Front), dealing with the battles of Czechoslovak soldiers during
the Second War in the West, appeared in three editions, totalling more
than 20,000 copies, first edn. 464 pp. (Prague, 1963); K. Bartošek,
Pražské povstání 1945 (The Prague Rising in 1945), also in three editions
and more than 20,000 copies—first edn. 1960, third 1965, 304 pp. This
book has also been published in English and German.

[8] Cf. J. Křen, *Do emigrace—buržoazní zahraniční odboj 1938–39* (Into
Emigration—Bourgeois Resistance Abroad), 579 pp. (Prague, 1963).

[9] Cf. V. Král, *Zločiny proti Evropě* (Crimes Against Europe), 444 pp.
(Prague, 1964); *Osvobození Československa Ruduo armadou 1944–1945*
(Liberation of Czechoslovakia by the Red Army) by a collective of military
historians; vol. I, 464 pp., vol. II, 448 pp.

[10] *Odboj a revoluce 1938–1945* (Resistance and Revolution),
440 pp.

[11] One of the most important, besides the book by Husak already
mentioned, is the essay by E. Friš, *Povstanie zdaleka i zblízka* (The
Rising from Far and Near), 121 pp. (Bratislava, 1964); a collective work
by Czech and Slovak historians, *Dejinna křižovatka* (Historic Crossroads
—the Slovak National Rising, prerequisites and results), 519 pp., 1964;
report on the Conference of Historians on the twentieth anniversary of the
SNR, *Slovenske narodne povstanie 1944* (Slovak National Rising 1944),
741 pp. (Bratislava, 1965). The best book on *DAV* is the collection of

studies, *DAV—zpomienky a studie* (DAV—Recollections and Studies), 496 pp. (Bratislava, 1965).

[12] During the 1950s historians defended and 'documented' theses invented by the political leadership of the day. These rested on accusations against a large group of progressive Slovak politicians and intellectuals who were alleged to hold anti-Czech, bourgeois-nationalist views. The consequences were far-reaching—from an under-estimation of the co-operation of democratic forces in politics to rigid views on aesthetics and culture.

[13] Cf. M. Otáhal, *Zápas o pozemkovou reformu v ČSR* (The Struggle for Land Reform in Czechoslovakia), 268 pp. (Prague, 1963); K. Kratochvíl, *Bankéři* (Bankers), 460 pp. (Prague, 1962); O. Mrázek, *Vývoj průmyslu v Českých zemich a na Slovensku od manufaktury do roku 1918* (Development of Industry in the Czech Lands and in Slovakia from Handicraft to 1918), 491 pp. (Prague, 1964); R. Olšovsky, V. Průcha, H. Gebauerová, and others, *Přehled hospodářského vývoje Československa v letech 1918–1945* (Survey of the Economic Development of Czechoslovakia, 1918–45), 741 pp. (Prague, 1964); J. Mlynarik, *Štrajkove boje na Slovensku* (Strike Struggles in Slovakia), vol. I (industry, 1921–24), 227 pp.; vol. II (agriculture, 1919–20), 1961, 440 pp.; K. Kořalková, *Hnutí nezaměstnaných v Československu v letech 1929–1933* (Movement of the Unemployed in Czechoslovakia, 1929–33), 372 pp. (Prague, 1962).

[14] Cf. V. Mencl, *Na cestě k jednotě—Komunistická strana Československa v letech 1921–23*) (On the Path to Unity—the Communist Party of Czechoslovakia, 1921–23), 388 pp. (Prague, 1964); and the studies by M. Klier of B. Smeral, an outstanding leader of the workers' movement.

[15] Cf. the studies by M. Hájek, also V. Suchopár, *Komunistická internacionála proti fašismu v letech 1921–1935* (The Communist International against Fascism, 1921–35), 329 pp. (Prague, 1964).

[16] Cf. the study by M. Reiman of the October 1917 rising in Petrograd, published in 1966 in the journal *Příspěvky k dějinám KSČ*.

Hungary
ZOLTÁN HORVATH

Recovering from the Past

Small nations with a relatively short past always have the greatest difficulty in developing a historiography that is independent of the state and its institutions, detached from party politics and the pressures of powerful groups. This being so, it tends to become a mere tool in their hands and a reflection rather of current interests than of actual conditions.

Balint Homan, the Hungarian historian who later, as minister of education in several Horthy governments, became notorious as a partisan historian, wrote in 1931 that the earlier historians 'by means of anachronisms which make a mockery of history try to transpose the aims, ideas, and principles of their own era to days long past, although not a jot or particle of them are actually to be found in those times'.

Josef Révai (1899–1959), the communist ideologist, commented on this attitude to history: 'We do not want to be observers after the event. Our approach to history is that of participants in the struggles of today', for 'only a fighter can understand other fighters'.

Homan continually violated his own principles, and deliberately tried to deceive his readers, but what he said is the only true basis for all historiography. Révai, on the other hand, announced quite openly that for him the purpose of writing history was to serve the politics of the present. But the true mission of the historian cannot be accomplished in this fashion. The historian must describe the events with which he is concerned with as much fidelity to truth as possible, although he has the right to add such comments and interpretations as he considers necessary. In no circumstances, however, may he do what Révai suggests—namely, distort reality and manipulate past events to fit into the framework of his *a priori* thesis.

This had to be said before starting to examine the actual state of Hungarian historiography, the problems with which it has to cope, and the obstacles which hinder it in the fulfilment of its task.

Henrik Marczali, a distinguished liberal historian, wrote in his book *Die Nationalität als geschichtsphilosophisches Problem* (1905):

It is the tragedy of the Hungarian nation that for a full three hundred years (that is, from Turkish domination in 1526 until the treaty of 1867), the sense of being a Hungarian had to transcend all feelings of human brotherhood, for in order to hold out, the Hungarian had to concentrate on remaining a Hungarian. ... He saw a threat in everything foreign regardless of whether it was in itself good or bad.[1]

These words are enlightening, for it follows from them that in Hungarian historiography events, people, and their interrelationships are judged not by moral, humanitarian, or even utilitarian standards, but that a special Hungarian yardstick is employed. In Hungarian historiography, or rather in the national consciousness that developed under its influence, anything was good insofar as it was Magyar, and at the same time everything which was Magyar must of necessity be good.

Thus it could and did happen that Gyula Szekfü, a strong supporter of the Habsburgs and the Church, was virtually banned from Hungarian cultural life because he had had the courage to mention in his writings that the national hero Ferenc Rákoczi II (a leader of the anti-Habsburg uprising at the beginning of the eighteenth century) lived as an exile in Paris on the proceeds of a house of prostitution and of gambling.

To take another example: Sándor Károlyi—Rákoczi's commander-in-chief during the same period—has survived in the national consciousness as the basest of traitors, because when he realized in 1711 that the uprising had been defeated and that his forces were nearing exhaustion, he made peace with the dynasty (thereby ensuring that the country retained as much independence as before and that the privileges of the nobility were secured).

Gyula Szekfü, who, 200 years after the event, had the temerity to speak up for the truth, was practically expelled from the ranks of the Hungarian historians, just as half a century earlier Béla Grunwald, who was himself not free from chauvinism and had not originally been a professional historian, was driven to suicide because of the reaction to his comments on the Hungarian nobility in his work on the reign of King Josef II.

The result of all this was that professional historians hesitated to embark on big, comprehensive tasks and devoted themselves rather to the study of sources and to questions of detail, retreating on to territory which was less exposed to attack. The only exceptions were the historians who were prepared to submit to the demands of the chauvinists, but they too were unable to produce works of significance. Much of the important source material was held at Siebenbürgen, and even more was in Vienna. It was not easy to get access to it, nor to the private archives of the great aristocratic houses. The fact that they were almost all closed to professional research was to have fateful consequences, for in the campaign of 1944-45 most of the archives were destroyed without ever having been examined. Thus contemporary historical research has lost some irreplaceable and indispensable documentary sources.

In the 1870s Mihály Horvath pointed out that 'only if borne aloft on the wings of public interest can our historiography reach the heights that nations of culture have already attained'; and Imre Madzsar wrote in *Szasadok* (1908), p. 483, that 'in our country scientific historical research has yet to solve the problems of the critical examination and compilation of source material'.

It was only to be expected that although in the years before 1914 some original and reliable works of history were produced, free of both nationalist and class prejudices, these did not fully come into their own. Erwin Szabó's work—*Gesellschaftliche und Parteikämpfe im Freiheitskampf von 1848-49*—could not be published until 1920, after his death in exile in Vienna in 1918. *Die Geschichte der Leibeigenschaft* by Ignac Acsádi (Budapest, 1906), and *Die Geschichte des ungarischen weltlichen Grossgrundbesitzes* by Péter Ágoston (Budapest, 1913), were important comprehensive works, but they were the exceptions and not characteristic examples of the output of research as a whole.

After the First World War, particularly from the autumn of 1919 onwards, that is to say in the Horthy period, the situation became even worse. The revolutionary interval was too short for any major work to be produced. Defeat in the war brought in its train the loss of two-thirds of the nation's territory and the only result of the two revolutions was the reconquest of the state by the former ruling classes, which, as a result of the war and of their terror of another revolution, wielded their power more brutally than ever before. The great landed estates were kept intact and the government remained in form a monarchy. In this situation, not only did the rulers force the historians into their service, but they also induced them without much difficulty to support the popular agitation of the irredenta movement.

Thus in the twenty-five years between the two world wars historiography made no progress in research or in uncovering the facts. It was prevented on the one hand by the terrorism of the counter-revolutionary regime, and on the other by the policies of the Succession States—the Little Entente—set up under the Paris peace treaties, which were hostile to Hungary and bent on the assimilation of their new territories.

The most eminent historian of this epoch, Gyula Szekfü, realized clearly enough (and indeed put down in writing), that the greatest danger for the historians lay in sectional influences of every kind. Nevertheless, he himself fell to a remarkable degree under the influence of the Catholic Church (not of the religion!) which played a leading role in the counter-revolution, and wrote a misleading work that could be and was used as propaganda in support of the 'Christian course' of the counter-revolution. *Drei Generationen* (Budapest, 1922) dealt with the history of Hungary from 1825 to 1918 and made a deep impression on its readers. It went through several editions and practically became the Bible of the Horthy era.

Szekfü belonged to the school of historical thought which tries to avoid a purely political view of history and to gain a better understanding by a clarification of its ideological, economic, and social aspects. This work was consciously designed to propagate a certain point of view, without using falsifications and lies in the presentation of facts. The pragmatic narrative of events was, however, completely overshadowed by his tendentious, pro-clerical, and chauvinistic comments. The causes of the catastrophe, he declared, were not the policies of the ruling classes and the maintenance of a semi-feudal social system, not the unjust apportionment of the land nor the poverty of the three million landless rural proletarians, nor the failure to understand and meet the needs of the various minorities, nor the squabbles of the gentry; he attributed Hungary's situation to the radicalism of the middle class (in fact, it was very weak), to urbanization (which in fact had not proceeded very far), and not least to the increase in the influence of the Jews.

When, after 400 years, the Hungarians regained their political independence (not indeed by their own efforts, but as a consequence of the disintegration of the Habsburg empire), their defeat in the war and the dismemberment of their national territory, whereby 2,500,000 Hungarians were forcibly turned into a minority group, prevented any real progress being made towards the construction of a true historiography. The nation came no nearer to the formation of a public opinion and a national atmosphere which would reflect and embody the course of its historical past. On the contrary, the writing of history became even more markedly shaped by its 'Hungarocentric' outlook, even more complacent and chauvinistic; against the background of its distorted picture of the past, it conjured up unrealistic visions of the nation's future.

As in all other sectors of public and private life, the great break came first with the ending of the war in 1945 and the occupation by the Soviet army, and later with the upheaval in 1949, with the advent of the dictatorship of the proletariat and the first terror trials.

In 1944–45 the Soviet forces drove out the armed gangs of Hungarian fascists together with the German army, and the new government put an end to the counter-revolution and the outdated overlordship of the landed nobility. From 1945 to 1949 Hungary had a parliamentary and republican form of government and was a sort of middle-class democracy, with a tendency however to more and more centralization. From 1948 onwards, after the two workers' parties, the social-democrats and the communists, amalgamated, there was a step by step development towards the dictatorship of the proletariat and a people's democracy. The system which came into being in 1949 was abolished in 1956 following the well-known events in the autumn of that year. Amends were made as far as possible for the cruelties and illegalities of the past, but the principles of government of a people's democracy and a dictatorship of the proletariat were retained. Thus in the history of the two decades following the defeat of 1945 we can distinguish three distinct periods: (a) The period of bourgeois democracy; (b) the Stalinist years 1949–56, during which Mátyás Rákosi ruled by savagery and terror; and (c) the new post-1956 system of government, which is also Marxist-Leninist.

In 1945, after the liberation, those historians who had not compromised themselves during the counter-revolution and the nazi period, went to work enthusiastically to seek out the sources which had hitherto been closed to them and to do as much research as was possible in their devastated land. On the one hand they wanted to settle accounts finally and completely with Hungarian fascism and the followers of the Arrow Cross; on the other they were anxious to do the research that should have been undertaken years before but had always been neglected.

Gyula Szekfü, in a study published in 1942 entitled *Somewhere along the road we lost our way*, actually criticized his own activities during the counter-revolutionary era. He now disowned the views which he had formerly proclaimed and openly acknowledged that the path which had been followed for a quarter of a century was bound to lead to fascism and catastrophe.

The period between the end of the war and 1948 was too short to yield any works of basic importance; it was taken up with preparatory studies, but conditions gradually became more difficult and more dangerous. By 1949 the Zhdanov spirit was completely in the ascendant and once more, though under different slogans, free research and a genuine historiography were abandoned in favour of subordination to the requirements of politics.

After 1956 there was much more freedom of thought and criticism. The end of the 'cult of personality', the fall of Rákosi, and the resignation and subsequent death of Josef Révai, who in spite of his great talents had exerted a harmful influence on Hungary's intellectual life, all had their share in these developments and the great improvements which resulted from them. Yet it must be made clear that the effects of years of terror on cultural life, and thus on historiography also, have not been eliminated merely because certain decrees have been passed or even because certain books have been published. A fundamental change of atmosphere and determined efforts over many years are necessary if the air is to be thoroughly cleansed. Such changes bring grave and difficult problems in their train.

'History happens', wrote Karl Marx in one of his letters. The meaning of this pithy saying is—at all events for Marxist historians—that, however arbitrarily we try to interpret and distort history after the event, the sequence and finality of what has taken place are unalterable.

The historian is able to fulfil his task only if he has a passion for research and for the discovery and presentation of the truth. It is by no means sufficient to write *without actually lying*—the whole truth, if it can be established, must be told and nothing must be concealed.

During the periods of which we have spoken, before 1914 and even more between the two world wars, the truth was not acceptable, for just as it was more important to be a Hungarian rather than merely a human being, so it seemed more vital to preserve supposed class interests rather than to face the facts. Equally, during the years in which the 'cult of personality' flourished, it was just as impossible to have a free and truthful historiography as it had been in the earlier periods which had seen the other extreme of a feudal and reactionary social system.

A false slogan—incorrectly attributed to Lenin—was blazoned forth, declaring that art and science must be partisan; the political manipulators of cultural affairs poured scorn on so-called 'objectivism'. They determined in advance the results that art and scholarship were to achieve and thus succeeded in destroying both. Of course, it was never openly admitted that scholars and scientists were forbidden to search for the truth or to publish it. Yet in the majority of cases, and in all the subjects studied, it was quite unscientifically laid down in advance *what* should be declared to be the truth, *what* aspect should be given to reality, who should be condemned and who praised both in the past and in the present. The result was the triumph of deductive servility over inductive inference, and quite often these performances, however ingenious, bordered on the ridiculous.

There were no decrees obliging people to produce works of this kind, but the atmosphere had an oppressive, intimidating effect on individuals who were otherwise worthy and well-meaning. It is difficult to analyse the reasons that induced them to make statements on which they must now look back with shame.[2] It was characteristic of this state of affairs that political opportunism was the sole criterion in delivering historical judgments. Béla Kun was the undoubted political and intellectual leader of the Hungarian Soviet Republic of 1919. In the course of the 1930s, Kun became a victim of the Stalinist terror after he had been quite unjustifiably accused of treason and espionage. Upon this Rákosi and his accomplices considered it their duty simply to omit Kun from the history of the Hungarian workers' movement. Until 1956–57 it was forbidden even to mention his name. Dozens of such examples could be cited, and it is not surprising that in these circumstances historiography could not match up to Marx's aphorism. Moreover, if one considers that from about 1949 to 1954, or indeed until 1956, anyone who gave rise to the suspicion that he was opposing official doctrine was risking his liberty or even his life, it is clear why almost all the works of that period must today be discarded as worthless falsifications. It is interesting to note that the further back the period that was being studied lay in the past, the more possibility there was of forming and pronouncing an independent judgment on it. Several works were published on Hungary in the Middle Ages that are still of value today, but practically all the studies of the Habsburg era in the eighteenth and especially in the nineteenth century are pervaded throughout by the corrupt atmosphere of the time.

The consequence for historiography was the almost complete absence of any comprehensive works, although it was clearly impossible to transform public opinion without them. Historians expended their energies on trivialities, on documentation, on monographs concerned with uncontroversial questions, for these things entailed fewer risks and there was less danger in speaking the truth about them. But it was impossible to try to eliminate the mistaken historical conceptions of the last few decades or to edit new school books in a spirit of liberty. During these years there were many opportunities of completely altering Hungarian historiography and directing it onto new paths, but they had to be ignored.

After Stalin's death, but more especially after the autumn of 1954 when the first amnesties had been reluctantly conceded, unrest and impatience in the ranks of the scholars and artists began to grow. There were loud demands for the elimination of the false and mendacious leaders who had been endured for so long. After the shocking revelations of the Soviet Union's twentieth party congress, events moved more swiftly in Hungary, and in the spring of 1956 the historians insisted on a public discussion and showdown about past errors. Those among them who had hitherto, like absolute dictators, pronounced historical judgments against which there was no appeal, were now forced to confess that they had 'corrected' historical facts and had obliged others to do the same. So the way was opened for better things.

The movement which had brought about these changes in the field of historiography also led to the complete collapse of the system introduced by Rákosi and his crew. There followed the events of October 1956, and the government which afterwards came into being learnt from the mistakes of its predecessors. It soon became obvious that the methods employed by Rákosi and his servile followers were disappearing from public life together with terrorism and intimidation, that the atmosphere in learned circles was gradually improving, and that the Rákosi group had no chance of regaining power, although some of them have been able to hold on to certain key positions.

It again became more natural to feel personally safe and slowly people grew accustomed to the fact that it was no longer dangerous to utter fair and well-disposed expressions of opinion. After several previously convicted writers had been amnestied, the feeling of security became even stronger.

Yet historians and other scholars, who seek the truth in peaceful study, are slowly becoming aware that the sins of the Rákosi regime were not confined to administrative actions and illegalities, for which reparation could quickly be made—even if only to those who had survived, but that they had also infiltrated areas from which they could not later be easily banished. It seemed that the acts of violence, the threats and deceptions, must have exerted a stronger influence on the thoughts and attitudes of people than had been imagined; they had generated a system of auto-censorship so efficient that it has not yet stopped functioning today. In any case it is not so easy to put an end to such things, since certain restraints are still in force. There are even now quite a number of works of distinction which cannot see the light of day, simply because the functionaries of the publishing houses or of newspaper editorial boards refuse to accept the responsibility of publishing them. These are, however, exceptional cases, which have been mentioned only for the sake of absolute frankness.

For historians, as for all those whose labours are embodied in their writings, it is an indispensable condition of existence that their word is accepted and that they are trusted. Since 1956 the intellectuals have had to learn that though such trust is easily lost, much labour and effort is needed to regain it. Ten years after Rákosi's fall and the retreat of Révai, whose disciples had been active in nearly all sectors of cultural life, our historiography— more perhaps than any other discipline—is still fighting desperately to regain its public standing, or rather to win a greater trust than it has ever before enjoyed.

Consider only the traces left by the false doctrines that were inculcated for so many years. During these fifteen years or so a new generation has grown up—the generation of today's young historians. It is only with the greatest difficulty and by bitter inward conflict that they are managing to shake off the false dogmas with which they had been indoctrinated—and not all of them can or want to make the effort. It must be remembered that not all who flourished during the bad years have resigned or been relieved of their posts. In our universities we can still find many a historian who was a leading functionary during the worst periods of all. People like this—even supposing they really want to—will hardly go further in self-criticism than mouthing insincere confessions of error, and so they act as brakes on healthier developments.

Our historians are today faced with three difficult basic problems. At the head of them stands the question of home-grown nationalism and the collateral question of the relationship with the other peoples of the multi-national Danube basin. The infection of nationalism has gone very deep and the socialist leadership has hitherto failed to find the road to a peaceful solution. Lately in Hungary there has been an intense and systematic struggle against a parochial, Hungarocentric historiography. The fight is led by Professor Erik Molnár, one of the most distinguished of communist historians and Marxist theoreticians. His attitude has aroused lively, not to say bitter, controversy, and the discussions showed how deeply the youth was still imbued with the nationalistic, complacent outlook embodied in Révai's directives, drawn up purely for the furtherance of current political aims.

This problem becomes even more complex by reason of Hungary's relations with the other peoples and states of the Danube basin and by their behaviour. Hungarian historians are agreed that before 1918, when many small nationality groups were still under Hungarian rule, the chauvinistic, aristocratic governments of the Dual Monarchy made some very serious mistakes. Acknowledgement of this fact has had the curious effect of creating new errors of judgment and new distortions of the truth. In the admirable desire to avoid even the shadow of irredentism, the various nations of the Danube basin are all turned into models of correct behaviour whose actions have always been impeccable and whose desires have always been virtuous. There is a tendency to load the whole burden of past wrong-doing on to our own shoulders. So much so that when individual leaders of the various states put forward suggestions for solving the problem of inter-group relations, these are immediately acclaimed without further examination, although they are in no way superior to similar proposals by

Hungarians. For example, the confederation schemes of the Hungarian politicians Count Lászlo Teleki, Georg Klapka, and later even of Lajos Kossuth, are in no way inferior to the 1852 confederation plan of the Rumanian Nicolae Balcescu. But the Hungarian schemes are generally either condemned or ignored, whereas Balcescu's plan, strongly tainted though it is by Rumanian nationalism, is extolled. Each of the planners, with the possible exception of Count Teleki, wanted to ensure the supremacy of his own nation in the disputed territory and this was, of course, no way to solve the problem. The historians should have made it their business to clarify the whole subject, but this task was neglected owing to concern with less vital matters.

The Hungarian ruling classes in the eighteenth and nineteenth centuries made a bad mistake when they advanced the theory of the 'unitary Hungarian national state'. According to this, some of the citizens might have a different mother tongue, but they were all equally Hungarians. This sort of reasoning was mistaken and un-justifiable, but equally unjustifiable were the claims of the Rumanians, South Slavs, and Slovaks, who wanted to replace the minority groups of their own people in Hungary with Hungarian minorities in their own countries. They wanted to bring this about by annexing territory in which the Hungarian national group was by no means always in a minority. Hungarian historians have hitherto failed to clear these questions up. This could be done only if less consideration were shown for the various national suscepti-bilities. However, it should not be forgotten that historians have to be specially tactful and humane in their discussion of these delicate problems if they wish to avoid wounding the national sentiments of others, or themselves becoming the victims of their own nationalism.

The second important problem facing the historians of modern Hungary is how to detach themselves completely from the current political scene when they pronounce judgment on certain out-standing historical personalities. Béla Kun has already been given as an example, but just as good a one would have been Count Mihály Károlyi, the first president of the democratic bourgeois republic of 1918–19. He openly condemned Rákosi's terrorism, and was therefore compelled to go into exile (for the second time) in 1949. Until quite recently any discussion of his true role in the country's history has been taboo. Again, we can enumerate person-ages both of earlier and more modern times—from Count István

Széchenyi, the most important champion of civil progress in the first half of the nineteenth century to the leaders of the bourgeois revolution of 1918, from Lajos Kossuth, the leader of the 1848 uprising, to the prominent social democrats of the present century, not to speak of the communists who for one reason or another came into conflict with the rulers of their own regime, all of whom must still perforce be evaluated according to standards which have been decided upon in advance. Their true historical role cannot be judged with the necessary objectivity because of the constant interference of contemporary politics.

For instance, Oszkár Jászi, a man of great distinction, who after the turn of the century was the leader of the bourgeois radical movement and one of the first to draw attention to the dangers of leaving the minority problems unsolved, who, without fully discarding Hungarian nationalism, nevertheless proposed some kind of confederation, who far earlier than the socialists tried to alert public opinion to the evils of the prevailing agrarian system and took up the cause of land reform—this same Jászi and the bourgeois radical movement are still not being judged in the light of the part they played in their own time, but are condemned for not having been Marxists who accepted the doctrine of class warfare, and for having joined the anti-communists after their exile.

The situation has improved considerably since 1956, but not all the pretensions of dogmatic hindsight have yet been discarded. And, as already mentioned, there is still in the breast of every historian an active censor who must be banished if the way is to be cleared for the truth. For even though we do not believe that history is made by individuals, nevertheless we do believe that historical events and situations can best be demonstrated and understood in the person of individuals. The parts played by Széchenyi and Kossuth respectively in preparing and carrying through the uprising of 1848–49, cannot simply be left out of the history of this event; nor, unless the account is to be completely devoid of depth and sense, is it possible to omit from the history of the beginning of the century personalities like the bourgeois radical Jászi, the social democrats Ernö Garami and Zsigmond Kunfi, the Catholic bishop Ottokar Prohaszka, or the farmer István Nagyatádi Szabó, just because their roles are judged according to what is considered desirable today and not according to what was possible in their time.

There are still a number of functionaries, survivors of the

Rákosi era and the school of Révai, who react with anguish each time the verdict on some outlawed personality is at last reviewed with the requisite objectivity, but their numbers are decreasing day by day. They have been forced to accept the rehabilitation of Kun and Károlyi; if this kind of work is carried on steadily and devotedly they will be kept on the defensive.

The third complex of problems, which will certainly not be easily unravelled, is bound up with the history of the workers' movement. On this subject dogma is still in the ascendant, the whole of the nation's history is judged in the light of the workers' movement, and for the period of the last century the two are considered to be practically identical.

We, too, hold the opinion, which we have often expressed, that the workers' movement has been the most important economic, cultural, and social phenomenon of the last hundred years. The organization of the working class into trade unions and later into a powerful political party marks the turning point, but we do not believe that it was the *only* important development. We are of the opinion that it is not feasible to judge all important economic, cultural, and social developments solely in relation to the progress of the workers' movement, for by doing this we would learn merely the history of this body and not of the whole nation. The former ruling classes, the landowners and landed gentry, the princes of the Church, the big capitalists, bankers, and industrialists, even the tradesmen and the man-in-the-street, finally the 'freelance intellectuals'—they were all part of the nation and their actions were not always pernicious and oppposed to the public good. It is not possible to eliminate or suppress their existence without falsifying history.

Rákosi's declaration in 1955 that 'the history of Hungary is the history of the struggle for freedom' must be labelled as an untruth replete with dangerous illusions. Its only purpose was to delude the nation into believing that he, Mátyás Rákosi, had brought to fulfilment the aims which none of the leaders of the earlier anti-Habsburg movements—Bocskay, Bethlen, Rákoczi, the dukes of Siebenbürgen, and Lajos Kossuth—had been able to achieve.

Our purpose in discussing these problems was to pinpoint the difficulties with which Hungarian historians have to cope. However, during the last few years much has been accomplished and several valuable publications have appeared. Of these we will mention only the most important: first, the two-volume *History of Hungary*, edited by Erik Molnár (1964). Although this enormous work, written by twelve historians, has many faults, it is the best and most reliable of all the comprehensive histories so far published. Its main weakness—both characteristic and understandable —is that the nearer the history approaches the present time, the less objective and reliable it becomes. Unfortunately, the period covered by the work comes right up to the present and it is inevitable that the events of these turbulent years are not seen in a perspective which can be produced only by the lapse of time.

We have said that the methods of the years of terror have gone for good and no responsible leader wants to bring them back, but the atmosphere has not yet been fully cleansed and former prejudices and inhibitions have not been wholly discarded. The results are obvious in the Molnár volumes. The story of the middle ages and of modern times until the nineteenth century, indeed until the outbreak of the First World War, is very well done—in fact the analysis of the Treaty of 1867 and of the era of the Dual Monarchy from 1867 to 1918 is quite excellent.

The realization that the best service that historiography can render to any ideal or ideology is to present the truth as faithfully as possible has still not penetrated deeply enough into the consciousness of the historians. Truth is, of course, not a simple thing; on the contrary, it is very complex and has many different facets. It is only by the greatest concentration of effort that it is possible to ascertain at least a great part of the truth. Hungarian historiography has reached the stage where it has been freed from terror and intimidation. It is now the task of the historians to rid themselves of traditional prejudices and false illusions.

There is still much to be done if the trust and faith of former days is to be regained and progress in the right direction is to be made. This is the desire of all those of us who seek the truth.

NOTES

[1] František Palacky, an eminent Czech writer, expressed the same thought in *Gedenkblätter* (Prague, 1874), p. 154: 'There can be no question of the Slavs of the Danube Basin, the Wallachians, or even the Poles voluntarily acceding to a state which has set up the principle that the first duty of a citizen is to be a Magyar and to be a human being comes

only second to that . . .' The Czechs, to be sure, were under the domination of the Hapsburgs for centuries, but to begin with they belonged to the Indo-Germanic family of nations, and secondly their national territory remained undivided and was never torn to pieces. Hence the great differences in the development of the two peoples.

[2] Here is one particularly crass example: an eminent Professor of Romance culture at the University of Budapest wrote in his preface to a collection of Leonardo da Vinci's letters that Leonardo was the greatest and most gifted scholar-artist of the Renaissance; yet he could not develop his genius to its fullest extent because 'this was never possible before the great socialist October Revolution'.

Poland

FRANCISZEK RYSZKA

Some Recent Revaluations

The deep attachment of the Polish people to their literature and history is probably due to their cultural tradition, dating back to the Middle Ages when the Polish state, barely united after two centuries of feudal division, was forced to defend its national integrity, its very existence, against expansion by the Teutonic Order. It is commonly held by Polish historians that the beginnings of Polish national identity, which was something more than the awareness of belonging to a separate cultural or religious group, have their origins in that period.

On the other hand, just as in other countries of Europe, Polish awareness of itself as a modern nation developed in the course of the nineteenth century. What made the process different in Poland from what it was in the rest of Europe was that it spread throughout Polish society in the course of a struggle for independence which, except for short intervals, lasted an entire century. Literature played an important part in this process, both belles-lettres and historiography, as seen in the work of Joachim Lelewel (1786–1861), the father of history as a science in Poland.

A contemporary, more or less, of Ranke and Niebuhr, Lelewel was the first to apply the critical method to source material, as shown in his work in the field of the sciences which aid history. Unlike Ranke, however, Lelewel understood the didactic role of history, its significance for people oppressed by foreign rule. This did not mean that history was to be prepared '*ad usum delphini*'. To select as themes those subjects and ideas which represented Poland's remarkable past was one way of instilling hope into the hearts of Poles and reinforced their opposition to attempts by the partitioning powers to destroy their morale.

The historical sciences actually took shape in the second half of the nineteenth century. They owe their development to the so-

234

called Cracow School (J. Szujski, W. Kalinka, M. Bobrzyński, *et al.*), often called the pessimistic school. The scholars from Cracow, professors at the oldest university in Poland, the Jagellonian University (one of the two Polish universities with full legal rights under the partitions), represented an ideologically conservative movement, and stood in opposition to those whose aim was to achieve national independence as well as those who were dissatisfied with the political situation at the time. The suppression of the January 1863 uprising in those territories annexed by Russia, Prussia's increased power after achieving victory in its wars with Austria and France, and the autonomy granted to Galicia by the Viennese government in 1867—all this bode ill for those who dreamed of an uprising. Instead it induced the Poles to accept the *status quo* and come to terms with the partitioning powers, especially in those territories under Austrian domination. The Cracow School rationalized these views to a certain extent. Their analytical, even punctilious, studies of the various historical periods indicated the reasons for the fall of the Polish state; they saw the seeds of the partition of Poland in the sins of the Poles themselves, in the anarchy rampant in Poland in the seventeenth century, and in the lack of respect for the authority of the state.

The views propagated by the Cracow School did not withstand the test of time; though they made a lasting contribution, no one was found to take up their cause. Their work greatly increased interest in the past, contributed to the formulation of research methods, and promoted the search for source material. Indeed, it was only with this school that the study of recent history became a university discipline.

The Cracow School may have been critical and pessimistic, but the zeal with which it investigated the history of the Poles was no less fervent than that of Lelewel and his disciples, while both groups understood the importance of history as education. This idea was to reappear in Polish historiography, in various movements, schools, and specialities: economic history (F. Bujak in Lwów, J. Rutkowski in Poznań from the founding of the university in 1919), political and legal history (O. Balzer, B. Ulanowski, St. Kutrzeba), and the history of Polish culture (A. Brückner, K. Estreicher). Polish historiography was closely involved with law, economics, ethnography, and sociology perhaps much earlier than in other countries, and certainly long before it became programmatically and institutionally connected with the other humanities. The outstanding sociologist, Ludwik Krzywicki (1859–1941), a pioneer of Marxist thought in Poland, was interested in history, as was another outstanding sociologist, Florian Znaniecki (1882–1941), one of the founders of the school of empirical sociology and the teacher of a whole pleiad of scholars, both in Poland and in the United States, to which country he emigrated in 1939.

None the less historiography in the strict sense developed independently. It continued to explain the reasons for Polish failures; it continued to involve itself in political matters vital to the Polish nation. Even after 1918, when Poland regained its independence, it would be difficult to name many historical works published in the country which were not concerned with the history of Poland. Those few which did appear were written with the object of examining Poland's role in the wider arena of political history. Szymon Askenazy (1866–1935), an outstanding representative of the comparative method in history, was the author of one such work, *Napoleon a Polska* (1918–19). This had been preceded a few years earlier by a book on a similar subject, written by Marceli Handeslman (1882–1945). Poland in the Napoleonic era is a theme close to the heart of the Polish historian. The reason for this may be that it was a period of great enthusiasm and effort on the part of the Poles, though one which yielded few results. It may also be due to the strong influence of French culture in Poland, which dates back at least to the middle of the eighteenth century.

To return to Marceli Handelsman for a moment: he was the author of the definitive work on the methodological approach in history, *Historyka* (1921) which, by virtue of its clarity, not to mention its pedagogical value, stands out as one of the most remarkable works ever to appear in this field. For many students of history it has been the basis of their education.

The study of Polish history could hardly fail to pay considerable attention to Polish-German relations. Centuries of proximity, more exactly, of German expansion to the east, generated continual conflict. An entire literature has been devoted to Poland's struggle against the Teutonic Order. The works of Józef Feldman (1899–1946) rank high among those written on modern and recent history. He wrote an excellent book on Bismarck's policy towards Poland, *Bismarck a Polska* (1939), and was one of the few scholars to do research on Polish-English relations during the eighteenth and nineteenth centuries. He belongs to that generation of scholars whose fate was especially cruel. Nazi policy, from the very beginning of the German occupation of Poland, was directed to the extermination of the Polish *élite*, first through 'Aktion AB' (*ausserordentliche Befriedigung*), and from then on without a break to the day of liberation. Historians were the object of special persecutions as investigators of the past of a nation deemed inferior by the nazis, and destined to be nothing more than slaves. Scholars who were engaged in research on the early Slavs were ruthlessly persecuted for daring to oppose the official nazi version of the past of the Slav territories, which described that past as German. Except for those who were abroad and those who could remain in hiding, everyone in this field was murdered. A typical example of nazi behaviour in Poland was the campaign to eliminate the professors of the Jagellonian University of Cracow in November 1939. During that campaign, known as '*Sonderaktion Krakau*', almost all the professors and lecturers of that university were imprisoned and then deported to the concentration camp at Sachsenhausen. Stanislaw Estreicher, the outstanding legal historian, was among those who perished there. Many other distinguished scholars suffered a martyr's fate. The hardships, the need to hide, the deprivation endured during the occupation, all took their toll of men who were in their prime. All institutions of higher learning and almost all of the secondary schools were closed. All scholarly or scientific activities, even when conducted privately, were forbidden. Libraries and archives were confiscated and a part of the collections sent to Germany. Many of them were destroyed or damaged in military operations, which were especially intense during the Warsaw uprising of 1944. Only some of the collections were hidden, often at great personal risk to librarians and archivists, and thus managed to survive the war.

Although the conditions might have appeared hopeless, historical research went on. Difficult as it may be to believe, almost every kind of activity was pursued—the collection of sources, research, and teaching. All this was of course done in the utmost secrecy, for the penalty was death. The conduct of conspiratorial scholarly and educational activity is probably a unique phenomenon in the history of Poland under the nazi occupation. The fact is, however, that seminars were conducted, examinations held, records sedulously kept (chronicles of life in the ghettos, for instance, a few of which survived the war), and archives secretly researched. One of the most interesting documents concerning everyday life during the occupation is the diary kept by the Warsaw economist and sociologist, Ludwik Landau. It covers the period from the beginning of the occupation to the day he was arrested in 1944. Those parts which were discovered were published in three volumes (1959–61). They are an invaluable source for day-to-day life and the moods of the people at that time, as are the notes found in the ghettos. The diary of a teenage boy, David Sierakowiak, discovered after the war, surpasses in its tragedy the famous diary of Anne Frank.

Even before the commission headed by Lord Vansittart was formed, evidence of crimes perpetrated by the nazis was being gathered by Poles, a task which required great effort and entailed great personal risk. Today they are housed in the archives of the Nazi War Crimes Commission, formed immediately after the liberation of Poland. These, and the documents captured during the German retreat, serve as evidence in proceedings against persons accused of war crimes, but they are also, and will remain, a source for the historian.

If we have dwelt on events that are well known to the Poles (though possibly less so to foreign historians), it was in order to demonstrate what tremendous difficulties faced Polish historians. True, their country was free again, but terribly ravaged by war. Against dreadful odds, they had struggled to remain alive in the underground and not to admit defeat. But the losses were heavy, whether they took part in conspiratorial activity or simply tried to survive.

Those who did survive saw victory, and the circumstances accompanying and following it gave a great impetus to their work. The new political system, the entirely new international relations, the new national boundaries, the social and political revolution— all this raised many questions which required old views to be revised and the past re-examined. From this moment Polish historiography begins to develop as never before.

Recent history (the equivalent of the French *histoire contemporaine*, the German *Zeitgeschichte*, the Russian *noveishaya istoriya*, and the Italian *storia contemporanea*) is generally understood as the history of living generations whose *dramatis personae* dwell in our midst or in the memory of the living. Polish historiography has as its *a quo* limit the re-establishment of Poland as an independent nation in 1918, which came about as the result of the First World War and the Russian Revolution, with the deposition of the tsar and the defeat of the other two partitioning powers.

Between the wars work on recent history developed very slowly and with great difficulty in Poland. As in other countries, it was refused recognition by the academic historians, and denied acceptance as a scholarly discipline on the ground that the necessary distance was lacking and emotions were too deeply involved. Moreoever, the need for discretion in regard to still living historical figures made it impossible to be objective, and threatened to turn historical literature into mere journalism. The conservative judgment of what constitutes a truly reliable source also entered into play. Such a source were the documents kept in the archives of the political authorities, which obviously were not available to the historian. The governments set up by the partitioning powers left little material behind, while the political authorities of newly-independent Poland refused to open the archives to historians. Memoirs were published, of course, but very few in comparison with other countries, where they poured out in a veritable avalanche.

It is little wonder, then, that the first serious attempt to reconstruct recent history was made not by a university historian, but by a socialist journalist (although a historian by training), Adam Próchnik. His *Pierwsze Pietnastolecie Polsk i Niepodległej* (1933) is actually a history of the Polish political parties and the parliament, whose activities were drastically limited by Pilsudski and his adherents. The book was a sharp attack on the government's policies and was subsequently banned, an action which discouraged further effort along these lines.

However, a good deal of work was done in the field of economic and social history. Sociologists trained in the traditions of the Krzywicki and Znaniecki schools investigated major social processes at work in Poland (emigration, changes among rural youth), and the microstructures of various situations which were the source of conflict. The material gathered provides valuable information on the social situation at the time, compelling the sociologist to look to the past (as in the works of Nina Assorodobraj), and the historian to use new research methods. This trend in studying the history of recent times was to come clearly in evidence only after the war, and was to be the reason why many historians turned to Marxism, first in economic and social history, later in other historical fields.

Today the Marxist approach to the past undoubtedly predominates among Polish historians, although Marxism does not hold a monopoly in the interpretation of history. The simple explanation given to this in many quarters in the West is erroneous; too neat a version of causal relationships is generally false. The Marxist approach was not forced upon historians (because it proceeded from official doctrine), and they did not have to conform to it for fear of having their careers destroyed or other more frightening consequences.

Marxist methodology did not become popular among historians overnight; controversy and polemics were not avoided. A good example of this is the first post-war Congress of Polish Historians, held in Wroclaw in 1948. The first works to be published in post-war Poland on periods close to recent history, such as the books by Professor Wereszycki and Professor Kula on the political and economic history of Poland at the turn of the century, were not at all Marxist, though the views expressed by the latter are very close to those advanced by Marxists. It was the younger generation of historians who began to write from the Marxist point of view, and that in research on recent history. The expansion of research in this area was not the result of ideological pressure either, nor of any other form of coercion, although it cannot be denied that the political authorities gave it encouragement and support. The principal reason was the desire to find an answer to the question which plagued the nation: What was the source of Poland's weakness which ended in tragic defeat in September 1939? In order to satisfy this need the authorities gave access to practically all the archive material up to 1945.

Historians turned their attention first to economic and social questions. They saw the source of the country's weakness in its economic backwardness, the outdated social structure (especially in the rural areas where a large part of the land was owned by wealthy landowners), and foreign influences in industry, finance, and commerce. Many studies of value appeared in the 1950s: L. Grosfeld's work on the economic crisis in 1929–33; F. Ryszka and J. Popkiewicz on heavy industry in Upper Silesia; C. Madajczyk on the rural reforms of 1925. Shortly thereafter more detailed studies began to appear: by Z. Landau, J. Tomaszewski, M. Mieszczankowski, M. Drozdowski, etc. Regional studies rank high in work done on economic and social history: monographs on the industrial system, banking institutions, maritime trade, and rural regions. The careful analytical studies by the late Professor

Stýs on the demographic processes in the villages of Little Poland, covering the period from the reforms of Joseph II to the present day, are still insufficiently appreciated. Stýs was not a Marxist; he was rather a neo-Malthusian. His great error lay in making far-reaching generalizations on the basis of his research of micro-structures. None the less he was a master of the technique of investigating economic phenomena, and his work reveals a care for detail and precision unmatched in the works of contemporary economic historians. He was one of the first to apply higher mathematics to historical research, a technique only now being adopted by historians in other fields.

Whilst it cannot be denied that these historical, economic, and social studies represented an important scholarly achievement, there was much in them that was superficial. This can possibly be explained as the result of their too great desire to synthesize—the authors were at times fascinated by the wealth of sources made available to them. In any case they paved the way for more solid and more critical studies, in which many of their views were attacked. The worth of a historical study is measured, however, by the creative inspiration it is capable of arousing long after it has become outdated. It is not unknown for the work of one man to give rise to a movement in which the disciples destroy the product of the master.

One fault of the work written in this earlier period is the over-emphasis on the economic aspect of historical processes and the under-estimation of political elements, especially those of a national character. Some authors proved incapable of correctly assessing the great (though negative) effect that the absence of a state of their own and their dependence on the economies of the partition-ing powers had on the Polish economy. Their interpretation of the role of state initiative in the pre-war Polish economy was far too limited, and they failed to appreciate the real economic achieve-ments of the time. This provoked an interesting controversy on the evaluation of production indices. Though the question was not resolved, it did encourage historians to make greater use of theoretical economic studies, and as a result the study of recent history has been enriched by an understanding of political economy.

The history of the working class has also become the subject of a growing number of socio-economic studies, concentrating on their material situation and working conditions, and on the social movements which eventually were transformed into organized political activity. The research conducted by the university research centres in Warsaw and Lódz, under the direction of the late Professor Natalia Gasiorowska, is very important in this respect. Obviously, in a country where the government is headed by the party which represents the ideals of the working class, the past history of that class attracts special attention.

This interest finds its expression in the publication of numerous source books, monographs, and articles on the history of the socialist and communist movements. A special institute attached to the Central Committee of the Polish Workers' Party is engaged in this work; it employs a great many specialists and has its own library and archives, consisting of original documents and microfilms of documents from other archives, as well as manuscript memoirs, diaries, reports, conspiratorial periodicals and leaflets. It publishes its own quarterly, *Z pola walki* (From the Battlefield). It is not the only body interested in research into the history of the working-class movement: the staffs of other institutes and universities have also made their contribution. The total published output is imposing: of special importance are those works dealing with the history of the Polish Socialist Party, the Revolution of 1905–07, and the strikes and workers' demonstrations in the 1930s, when the idea of a popular front was coming into existence (the studies of H. Jablonski, T. Daniszewski, Z. Kormanowa, F. Tych, *et al.*). As for the right-wing and centre parties, they have been poorly investigated, although a number of interesting studies can be found in this area, too.

There is a strong demand for a comprehensive history of the Polish working-class movements from its beginnings in the 1870s to the present day. This drive towards presenting a synthesis is not confined to the history of the Polish working-class movement. Polish historiography in general today is characterized by a tendency towards synthesis. This is an inherent feature of Marxist historiography. For Marxists, after all, history is not a mere collection of accidental and isolated facts, but is composed of dialectically interwoven relations of cause and effect, the source of which lies in the economic structure of society. Consequently, the task of history is to explain the past as well as describe it. Having survived a brutal war and occupation by a foreign power, the Polish people are especially predisposed to searching for the meaning of history. They need to understand how such cruelty and disregard of the law came about, how it was possible for crimes on such a mass scale to take place; they need to know what is a historical regularity and what is a denaturalization of history. Their interest goes beyond mere curiosity, such as is common in stable societies. They are not interested merely in how it was—*'wie es eigentlich gewesen ist'*—to use Ranke's formula. This every Pole knows, for history marched ruthlessly and brutally into every Polish home. Rather he asks himself why it was so. Marxism gives him a rational answer: it presents history as a rational and logical field into which a phenomenon like nazism can be placed without going into involved metaphysical speculations.

The ambition of Polish historians to synthesize is conditioned by purely practical considerations as well. The war and occupation reduced the teaching staff at universities and in schools (school teachers at all levels were considered a highly dangerous and harmful element by the nazis), and many university library collections were destroyed or damaged. After the war there was a lack of textbooks and materials at all levels. Before the war contemporary history was not taught. After the war it was decided to teach this subject at all levels up to and including the university.

Through the combined efforts of the scholars at the Polish Academy of Science Historical Institute (founded 1953), work was begun on a multi-volume history of Poland. At the present moment the volume devoted to the period 1918–21, that is, the period in which the new state was formed and in the process of consolidation, is being discussed. The authors are H. Zielinski, T. Jedruszczak, *et al.*

Many monographs in all fields of history would have to be written to do justice to this short though crucial period. It was then that Poland regained her independence, fought battles to establish the limits of her territory, even fought a regular war with Soviet Russia, took part in the Paris Conference, was a signatory to the Versailles Treaty, and signed several international agreements (principally with France), only to have them become a burden on the foreign policy of later Polish governments. In internal affairs it was a period of sharp social conflict (as it was throughout Central Europe, largely under the influence of the revolution in Russia), when the shape of the state and the political structure were being decided. The first constitution was ratified in 1921 (it was to remain in effect until 1935, though with great changes). Finally, the first attempts at integrating the Polish economy were being made.

Thus there is no lack of subjects to engage the attention of the historians. The synthesis being prepared by the Historical Institute can be no more than introductory. There is a great deal of archival material which has not yet been used (for example, the content of hitherto unknown treaties between Poland and France concerning Upper Silesia), and foreign as well as domestic archives have still to be studied. The exchange of information and archive material has been proceeding favourably, especially with the other countries of the socialist bloc. Contacts with archivists in the German Democratic Republic have been very fruitful; the archive material in that country for the period 1918–45 has been made accessible to Polish historians.

To return, however, to research on the early period in independent Poland (conventionally known as the Second Commonwealth), the preparatory work does not exclude the discussion of controversial views, in particular regarding the effect of regaining independence on the later history of the country. It is generally agreed that Poland was governed by nationalistic and anti-communist right-wingers who were intolerant towards national minorities (approximately 30 per cent of the population), especially in the eastern provinces, and suffered from a dangerous power-politics megalomania, far from the ideals of those who had fought and died for Poland's freedom. In the opinion of the present generation the blame for the catastrophe which destroyed the nation in 1939 falls on them. But historians cannot be guided by their emotions, nor allow themselves to fall under their influence into an over-simplified causalism. Today most historians admit that regaining independence was of colossal importance, and the inter-war period one in which Poland developed her culture and her art. Above all it was a period when the sense of national identity increased both in the cities and the villages. Poland was a predominantly agricultural nation, and as the peasants were kept in ignorance by the partitioning powers, the consciousness of national identity was not widespread. With independence, however, both peasant and worker acquired those sentiments of patriotism which were so strongly manifested during the nazi occupation. Much of this must be attributed to the influence of the Second Commonwealth.

As historians learn more about this period, pre-war Polish

history is being revaluated. But there is one important link missing. I have in mind biographical writing, which is sadly neglected by the historians. Not only is it a genre especially attractive for the reader, but in the proper proportions it helps to fill the gaps in our knowledge of the past which cannot be filled by even the most thorough analysis of mass phenomena. It is beyond doubt that individuals can act as catalysts in certain historical processes, while at other times they can check them. But Polish historiography has not yet produced a biography of such an important character as Józef Pilsudski, nor of his chief antagonist, the head of the nationalist bourgeois party and its ideologist, Roman Dmowski; the peasant leader, several times head of state, Wincenty Witos, the socialist leader and parliamentarian, Ignacy Daszyński, and finally, the head of the Christian Democratic Party and political leader of the Silesian rebellion, Wojciech Korfanty, still await full treatment. Not only are they important figures, they are exceptionally colourful ones as well.

Nor have the biographies of outstanding communist leaders yet been written. There was Adolf Warski, an outstanding theoretician and politician, Maria Koszutska, a person of great personal charm, Jerzy Lenski, and others. Their works have been published, their speeches and correspondence will soon be issued, but no historian has yet been tempted to write their biographies and establish their place in the history of the nation. The reasons for this are understandable. Almost all the leaders of the Polish Communist Party suffered a tragic end; as victims of the Stalinist purges they either died in prison or were executed. Another barrier to the writing of biographies has been the misguided views concerning the role of the individual, which was thought to be minor in comparison with the role of the masses. Fortunately, this view no longer prevails, but the fact remains that biographical literature continues to be more than poor.

Until recently there has been very little on the Second World War and the participation of Poles in the ultimate victory of the Allies. An exception are the works devoted to the martyrdom of the Poles and the terror they experienced under the nazis, but documentation continues to be of greater importance, beginning with *Documenta Occupationis Teutonicae*, published immediately after the war by Professor K. M. Pospieszalski of Poznań. Monographs are still rare, in spite of the effort put into research, especially within the last few years, and have tended to be regional in character.

The reasons for this delay are very complicated, and psychological factors are not to be excluded. Awareness of the defeat suffered in September 1939 clouded all appraisals of the Polish military effort. At the end of the 1940s and the beginning of the 1950s historians were concerned principally to reveal the shortcomings and weaknesses which led to defeat in order to find a rational explanation for it. The view they took of the recent past was on the whole very critical, as though the Cracow School had come to life again. Research concentrated on the military errors and the tragic political isolation which resulted from the government's foreign policy. The Warsaw uprising of 1944 was also regarded as a national defeat, although in both these campaigns the enemy suffered heavy losses and the moral victory was on the side of the Poles, something whose importance was fully recognized by that great political pragmatist, Winston Churchill.

Another reason for the delay was the lack of source material. The remaining archives and reports and the material left behind by the Germans had not yet been put in order; contact had not yet been made with foreign centres, in particular the microfilm library of German documents at the National Archives of the United States. Until recently there were not even enough experts in military history; these have only recently been trained in special institutes. Equally handicapping, especially for political and diplomatic history, was the lack of contacts with western historians and their work. This is no longer the case; contacts are now numerous and lively, but their absence was felt in earlier years.

So far there has been little in the way of discussion and debate with Western historians concerning the genesis of the Second World War and the course it took. An exception to this has been the group of historians attached to the Western Institute in Poznań, where much research has been going on into Western publications on these questions. Unfortunately, most of it has concerned German publications. Towards the end of the 1950s such discussions began to appear in other periodicals as well, starting with the *Kwartalnik Historyczny* (The Historical Quarterly) which published a long essay on the collective publication, *The Third Reich*, sponsored by UNESCO. A year later there appeared an article on the main trends in world historiography dealing with the Third Reich and nazism.

Polish historians, like the Polish public as a whole, are very sensitive to what is happening in the German Federal Republic, especially as there are historians there who are attempting to justify the institutions of the Third Reich. (This sensitivity is as marked on matters that do not necessarily concern nazi actions in Poland.) Some German historians are inclined to accept the nazi claim—with minor corrections, of course—that the Poles murdered 50,000 German nationals in the early stages of the war. This estimate is ten times that made by the nazis themselves, though both are complete nonsense. K. M. Pospieszalski has undertaken to prove the claim false; others have followed his example. Unfortunately, Poles are often seduced into polemics with German publications undeserving of the title historical, though this is understandable. One bad tradition of German historiography has been its rationalization of German expansionist policy, especially as concerns the East. No less a historian than Heinrich Treitschke supported these policies. Pseudo-historical studies aside—though they proliferate in West Germany and are very popular—serious historians in the German Federal Republic have made claims and advanced interpretations with which Polish historians cannot agree. The work of Gerhard Ritter on the German army and its relations with Hitler can serve as an example. On the appearance of J. W. Wheeler-Bennett's book, *The Nemesis of Power*, views were expressed which rehabilitated the traditions of the Wehrmacht.

Work done by Polish historians in this area is not limited to criticism of and polemics with foreign publications. Of late many studies have been written of the fronts on which Poles fought and on the events connected with the genesis of the Second World War. The crowning achievement of research on the Second World War has been the publication of *Wojna Wyzwolencza Narodu Polskiego w Latach 1939–1945* (The Polish Struggle for Freedom 1939–1945), by T. Rawski, Z. Stapor, and J. Zamojski, in which particular attention is paid to the activities of the partisans. Shorter monographs and articles of unequal merit have also appeared, of which some (e.g. the history of the Warsaw operation in 1944–45 by K. Sobczak) are of undoubted value, though they make no great pretensions to scholarliness. Taken as a whole, they show that the uniform view of the Polish contribution to the war effort is definitely a thing of the past. Opinion today is rather that this effort was greatly exaggerated from the military standpoint. It is the subject of animated discussion, however, as shown by the heated polemics over the books written by the military journalist

247

Z. Zaluski, who passionately, though not always very critically, defends the traditional view of the Polish armed struggle, an attitude close to the heart of the Poles.

Professional historians, that is university historians, do not as a rule take part in these polemics. Their reluctance to do so is completely understandable, though they cannot cut themselves off entirely, since the public turns to them as experts and arbiters. Hence the marked participation of historians in discussions in the press and on radio and television, on matters not always concerned with recent history.

The atmosphere is much calmer when it comes to work on political history. Here the past few years have seen the publication of several very valuable books: on Polish-German relations during the inter-war period (J. Krasucki, M. Wojciechowski), diplomatic history just preceding the war, from the point of view of Polish affairs (M. Turlejska, St. Stanislawska, K. Lapter, H. Batowski), the Polish question during the war (St. Jabiello, W. T. Kowalski).

M. Turlejska and Cz. Madajczyk have written a large study of Poland during the occupation, attempting a synthesis of the period. Turlejska, concerned with political and social history, is the first Polish historian to tackle the difficult question of German-Soviet relations from 1939 to 1941. Madajczyk writes more of economic and demographic problems, attempting—also for the first time—to establish exactly the losses in human life and the economic losses suffered by Poland in the war. A. Eisenbach has devoted himself to research on the tragic fate of the Polish Jews. Foreign authors have also written on this, and though they tried to be as objective as possible, their work suffers from their ignorance of Polish sources.

That Polish historians should devote themselves to a period in Polish history as dramatic as the Second World War is understandable. It is no different in other countries which suffered the same fate as Poland. Yugoslav historians have made an impressive contribution to the history of the nazi occupation of Europe and of the resistance movement, and much is being written on the same subjects in France and Italy. None the less, one can rightly criticize the Poles for their half-hearted interest in questions which do not directly concern Poland, even though they may be among the central problems of the epoch and must therefore have influenced the history of Poland. The internal history of the Third Reich has been treated, but not often. L. Hirszowicz has written on the

Near East policy of the Third Reich (this has appeared in English translation), and the present writer has published work on the governmental and legal systems of the Third Reich.

As much time has now elapsed since the end of the Second World War as separated the end of the First World War and the invasion of Poland in September 1939. This does not entitle us to draw any conclusions save that the events which have occurred since 9 May 1945 are now a proper domain for research. For this the atmosphere in Poland is now favourable, though it must be remembered that the use of archive material will of necessity be limited. This is dictated by reasons of state, and for all practical purposes research must be limited to the early stages of the new government. (May I state by way of reminder that the date for the formation of the new government in Poland is accepted as 22 July 1944.) So far the output on this period is still very meagre. Apart from the publication of some source material (more of which is now being prepared), one can note several monographs on social and economic problems (W. Góra on the rural reforms, J. W. Golebiowski on the nationalization of industry). Some political studies have also appeared, e.g. the much discussed, though inconsistently written book by K. Kersten on the Polish Committee for National Liberation.

There is the danger that the historian will be influenced by the situation at the time he is writing, but it is no greater than the dangers which face any historian, regardless of where he writes, who undertakes work on recent history. Whether he wants to or not, he is influenced by current politics, and this makes its mark on his personality. Polish historiography has no tradition of a court historiography, unless, of course, we are to count the Middle Ages. But then this was the same throughout Europe at that time. On the other hand, it has a tradition of service to the nation; that is how it developed into a modern scientific discipline. This might lead to deformation, or to its enclosure within the confines of national history. Within these confines, however, it can be extremely critical, and a critical attitude in regard to one's own past is healthy above all for the historian.

Yugoslavia

DIMITRIJE DJORDJEVIĆ

Work in Progress

In the course of the two post-war decades, Yugoslav historiography has shown marked progress, with respect both to the organization and the scope of research. This is reflected in the growing number of scholarly institutions, in the organization of archivist services, in the emergence of a considerable number of young historians, and in the publication of the results of their work.[1] The aim of this brief survey is to present, in a concise form, the main characteristics of this development, referring only to work on recent history.

Modern history is the subject of research conducted in the Yugoslav Academies of Sciences (the Serbian Academy of Sciences in Belgrade, the Yugoslav Academy in Zagreb, and the Slovene Academy in Ljubljana), in their departments of social sciences, as well as in inter-academic committees. The greater part of these studies is carried out in historical institutes, which are exclusively research institutions. In each constituent republic of Yugoslavia there are institutes for the study of the history of the Yugoslav peoples and institutes for the study of the labour movement. There is also a federal institute doing research into the history of Yugoslavia after 1918, and the Military Historical Institute. In addition to training young historians in their special subjects,[2] all of them are engaged in systematic and planned research into the history of the peoples of Yugoslavia and their relations with neighbouring nations. The work of all institutes is co-ordinated by the republic councils for scientific work, which also allocate the necessary funds. The institutes are administered by their councils, consisting of delegates from academies, universities, and archives (or other similar institutions), as well as of members of the scientific staff of the institutes. In this manner, collaboration with related institutions is encouraged. This method of work, with teaching left exclusively to universities, enables the staff of the institutes to concentrate all their efforts on research.

Recent and modern history is taught, in general and special courses, at the faculties of arts of eight Yugoslav universities (Belgrade, Novi Sad, Zagreb, Zadar, Ljubljana, Sarajevo, Skoplje, Pristina), in their departments of national and general modern history. In addition to their teaching duties, the university staffs undertake historical research, either within their own departments, or as external associates of historical institutes, from which they can obtain material or other kinds of assistance for archive research at home or abroad. Finally, historical research is also conducted in archives, and to some extent in libraries and museums (the museums of the Yugoslav socialist revolution are particularly active in the field of recent history).

Post-war historiography was given a strong impetus by the establishment of large-scale archivist services. Yugoslav archives, especially those in Serbia, suffered grave damage during the two world wars. One of the chief Serbian archives, that of the Ministry of Foreign Affairs, was burned twice (1915 and 1941), and during the occupation in the Second World War parts were removed to Austria and Germany. The documentation from another important source, the Serbian State Archives, containing materials from all Serbian ministries up to 1918, was taken from the building during the last war and stored in the cellars of neighbouring houses, with the consequence that all the files, registers, indices, etc. were seriously damaged.[3] Among the heaviest losses incurred during the Second World War was the destruction of the National Library in Belgrade, whose contents—500,000 valuable copies of books and periodicals—were burned during the bombing raid on 6 April 1941. After the war, long and patient work was required to reassemble the materials taken out of the country and to list and classify them again. Today, there are some seventy state, regional, and special archives in Yugoslavia. Among them are the republic, regional, and town archives, with documents on the national history of the peoples of Yugoslavia as well as materials on the economic, social, and cultural life of particular regions or towns. Important documents from the recent past are contained in the archives of the academies of science and historical institutes, with original documents about prominent personalities from the Yugoslav public and political scene. Substantial documentation about Yugoslavia in the period 1918–41 and about the war and the socialist revolution is to be found in the archives of the central organizations of the League of Communists of Yugoslavia, the institutes for the study of the labour movement, and the Military Historical Institute. In addition Serbian Orthodox and Catholic dioceses, as well as museums and libraries, also have archives, mostly with collections of manuscripts.

All archives are under the control of state authorities, and are run by archives councils. The majority of archives containing documentation for the period up to 1918, including the Yugoslav State Archives, with materials for the period after 1918, admit research workers without any restrictions, and permission to work in them is easily obtained. An exception, for obvious reasons, are the archives of the Secretariat of State for Foreign Affairs, the Military Historical Institute, and the League of Communists. Permission to work in them can be obtained for certain historical periods by submitting an application with a detailed description of the research to be done.

A substantial portion of the work being done is devoted to editing collections of domestic and foreign sources. They cover mainly important periods in recent Yugoslav history, the liberation uprisings in the early nineteenth century, the national renaissance, and economic, social, political, and cultural developments, the establishment of Yugoslavia (1914–18), the two wars and the socialist revolution. Thus, for example, Austrian, French, and Turkish sources about the Serbian uprising of 1804 are being systematically published.[4] Negotiations are conducted between the Serbian Academy of Sciences in Belgrade and the Institute of Slavonic Studies in Moscow on the joint publication of Russian sources about the first Serbian uprising (1804–13). Another broad area about which source material is being published is the national renaissance of Yugoslavs, the formation of the Yugoslav movement, the establishment of a modern society, and the organization of the first free states. A special place in this renaissance is taken by the development of the state of Montenegro, by the Illyrian movement in Croatia, and by the national awakening in Dalmatia.[5] From the history of Serbia, sources have been published providing data on its economic and social growth and on the influence of liberal ideas penetrating from Europe, especially after 1848.[6] Sources on the development of the Yugoslav movement in the 1860s and 1870s, the wars of Serbia and Montenegro, and the impact of the unification of Italy and Germany on the Yugoslav movement, are of a broader importance for the study of the history of the Balkans and of Europe in general. In 1965, the Serbian Academy of Science published an important collection of documents which throws new light on the integration of the Yugoslav movement in the nineteenth century.[7] A special committee of the Serbian Academy is collecting and editing documents on *Serbia and the Liberation Movements in the Balkans from 1856 to 1878*. The efforts to throw more light on the recent history of Macedonia, which have been greatly intensified during the past twenty years, have resulted in the publication of documents, letters, and memoirs of Macedonian revolutionaries of the late nineteenth and early twentieth century.[8] Side by side with the domestic sources, foreign documents have also been published, particularly those from the Viennese archives.

Following the publication of German, French, Austrian, English, Russian and other sources for the early years of the twentieth century, the Serbian Academy of Science in Belgrade is preparing for publication, in three series, documents from the Ministry of Foreign Affairs dealing with the foreign policy of Serbia from 1878 to 1918. The first volume of the third series (covering the year 1914) is to come out in 1967. The Historical Institute in Belgrade is preparing an edition of Viennese sources for the period after 1903.

Special attention has been given recently to the publication of sources concerning the formation of the Yugoslav state during the war of 1914–18, covering both politics and socio-economic trends in the Yugoslav region. The editorial work of the late Professor Šišić has been continued by a number of historians from Zagreb and Belgrade (A. Mandić, B. Krizman, B. Stulli, D. Šepić, J. Vidmar, D. Janković); the historical department of the Institute of Social Sciences in Belgrade is particularly active in this work. Materials from the 1919 peace conference of Paris have also been published.[9]

The research staff of the Institute for the Study of the Labour Movement collect, classify, and edit documents about the history of the labour and socialist movement. The historical section of the Central Committee of the League of Communists is also active in this field. The result of this work is the collection *Historical Archives of the Communist Party of Yugoslavia*, containing documents on the development of the socialist movement in all Yugoslav regions, on trade union organizations, on the economic and political struggle of the Yugoslav working class, etc. Considerable efforts have been made in publishing sources from the period of the Second World War and the socialist revolution in Yugoslavia. A large number of diaries, memoirs, records, and chronicles have been printed, a list of which can be found in the *Selection of Bibliography of the National Liberation War and Revolution 1941–1945*, prepared for the twelfth international congress of historians in Vienna 1965. Special teams worked for several years in the regions where military operations had been conducted, recording on the spot first-hand information and memories of the participants in the national liberation war. The Military Historical Institute has published a large part of this documentation in 116 volumes, grouped in nine books.[10] Documents on the history of the youth movement have also been issued, as well as papers of Yugoslav war and revolutionary leaders, Marshal Tito, B. Kidrić, M. Pijade, and others. A specially useful contribution is provided by the *Chronology of the Liberation Struggle of the Peoples of Yugoslavia 1941–45*, published in Belgrade in 1965. Joint collections of sources by more than one country would undoubtedly contribute not only to a more complete understanding of certain aspects and periods of history, but would also provide a link between national historiographies in the common effort to arrive at the historical truth.

Yugoslav historians today, with the exception of some remaining adherents of the old positivist school, use Marxist concepts in their studies; that is to say, they employ the dialectical method in studying economic and social phenomena. The task of historical research is not only to tell us *what* happened in the past and *how* it happened, but also *why* history took that particular course. To answer this last question, the historical process must be seen in the context of the economic, political, and cultural development of a society, and within the broader context of general world historical trends. In this respect, the tasks of contemporary Yugoslav historiography are threefold: (*a*) to re-examine the results of earlier work; (*b*) to broaden the range of subject-matter under research so as to cover all historical manifestations; and (*c*) to examine the greatest possible amount of historical sources, in keeping with the growing availability of materials in domestic and foreign archives.

In pursuit of these tasks, the earlier studies of the Serbian uprisings of 1804 and 1815 have been expanded to become the study of the Serbian revolution at the beginning of the nineteenth century; in other words, the rising against the Ottoman Empire expressed, from the economic point of view, the struggle of the peasantry against Ottoman feudalism and was intended to pave the way for the penetration of new, capitalist, relations; from the national point of view, it represented the renaissance of the Serbian people and the early beginnings of a free, independent state. One of the consequences of the uprising was the establishment of conditions for the development of the national culture and for its integration into European cultural trends. Modern Serbian historiography investigates the changes occurring in Serbian society in the course of the agrarian revolution in the early nineteenth century, the establishment of the new central authority in the conflict with the patriarchal rural democracy, the penetration of new economic relations into its agricultural economy, the political struggle for full independence, as well as the impact of the uprising on the situation in Yugoslavia and in the Balkans in general. A number of historical works examine specifically the agrarian or middle-class character of the Serbian revolution, as well as the role and significance of rural communities in the formation of the new state.

Similar fresh work has been undertaken in the study of Serbian history between 1840 and 1880, covering the formation of the Serbian society and state, of the influence of European liberal movements after 1848, and the liberation activities of the Serbian agrarian movements and middle-class organizations in Ottoman territory, whose aim was to prepare the ground for the general Balkan uprising. These studies have revealed new data, and at the same time make it possible to examine the subject within the broader, integrated framework which shaped the national and social development of the Balkans in the nineteenth century. New light has been thrown on a number of major issues of the 1860s and 1870s: the actions of Serbia in the Yugoslav and Balkan regions, the influence of the Italian Risorgimento, and the intervention of the great powers in the Eastern Crisis 1875–78.

A new, almost unexplored field has been opened by research into the penetration of foreign capital in Serbia at the end of the nineteenth century (particularly in the form of foreign loans), the beginnings of industrialization, the construction of railways, the development of banking, the crisis of the craft guilds, and expropriation in rural communities.[11] The establishment of political parties, their programmes and political activities, are viewed from two angles: in relation to the development of parliamentarianism and constitutionality in the conflict between progressive and conservative forces; and from the point of view of the socio-economic base on which these parties developed and of the social interests whose protagonists they were.[12]

Until some ten years ago, the history of Serbia between 1903 and 1914 had been somewhat neglected. For that reason, the Historical Institute in Belgrade undertook a systematic study of the period in the form of a series of monographs, which will eventually make it possible to provide, by means of synthesis, a complete picture of that extremely eventful period of history. The finished papers are being published in a special series under the title *Yugoslav Countries in the Twentieth Century*; three have appeared so far.[13] The monographs will deal with finance-capital in Serbia, the position of the peasants, the role of foreign capital, trade in the Balkans, political parties, the growth of the labour movement, relations between Serbia and the great powers and between Serbia and her Balkan neighbours, and the Yugoslav revolutionary youth movement in the early twentieth century.[14] The participation of Serbia and Montenegro in the wars of 1912–18 is being studied by the Military Historical Institute.[15]

The study of the socialist movement in Serbia covers the age of Svetozar Marković and his followers, tracing the development of the movement from the end of the nineteenth century to the establishment of the Serbian Social Democratic Party 1903–19, when it became a modern socialist movement and part of the international labour movement. Special study groups are organized from time to time to discuss specific questions (the relations between the labour movement and the rural areas, relations between the Social Democratic Party and the trade unions, the activities of the party during the First World War, etc.).[16]

Contemporary Croatian historiography has studied the growth of Croatian towns (Zagreb, Rijeka, Split, etc.), the influence of the ideas of the French Revolution in Croatia at the beginning of the nineteenth century, and the national Croat revival in the 1830s. The Illyrian movement is studied within the context of its all-Yugoslav significance, covering its South Slavistic ideology, its links with Serbia, the attitude of the peasants towards the nationality policy, etc. In the last few years several papers have been published on political conditions and parties in Croatia in the nineteenth century, and its status within the Dual Monarchy, and a number of studies on the agrarian problem in Slavonia have also appeared.[17]

The hundredth anniversary of the 1860 national revival in Dalmatia was the occasion for the publication of numerous papers which considered that event from the point of view of its Slavonic and Yugoslav manifestations.[18] A great deal of research has also been done on the political and social history of Croatia in the second half of the nineteenth century, from the establishment of dualism in 1867 up to the new national movement at the beginning of the twentieth century. Work has been done, with the use of new materials and new methods, on the national movement in Croatia from 1903, the genesis of Franko's party, and especially on the Croat-Serbian coalition, whose establishment and activities are regarded not only as a political but primarily as a socio-economic manifestation.[19] Research into the modern history of Istria has also been initiated but, with the exception of some papers, no attempt at a synthetic presentation has been made.

As compared with other Yugoslav areas, historical research in Slovenia devotes a great deal of attention to the region's cultural development; its national revival in the nineteenth century was indeed predominantly of a cultural-economic character. There have been a number of demographic studies, particularly about urban communities, economic development, trade, transport, and industrialization. In the field of political history, the status of Slovenia in the Habsburg monarchy has been examined;[20] an important contribution to the study of the general history of Slovenia is the work by I. Prijatelj, *Slovenska kulturnopolitična in slovstvena zgodovina 1848–95* (Cultural, political, and literary history of Slovenia) in four volumes, published 1955–61. A great deal has been written about the development of the labour movement in Slovenia and about the underlying socio-economic processes.[21]

The historians of Montenegro have concentrated on the extremely complex sociological, economic, and political problem of the transformation of its tribal society into a modern state. This covers the disintegration of the patriarchal mountain tribes and the emergence of a central state authority in the years between 1796 and 1860. Other historians have dealt with the relations between Montenegro and Serbia in the middle of the nineteenth century, the participation of Montenegro in the wars against the Ottoman Empire in the 1860s, the social-political crisis at the beginning of the twentieth century, and the unification of Montenegro and

Serbia.[22] There still remain numerous interesting themes in the history of Montenegro to be explored, particularly the penetration of Italian capital in the region of Montenegro, Lake Scutari, and Albania in the early twentieth century.

The central place in the work of historians in Bosnia and Herzegovina is taken by the agrarian uprisings in the nineteenth century, and by the situation in the two provinces under Austro-Hungarian rule 1878–1918.[23] Considerable research has been done on the national-revolutionary youth, its ideology, organization, and links with other national movements on the Yugoslav territory at the beginning of the twentieth century.

Historical research in Macedonia, which has developed particularly rapidly during the last twenty years, had to undertake the twofold task of revising earlier works which did not recognize that the Macedonian nation had had a separate history, and of making a scientific study of that history. Old misconceptions were removed and the foundations of the new national Macedonian historiography laid. It concentrates mainly on research in the four major phenomena in the history of Macedonia: the period of cultural and educational struggle, out of which emerged the Macedonian national revival in the nineteenth century; the period of the political and national-revolutionary development of that revival within the Internal Macedonian Revolutionary Organization; the uprisings of the Macedonian peasants in the nineteenth century, culminating in the Ilinden uprising in 1903;[24] and the impact of the Young Turks revolution of 1908 on the internal development of Macedonia. Although a comprehensive general history of Macedonia has not yet been written, work has been done on a large number of particular aspects of its economic and social history, migration and emigration, the activities of the Balkan states on the territory of Macedonia, and the development of the Macedonian labour movement and its links with the Serbian and Bulgarian Social Democratic Parties.

The results of all this work referring to the nineteenth century and up to 1918 will be published in the third volume of the *History of the Yugoslav Peoples*, on which work was resumed in 1965. The fourth volume is to cover Yugoslav history from 1918 to 1941, and the fifth volume from 1941 until the present time.

The First World War was extensively treated in pre-war historiography, and the work has continued, with emphasis laid on new aspects, especially social and political trends behind the lines of the occupied Yugoslav territories, and the resistance movement.[25] Studies have been made of the political conditions prevailing at the time of the retreat of the Serbian army to Corfu, and especially of the Saloniki trial in 1917.[26] The majority of the papers deal with the development of the Yugoslav movement, the role of Yugoslav volunteers in military operations, the activities of the social democrats during the war, the influence of the Soviet revolution, and the attitudes of the Yugoslav Committee and of the Serbian government on the question of the establishment of Yugoslavia.[27] Although no comprehensive work on the establishment of Yugoslavia has yet been written, numerous partial research papers exist, for example about the Geneva conference (D. Janković) and the National Council in Zagreb (B. Krizman).

Before the establishment of the historical department at the Institute of Social Sciences in Belgrade in 1958, the history of Yugoslavia between the two wars had not been systematically studied.[28] The Institute has drawn up a comprehensive long-term plan of research into the history of Yugoslavia from 1918 to 1941, its relations with the great powers and the neighbouring Balkan states, the economic, political, and social development of the Yugoslav peoples, the history of the Communist Party, trade unions, and of the labour movement as a whole. Analytical studies treat the period of the Vidovdan constitution, political relations in the first days of the development of Yugoslavia, the appearance of right-wing and pro-fascist organizations, the activities of the middle-class opposition, changes in Yugoslav policy under the regency (1934–41), etc. A large part of these papers has been published in the periodical *History of the Twentieth Century*, issued by the Institute of Social Sciences. *A Survey of the History of the League of Communists of Yugoslavia*, written by a group of authors, was published in 1963. The economy of pre-war Yugoslavia and the role of foreign capital represent a separate field of investigation.[29]

The history of the Second World War, of the national liberation movement in Yugoslavia, and of the socialist revolution is being studied at the Military Historical Institute, the institutes for the study of the labour movement, and at the Institute of Social Sciences. This research covers the course of military operations, the fighting in Yugoslavia in April 1941, the occupation, collaboration, the uprising of the peoples of Yugoslavia and the development of the national liberation war, and particularly the growth of the socialist revolution during the war and the formation of political organs of popular authority. There are also numerous papers dealing with the different Yugoslav regions during the war and the revolution.[30]

It is hoped that this brief survey will convey a general idea of the development of modern Yugoslav historiography. In the course of the last two decades it has grown in scope and gone deeply into a series of problems of contemporary history which had formerly been neglected. Research has become broader and more systematic, and the number of historical institutions and of their staffs has been greatly expanded. This represents the first stage in the analysis of the historical development of the Yugoslav region. The second stage, on which the historians are now entering, is the integration of the work of national historiographies into a general Yugoslav whole, which will provide a realistic and critical appraisal not only of the recent history of the Yugoslav region but also of its contribution to the development of the Balkans and of Europe in the twentieth century.

NOTES

[1] These results are published in two volumes presented at the International Historical Congress in Rome (1955) and Vienna (1965), under the title: *Ten years of Yugoslav historiography 1945–1955* (Belgrade, 1955), pp. 685; and *Historiographie yougoslave 1955–1965* (Belgrade, 1965), pp. 525. There are nineteen Historical Institutes, covering all aspects of the discipline, archaeology, Byzantine and medieval studies, Ottoman period, modern history, workers' movement, etc.

[2] Between 1948 and 1966 nineteen young scholars defended their doctoral theses in the Historical Institute in Belgrade.

[3] See: *Državna arhiva NR Srbije 1900–1950* (Belgrade, 1951).

[4] A. Ivić, *Spisi bečkih arhiva o prvom srpskom ustanku, 1804–09*, 8 vols. (Belgrade, 1935–65); H. Šabanović, *Turski izvori o srpskoj revoluciji 1804. Spisi carske kancelarije 1789–1804* (Belgrade, 1956); G. Jakšić and V. Vučković, *Francuski dokumenti o prvom i drugom ustanku 1800–1830* (Belgrade, 1957); D. Janković, *Francuska štampa o prvom srpskom ustanku* (Belgrade, 1959); Istorijski arhiv Beograd, *Gradja iz Zemunskih arhiva za istoriju Prvog srpskog ustanka*, vol. I (1804–08) (Belgrade, 1955); R. Perović, *Gradja za istoriju Prvog srpskog ustanka* (Belgrade, 1954); ibid., *Prilozi za istoriju Prvog srpskog ustanka: neobjavljena gradja* (Belgrade, 1954); Sl. Gavrilović, *Gradja o Sremu i njegovim vezama sa Srbijom 1804–15* (Sremski Karlovci, 1965); Z. Sečanski, *Gradja o Ticanovoj buni u Sremu 1807 godine* (Belgrade, 1956).

[5] Illyrian movement: J. Horvat and J. Ravlić, *Pisma Lj. Gaju* (Zagreb, 1956); Montenegro: M. Kićović, *Petar II Petrovic-Njegoš* (Belgrade, 1955); V. Novak, *Valtazar Bogišic i Franjo Racki, Prepiska 1866–93* (Belgrade, 1960); Dalmatia: I. Palavršić and B. Zelić, *Korespondencija Mihovila Pavlinovića* (Split, 1962).

[6] On economic development: R. Marković, *Kragujevacka nahija 1815–39* (Belgrade, 1954); D. Vulović, *Nahija Požeška 1815–39*, vol. I (Belgrade, 1953). For the study of 1848: *Gradja za istoriju srpskog pokreta u Vojvodini, 1848–49* (Belgrade, 1952). On the liberal movement: A. Radenić, *Svetoandrejska skupština* (Belgrade, 1964); peasant movements in the second half of the twentieth century: M. Nikolić, *Timočka buna 1883*, 2 vols. (Belgrade, 1954–55).

[7] V. Vučković, *Politička akcija Srbije u jugoslovenskim pokrajinama Habsburške monarhije 1859–74* (Belgrade, 1965). See also G. Jakšić, *Pisma Filipa Hristića* (Belgrade, 1953), and *Prepiska Ilije Garašanina* (Belgrade, 1950).

[8] Lj. Lapc, *Današeni izvori na makedonskata istorija* (Skopje, 1951); ibid., *Pismata na Goce Delčev* (Skopje, 1951).

[9] A. Mandić, *Fragmenti za historiju ujedinjenja* (Zagreb, 1956); D. Šepić, *Iz korespondencije Frana Supila, Arhivski vjesnik*, 1958, 1959; D. Janković-B. Krizman, *Gradja o stvaranju jugoslovenske države* (Belgrade, 1964); B. Krizman-B. Hrabak, *Zapisnici sa sednica delegacije Kraljevine SHS na Mirovnoj konferenciji u Parizu 1919–21* (Belgrade, 1960).

[10] *Zbornik dokumenata i podataka o narodno-oslobodilačkom ratu jugoslovenskih naroda*, I–IX, 1–116 (Belgrade, 1949–65).

[11] A. Radenić, *Polozaj i borba seljaštva u Sremu od kraja XIX veka do 1914* (Belgrade, 1958); N. Vučo, *Raspadanje esnafa u Srbiji*, 2 vols. (Belgrade, 1954, 1958); ibid., *Položaj seljaštva, I, Eksproprijacija zemlje u XIX veku* (Belgrade, 1955).

[12] V. Čubrilović, *Istorija politicke misli u Srbiji XIX veka* (Belgrade, 1958); D. Janković, *O političkim strankama u Srbiji XIX veka* (Belgrade, 1951).

[13] D. Djordjević, *Carinski rat Austro-Ugarske i Srbiji 1906–1911* (Belgrade, 1962); M. Zivanović, *Dubrovnik u borbi za ujedinjenje 1908–1918* (Belgrade, 1962); Lj. Aleksić, *Odnosi Srbije sa Francuskom i Engleskom 1903–1914* (Belgrade, 1965).

[14] See D. Djordjevic, 'The Historical Institute in Beograd', *Balkan Studies* (Thessaloniki), 5, 1964, pp. 139–44.

[15] Vojno-istorijski institut: *Prvi balkanski rat 1912–13. Operacije srpske vojske* (Belgrade, 1958).

[16] See S. Dimitrijević, *Bibliografija socijalističkog i radničkog pokreta u Srbiji s osvrtom na ostale krajeve naše zemlje* (Belgrade, 1954); R. Perović, *Prilog bibliografiji srpskog radničkog pokreta (do 1919)* (Belgrade, 1957).

[17] J. Šidak, 'Hrvatsko pitanje u Habsburškoj monarhiji', *Historijski pregled*, 1963, IX. See on Slavonia the works of Sl. Gavrilović and I. Karaman.

[18] See the works of G. Novak in *Radovi Jugoslovenske akademije znanosti i umjetnosti u Zadru*, Nos. III–X, 1957–63, and also the writings

of K. Milutinović and M. Gross. For Croatia see the works of V. Bogdanov and J. Horvat.

[19] M. Gross, *Vladavina hrvatsko-srpske koalicije 1906–07* (Belgrade, 1960).

[20] F. Zwitter, J. Šidak, V. Bogdanov, *Les problèmes nationaux dans la Monarchie des Habsbourgs* (Belgrade, 1960).

[21] The works of D. Kermavner, J. Pleterski, I. Regent, B. Zicherl, B. Kidrić.

[22] Studies by B. Pavicević, P. Popović, S. Stanojević, D. Vujović.

[23] See the studies by H. Kapidžić, F. Hauptmann, M. Ekmedžić, I. Kecmanović, V. Bogičević.

[24] See the works of B. Koneski, D. Mitrev, H. Polenaković, A. Spasev; H. Poljanski, I. Katardžijev, M. Pandevski, S. Dimevski, A. Hristov, V. Ristovski; D. Zografski, Lj. Lape, K. Džambazovski.

[25] In particular, B. Stulli, *Ustanak mornara u Boki Kotorskoj 1–3 februara 1918* (Split, 1959); M. Perović, *Toplički ustanak* (Belgrade, 1959).

[26] M. Živanović, *Solunski proces* (Belgrade, 1955).

[27] D. Šepić, *Supilo diplomat* (Zagreb, 1961); M. Marjanović, *Londonski ugovor iz 1915* (Zagreb, 1960); F. Slipičević, *Prvi svjetski rat i stvaranje države jugoslovenskih naroda* (Sarajevo, 1957); S. Budisavljević, *Stvaranje države Srba, Hrvata i Slovenaca* (Zagreb, 1958).

[28] There is only one general work: F. Čulinović, *Jugoslavija izmedju dva rata*, 2 vols. (Belgrade, 1961).

[29] S. Dimitrijević, *Strani kapital u privredi bivše Jugoslavije 1918–1941* (Belgrade, 1958).

[30] The Institute of the Army published a history of the Second World War, *Istorija Drugog svetskog rata* (Belgrade, 1957–64) in three volumes. See also V. Terzić, *Jugoslavija u aprilskom ratu 1941* (Titograd, 1963); *Les systèmes d'occupation en Yougoslavie 1941–1945* (Belgrade, 1963); Vojno-istorijski institut, *Oslobodilacki rat naroda Jugoslavije 1941–45*, 2 vols. (Belgrade, 1957–58); F. Tudjman, *Stvaranje socijalističke Jugoslavije* (Zagreb, 1960); J. Marjanović and P. Morača, *Naš oslobodilački rat i narodna revolucija 1941–45* (Belgrade, 1958); V. Strugar, *Rat i revolucija naroda Jugoslavije 1941–45* (Belgrade, 1962); L. Geršković, *Historija narodne vlasti* (Belgrade, 1957).

USSR

ARTHUR P. MENDEL

The Current Theory of Soviet History: New Trends or Old*

Over the past few years, Soviet historians and philosophers have been carrying on a curious discussion about the nature and methods of historical inquiry. It is too early to say with any confidence what the outcome will be. Taken by itself or set in the context of the 'thaw' the discussion encourages cautious optimism. Still, historical publications look much the same as they did in Joseph Stalin's time, and many of the concepts and arguments I will be reviewing seem more like further developments of revisions in historical theory introduced under Stalin in the 1930s than reactions against them. It is also reasonable, although not necessarily correct, to claim party-political interests behind everything written in this field. But, however interpreted, the current discussion is remarkably fresh and interesting compared with customary Soviet publications on historical theory, the sacred domain, after all, of the *istmatchiki*, the historical materialists.

To judge from official party pronouncements, the aims and methods of Soviet history remain what they were under Stalin. 'A historian is not a dispassionate reporter who identifies facts or even places them in a scientifically valid pattern,' declared Central Committee Secretary and Academician B. N. Ponomarev in his opening address to the all-union conference of historians in December 1962. 'He is a fighter who sees his goal in placing the history of the past at the service of the struggle for communism,' and whose purpose it is to promote 'a firm conviction of the inevitability of the triumph of communism'. Similarly, we learn from a party Central Committee decree of October 1959 that secondary-school history courses should develop in students 'a

* Reprinted from the *American Historical Review* LXXII (No. 1, October 1966). The *American Historical Review* disclaims responsibility for statements, either of fact or of opinion, made by contributors.

scholarly understanding of the laws of development of society, implant in them the conviction that the doom of capitalism and the victory of communism are inevitable. . . .' Since this is the task to be met by historians, the 'obsolete, sterile problems and overly narrow, insufficiently topical, private, and incidental themes, which here and there still divert historians from the treatment of the pressing problems of historiography, must be resolutely swept aside'.[1]

The dominant character and central concerns of the official declarations are represented by the above quotations, and only rarely does one encounter a hint of less doctrinaire judgments. In the current discussion on historical theory and methods by the historians themselves it is the other way round; the prevailing tone, the specific topics, and the quality of thought and argument are, relative to the official statements, refreshingly undoctrinaire; only occasionally do we find ourselves back in the dark age, usually at the beginning or end of an analysis or when some protection is required to cover too flagrantly 'bourgeois' ideas.

Consider, for example, one of several less doctrinaire points made in Ponomarev's speech. As part of the general anti-Stalin campaign that was given an added thrust at the Twenty-second Party Congress in 1961, the party has continued to attack Stalin's 'arbitrary', 'subjective' distortions of history and has encouraged a limited return to the archives. Ponomarev, accordingly, decried the time when 'as a rule, material in the archives was employed only to illustrate commonly-known propositions', and when 'respect for facts, without which history as a science is unthinkable, was lost'. Also, at the close of his speech, he quoted Lenin's exhortation to scholars 'to take not individual facts, but the *entire totality* of the facts bearing upon the problem under consideration, *without a single exception.* . . .'[2] These admirably liberal comments stand out in glaring contrast to the rest of Ponomarev's speech. When they appear in the recent publications on historical theory, however, the contrast, while still there, is far less extreme.

First of all historians have naturally welcomed with enthusiasm the opportunity to attack Stalinist repression and intellectual corruption. At a conference on historical method arranged by the USSR Academy of Sciences in early 1964, for example, participants repeatedly denounced Stalinist historiography for its 'arbitrary attitude towards the facts'. Under Stalin 'the most fundamental norms of scientific ethics were violated', one historian recalled, going on to remind the conference that 'the value, the authority of historical investigation lies in its objectivity, in the truthfulness of the description of events and phenomena'. History teachers were similarly criticized for confining their lectures within the 'framework of a special set of ideas, quotations, and propositions' and were urged to expose students to 'doubts and unsolved problems' and to 'the controversial ideas that promote independent thought'.[3]

This concern for more scholarly objectivity (or, perhaps, only for works that appear to be more objective) is reflected in a number of recent tendencies familiar to students of Russian history, particularly the campaign against doctrinaire 'quotism', that is, 'proving' arguments by quotations from Marxist classics, and the related insistence on the careful study of primary sources. Both tendencies have received considerable attention in the West and need not concern us here, other than to mention that they continue to be prominent.[4] Another less familiar but perhaps more important expression of what seems to be a growing respect for scholarly objectivity is the current treatment of opposing views. Those who have not read recent Soviet reviews of Western thought, even anti-Marxist 'idealistic' historical theory, would be surprised at both the completeness and the fairness of summaries and excerpts.[5]

Next to this apparently enhanced regard for professional integrity,[6] the most persistent theme in the current discussion is the 'respect for facts', the criticism of historians who use facts 'only to illustrate commonly-known propositions'. Both quotations, it will be recalled, are from Ponomarev's official party declaration. In making these statements, however, he was careful to associate them specifically with the attack against Stalin's abuses, and he avoided any inference that might undermine the 'laws' and 'commonly-known propositions', which, as we have seen, are still the *sine qua non* of the ideologists. In the analyses by the historians themselves, on the contrary, inferences drawn from the admonition to 'respect the facts' are having precisely this effect.

A. V. Gulyga, of the Institute of Philosophy, touched the essential point when he maintained at the 1964 conference that 'the fact in historical science is not supplanted by the generalization; it is an end in itself (*samodovleiushchaia tsenost*').[7] In a field such as history, he wrote elsewhere, 'which, along with generalization, also aims at description, factual material plays a special role, one that is different from that played in purely theoretical disciplines. The latter use factual data only to support generalizations.' 'For the historian,' he continued, 'the fact is not only material for generalization, not simply an example illustrating the action of a general law which can be left out or replaced by others.'[8] The director of the Institute of History, Academician V. M. Khvostov, referred approvingly to Gulyga's statement about facts being ends in themselves in order to justify the historian's right to study facts simply for the sake of 'enriching our factual knowledge'.[9] The subjects historians study might seem petty and unrelated to specific problems, B. F. Porshnev, also of the Institute of History, added, but such themes are similar to the 'preparatory experiments' in natural science necessary before more general studies are undertaken.[10] The main point, restated endlessly, is that the familiar, sweeping Marxist generalizations will no longer do: 'History is concreteness at its maximum.'[11] A lead article in *Voprosy istorii* on the treatment of historical subjects by Karl Marx and Friedrich Engels referred to their concern with specific, concrete facts, and praised this attitude as 'the categorical imperative of scientific ethics' and 'the methodological requirement for scientific knowledge of the historical process'.[12]

The most explicit and elaborate example that I have found illustrating this attempt to liberate the study of concrete historical facts from submission to Marxist laws and generalizations is contained in a prominently placed article by A. Ya. Gurevich, one of the most thoughtful contributors to the discussions. The general laws of historical materialism regarding the transition from one social system, or 'formation', to another are true, Gurevich readily acknowledged, but they are simply not immediately relevant to the historian's inquiry.

Most often, a scholar is necessarily concerned with a geographically limited and relatively brief phase of the historical process during which a general law may be only partly expressed by merely a few of its aspects or even a single one or it may not appear at all. ... Does the scholar search his empirical data only for manifestations of the general law discussed above [that of transition from one system to another]? It is obvious that History requires concrete explanations of occurrences, and mere references to sociological laws do not solve the problem.

As a specific example, Gurevich discussed the historical materialist interpretation of the fall of the Roman Empire. After summarizing the familiar Marxist picture of socio-economic develop-

266

ment, class struggle, and revolution, he went on to write: 'It is well known that for a long time this was how Soviet historiography explained the fall of the Roman Empire. However, this kind of approach failed every time one took into account concrete facts and processes of history.' Above all, Gurevich insisted, the historian must regard categories of historical materialism simply as epistemological guides to research and not *a priori*, ontological descriptions of reality, which they are for philosophers. He rejected, furthermore, the 'proposition long dominant in our intellectual life that there are no other laws of history besides the laws of historical materialism, interpreted and edited, moreover, subjectively'. On the contrary, he argued, there is a great variety of causal patterns (which he considers synonymous with laws) besides those associated with production, the focus of historical materialism. Whatever the general sociological law might say about the economic base of historical developments, 'the concrete historical actions of people depend on the most diverse causes, among which, besides production, one must find a place for natural environment, national characteristics, psychology, ideology, external influences, all sorts of traditions, the level of cultural development, biological and demographic factors, and many others'. As to the problem of deciding which are the most important: 'It is hardly possible to establish a scale of factors *a priori*, to determine degrees of significance apart from a concrete empirical analysis of the interrelationships of these factors in a particular period and particular country.' The historian must also realize, he noted, that different factors play dominant roles at different times.

Concerning the question of 'accidents' and unpredictable, alternative paths of historical development, Gurevich was particularly frank. After indignantly denouncing attempts to portray Marxism as a 'materialistic interpretation of Biblical eschatology', a secularized faith in 'providential history', he analysed at length the category of 'possibility' in history. There is nothing at all predetermined in history, he insisted, and simply because something actually happened does not mean that nothing else could have happened. For example, neither Hitler's rise to power nor the Second World War was inevitable, and merely because the 'basic conditions' for revolution were present did not mean that revolution must occur. Without specific reference to Engels, Gurevich criticized his contention that 'historical law cuts a way for itself through the chaos of accidents'. As with the general law on transitions, Gurevich considered this theory correct, 'but only on the level of sociology'. Such 'macro-laws' are not the immediate concern of historians who study specific events and for whom 'the possible varieties of historical process are extremely diverse and pregnant with the most serious consequences for its later development'.[13]

Every historical event is the result of a convergence of many contributing conditions. A different convergence might result in a different event which, influenced by all the remaining factors, would in turn lead to consequences different from those that in fact occurred and, thus, there would begin an entire chain of events and phenomena—a different variant of development . . .[14]

Thus, once interest focuses on specific facts, their individual attributes and kaleidoscopic conjunctions cannot so easily be encompassed by general laws. Reality becomes complex and elusive. And, indeed, the words 'complex' and 'diverse' appear as frequently in recent Societ historiography as do 'concrete' and 'specific', and usually in association with them. The good Marxist historian presents history 'in all its immense diversity', while the bourgeois scholar is accused of squeezing complex reality into narrow schemata. Even the great social transformations that used to unfold, at least in theory, so neatly and orderly are now set in a context of 'the most variegated assortment of different economic systems, social systems, unprecedented diversity of traditions, customs, and living conditions'. Consequently, the author of this statement continued, a major task facing Soviet historians is 'the reconsideration of the theory of knowledge and the problems of its application in analysing the particularly complex and variable phenomena of social life'.[15] The following statement by Gulyga represents an adequate summary of this part of the current discussions:

[The historian's] task is to re-create historical reality through a unity of necessity and contingency, to reconstruct the course that humanity has actually traversed, with all its zigzags, all the diversity and unique individuality of the events that have occurred. A pattern of the historical process is not yet history, just as the subject and the concept do not yet make a work of art. Each historical event possesses individual attributes characteristic of it alone, and to disclose these and preserve them for posterity is just as much the responsibility of the historian as is the generalization of materials studied by him.[16]

Is this what Ponomarev had in mind when he talked about 'respect for facts'? It would seem to be one thing to use this line as part of the campaign against Stalin, but quite another to use it as part of an argument that is increasingly separating historical research from the Marxist laws and predictions that have from the beginning provided the principal source of legitimacy for party rule.[17]

At several places in Ponomarev's speech he also commented on another theme that has become a leitmotiv for the methodologists: the historian's return to 'the richness of colours and gradations that one finds in real life'. He urged historians to show more concern for style, and he warmly recommended 'pre-revolutionary Russian, Soviet, and foreign' historical works as 'first-class models'.[18] In his response to the principal paper delivered at the 1964 conference, the editor of *Voprosy istorii*, V. G. Trukhanovsky, echoed these views when he said that he was 'most pleased by the appeal of the speakers to historians to write living history, with flesh and blood, emotions and passions'. Explicitly associating the 'living' quality of history as it should be written with the emphasis on the 'concrete facts', Yu. S. Borisov asserted that 'authentic historical scholarship excludes stilted schematism and illustrationism: it is always factual in the best sense of the word, because it reconstructs the past in all its full-bodied, many-coloured, living clarity'.[19]

L. V. Cherepnin, long a leading Soviet medievalist, used an article on N. V. Gogol as a historian to argue the need for historians to capture the unique, vital, personal aspects of their subjects: 'Gogol was interested in everything, the people's customs, ceremonies, holidays, superstitions, clothing, and the like'. He avoided 'bare abstractions', wanted to know '"the true existence, the essential characteristics, all the shifts and shades of feeling, excitement, suffering and joys"' of his subjects, and gave special attention to such things as music, art, and fashions as sources for what was worth knowing about people. In Cherepnin's words, Gogol believed 'that the work of a historian should not merely provide material for the literary writer but should itself, without losing its own specific character, represent an artistic production affecting the feeling and imagination of the reader as well as his mind'. How wonderfully different Soviet historical works would become if Soviet scholars took heed of Cherepnin's implicit prompting here, through the medium of Gogol, to involve themselves in 'the expressiveness, colour, diversity of the unfolding pictures of the past, whose incessant change provides such a fascinating study. . . .'[20]

Both here and to a lesser extent in the concern for more factual and less dogmatic history one can easily appreciate the party's motives for promoting these arguments. History books written in the familiar Soviet manner are simply not read. Compared to the citizen of the 1930s and 1940s there is indeed a 'new Soviet man', and the change affects the consumption of literature and history no less than shoes: the shoddy and crude stay on the shelves.[21] But here again, as in the preceding theme, the historians seem to go farther than necessary in supporting the party's interests. And, after all, party interests or not, historical works that are closer to the facts and that are written in a way that brings alive the events of the past are better history than those written in the Stalinist manner. The question becomes who is using whom. Are the party ideologists using the historians to make their propaganda more effective, or are the historians taking advantage of a fortunate conjunction of interests to improve the quality of Soviet historical research and publication?

The same question can be raised with regard to another major theme in these recent publications on historical theory: the emphasis on the role of human will and goals in determining the course of historical development. 'History is *nothing but* the activity of man pursuing his aims'—such is the classic quotation from Marx most often brought in to legitimize this voluntarist position. There has always been, of course, a tension in Marxism between an emphasis on objective, ineluctable economic laws necessary to guarantee victory and a large role for political initiative demanded for revolutionary leadership and self-sacrifice. Leninism and Stalinism represent successive heightening of the tension, with the advantage steadily increasing on the side of voluntarism. Essentially the reverse side of the attack on abstract, 'sociological' generalization, this voluntaristic theory of history (as well as of politics, economics, and psychology) was a fundamental part of Stalin's 'great retreat', and it is important for an understanding of the main trends of Soviet life and thought to appreciate the persistence of this theme. Party leadership, the vanguard of the proletariat, consciousness over spontaneity, the primacy of politics over economics in socialist revolution and 'communist construction', the socialist hero in literature, the high rewards for those who do well in all spheres of Soviet life—these and many other characteristic aspects of Stalin's Russia were associated with such voluntarism or, better, idealism.[22]

What are the theorists doing with it now? The theme itself appears constantly. Such statements as the following, made at the 1964 conference, are common: 'Gifted with consciousness and will, people make their own history and in this sense appear not as the passive objects of history, but as its subjects, as its active, creative force, transforming reality in the course of historical practice.'[23]

This emphasis on will as a determinant force in history obviously continues to have great political value. In his outspoken article directed against those exaggerating the place of objective social laws or alleged inevitabilities in history, Gurevich repeatedly stressed the importance of 'energy and enterprise of leaders, parties, and classes'. With such activism, Hitler and the Second World War could have been stopped, and, without it, revolutions do not occur even if the 'basic' objective conditions are present.[24] The Bolshevik victory in 1917 provides a fine example, for it was due above all to Lenin's ability to appreciate the role of the 'subjective' political factor, in decisive contrast to the 'turgid dogmatism' of the Mensheviks, who thought only about the 'insufficient development of productive forces and the small number of proletariat', and the 'metaphysical approach' of the 'Right Opportunists', like Lev Kamenev and Alexei Rykov, who were against moving from the 'democratic' to the 'socialist' phase of revolution after the February upheaval.[25]

Understandably it is with reference to the 'liberation movement' that such voluntarism now finds its most frequent and unmistakable expression. There is no longer any doubt about skipping the 'stage of capitalism' or, with regard to Africa, both feudalism and capitalism, of advancing directly from feudalism or tribalism to socialism.[26] The theory holding that 'the whole world follows one and the same series of stages' must be rejected, according to K. A. Antonova, because 'before our very eyes the industrial development of new Asiatic and African nations is occurring in a manner so very unlike that of the classical European model. . . .'[27] It is frankly acknowledged, moreover, that the key factor allowing this extraordinary violation of objective Marxist 'laws' is the contribution of external influences. M. I. Braginsky, of the Academy of Science's African Institute, argued the case quite reasonably. The Marxists were right and the populists wrong in their debate over the chances of Russia's skipping the stage of capitalism, he writes, because such a leap could only occur if Russia had the support of an advanced society that had already moved on to socialism. Sadly, this had not happened. But things were different now: socialist Russia could provide the helping hand to under-developed economies lacking just about all the necessary, objective conditions for a Marxist socialist revolution.[28] Braginsky brings out clearly the relationship between this argument and idealistic voluntarism: 'When we speak of a non-capitalist path of develop-ment, we must keep in mind not only the objective factors, but also the subjective.'[29] Gurevich gave historical examples to illustrate this view when, in connection with his emphasis on the importance of 'accidents' in history, he referred to the impact of foreign colonial powers on the development of native societies. Similarly, he considered the decisive factor in the fall of the Roman Empire (the factor neglected by the customary Marxist picture of transitions generated from within a given society) to be the barbarian invasions.[30]

Besides this relationship between theoretical voluntarism and the practical politics of 'national liberation', one might argue a similar connection between the latter and the shift by historians from the 'general' to the 'concrete' discussed above. The paramount con-cern of Russian Marxists before and immediately after the October Revolution was to prove both the universality of Marx's historical patterns and the orthodoxy of the Bolshevik victory. The result of this was to exaggerate to absurd degrees the 'capitalist' develop-ment of pre-revolutionary Russia. Today the main political con-cern is to present Russia as a model for the underdeveloped economies, an example of rapid progress from an underdeveloped economy to a highly advanced one. Consequently, one finds historians criticized for underestimating the persisting feudal elements in pre-revolutionary Russia as well as a new emphasis on the similarities between Russia on the eve of the Bolshevik Revolu-tion and present-day underdeveloped societies. For example: 'While linked through its monopolies with the Imperialist West, Russian capitalism as an object of study is far more relevant and instructive for contemporary developing countries because of its contradictions, its social complexity, the immense gentry lati-fundia, the adaptation of the wealthy bourgeoisie to fit the rem-nants of serfdom, the union between the landed class and the wealthy capitalists, with political predominance for the land-owners and economic predominance for the capitalists.' To illustrate his point, the author went on to note the remarkable similarities between conditions of Russian life as described in the works of L. N. Tolstoy and A. P. Chekhov and those prevalent today in the underdeveloped societies.[31]

Still here, as in the case of preceding topics, theorists seem to go beyond the point necessary for meeting political interests, in the direction, that is, of serious methodological reflection. In the article just discussed, for example, Gurevich suggested that objective tendencies, where they did obtain, were the remnants, or the 'statistical average' of different individual 'wills, emotions, ideas, predispositions, and personal, social, and class interests'. Also, he continued, while such individual actions are based on conditions, that is, determined in the sense of being caused, 'this determinism can never be complete, totally reducible to the influence of sociological laws: to one degree or another human action is autonomous, both with regard to its causes and to the results it achieves'. History, he wrote towards the end of the article, and I am uncertain of the level of insight involved, is not the memory of humanity and society so much as it is their 'self-consciousness'.[32] In a footnote, Gurevich makes it explicitly clear that by autonomy here he means more than the familiar Marxist 'reciprocal relationship' between the substructure and the superstructure. Existence does determine consciousness, he agreed, in the sense that the 'spiritual life of society' is influenced constantly by 'economic, social, biological, and natural-geographical' factors. (Even this listing is remarkable.) Nevertheless, he continued, this spiritual life is 'to a certain extent self-determined, possessing its own laws', and the historian should keep this self-determination of the spiritual life in mind and not only its 'interrelationship with the base'.[33]

As noted earlier, Soviet historians are finding a fundamental difference between history and natural science in their contrasting approaches to individual events. In the 'colossal degree', as Gurevich put it, to which events and conditions in history depend on human will and aims,[34] they now see another distinction between these two realms of being and inquiry. Whereas forces in nature 'are blind and unconscious', Gulyga wrote, 'society consists of people endowed with consciousness and will who set for themselves specific aims and strive to realize them'. Consequently, he continued, in virtually the same phrases that Gurevich used, 'regularity emerges as a kind of resultant of millions of individual actions. A social law, therefore, is realized only in an approximate way'.[35] G. E. Glezerman seems to go a step further by spelling out the separation between historical study and dialectical materialism implicit in these definitions:

Dialectical materialism regards as materialistic those objects, phenomena, and relationships that exist apart from and independent of human consciousness. But social life is different from that in nature, since social phenomena and relationships are the result of human actions, and people are conscious beings.[36]

Making explicit the question begged by all this, M. T. Yovchuk declared: 'It is now necessary to concern ourselves with creating—if it can be so expressed—a Marxist, scientific phenomenology of the spirit. . . .'[37]

In what is perhaps his most important article, Gurevich boldly pressed on toward precisely such a 'phenomenology of the spirit' by urging Soviet historians to pay more attention to psychology. Since individuals and masses 'are the subjects of historical actions, their authors and executors', he wrote, the historian

must consider in each concrete case how the social life he studies is reflected in the minds of people, articulated into concepts, images, and feelings and how, after undergoing an appropriate subjective transformation, these factors determine people's actions, moving separate individuals as well as social groups and masses to one or another activity.[38]

The central theme of Gurevich's argument lies in the phrase 'subjective transformation', found near the end of the last quotation. It is not enough to study such 'objective factors' as the 'economic, social, political, and ideological', since these do not act 'mechanically and directly' but rather through the minds of people, through the prism of a particular social psychology. As an illustration, Gurevich described at considerable length the way economic aims and activities in ancient and medieval societies were 'linked with a complex of images and instincts unrelated to economics'. 'For the member of such a society, ceremonies and magic were as essential as (and perhaps even more important than) production itself in agriculture, cattle breeding, and handicrafts', and economic activity was closely interwoven with religion, both directly through morality and indirectly through law.[38a]

It may be more than coincidence that Gurevich chose for this exercise in psychological reductionism those very economic activities that had for so long reigned in the realm of 'the final analysis', the irreducible, ultimate motivating force of all social and historical processes. As recommended examples of historians who made use of psychology in historical analysis, he noted Georges Lefebvre and his 'Marxist' students Albert Soboul and George Rudé. But he urged as well the study of Western bourgeois scholars, including Max Weber, Georg Simmel, Werner Sombart, Lucien Febvre, and Johan Huizinga.[39] Of these, he gave particular attention to Huizinga and his psychological analysis of the waning of the Middle Ages. From Gurevich's excellent summaries of Huizinga's argument one sees a willingness to give fair treatment to non-Marxist, even idealistic and Freudian, interpretations, and, when considered along with the rest of his article, perhaps also Gurevich's own inclination toward the same approach.

A fear of hell and a naïve joy of life were so close in the minds of the people of the time that they sometimes merged. Cruelty and kindness, vengeance and indulgence, love and hate, greed and generosity—these abruptly interchanged. Emotional tension was extraordinarily great. . . . Man swayed between extremes of behaviour, between the ideal and the base. On the lower, unconscious level of the psyche were all shades of desire and inclination, repressed by a conformist society and its severe ethics. On the higher level of conscious aims, only the most elevated motivations, the Christian virtues, approved by society and morality were permitted. The split between the two levels of the psyche, the intense strain arising between them was the source of the intense emotionality and the fluctuations from one extreme to the other.[40]

If the emphasis on will and emotions and the consequent search for a 'phenomenology of the spirit' help undermine oversimplified categories of historical materialism by directing attention to complex personal motivations, they also do so by encouraging an awareness of ethical and intellectual themes that have accompanied the evolution of the human spirit throughout its history, disregarding 'class' division, contrasting socio-economic 'formations', and Marxist 'periodization'. A fascinating article by the Orientalist N. I. Konrad provides a fine illustration.[41]

Konrad's concern is to find the meaning of history. As one might expect, he finds the meaning in progress. But throughout the essay both the content and the dynamics of progress are described in a remarkably unmaterialistic manner. Only midway in the article do we find as a sign of progress the theme with which one would expect a Soviet article like this to begin: economic advance. And even this is treated in a strangely un-Marxian manner. We are told

275

that from the beginning man had to assure his material conditions, but the supporting quotations come not from Marx or Lenin but from ancient Chinese proverbs. The criterion recommended for the definition of economic periods is, moreover, totally unrelated to the usual Marxian categories of class theory: Konrad suggests the division of history into the era of natural materials and the 'polymer age' of synthetics.[42]

The major index of progress, to which virtually the entire article is devoted, is the gradual extension of culture and, especially, the growth in man's knowledge of nature, society, and man himself. We meet little from Marx, Engels, or Lenin in all this. By way of introduction to each area of progress in knowledge (nature, society, man himself), we find instead quotations from ancient Chinese wisdom, and throughout this section the reader passes through a fine array of illustrative references to mythology, religious symbolism, and classical philosophy.[43]

The most striking theme of the article comes in the final section. Man's conquest of nature and his rational achievements in general are judged inadequate in themselves as evidence of progress. The advance of rational knowledge can be considered truly progressive only when united to 'the social principle in man's nature'. To show that for him this is more than the usual propaganda slogan, Konrad again surveys the sweep of history and relates his 'social principle to the Confucian pictogram for 'sympathy', Buddhist 'compassion', the teachings of Jesus, and the ideals of the Renaissance. Toward the end of the article, the ethical factor emerges as the essential and distinguishing one in human history: 'the truly great achievement of mankind and, perhaps, the highest manifestation of progress is the fact that people . . . . called evil, evil; coercion, coercion; crime, crime. The very appearance of the concepts denoted by these terms is proof of progress, for these words did not merely describe phenomena and actions, but evaluated and drastically condemned them'.[44] Thus, notwithstanding his explicit emphasis on 'progress', Konrad's splendid essay surveys and honours the fundamental human values that have persisted through the course of history. At the end of the article he offers elaborate homage to the concept that represents for him a unity of the two values that pervade the essay as its central themes: reason and charity. The concept is humanism, and in his lengthy praise of it, it seems to me, one finds a meeting of Soviet idealism and the heritage cherished by the West.

The above themes concern current Soviet theories on the proper subject matter for historical inquiry. But theories of the known and theories of knowledge go together. When the selection and treatment of subjects are guided by pre-established patterns, abstracted from individual events, historians can easily claim the attainment of objective, 'scientific' laws. Indeed, the entire process is notoriously circular. A host of epistemological problems arises, however, when the concrete facts are brought back in, when an effort is made to grasp and communicate the dynamic complexities and the 'living', elusive quality of reality, and when the ideological 'superstructure', including even unconscious motivations, not only gains autonomy, but becomes increasingly a major 'moving force' in history.

First of all, to 'respect the facts' means to raise that essential problem of all historical study, the problem of selection. As Gulyga wrote, 'the historian must select facts and interpret them. He faces a problem in logic. What criteria should be used in the selection of factual material?' [45] Elsewhere, Gulyga elaborated on this view somewhat: 'One can determine the actual facts but present a distorted picture of the events, because all facts are not equivalent. There are important, determining facts and there are facts of secondary importance. . . . What criteria are there for selecting facts? How can one avoid here subjectivism and arbitrariness?' [46] Others as well are raising this fundamental question, which in Western historiography fostered relativism, subjectivism, and scepticism. The phrasing of a similar statement by Glezerman is even more reminiscent of the early years of relativist thought in the West.

I would like first of all to say something about the theory of knowledge in historical science. There is much here that still remains meagrely studied, particularly concerning the epistemological analysis of the nature of the historical fact. The special character of history as a science consists in the fact that it is mainly concerned with the past, with that which has left its imprint on contemporary conditions of society, but which no longer exists. In contrast to the natural scientist, who has immediately before him the object of his investigation, and in contrast with the sociologist, whose subject is society after it has attained a certain level of development, the historian is concerned with historical facts belonging mainly to the past. Consequently we face here the task of re-creating the historical fact. What should be the criteria for selection from the endless diversity of phenomena those that are most characteristic, those we call historical fact? [47]

In an article on Lenin as a historian, G. M. Ivanov attempted to reconcile objectivity and subjectivity by proposing an approach that he called 'retrospective knowledge', by which the historian is to use insights and concepts reflecting the later development of a particular phenomenon in order to understand its earlier phases, taking care, however, not to read back present meanings into the past. As one might imagine, it is no simple matter for Ivanov to prove that this is entirely different from the presentist position.[48] Ivanov here also expresses another of the difficulties that fostered historical relativism in the West. 'Of course, since man is both the subject of historical development and, at the same time, the subject of historical knowledge, he is learning his own history when study- ing the past, and, in this sense, historical reality and historical consciousness coincide. . . . Since the object of investigation is the history of human society and not the history of nature, it is signi- ficantly more difficult in historical science than it is in natural science to solve the problem of the relationship between the object and the subject.'[49] In his usually frank manner, Gulyga dots the 'i' when he states simply that 'history makes no claims to the laurels of natural science; it has other possibilities and problems'.[50] Since it is common knowledge that much of Soviet ideology and political practice rests ultimately on the assumed affinity between history and natural science, the significance of this line of thought should be self-evident.

An acceptance of part of the relativist argument seems implicit also in V. F. Asmus's statement that ideas 'are never simply selected, but undergo a certain change, a re-evaluation', that besides being chosen because they 'are suitable for supporting present-day views about reality', they are 'brought nearer the present by means of a particular kind of revision, of alteration'.[51] We have already met the same view in Gurevich's article on social psychology. In an article on French archival studies, O. M. Me- dushevskaia offered still another example when she wrote that 'before either serving as the cornerstone of investigation or being thrown out as insignificant, the fact must pass through the prism of the historian's consciousness, become known to him and evalu- ated by him.[52]

One may suggest a variety of factors contributing to the emer- gence of such subjectivism, besides, that is, the strong tendencies in that direction in Marx's relativistic sociology of knowledge.[53] It may well result from the problems of selection, once guiding 'laws' are abandoned in favour of a 'respect for facts', and empathy, once the historian turns his attention to human will and to the 'richness of colour and gradations' in human experience. Such, at any rate, was the case in Western historiography. Or, perhaps, the impact of the 'new physics' on social and historical thought that has been so long familiar in the West is beginning to be felt by Soviet theorists. Since the victory of Soviet scientists over the 'philosophers' and the consequent acceptance of relativity theory, indeterminateness, and so forth, this would seem a likely development.[54] In this connection one should keep in mind the monistic character of Marxist and Soviet epistemology, according to which the science of nature and the 'science of society' share common assumptions, 'categories', and methods.[55]

If something of this sort is occurring, it would certainly be helped by the remarkably full and fair summaries and quotations of Western 'idealistic' historiography in works designed to 'unmask' such theories. As long as Soviet students and scholars knew little or nothing about Benedetto Croce, R. G. Collingwood, Heinrich Rickert, Charles Beard, Carl Becker, and the like, the dogmatists could more easily get away with ritualistic pronouncements and *ad hominem* denunciations. But the contrast between such primitivism and the sophisticated Western thought and argument now openly displayed in extended paraphrases and quotations is too crudely glaring. Having presented these Western views,[56] Soviet theorists seem to feel the need to work out more imaginative responses.

In Gurevich's discussion of general laws, multiple causation, accidents, statistical 'resultants', and alternative possibilities in history, we see one such approach towards a more sophisticated analysis of the individual-general problem. But some theorists have recently become particularly attracted by another approach: the concept of 'ideal type'. Since the central concern that pervades virtually all that is written in this field by Soviet theorists is the need to reconcile the historian's focus on concrete events with the ideological and methodological interest in generalization, the appeal of this approach is understandable. With reference to Goethe, Rickert, and, most of all, Weber, Gulyga devoted an entire article to this theme. It is important to add that it was the lead article in *Voprosy istorii*, a place usually reserved for authoritative party editorials. Weber's essential and valuable contribution, according to Gulyga, was his distinction between the ideal type or form of some phenomenon and its actual existence. Since the ideal type was essentially a 'protoimage' permitting wide deviations from it in reality, Gulyga urged historians to remember that the ideal type was only a useful guide, an epistemologically valuable construction and not a picture of actual patterns and processes in historical reality. (Gurevich, it may be recalled, gave the same warning.) Marx's logical analysis of capitalism, for instance, 'while for sociology a concrete picture of the structure and functions of this society, is for the historian only an abstract point of departure for the reconstruction of the concrete origins of capitalist relations in one or another country, in one or another epoch'.[57]

Here, it would seem, we might have a meeting point between at least some Soviet theorists and one school of thought among our own historians. Ironically, what might stand in the way of such co-operation, assuming this optimism warranted, is the reorientation of those Soviet historians who write about concepts like 'ideal type' away from scientific models of knowledge toward aesthetic.

As in the case of other themes discussed in this study, Gulyga expressed this reorientation with particular clarity. History, he wrote, represents 'a special kind of synthesis between the theoretical and the artistic apprehension of the world. It is dualistic by nature. There co-exist here the abstract and the sensitively concrete, the conceptual and the visual picture of the past.' In its characteristic use of 'ideation in the form of imagery and emotions' he saw one more way in which history differed from 'the majority of the sciences', and he went on to attribute this difference to the special subject matter of history, the 'unique lives of individuals, their intentions and achievements'.[58]

S. O. Schmidt had some still more intriguing thoughts along these lines. Because of the vast accumulation of facts, he said, it was becoming increasingly necessary to 'crystallize' in our minds some stable historical types, and he advised historians to look to creative literature for help in this. In addition, he noted that historical types, 'freed from the narrow framework of specific time and place, and turned into something like timeless symbols, have an effect similar to that of literary-artistic images'. Examples from history, he went on, provide people with types by which they classify real life experiences in the same way that literary characterizations often provide the historian with types around which he crystallizes his historical data. What the historian and writer have most in common, however, is their desire 'to convince the reader of the authenticity of their characterizations'.[59]

In Cherepnin's article on Gogol, we have already seen a full treatment of this theme, associating artistic and historical creativity. Only by following such methods as Gogol adopted in creating concrete, living individuality can the historian fulfil his proper task:

The task of the historian-artist, according to N. V. Gogol, was to draw from his multicoloured palette, and to make use of, the most suitable colours for depicting one or another national image on the historical canvas. One should not 'accumulate a great number of features, but only those that would reveal much, the most original characteristics, the most distinctive, those possessed only by the people described'. To reproduce past phenomena, N. V. Gogol considered necessary a fusion of 'historical' truth and artistic, 'poetic' truth. The study of past facts and the penetration into the depths of the past with the artist's eye—here were the two sides of the creative process, the two paths to historical knowledge.[60]

But the next question immediately arises: how is the historian to apprehend the 'typical'? What is there to replace the, at least allegedly, objective analysis, the dispassionate rationalism that the historian could claim as his guide when he looked to natural science for his method and chose the general as his subject? There are hints of the kind of answers that lie ahead for Soviet historians and philosophers who pursue this line of thought. It is no easy task to 'feel about for' (*nashchupat*) the regularities in the complexity of individual events, Academician P. N. Fedoseev said at the 1964 conference. He then went on to quote V. G. Belinsky's description of the proper historical method:

The difficulty in the prerequisites for a good historian consists in the necessity of joining a rigorous study of historical facts and materials, a critical, cold, dispassionate analysis, with poetic inspiration and a creative capacity to combine events, forming from them a living picture, in which all the principles of perspective and chiaroscuro are observed.[61]

In all this we have left far behind the traditional Marxist picture of both natural and social 'science' and have entered the realm of aesthetics. Gulyga does not balk even here:

Speaking of the particularities of historical science, one must stress the special role played in it by imaginative thought. The questions of imaginative thought, the aesthetic apprehension of reality in the work of the historian is a theme for thought and investigation. Categories of aesthetics belong to reality and consequently to history. They are concerned not only with art, but with the knowledge of reality in general, with the knowledge of the historical process.[62]

In a later article, Gulyga nicely merged together the various approaches with which he has been closely associated. The 'typical' in history, the image that permits a fusion between the specific and the general (which is, in turn, the historian's main concern), is identified by him as an 'aesthetic category', as a means for expressing the 'essence' of a phenomenon 'in its most complete and clearest form'. The processes of apprehending the 'typical', of 'finding material and giving it meaning', he refers to as an 'intuitive act'.[63] Thus, from an admonition to 'respect the facts', through an appeal for a 'phenomenology of the spirit', we arrive at an appreciation of the need for 'an aesthetics of history'.[64] Again, one can reasonably ask, is this what Ponomarev had in mind?

How much of this is new and how much old? Does current Soviet historical theory deserve a place in the 'thaw', or does it continue to fulfil the familiar political and ideological functions, those so clearly laid down in Ponomarev's speech? Do the apparently novel themes indicate a serious reorientation on the part of some Soviet historians and philosophers, or do they merely indicate efforts to provide a cloak of sophistication for official doctrines and thereby more subtly and effectively to satisfy party directives.

Certainly caution is the first principle to be followed when interpreting seemingly novel and hopeful trends in Soviet thought, and throughout this article I have suggested arguments favouring the cloak of sophistication theory. But the second principle is to be aware that such caution may be unsound as well as deeply unjust to Soviet scholars, trying courageously, perhaps, to inch their way out of still vastly powerful ideological controls. One can, of course, find all manner of tediously orthodox statements in even the most revisionist of Soviet publications, but this has always been a form of political insurance, and, moreover, none of the already numerous changes in Soviet theory and practice have ever lacked supporting quotations from the classics. The orthodox comments are also at times so flagrantly inconsistent, either logically or in style and quality of thought, with the rest of the publication (as they are not in such pronouncements as Ponomarev's) that it is hard to take them seriously. Finally, it is less weighty an argument than it might seem to note that some of the liberal statements are expressed by highly placed and long-familiar party functionaries in the historical profession whose major achievements lie well within the Stalin era. For one thing, there is something encouraging in the fact that the liberal bandwagon is considered the profitable one to jump on. In any case, anyone sensitive to the endless combinations of personal motivation and rationalization as well as to the character and intensity of Stalinist oppression would hesitate to pass judgment here or hurl abusive epithets.[65]

My own bent, therefore, is towards a qualified optimism. All potential or actual service to the party notwithstanding, both the tone and the quality of the current discussion lead me to take much of it at face value. But besides the impression made by the publications on historical theory themselves, I am encouraged in this judgment by parallels between them and current developments elsewhere in Soviet life and thought. The exigencies of national defence and economic growth have forced the liberation of the natural sciences from the control of dogma and also a significant and increasingly broader tolerance for experimentation in economic theory and practice. It is hardly likely that professionals in other fields, including history, who have equivalent training, background, and aspirations are unaffected by the return to reason in these favoured disciplines.

Still more indicative of the tendency involved, however, since it is less clearly attached to practical gains, is the veritable obsession with 'truth' that pervades the 'thaw' literature. That the trends toward professional integrity in history are part of this massive reaction against Stalinist mendacity seems to me very likely. I have referred already to a related pressure in this same direction: change in the reading public. To inculcate desired attitudes and ideas in the minds of Soviet readers, the books have to be read, but to get them read, the style and content of the message must be radically altered to suit far more critical, self-confident, and sensitive readers.

There is, finally, another way, less obvious but more basic, in which the achievements in Soviet science and economy may be contributing to the present state of Soviet historiography. Historical and economic determinism, with all their derivative categories, patterns, and laws, provided together an encouraging crutch for powerless Russian Marxists in the last decades of the nineteenth century. Having nothing, they looked to inevitable historical and social processes to guarentee them all. Soviet society is now more than strong enough to throw the crutch away. Present achievements are providing realistic grounds for the hope and expectation that the first Russian Marxists could derive only from Marxist historical mythology.[66] With tangible scientific and economic success winning allegiance for the regime from those who matter politically, the authorities may feel secure enough to lessen their dependence on Marxist eschatology. Consequently, if this is correct, the historian can begin to withdraw from service on the 'historical front' and to return, at least partly, to his traditional pursuit of historical truth.

The hesitant re-emergence of sociology as an acceptable field may be the other side of the coin of history's return to its customary enterprise. Boundaries seem in the process of being drawn: historians study specific events; sociologists focus on general trends, patterns, and laws. As for historical materialism, it is quite possible that under the combined blows of rational history and rational sociology its fate will be the same as that suffered by its mate—dialectical materialism—under the blows of demythologized science. Perhaps the coffin for historical materialism is already being prepared under the title 'scientific communism', to which the familiar propaganda slogans and clichés are now being consigned, leaving history and sociology somewhat freer to engage in, or at least to search for, their proper concerns.

NOTES

[1] B. N. Ponomarev, 'The Tasks Facing Historical Scholarship and the Training of History Teachers and Researchers', tr. from *Voprosy istorii* (No. 1, 1963), in *Soviet Studies in History*, II (No. 1, 1963), pp. 5, 6; 'Soviet Historiography at a New Stage of Development', tr. from *Voprosy istorii* (No. 8, 1960), in *Current Digest of the Soviet Press*, XII (2 Nov. 1960), p. 11; 'The Party Central Committee Resolution "On the Tasks of Party Propaganda in Present-Day Conditions" and Historical Science', tr. from *Voprosy istorii* (No. 6, 1960), ibid. (31 Aug. 1960), p. 8. In 1957 Soviet historians were sharply reprimanded for moving too near 'bourgeois objectivity' during those hopeful months surrounding the Twentieth Party Congress. For an account of this repression, see Merle Fainsod, 'Soviet Russian Historians, or the Lessons of Burdzhalov', *Encounter*, XVIII (Mar. 1962), pp. 82–9, and Alexander Dallin, 'Recent Soviet Historiography', in *Russia under Khrushchev*, ed. Abraham Brumberg (New York, 1962), pp. 470–88.

[2] Ponomarev, 'Tasks', pp. 8, 26.

[3] Excerpts and summaries from the discussions at the 1964 conference were published in 'O Metodologicheskikh Voprosakh Istoricheskoi Nauki' (Concerning the Methodological Problems of Historical Science), *Voprosy istorii* (No. 3, 1964), pp. 3–68. Later that year, a much fuller compilation was published as a separate volume, *Istoriia i sotsiologiia* (History and Sociology) (Moscow, 1964). For these and similar 'anti-Stalin' declarations, see the conference coverage in *Voprosy istorii*, pp. 4, 6, 8, 26, 33, 34, 38, 39, 44, 51, 53, 55, 57–9; and in *Istoriia i sotsiologiia*, pp. 230, 234–35, 244–45.

[4] For a discussion of the return to the archives, see the relevant articles, particularly S. V. Utechin, 'Soviet Historiography after Stalin', and George Katkov, 'Soviet Historical Sources in the Post-Stalin Era', in *Contemporary History in the Soviet Mirror*, ed. John Keep and Lilianna Brisby (New York, 1964); see also translations in *Current Digest of the Soviet Press*, e.g., VII (No. 15, 1955), pp. 20–1, and XIV (No. 8, 1962), pp. 18–21. Here are two samples of current Soviet criticism of 'quotism', both drawn from the 1964 conference. 'Naturally, historians are no longer satisfied with stock formulas, based on nothing but a clever selection of quotations and often having nothing at all to do with the circumstances, country, or period about which a particular historian is writing.' 'Can one really limit oneself when explaining one or another set of historical phenomena to a few statements from the classics of Marxism that were relevant to concrete situations, and that were, moreover, based on a study of sources and literature accessible to them at that time, before the appearance of a great deal of new factual data?' (*Istoriia i sotsiologiia*, pp. 274, 292.)

[5] One of the most remarkable illustrations of this tendency is a study very frequently cited by Soviet historians: I. S. Kon, *Filosofskii Idealism i Krizis Burzhuaznoi Istoricheskoi Mysli* (Philosophical Idealism and the Crisis in Bourgeois Historical Thought) (Moscow, 1959).

[6] It may well be this concern that makes Soviet historians now so uncomfortable with the slogan attributed to M. N. Pokrovsky according to which 'history is politics projected back into the past'. See their rejection of this view of history and their denial that Pokrovsky ever expressed it in 'Obsuzhdenie Stati S. M. Dubrovskogo "Akademik M. N. Pokrovsky i Ego Rol v Razvitii Sovetskoi Istoricheskoi Nauki"' (A Discussion of S. M. Dubrovsky's Article 'Academician M. N. Pokrovsky and His Role in the Development of Soviet Historical Science'), *Voprosy istorii* (No. 3, 1962), pp. 34, 35, 37; and A. V. Gulyga, 'O Kharaktere Istoricheskogo Znaniia' (On the Character of Historical Knowledge), *Voprosy filosofii*, XVI (No. 9, 1962), p. 33. (Here and elsewhere in this article the 'soft sign' has been omitted in transliterations.)

[7] 'O Metodologicheskikh Voprosakh', p. 37.

[8] Gulyga, 'O Kharaktere', pp. 32–3.

[9] *Istoriia i sotsiologiia*, p. 101.

[10] 'O Metodologicheskikh Voprosakh', p. 48.

[11] *Istoriia i sotsiologiia*, p. 313.

[12] N. E. Zastenker, 'Problemy Istoricheskoi Nauki v Trudakh K. Marksa i F. Engelsa' (The Problems of Historical Science in the Works of

K. Marx and F. Engels), *Voprosy istorii* (No. 6, 1964), p. 19. The current attitude toward Pokrovsky is relevant here also. Although rehabilitated with praise and honours, he continues to be criticized for his 'naked' or 'abstract' 'sociologizing', and the dominant role he played in the twenties and early thirties is attributed to 'the inadequate scientific preparation' of young historians at the time. ('Obsuzhdenie Stati S. M. Dubrovskogo', pp. 34–5; 'O Metodologicheskikh Voprosakh', p. 53.)

¹³ A. Ya. Gurevich, 'Obshchii Zakon i Konkretnaia Zakonomernost v Istorii' (General Law and Concrete Regularities in History), *Voprosy istorii* (No. 8, 1965), pp. 15, 16, 19, 22, 23, 26. Gurevich, a professor at Kalinin Pedagogic Institute, is a specialist in medieval English and Norwegian history.

¹⁴ 'The historian who regards the historical process as something ineluctable', Gurevich continued this argument, 'and begins with the conviction that what in fact occurred was the only possible result of all that came before, incorrectly ignores other, unrealized possibilities, does not study different and, perhaps, mutually contradictory tendencies of development.' (Ibid., pp. 26–7.) Gurevich is hardly alone in this shift away from determinism and inevitability. The same point is argued by M. Ya. Gefter, 'O Metodologicheskikh Voprosakh', p. 48; Zastenker, 'Problemy', p. 20; E. N. Gorodetsky, 'Voprosy Metodologii Istoricheskogo Issledovaniia v Posleoktiabrskikh Trudakh V. I. Lenina' (Questions concerning the Methodology of Historical Research in the Post-October Works of V. I. Lenin), *Voprosy istorii* (No. 6, 1963), p. 32. Near the close of a lengthy survey of the evolution of Soviet historiography published in the leading party journal, *Kommunist*, we find the authors lamenting the absence of 'a scholarly work containing a comprehensive answer to the question of why it should have been Russia that became the birthplace of Leninism and that was the first to throw off the domination of the exploiters'. (*Current Digest of the Soviet Press*, XIII [23 Aug. 1961], pp. 17–18.) Even more surprising is G. E. Glezerman's complaint that 'the particular characteristics of causal relations in history have been very little studied', that 'there is not a single work' on this theme by a Soviet author. ('O Metodologicheskikh Voprosakh', p. 43; for further comment on this important theme, see note 17, below.)

¹⁵ 'O Metodologicheskikh Voprosakh', pp. 5, 8, 47–8.

¹⁶ Gulyga, 'O Kharaktere', p. 32.

¹⁷ The sad state of *zakonomernost*, the term used to denote historical and social 'laws', is a revealing indication of the demise of rigorous determinism. It would be worth a separate study to show the different ways the term is used, since each new usage increases the ambiguity and undermines the essential purpose of the concept, which is, to recall Ponomarev's injunction, to inspire 'a firm conviction of the inevitability of the triumph of communism'. It is now used to refer to constants persisting through history, to typical or repeated social relations, or to the core attribute of a society reflected in its various facets. Most often, 'laws' are mentioned briefly as the 'essence' 'hidden' somewhere within the complex fabric of events then dismissed as the historian turns to the serious business of working with the factual events themselves. Perhaps

its most general usage is as a synonym for causal relation of any kind, permitting the statement, for example, that realism in art is the 'lawful (*zakonomernyi*) result of an artistic comprehension of life'. In fact there seems now to be little that distinguishes the term from its common meaning of reasonable or intelligible, as in the phrases 'We consider this completely reasonable (*zakonomerno*) for the progress of social science', or 'It is entirely reasonable (*zakonomerno*) to put the question: what is historical methodology?'. In short we have come a long way from the time when Plekhanov proclaimed euphorically that history à la Marx was 'moving to its logical conclusion with the ineluctable character of astronomical phenomena'.

[18] Ponomarev, 'Tasks', pp. 15, 26.

[19] 'O Metodologicheskikh Voprosakh', p. 44; *Istoriia i sotsiologiia*, p. 322.

[20] L. V. Cherepnin, 'Istoricheskie Vzgliadi Gogolia' (The Historical Views of Gogol), *Voprosy istorii* (No. 1, 1964), pp. 77–8, 82, 90–1.

[21] For references to the poor response of Soviet readers to Soviet history books, see 'O Metodologicheskikh Voprosakh', pp. 21, 57, 59, and *Istoriia i sotsiologiia*, p. 285. For a Madison Avenue approach to this problem, see ibid., p. 248, where we find one enterprising participant in the 1964 conference urging history publications 'on good paper, illustrated with colourful pictorial reproductions and at an inexpensive price'.

[22] Still the best analysis of Stalin's radical 'idealization' of Soviet historiography is Klaus Mehnert, *Stalin versus Marx* (London, 1952). For the complete account of this transformation through its several stages, see Konstantin F. Shteppa, *Russian Historians and the Soviet State* (New Brunswick, N.J., 1962).

[23] G. M. Ivanov, 'Svoeobrazie Protsessa Ostrazheniia Deistvitelnosti v Istoricheskoi Nauke' (The Particular Process of the Reflection of Reality in Historical Science), *Voprosy istorii* (No. 2, 1962), p. 21.

[24] Gurevich, 'Obshchii Zakon', pp. 24–6.

[25] 'O Metodologicheskikh Voprosakh', pp. 31–32; Gorodetsky, 'Voprosy Metodologii', pp. 23, 30; *Istoriia i sotsiologiia*, pp. 271, 307, 317.

[26] 'O Metodologicheskikh Voprosakh', p. 27; *Istoriia i sotziologiia*, p. 273.

[27] Ibid., p. 282. An interesting expression of this more flexible approach to social development is the revival of Marx's 'Asiatic Mode of Production' theory, repressed by Stalin. Ibid., p. 275; Gulyga, 'O Kharaktere', p. 30; Zastenker, 'Problemy', p. 5.

[28] *Istoriia i sotsiologiia*, pp. 265–74.

[29] Ibid., p. 271. See also, G. E. Glezerman 'K Voprosu o Predmete Istoricheskogo Materializma' (Concerning the Question of the Subject of Historical Materialism), *Voprosy filosofii*, XIV (No. 3, 1960), p. 12.

[30] Gurevich, 'Obshchii Zakon', pp. 15, 16.

[31] A. Ya. Avrekh, 'K Voprosu o Metodakh Istoricheskogo Issledovaniia' (Concerning the Question of the Methods of Historical Research), *Voprosy istorii* (No. 10, 1963), pp. 110–20; *Istoriia i sotsiologiia*, pp. 308–10. Politically motivated or not, this return to 'concrete' Russian realities can only be welcomed by Western scholars.

[32] Gurevich, 'Obshchii Zakon', pp. 17–18, 29.

[33] Ibid., p. 18, n. 14.
[34] Ibid., p. 27.
[35] Gulyga, 'O Kharaktere', p. 31.
[36] Glezerman, 'K Voprosu', p. 9.
[37] 'O Metodologicheskikh Voprosakh', p. 58. The way towards such a 'phenomenology' was paved by Stalin's long and emphatic stress on ideological and political superstructure. Although Stalin's last party congress, the nineteenth, and his last ex-cathedra pronouncement, *Economic Problems of Socialism in the USSR* (New York, 1952), gave evidence of a return towards the 'objective' and 'lawful', the subjective idealistic position has become increasingly bold since his death. In addition to publications already cited, particularly that of Gurevich, see, e.g., the attack by philosophers V. F. Asmus and M. M. Rozental on those who try to derive philosophy from class or other economic categories. (V. F. Asmus, 'Nekotorye Voprosy Dialektiki Istoriko-Filosofskogo Protsessa i Evo Poznaniia' [Several Problems of the Dialectics of the Historical-Philosophical Process and Our Knowledge about It], *Voprosy filosofii*, XV [No. 4, 1961], pp. 111–12, 115–17, 121–23; M. M. Rozental, 'O Sviazi Filosofskikh Teorii s Ekonomicheskim Bazisom' [On the Connections between Philosophical Theory and the Economic Base], ibid., XIV [No. 3, 1960], pp. 146–7.) A. M. Deborin similarly warns against considering philosophy exclusively from the point of view of its relationship to extraneous factors and giving too little attention to the 'relatively independent, inner, logical development, the historical continuity of universal scientific thought'. (A. M. Deborin, 'Ob Istorizme Vozzrenii V. G. Belinskogo' [On Historicism in the Views of V. G. Belinsky], *Voprosy istorii* [No. 3, 1962], p. 53.)
[38] A. Ya. Gurevich, 'Nekotorye Aspekty Izucheniia Sotsialnoi Istorii' (Several Aspects of the Study of Social History), ibid. (No. 10, 1964), p. 55. This article appeared approximately a year before the article by Gurevich discussed above. The articles are obviously two aspects of a single and dramatically idealistic argument. Unless the themes in this 1964 article had the complete approval of party authorities, it is hardly likely that Gurevich's 1965 article would have been published at all, much less honoured with first mention on the cover list of contents.
[38a] Ibid., p. 59.
[39] Ibid., p. 54, 66.
[40] Ibid., p. 66. It has been a long time since anything of this sort appeared in a Soviet publication.
[41] N. I. Konrad, 'Notes on the Meaning of History', tr. from *Vestnik Istorii Mirovoi Kultury* (No. 2, 1961), in *Soviet Studies in History*, I (No. 1, 1962).
[42] Ibid., p. 13. Konrad's discussion of economic exploitation, when it does come, could be interpreted as an attack on the Soviet system as much as on any other: 'Exploitation results in various forms of social relations, of which two are the most clearly defined—exploitation by non-economic compulsion, i.e., outright force, and exploitation by economic compulsion. *Both forms include variants determined by different relationships of the exploited to the tools and means of production* and, in conjunction therewith,

288

different situations relative to the exploiter.' (Ibid. [italics mine].) Whether intended or not, there is present in this abstract formulation the system of economic and/or political compulsion *without* private property which has always been a central theme in the revisionists' contest with Soviet Marxists.

⁴³ Ibid., pp. 14–17.
⁴⁴ Ibid., pp. 20–21.
⁴⁵ 'O Metodologicheskikh Voprosakh', pp. 36–7.
⁴⁶ 'O Kharaktere', p. 34.
⁴⁷ 'O Metodologicheskikh Voprosakh', p. 43.
⁴⁸ Ivanov, 'Svoeobrazie Protsessa Otrazheniia', pp. 31–5.
⁴⁹ Ibid., pp. 21, 22.
⁵⁰ Gulyga, 'O Kharaktere', p. 31.
⁵¹ Asmus, 'Nekotorye Voprosy', p. 112.

⁵² O. M. Medushevskaia, 'Voprosy Teorii Istochnikovedeniia v Sovremennoi Frantsuzskoi Burzhuaznoi Istoriografii' (On the Question of the Theory of Source Research in Contemporary French Bourgeois Historiography), *Voprosy istorii* (No. 8, 1964), pp. 81–2.

⁵³ In connection with the current emphasis on greater objectivity, Soviet scholars like to recall Marx's attack on those 'base' persons who 'subordinate facts to predetermined aims' drawn from other than scholarly considerations, or Engels's similar judgment that 'any scholar who subordinates science to his ideal "cannot be considered a man of science since he begins with preconceived ideas"'. But how can the Soviet historian heed these commendable exhortations when he is so often reminded that 'one of the particular characteristics of the reflection of reality in historical science consists in the fact that it always takes place, consciously or unconsciously, through the prism of class interests; since it is not people in general, not some general subject, but a completely concrete subject, the bearer of the interests of a particular class, who apprehends historical reality and the struggle of social classes, in regard to which he cannot be impartial'. (Ivanov, 'Svoeobrazie Protsessa Otrazheniia', pp. 24, 31; Medushevskaia, 'Teorii Istochnikovedeniia', p. 81; Zastenker, 'Problemy', p. 23; *Istoriia i sotsiologiia*, p. 244.)

⁵⁴ The Polish physicist Leopold Infeld said it all in a sentence: 'As one of the most distinguished Soviet physicists informed me, physicists no longer read the Soviet philosophical journals and they don't care a damn what the philosophers [i.e., dialectical materialists] have to say.' (Leopold Infeld, 'As I See It', *Bulletin of the Atomic Scientists*, XXI [Feb. 1965], p. 14.) The Russian physicist, P. L. Kapitsa, is no less explicit. 'If, then, our scientists had listened to the philosophers in 1954 and had accepted this definition [of cybernetics as 'a reactionary pseudo-science'] as a guide for the further development of this science, it can safely be said that the conquest of cosmic space, of which we are all legitimately proud and for which the entire world respects us, could not have taken place, because it is impossible to direct spaceships without cybernetic machines.' Or again: 'It is still fresh in many people's minds how a number of our philosophers, dogmatically applying the method of dialectics, demonstrated that the theory of relativity was without foundations. . . . And so the physicists

carried out a number of nuclear reactions and verified Einstein's law not with individual atoms but on the scale of the atom bomb.' (P. L. Kapitsa, 'Theory, Experiment, Practice', tr. from *Ekonomicheskaya gazeta* [26 Mar. 1962], in *Current Digest of the Soviet Press*, XIV [No. 19, 1962], pp. 14–15.)

[55] Here, too, politics may be served. If, as discussed above, the stress on 'energy and enterprise' and other subjective factors in history has political value, so, clearly, does the emphasis on epistemological subjectivism. In listing criteria for selecting data, Gulyga included the 'criterion of value' and went on to explain this by saying that 'the historian frequently turns his attention to facts that play no role in the causal chain of past events, but that are of interest to contemporaries'. In a later article, after restating this theme, he compared such historical events as displays of military heroism with artistic productions, since both were valued not for their place in a past causal pattern but for their effect on people today. This calls to mind a reference by Ponomarev to earlier Russian military battles with Germany, since 'they alert the people to vigilance against the revival of aggressive forces in West Germany'. Is the criterion for selecting facts and events still to be, and now admittedly, only propaganda potency? ('O Metodologicheskikh Voprosakh', p. 37; A. V. Gulyga, 'Poniatie i Obraz v Istoricheskoi Nauke' [Understanding and Image in Historical Science], *Voprosy istorii* [No. 9, 1965], pp. 10, 14; see also Gurevich, 'Obshchii Zakon', p. 29.)

[56] Unfortunately space does not permit a discussion of this welcome tolerance of Western thought. For example, see Asmus, 'Nekotorye Voprosy', p. 123; Deborin, 'Ob Istorizme', pp. 62–3; *Istoriia i sotsiologiia*, p. 275; 'Obsuzhdenie Stati S. M. Dubrovskogo, p. 38; Medushevskaia, 'Teorii Istochnikovedeniia', p. 88; Zastenker, 'Problemy', pp. 21–2. During the first, tense weeks of the Vietnam crisis, in February 1965, a group of about fifty books on American history written mainly by American 'bourgeois' historians was on display in one of the most conspicuous sections of the Lenin Library in Moscow, visible to everyone passing from the main catalogue halls to the central reading room. The revival in Soviet dialectics of the 'negation of the negation' concept, suppressed by Stalin, seems at least in part due to this willingness to accept the emergence of bourgeois tendencies in Soviet life and thought. 'The "second negation" represents a surmounting of the limitations of the "first", a particular kind of necessary "historical corrective" to it', correcting the excesses committed by the first negation in its too thorough destruction of the 'thesis'. (O. O. Yakhot, 'Otritsanie i Preemstvennost v Istoricheskom Razvitii' [Negation and Continuity in Historical Development], *Voprosy filosofii*, XV [No. 3, 1961], pp. 147–8, 151.)

[57] Gulyga, 'Poniatie i Obraz', pp. 5, 7–8.

[58] Id., 'O Kharaktere', pp. 36–8, and 'The Subject Matter of Historical Scholarship', tr. from *Voprosy istorii* (No. 4, 1964), in *Soviet Studies in History*, III (No. 4, 1965), p. 54. As an example of such artistic history, Gulyga referred to the works of the great pre-revolutionary 'bourgeois' historian, Vasily Kliuchevsky. (Id., 'O Kharaktere', p. 38.) In his most recent article on the subject, Gulyga goes on at some length illustrating how 'tragedy' and other literary categories are applicable to historical

interpretation, and why 'universal history is a superb poetess'. He even draws some support from H. Stuart Hughes, *History as Art and as Science* (New York, 1964). (Gulyga, 'Poniatie i Obraz', pp. 11–14.)

[59] *Istoriia i sotsiologiia*, pp. 294–5. Another member of the Academy of Science's Institute of History attending the 1964 conference supported this view of history by reminding the conference 'that "history" is a translation from the Greek word for "story"'. (Ibid., p. 320.)

[60] Cherepnin, 'Vzgliadi Gogolia', p. 83. And from whom did Gogol in turn learn 'the art of re-creating the historical past' ? From the great works of world literature beginning with Homer, we find from a letter from Gogol to the poet A. N. Zhukovsky quoted by Cherepnin. (Ibid., p. 79.)

[61] 'O Metodologicheskikh Voprosakh', pp. 10–11. Much the same terms are used by Cherepnin in describing the faculties employed by Gogol, who 'apprehended the past not simply through the eyes of a historian, but through the inspired sensitivity of the artist'. (Cherepnin, 'Vzgliadi Gogolia', p. 81.)

[62] 'O Metodologicheskikh Voprosakh', p. 37.

[63] Gulyga, 'Poniatie i Obraz', pp. 13–14.

[64] Id., 'O Kharaktere', p. 38. Were Soviet historians to heed these promptings from the 'methodologists', there would open to them a wide range of immensely fruitful sources of knowledge and insight so long blocked by dogmatic conservatism and obscurantism. From the manner of his presentation, there can be little doubt that Gurevich thoroughly approves of the way Huizinga and Febvre made use of 'works of art and literature for discovering, through analysis of a society's aesthetic values, a people's psychology, their forms of perceiving life and nature, and their normative systems'. 'In the works of creative writers, poets, intellectuals, theologians, historians, and scientists of the later Middle Ages', Gurevich continued, 'both Febvre and Huizinga are concerned not only, and perhaps not so much, with what people intentionally express, as with what they express unconsciously, without intent.' (Gurevich, 'Nekotorye Aspekty', pp. 60–1, 63, 66.)

[65] After all, it is Ilya Ehrenburg who gave the name to the 'thaw' and who by his public statements, fascinating memoirs, and personal interventions has done as much as anyone to keep it going. And speaking of literature, who would have expected that Stalin's 'engineers of the soul' would be carrying on as they have been over the last thirteen years ? For brief biographical sketches of the more prominent historians and philosophers mentioned in this article, see, among other such works, *Who's Who in the USSR* published by the Munich Institute for the Study of the USSR, a second edition of which was published in New York and London in 1966. Time will tell whether the exile of Andrei Sinyavsky (Tertz) and Yuli Daniel (Arzhak) will seriously impede the further evolution of the 'thaw' in Soviet literature. It has been argued that their defence and the absence of 'confessions' represent an improvement over Stalin's 'trials' of such 'enemies of the people'. Even more encouraging was the display of sympathy, both public and tacit, that the writers received both from their own countrymen and from Communist Party members abroad.

[66] In the light of all that has been said here about voluntarism and

subjectivism in Soviet historical theory, it might be more accurate to say that the myths have changed, that the symbol of Prometheus representing the transformation of nature, society, and man himself through endless conquests of conscious human will and reason has replaced the myth of that weird, impersonal, animistic material force that somehow guaranteed the realization of the good society. The current development of Soviet historical theory may, therefore, be viewed as one more phase, following quite consistently the Lenin and Stalin phases, in a process that is bringing Soviet theory in line with Soviet practice, which from the beginning so dramatically demonstrated the determining power of ideas and ideals in history.

D. M. SHAPIRO

Research into Contemporary History in the Soviet Union

Contemporary history in the USSR has been an essential part of the actual political system as in few other countries. Indeed the writing of history of whatever country, of whatever age, has had more political overtones than we commonly expect. This aspect of the writing of contemporary history in the Soviet Union has had its due share of notice in Western writing.[1] This aspect is also much stressed in Soviet surveys of historical writing. Recently, however, the tone of anniversary volumes on Soviet historical writing has begun to change. The change can be highlighted by comparing the tone of the volume issued in 1942 to commemorate twenty-five years of historical science in the USSR with that of the two volumes on writing between the Twentieth and Twenty-second Party Congresses.[2]

This paper will attempt to consider the writing of contemporary history in the Soviet Union purely as a contribution to the study of history and not to the study of contemporary or recently past Soviet politics. The pitfalls in this approach are obvious. One can too easily forget the constraints placed both on research and writing by current political preoccupations. Nevertheless, it may for once be worthwhile to ignore the better publicized facets of Soviet historical writing. Rather than asking why a given interpretation is offered at a certain moment of, say, the strategic planning of a phase of the Second World War, let us rather ask how far a real contribution to knowledge has been made.

It is unfortunately easy to ignore how much work has been done by Soviet historians. For one thing, relatively few Soviet intellectuals read much of it. This point is worth emphasizing. A controversial article in *Novyi Mir* needs no advertising. But comparatively few Moscow or Leningrad intellectuals would be aware of the unspectacular but serious writing on collectivization being

293

produced by the group of historians round V. P. Danilov. Soviet citizens do not read history for pleasure, with the possible exception of war memoirs. Textbooks, of course, are published in very large prints; but there is no equivalent of A. J. P. Taylor's *English History, 1914–1945* selling widely to the general public. In no other country has the writing of history become so completely professionalized as to exclude general interest. This applies quite as much to the writing of the history of the period before 1900 as to contemporary history. It is also independent to some degree of the constraints imposed politically on the writing of history. In part the lack of appeal is a consequence of a general debasement of Russian as written by scholars. The lack is felt by many Soviet intellectuals. They can read Solovyev and Klyuchevsky for pleasure (both have recently been reprinted) but can name no contemporary Soviet historian who interests them. This complaint is no doubt exaggerated. But together with political preoccupations, both theirs and ours, it explains why too much Soviet work has failed to receive due attention.

And yet, in a formal sense, there is little excuse for failing to keep abreast of current Soviet historical writing. The formidable Russian tradition in bibliography and historiography has been maintained and reinforced. The running national bibliography, the annual cumulations, the annual bibliographies of the Academy of Sciences publishing house, the running bibliographies of journal articles and reviews, all furnish the diligent scholar with unsurpassable bibliographical control.[3] Specialist bibliographies, for example, exist for those who wish to study Soviet writing on Africa, the Kurds, or the Bryansk *oblast* of the USSR.[4] It should be noted that Soviet bibliographies have been annually cumulated since 1946 in *Bibliografiya sovetskoi bibliografii* (a volume was issued also for 1939). Learned journals print lists of theses defended. It is, nevertheless, a matter for regret that the Lenin Library's catalogue of thesis accessions is not at the moment available for foreign subscription. (Access to theses is a topic that will be treated later.)

So much by way of prolegomena.

I. THE ORGANIZATION OF RESEARCH

The Soviet Union inherited an academic and educational system in which the Academy of Sciences and the universities dominated the study of history. This continued into the 1920s. A parallel system of research organizations was established in the 1920s, but at the end of that decade largely fused with a reorganized Academy of Sciences. The dualism of the 1920s has, however, reappeared. The party, while no longer doubting the Marxism of the academy, has created its own deposit archive and research institute in the Institute of Marxism-Leninism and, to some extent, its own university in the Academy of Social Sciences attached to the Central Committee of the CPSU. Meanwhile the spread of teachers' training colleges (*pedinstituty*) has created a network of places of higher education where research is carried on. Even more important is the development of specialist research institutes in the various social sciences that contribute to the study of contemporary history.

The Institute of History of the Academy of Sciences, both in Moscow and in Leningrad, dominates and organizes research into all periods of history. The domination is both in sheer numbers of research workers and hence in the ability to organize collective research and publication. Within the institute there are groups of historians assigned to regularly-constituted committees charged with oversight of research into certain topics. Academician I. I. Mints in Moscow has been responsible for the co-ordination of work on the October Revolution. V. P. Danilov, also of the Moscow Institute of History, has a group of historians working on the history of collectivization. The Leningrad branch of the institute has been notable for some time for the work done on the economic history of Russia immediately before the Revolution. The impression that this account may give is perhaps of overmuch centralization and direction. Nevertheless, such a system did allow for great and immediate concentration on more contemporary themes, once it had been decided in the late 1950s that this was desirable and necessary. It should be noted that the institute admits and trains its own graduate students; in recent years its intake into graduate work has probably exceeded that of the history departments of Moscow and Leningrad State Universities. The future contemporary historians in the Soviet Union are for the most part being trained in this and other institutions where the emphasis is on collective research.

Moscow and Leningrad State Universities preserve a somewhat different and older tradition of scholarly research in their history departments.[5] While it would be wrong to press the antithesis far, the organization of the teaching departments obviously does not lend itself to the creation of research teams. For the same type of organizational reason, the relatively recent concentration on contemporary history has been less noticeable in the universities. Until recently it has been held that serious research for practical purposes stopped at 1900. There were, of course, exceptions, Professor Chermenskii of Moscow State University being one; he has worked steadily since the 1930s on the history of the first decade of the twentieth century. The feeling that an interest in contemporary history is not for serious scholars is no doubt compounded in the universities by the fact that for so long the history of the Soviet Union was the province of departments charged with political instruction. Nevertheless, there are signs that the study of the 1920s has been taken up, and not only in history departments.[6] Much historical work is being undertaken by graduate students in economics.

Foreigners may perhaps be forgiven for discussing Soviet universities in terms of Moscow and Leningrad. These are the places we visit most. But they are also the universities with the most lively traditions of historical study. In prestige and in access to library and archive resources, they combine the strengths shared in Britain by London and Oxbridge. This is not to denigrate the other universities, from Kishinev to Vladivostok. But we need better access to these universities and to their publications. Their periodical publications (*uchenye zapiski*) are almost impossible to purchase through Soviet trading organizations and are rarely to be found complete in those Western libraries that obtain them by exchange. The Soviet authorities have also shown great, and surely unnecessary, reluctance in placing Western students outside Moscow and Leningrad.

The Institute of Marxism-Leninism is the centre of party archival administration and research. Of all the institutions engaged in historical research, IML is closest to the organs of ideological control. It therefore exercises a general supervisory function over the most political of the contentious issues in contemporary history. It was in IML that recent discussions took place on the historiography of 1941. In general IML is an institution to which access is difficult, though not of course for Eastern Europeans. It has played a large part in sponsoring multi-volume publications on the Revolution and in reprinting most of the stenographic reports of party congresses and conferences. But with these exceptions it is not an institution that as such has contributed much to recent developments in the study of Soviet history. Its personnel are ideologists more than historians, even if they have passed through the Academy Institute of History.

The Academy of Social Sciences attached to the Central Committee of the CPSU has played a much larger role in fostering research on recent Soviet history. It is the apex of a system of party education. The party has encouraged study of its own functioning; the quantity of theses presented is large, even if relatively few are published. Professor J. Armstrong's work on the Ukrainian apparat, *The Soviet Bureaucratic Elite*, gives some indication of the type of material that these theses provide. The difficulty now experienced in seeing copies of theses is offset by the new regulations requiring major publication before the candidate may submit a thesis for defence. Thanks to this, the work of the Academy of Social Sciences is much more available to Western scholars than that of the Institute of Marxism-Leninism. At the same time the Academy of Social Sciences directly sponsors a considerable amount of publication.[7]

As already mentioned, the spread of places of higher education throughout the Soviet Union, most notably of teachers' training colleges (*pedinstituty*), has developed a wide range of centres of research. All universities and training colleges naturally generate work on the local history of their region. For many years it was easier to write about the recent history of the Soviet Union on the local scale. Much of this writing is to be found in the *uchenye zapiski* of these institutions.[8] While I emphasize the role of the teachers' training colleges in fostering research since they have attracted little attention, it remains true, of course, that the major provincial universities such as Kiev, Kazan, Saratov, Tbilisi, and Tartu make a disproportionate contribution.

The most important recent development in the actual location of research has been the establishment of the Siberian branch of the Academy of Sciences at Novosibirsk. This has immediately led to some large-scale publications on the recent as well as on the pre-revolutionary history of Siberia. Novosibirsk has also led the way in fostering sociology and in demanding more accurate statistics for economic planning, both preoccupations that have contributed to the study of recent Soviet history.

Novosibirsk is only the latest, if most powerful, example of the geographical spread of the Academy of Sciences. Virtually every

K*

Union Republic now has its own Academy of Sciences, each with its own Institute of History. In many of the Union Republics these institutes play the same role *vis-à-vis* the other institutions of higher education as the Institute of History of the All-Union Academy in Moscow and Leningrad. The outsider also senses that in the Union Republics the Institutes of History play a larger role within the Academies of Sciences because these local academies have the politically important task of describing the ethnic national contribution of the Union Republics. The president of the Moldavian Academy of Sciences, for example, is a historian, A. S. Grosul. Nevertheless, these local academies have turned rather more slowly to the study of contemporary history than the parent body.[9]

More important even than the geographical spread has been the spread of disciplines now contributing to the study of contemporary history. The role of the Institute of International Relations is obvious; so is that of the Institute of World Economics and International Relations. The latter is an institution where the more historically-oriented members wish to emphasize the 'and' in the title—a phenomenon also to be found among political scientists at the London School of Economics and Political Science. The Institute of International Relations is not only a place of research but is also largely involved in the training of diplomats. Members of the Institute of World Economics are apt to suggest that their institution is the more scholarly. Since neither has been very notable in welcoming foreign scholars, it is hard to judge. Certainly a comparison of their publications does not suggest any great difference in this respect. Between them they dominate Soviet study of the history of the modern world, with the exception of the specialized Oriental and African Institutes.

Economics and sociology have largely influenced the availability of research materials for the contemporary historian of the Soviet Union. Economists' demands, and indeed the needs of the new types of planning, have elicited a mass of statistical material. The role of the sociologists is the more striking because it is the more recent. Their studies of workers' time-budgets, of the use of leisure, of educational opportunity and social occupation, of the extent of religious belief, all furnish valuable material and should encourage our historians of the Soviet Union to widen the range of our interests. The fashion for what are termed 'concrete social investigations' is now rampant; but the main centres of sociological research remain Moscow, Leningrad, and Novosibirsk.[10]

2. JOURNALS

The leading historical journal is *Voprosy istorii* (Problems—or literally Questions—of History). This is published monthly, issues average 220 pages, and its circulation is currently 23,000 copies. It covers all periods of the history of the whole world. The tone, as befits a central, more official journal, is responsible; since a troubled period in 1956–57, editorial policy has not been adventurous. *Novaya i noveishaya istoriya* (Modern and Contemporary History) appears six times a year, averages 180 pages an issue, and has a circulation of 12,500 copies; this is also a journal of world history.[11]

Among the more specialized journals, the most important are: *Istoriya SSSR*, the major journal on the history of Russia and the Soviet Union. It appears six times a year, averages 240 pages an issue, and has a circulation of 8,000 copies. One notable feature is the amount of attention given to foreign and Western writing on Russian and Soviet history. The tone of these reviews and surveys has in recent years become much more scholarly. The long review article on E. H. Carr's *Socialism in One Country* that appeared in 1963 contrasts notably with the passing treatment in a 1961 survey of foreign literature on the Revolution.[12] Professor Venturi has been given the opportunity in its pages to print some pointed criticism of Soviet writing of history. Altogether the journal gives an impression of liveliness. So did the short-lived *Istoricheskie nauki* (Historical Sciences) and the discontinued *Istoricheskii arkhiv* (Historical Archive); the latter was particularly valuable as the vehicle for the publication of archival material and its disappearance is most regrettable. To a minor extent the place of the latter is supplied by *Sovetskie arkhivy* (Soviet Archives), which continues from 1966 the journal formerly known as *Voprosy arkhivovedeniya*.

Two of the most interesting journals for recent history are, as is to be expected, concerned with party history and with military history; *Voprosy istorii KPSS* (Problems of the History of the CPSU) and *Voenno-istoricheskii zhurnal* (Military-historical Journal).

Finally one may note the largest of the purely university journals *Vestnik MGU*, Series IX. This is one series of Moscow State

University's periodical publication; it appears six times a year, with a circulation of 1,750 copies.

3. AREAS OF CONCENTRATION

In the pre-revolutionary period there has long been an emphasis on economic history. Financial policy has been well explored. Under titles that tend to include the phrase 'monopoly capitalism', the history of the major branches of industry in the period 1890–1917 has by now been written.[13]

The fortieth anniversary of the 1917 Revolution was heavily greeted—the adverb is intended literally—by the publication of a ten-volume set of documents and a very detailed chronology that so far has reached its fifth volume. There is still no good Soviet history of the Revolution; Academician I. I. Mints has written a three-volume history, of which the first volume should already have been published. In general, Soviet scholars have concentrated on publication of materials. This enables us to see in ever greater detail the actions of the Bolsheviks, even if contemporary publications must be checked against those of the 1920s.[14] Their opponents are not so well studied, but the rarer works on such themes as the SRs arouse useful as well as politically heated discussions.[15] The peasant anarchist movement of Makhno has recently (*Voprosy istorii*, 1966, No. 9, pp. 37–60) been treated at serious length. Nevertheless, the strength of Soviet writing on the Revolution remains in its treatment of the Bolshevik movement. This only in part reflects the availability of archive material. So far no serious use has been made by Soviet historians of the Prague archive presented at the end of the Second World War by the Czech government to the Soviet authorities. Nevertheless, there are signs of a welcome tendency for the economic historians of the earlier period to interest themselves in the politics of the Revolution and Civil War.[16]

The politics of the 1920s are just beginning to receive scholarly attention. The work of I. Ya. Trifonov should be noted; A. Ya. Vyatkin is also writing on the intra-party struggles of the 1920s.[17] Interesting material on this topic has begun to appear in the journal *Voprosy istorii KPSS*.

Collectivization has been made the subject of a historical drive largely under the supervision of V. P. Danilov. A large series of documentary publications is under way under the general title of

Istoriya Kollektivisatsii selskogo khozyaistva SSSR: Dokumenty i materialy (1962–). The pace is a good deal more measured than that of the events described; the results promise to be more fruitful. Admittedly the hardships suffered by the population are not prominent among the topics of research. Here is one aspect of Soviet history where the not so arid figures of statistical data can be brought into use to complete a picture. The scale of research can be indicated by the increasing specialization of the monographs.[18]

The latest subject to attract major attention is industrialization. A series of volumes of documents is planned, of which the first to appear was on the northwest region in 1925–28. The series is described in *Sovetskie arkhivy*, 1966, No. 1, pp. 68–71, and seems likely to become rapidly a bibliographical rarity unless the print order is increased.

The history of the Second World War is now a major Soviet industry and, as already suggested, the one aspect of contemporary history as now written in the Soviet Union that commands popular attention. The six-volume history, largely Khrushchevite in tone, is well known; it was largely used by A. Werth in his *Russia at War, 1941–1945*. Since this subject is so much that of John Erickson and has had so much Western attention in general, it is worth saying here only that the political swings have been much to the advantage of historical research. At various times writing has been dominated by Stalinist interpretations, then by Krushchevite. The rise and fall of Zhukov in the mid-1950s enabled rival and lesser commanders to have their say in a manner that yields nothing to the standards elsewhere of conflict in military history.

In 1945 the province of the Soviet historian reaches its limits. The study of the post-war period belongs to the party research workers, the economist, and the sociologist. It is, however, worth pointing out how the contemporary preoccupations of the economist and the sociologist give material needed by the historian of an earlier period. Two examples must suffice: the series of statistical handbooks that have been published for virtually all regions of the Soviet Union since the mid-1950s allow for retrospective computation.[19] The sociological investigations of religious practice in the Soviet Union give us a rare insight into one of the conditions of popular life, especially in the countryside.[20]

In the study of contemporary foreign history, the two Moscow institutes seem to have attained a workmanlike, if slightly dull, level of scholarship. But neither at the Institute of International Relations nor at the Institute of World Economics are there scholars who have attained the international eminence of, say, Professor Porshnev in the study of seventeenth-century France, or of the late Academician Kosminsky in medieval English history. Whatever the reasons, Soviet Marxism does not lend as ready an inspiration in the study of the twentieth century. More impressive work has been done on Soviet foreign policy. To date the principal publication is the series of documents on Soviet policy in the 1920s, *Dokumenty vneshnei politiki SSSR*, which it has been recently announced will be extended to twelve volumes. Nevertheless, Academician Maisky for the 1930s has still to rely on the British published documents.

4. ARCHIVES

The Main Archive Administration (*Glavnoe administrativnoe upravlenie*) is the central organizing institution. It was formerly attached to the Ministry of the Interior, but is now responsible to the Council of Ministers.

It does *not* control the archives of the Foreign Ministry. These are a law unto themselves. Since foreign researchers have had great difficulty with access even for the early nineteenth century, contemporary historians must presumably do without. If Academician Maisky may not use his own despatches in his memoirs, what can we expect? (That is not, however, a reason for not asking.) Other important archives not controlled by GAU are the MSS Divisions of the Lenin Library in Moscow and the Saltykov-Shchedrin Library in Leningrad. These, however, do not contain material of great significance to the contemporary historian. Finally, the archives of the Academy of Science, of which detailed descriptions are in print, may yield useful material for the intellectual historian.

GAU, however, controls the essential state, central, and local archives.[21] For the contemporary historian these are:

The Central State Archive of the October Revolution
(TsGAOR—in Moscow)
The Central State Historical Archive
(TsGIA—in Leningrad)
The Central State Military Historical Archive
(TsGVIA—in Moscow)

The Central State Archive of the Red Army
(TsGAKA—in Moscow)
The Central State Archive of the Navy
(TsGAVMF—in Leningrad)
The Central State Archive of Literature and Art
(TsGALI—in Moscow)

Each Union Republic, each *krai*, and each *oblast* has its own archive. For many of them detailed published descriptions exist, even if somewhat outdated.[22] As early as 1945 a guide was published to the Archive of the Red Army, listing largely materials of the 1920s.

5. THE FUTURE OF RESEARCH

The impertinence of suggesting future lines of research for Soviet scholars is fortunately no temptation. Advice would not be heeded; it may be doubted if it is necessary.

The ability of Soviet contemporary historians to contribute seriously to research would be hard to doubt. The work being done on the history of the Second World War, on collectivization, and on industrialization is of sufficient quality to substantiate that claim. Much of the work done on the history of the Revolution itself demonstrates that historical research can flourish even on the most political of themes.

The Soviet historian suffers from serious restrictions in access to material. He apparently has no access to the records of police administration, at any rate after the founding and Civil War operation of the Cheka. He likewise has access only to printed materials from the Foreign Ministry archives. These restrictions obviously would not preclude altogether the study of the intra-party politics of the 1930s, of the effects of collectivization, and of the Great Purges. For the moment these topics are the preserve of the Western historian.

If one reproach is to be made of Soviet historians it is that they are insufficiently Marxist. Togliatti demanded a Marxist analysis of the career of Stalin. Yet we wait in vain for an academic Soviet biography of Lenin. Surely the teasing problem of the relationship between society and the individual ought to encourage more scholarly writing about Lenin.

Meanwhile to the foreign researcher go the most delicate themes.

For the moment he need not fear that Soviet scholars will have greater access to materials. Indeed foreign work may well facilitate the opening of Soviet archives to Soviet scholars and this, surely, would be a useful and honourable role for foreign scholars. (One might look to the effect of Professor A. J. Marder on the British fifty-year rule.)

If one tries to list the possible deficiencies of foreign research, they might be over-concentration on the centre, over-ready acceptance of the theory of totalitarianism, and a failure to read Soviet materials in print. We need more attention throughout the whole period 1900–45 paid to what was happening outside Moscow and Leningrad. We need to investigate Soviet phenomena not so much with the preconceived notion that the totalitarian juggernaut works; we might then begin to write more plausible accounts of, say, the Komsomol. Finally we must use Soviet materials on the 1917 Revolution with due speed. Professor Harcave's book on 1905, *First Blood*, at last makes good use in English of documents published in the 1920s. Let us hope in future that our industry will be greater.

NOTES

[1] Among other works: K. F. Shteppa, *Russian Historians and the Soviet State* (Rutgers UP, 1962); on recent trends: K. Marko, 'Ghosts behind the Ghost—Stalin under Revision', *Survey*, No. 60 (July 1966), pp. 112–18.

[2] A. M. Pankratova *et al.* (eds), *Dvadtsat pyat let istoricheskoi nauki v SSSR* (Moscow, 1942); *Sovetskaya istoricheskaya nauka ot XX k XXII syezdu KPSS—Istoriya SSSR* (Moscow, 1962) and—*Istoriya zapadnoi Evropy i Ameriki* (Moscow, 1963).

[3] *Knizhnaya letopis* (1907–); *Ezhegodnik knigi* SSSR (1925–1919, 1935, 1941–); *Ezhegodnik knigi AN SSSR*; *Zhurnalnaya letopis* (1926–37) continued by *Letopis zhurnalnykh statei* (1938–); *Letopis retsenzii* (1934–). These dates refer to the years covered, *not* to the date of the edition. Note that the constituent Union Republics publish similar running bibliographies.

[4] *Bibliografiya Afriki*, vol. I (Moscow, 1964–); *Bibliografiya po kurdovedeniyu* (Moscow, 1963); V. Antoshina, N. Davydova, *Bryanskaya oblast* (Bryansk, 1958). Note especially for memoir material *Istoriya sovetskogo obshchesta v vospominaniyakh sovremennikov*, vol. I (Mocow, 1958–).

[5] To avoid possible confusion, it should be noted that *fakultet* is here translated by 'department'.

[6] Leningrad University Press is publishing I. Ya. Trifonov's *Klassy i klassovaya borba v SSSR*, of which the first volume (1964) deals with the period 1921–23.

[7] A typical example: *Ukreplenie soyuza rabochego klassa i krestyanstva v period krutogo podyema selskogo khazyaistva (1953–1958 gg.)* (The strengthening of the alliance of the working class and peasantry in the period of the sharp rise in agriculture.) Stodgy titles can conceal material of interest.

[8] These series can be checked in such bibliographies as *Periodicheskaya pechat SSSR, 1917–1949 . . . svodnye ukazateli* (Moscow, 1963). Note that this has a geographical index.

[9] This remark needs qualification. The Central Asian Academies, for example, in particular that of Kazakhstan, have sponsored much recent publication on the Soviet period.

[10] A two-volume work that summarizes work to 1964 is *Sotsiologiya v SSSR* (Moscow, 1965).

[11] *Mirovaya ekonomika* is the journal of the Institute of World Economics.

[12] I. I. Mints (ed.), *Zarubezhnaya literatura ob oktyabrskoi revolyutsii* (Moscow, 1961).

[13] The latest industry to be described in a monograph is textiles; V. Ya. Laverychev, *Monopolisticheskii kapital v tekstilnoi promyshlennosti Rossii, 1900–1917 gg.* (Moscow, 1963). On the economic policy of the Provisional Government; P. V. Volobuev, *Ekonomicheskaya politika Vremennogo pravitelstva* (Moscow, 1962). On the war period; A. L. Sidorov, *Finansovoe polozhene Rossii v gody pervoi mirovoi roiny, 1914–1917* (Moscow, 1960); also two volumes of well chosen documents: *Ekonomicheskoe polozhenie Rossii nakanune . . . revolyutsii* (Moscow, 1957); a third volume has just been announced for publication.

[14] This task of checking is aided by the bibliography of documentary publication, E. N. Gorodetsky (ed.), *Velikaya Oktyabrskaya sotsialisticheskaya revolyutsiya: Bibliograficheskii ukazatel dokumentalnykh publikatsii* (Moscow, 1961).

[15] For example, K. Gusev, *Krakh partii levykh eserov* (Moscow, 1963); discussion reported in *Voprosy istorii* (No. 10, 1964), pp. 176 ff.

[16] For example, P. V. Volobuev, *Proletariat: burzhuaziya Rossii v 1917 godu* (Moscow, 1964).

[17] I. Ya. Trifonov—see footnote 6 above. A. Ya. Vyatkin, *Razgrom kommunisticheskoi partiei trotskizmai drugikh antileninskikh grupp*, vol. I: Nov. 1920–25 (Leningrad, 1966).

[18] For example, Yu. A. Moshkov, *Zernovaya problema v gody sploshnoi kollektivizatsii . . . 1929–1932* (Moscow, 1966); P. N. Sharova, *Kollektivizatsiya . . . v tsentralno-chernozemnoi oblasti, 1928–1932* (Moscow, 1963).

[19] These handbooks are annually listed by M. Kaser in *Soviet Studies*. The eighth such list is in vol. 17 (Jan. 1966), pp. 391–3. Another example of the economist helping the historian is in the history of prices: A. N. Malafeev, *Istoriya tsenoobrazovaniya v SSSR, 1917–1963* (Moscow, 1964).

[20] These can be followed in the standard periodicals on religion and

CONTEMPORARY HISTORY IN EUROPE

atheism, both more interesting than they sound: *Voprosy istorii religii i ateizma* and *Exhegodnik Muzeya istorii religii i ateizma*. Another type of material of obvious importance to the historian, mentioned above, is the publication of the 1959 census data.

²¹ I am very unclear about the legal status of the Institute of Marxism-Leninism, but assume that it must be considered to be independent of the GAU. But it must also be presumed to be closed to foreigners except in cases such as the exchanges of copies effected by the Institute of Social History. A somewhat outdated account is G. A. Belov *et al.* (eds.), *Gosudarst vennye arkhivy SSSR* (Moscow, 1956).

²² G. A. Belov *et al.*, op. cit., pp. 484–8, list some publications of the period 1941–56.

USA

ALLAN G. BOGUE

The 'New' Political History*

Thousands of scholars study, teach, or write American history. Score upon score of commercial and scholarly presses speed the researches of these scholars to an audience provided by their professional colleagues and the general public. To search for trends or to look for common denominators in this massive outpouring is a task for the brave, the gifted, or the foolish. On occasion, however, accident or incident reveals a purposive current in the relentless tide even to those who lack the ideal qualifications of the historiographer. So was it recently, when a political scientist searched in his midwestern university for a scalogram computer programme and learned that the only deck on campus belonged to a historian. His discovery reflected the growing interest in quantification and social science theory and method that has been developing among American political historians for some years now.

American historians experimented with quantification in earlier years. Frederick Jackson Turner and some of his Wisconsin students, most notably Orin G. Libby, were industriously mapping election returns and analysing legislative roll calls at the turn of the century. Libby's plea for the systematic study of congressional roll calls appeared in the Annual Report of the American Historical Association in 1896.[1] Turner never lost his enthusiasm for such methods and the imprint of his influence shows in the major publication of a number of scholars. Work in this tradition appeared as late as 1941, but the early interest in quantification

* I am indebted to J. Rogers Hollingsworth and Joel Silbey for critical advice during the preparation of this article. I would also like to thank the many colleagues with whom I have discussed this subject, or who have replied to my inquiries, in particular Thomas B. Alexander, William O. Aydelotte, Lee Benson, Thomas C. Cochran, Merle Curti, Richard P. McCormick, and Rowland L. Mitchell.

and political ecology among historians subsided, perhaps because of the inadequate statistical methods of the pioneers.

At present a small number of historians are trying to apply social science methods and theory in American political history with varying degrees of rigour. The nine men who were early members of the American Historical Association's *ad hoc* committee for the collection of the basic quantitative data of American political history, and others who have since become associated with the committee's work in one way or another, are at the centre of the movement. Their seminars are producing recruits for the cause, as are the seminars of some other historians who allow their graduate students to apply methods learned in satisfying the requirements of minor or related fields. During the summer of 1965, thirty-five historians gathered at Ann Arbor for a three-week seminar on voting and legislative behaviour under the auspices of the Inter-University Consortium for Political Research.[2] This group certainly did not include all the professional historians who are interested in such matters and only representative doctoral candidates were invited. Not all those in attendance, however, were deeply dedicated to a quantitative approach. It was an assembly composed in undetermined proportions of prophets, converts, neophytes, seekers, and scoffers. In the argot of the political scientist, slightly corrupted, political historians today number an overwhelming majority of standpatters, a small group of dedicated switchers, and a growing number of their new votaries. Some believe that the members of the last two categories are sufficiently different from the majority of American political historians to justify calling them behavioural historians—understanding behavioural to connote, in this instance, a strong interest in the methods, results, and implications of measurement, combined with some desire to produce research that is respectable by social-science criteria.[3] I realize that the term raises problems, but for our purposes it is a convenient label.

The behavioural historians have not yet produced an impressive body of literature bearing upon American politics. There are in print various voting studies using ecological correlations, most of them quite simple in method;[4] two books and a number of articles in which scaling techniques or simpler methods of roll-call analysis are used;[5] a number of collective biographies of political elites;[6] a couple of articles dealing with the characteristics of the national electorate between 1800 and 1840 and another surveying voting

USA: 'NEW' POLITICAL HISTORY

trends in presidential elections;[7] a path-breaking monograph on
the importance of the time dimension in evaluating election
returns, as well as a major reassessment of the political ideology
and voting behaviour of the Jacksonian period;[8] and several contributions concerned with the methods, problems, and promises of
quantitative history.[9] This is the type of work which the behaviouralists have published so far.

What kind of findings are emerging from their endeavours? In
two important articles Richard P. McCormick has shown that the
Jackson elections did not represent the revolution in popular
voting behaviour that historians have so confidently assumed for so
many years, and that economic class affiliation apparently had
little influence in affecting the party choice of voters during the
early national period.[10] Lee Benson carried reassessment of
Jacksonian democracy still further when he found that content
analysis revealed basic ideological differences between Whigs and
Democrats, and particularly when he discovered that the multi-
variate analysis of election returns in indicator precincts in New
York showed ethno-cultural conditioning to have been the most
important variable associated with party choice in that state.

The writings of McCormick and Benson are perhaps the most
impressive exhibits of the new historical persuasion, but a few
other studies are representative. Using the Guttman scale as his
major analytical tool, Joel Silbey assessed the significance of sectional and party ties in Congress during the 1840s and early 1850s,
finding that party ties withstood the impact of the slavery expansion
issue much better than some of the conventional literature leads
one to expect. George Daniels probed the problem of ethno-
cultural loyalties and the 1860 election, and his analysis of precinct
voting returns in Iowa reinforced Joseph Schafer's rather neglected
findings of a generation ago that a majority of German voters in
Wisconsin and Illinois remained true to their Democratic Party
allegiance in the 1860 election.[11] Using multiple correlation techniques, Stanley Parsons destroyed a truism of Populist folklore
by showing that Populist votes in Nebraska and mortgage interest
rates were only slightly correlated, and that in so far as they were
associated the correlation was negative rather than positive. In one
of the better collective biographies published by a historian to date,
William T. Kerr, Jr has shown that the Progressive leaders of
Washington differed not only in the major sources of their support

from their conservative counterparts. Thomas B. Alexander and his students have published the initial results of what has since become an elaborate least-squares analysis of social and economic attributes and voting preference in ante-bellum Alabama and which contradicts the old generalization that the 'Democrats became the party of poverty and numbers, and the Whigs the party of property and talents'.

A number of theses and dissertations dealing with similar or related problems are now complete. Samuel P. Hays drew upon some of these in suggesting that the urban reform movement of the early twentieth century was essentially upper class in origin, and also in proposing an ethno-cultural interpretation of national voting behaviour in the period 1865–1929.[12] Joel Silbey found support in similar materials for his contention that sectionalism was not the only major influence shaping American politics during the 1850s.[13] Much other research with a strong quantitative element is under way. These studies include roll-call analyses of Congress in the early national period, during the 1850s, 1860s, and 1870s, and the progressive period, as well as of the Confederate Congress and midwestern state legislatures during the nineteenth century. Historians are preparing studies of the evolution of party structure during the nineteenth century, and others are studying popular voting behaviour in states and regions in the nineteenth and early twentieth centuries. There has also been completed, or is under way, work which has important implications for political history even though its focus is not primarily political—most notably research in historical demography and population mobility, both spatial and social.[14]

Much of the new quantitative history is unsophisticated in social-science terms. A member of the AHA committee on quantitative data estimated recently that there were no more than several dozen members of the history profession at the faculty level who are conversant with statistics through multiple correlation and regression analysis, and if one omits the new breed of economic historian that is, I am sure, true.[15] This state of affairs is changing as history graduates attend statistics courses and social science methodology seminars, but it will be some time before there is a sizeable cadre of historians confidently aware of both the promises and the pitfalls inherent in quantification.

Social scientists find the theoretical assumptions of the behavioural historians rather elementary. They are not trying simply to describe 'what happened', in the parlance of the old 'scientific' historian, but their methods hardly conform to the basic rules of the behavioural approach sketched by David Easton in *A Framework for Political Analysis*.[16] Few behavioural historians are consciously looking for findings with predictive value, or purposefully giving their research a theoretical frame which the results may in part verify, modify, or contradict. Instead, most are still problem or topic-oriented, using social-science techniques or theory to refute or build on the work of past historians or to probe new areas which catch their fancy. Lee Benson is an exception. To a far greater extent than any of the other historical behaviouralists, he tries to make his theoretical commitments explicit and believes that a historian can make a major contribution to the social sciences. He has for instance suggested certain basic propositions which, he argues, illuminate the behaviour of the founding fathers:

(1) The behaviour of men is determined more by the ends they seek than by the means they use to achieve those ends; specifically, men favoured the Constitution largely because they favoured a Commercial Society, they opposed the Constitution largely because they favoured an Agrarian Society. (2) The ends men choose are positively related to the 'modes and processes' by which they gain their livelihoods, the social environments in which they live, the social roles they occupy, the groups with whom they identify, and the groups with whom they regard themselves in conflict. (3) In certain historical situations, men who choose certain ends are more likely than their opponents to possess the qualities and resources needed for victory; specifically, in the United States during the 1780s, commercial-minded men like Hamilton possessed the qualities and resources needed to defeat agrarian-minded men like Clinton.[17]

Such behavioural models are rare indeed in the work of historians. Despite his concern for theoretical explication, Professor Benson's work sometimes falls short of the standards that many behavioural scientists consider essential. One searches the first edition of *The Concept of Jacksonian Democracy* in vain for any detailed discussion of the methods by which he selected his indicator precincts, or of the numbers of voters in his sample, or of correlations or significance tests underlying the party preference percentages which he ascribed to the various ethno-cultural groups living in New York during the 1830s and 1840s.[18]

It can indeed be argued that social scientists have written almost as much, if not more, behavioural history than have the political historians. Walter Dean Burnham, William Nesbit Chambers, Robert A. Dahl, Manning J. Dauer, V. O. Key, Theodore J. Lowi, Duncan MacRae, John Schmidhauser, and Ruth C. Silva, have all probed significantly beyond the contemporary scene and produced work that any political historian must use if he wishes to view this nation's political history in fullest perspective.[19]

More significant perhaps than the research achievements of behavioural historians has been their contribution to the building of the historical data archives of the Inter-University Consortium for Political Research, made in co-operation with political scientists. As a number of historians became interested in quantification some years ago, they discovered in discussion that they were wasting their time in searching out and processing quantifiable information which others had already recorded. They agreed that historians needed an inventory of the basic quantitative date of American political history and ultimately, perhaps, a central data archives on which all interested scholars might draw. Following such discussions, Lee Benson, Charles Sellers, Samuel P. Hays, and William Riker (three historians and a political scientist) submitted a memorandum to the Social Science Research Council. In response the Council invited W. Dean Burnham to assess the problems of collecting election statistics in a number of states.

While these developments were taking place, the Inter-University Consortium was also beginning to consider the establishment of a data archive, having as a nucleus the data collected by the Survey Research Center of the University of Michigan. When Professor Burnham's initial investigation was encouraging, the SSRC commissioned him to spend an additional year on the task of inventorying and undertaking an exploratory recovery of data. His labours were so successful that additional organization seemed necessary. Lee Benson organized a committee of historians to assist the consortium in developing a historical data archive, and the American Historical Association gave it status by designating it an *ad hoc* committee. In turn the committee organized state committees that undertook to exhume the county election returns from 1824 to the present and other materials. Under the imaginative leadership of its director, Warren Miller, the consortium obtained funds from the National Science Foundation for the development of the archives and the SSRC continued to be helpful. Dr Miller appointed a historian, Howard W. Allen, as director of data recovery at the consortium, and it was hoped that almost all the county election and referenda returns would be available for use by the late fall of 1966. The historians and archivists engaged in this work may be helping to transform one area of history into a cumulative discipline, in which, for the first time, the careful historian need not duplicate every step of the research of predecessors who were interested in the same problem.

While the work of collecting and recording has gone forward at the consortium, planning conferences have considered the problems of adding legislative materials, primarily roll-call votes, to the archive, and various types of economic and ethno-cultural materials which seem necessary for any considered analysis of the basic election data. At the Ann Arbor seminar in 1965, a number of historians expressed interest in essaying the difficult task of retrieving the election returns of the early national period and this work is now under way. The extent to which these collection and service programmes can be maintained and extended will largely depend, of course, on the willingness of granting agencies to subsidize the work and this in turn must depend to a considerable extent on the interest which historians and social scientists show in using the archive.

Its concrete achievements and the ambitiousness of its programme clearly mark the combined consortium-AHA committee project as the most impressive evidence of the development of a quantifying and behavioural bent in the historical profession. It is not the only organized effort in that direction, however. In 1964 the Mathematics Social Science Board, an offspring of the Social Science Research Council and the Institute for Advanced Study in the Behavioural Sciences, sponsored the organization of a history committee, headed by Robert Fogel of the University of Chicago.[20] The AHA *ad hoc* committee is concerned primarily with the development of a data archive and with training programmes geared to its use. The history committee of the MSSB is seeking ways of encouraging the spread of mathematical and statistical expertise within the history profession.

The behavioural movement among American political historians reflects in part a recent tendency among historians to draw more heavily upon the social sciences for method and theory. In his reader, *American History and the Social Sciences*, published in 1964, Edward N. Saveth presents two dozen historians, writing on concepts which are more usually considered to be of primary interest to social scientists. A large number of other scholars could be added to Saveth's list, whose writings in some way reflect the influence of social-science thought or methods. The political behaviouralists, however, are prepared to introduce considerably more quantification and rigour into their work than most such historians.

A few years ago, in a paper paying tribute to a successful revolution—the advent of behaviouralism in political science—Robert Dahl devoted some attention to the causes of this development.[21] He stressed the pioneering work of Professor Merriam at Chicago, the contributions of the European *émigré* scholars who came to this country during the 1930s, the practical experience of political scientists in government and military service during the Second World War, the empirical promise of survey research techniques, the leadership of the SSRC, and the helping hand of the foundations. No doubt he would agree that the recent tremendous advances in computer technology have helped to confirm the trend.

There are both similarities and differences between the early developments in political science and those now occurring in history. If political science lagged behind sister fields in moving towards behaviouralism, the lag in history has been greater. The commitment of historians to theory was of course typically less than that of political scientists even in the most unsystematic days of political science. There is among the behavioural historians no group analogous to the European *émigrés* of the 1930s, trained in a different tradition from their American colleagues. Nor can we point to any history department occupying the pre-eminent position of the political science department at the University of Chicago as a disseminating centre of behavioural ideas and methods. For a time in the late 1950s three historians at the University of Iowa were stressing quantification in their seminars and sending their graduates into the methods seminars of their colleagues in political science and sociology. But this group is now dispersed.

There is no pioneer of quantifying techniques in the historical profession comparable in stature to Charles Merriam. But there were a number of historians, active during the 1930s and 1940s, whose writings or seminar offerings anticipated a quantitative approach. During the 1930s James C. Malin used manuscript census rolls to prepare demographic studies that modified con-

ventional interpretations of frontier population movements and
influenced a considerable number of other scholars either directly
or indirectly. This work, plus Malin's emphasis on the intensive
study of the local and regional unit, make him one of the pro-
genitors of historical behaviouralism in America, even though in
his later work he specifically repudiated the aims and methods of
social science.[22]

In reaction against the conventional history fare that he had
suffered as a graduate student, Thomas C. Cochran immersed
himself during the 1930s in social-science literature, particularly
sociology. Exasperated by the traditional views of the craft which
several eminent historians expressed at the meeting of the American Historical Association in 1947, he advanced his rebellious ideas
in 'The "Presidential Synthesis" in American History' (*American
Historical Review*, July 1948). This article was a resounding
attack on the traditional method of describing American political
history, presidential administration by presidential administration,
and a plea for a '"social science" synthesis of American history'.
Cochran argued that our political history should be viewed as an
outgrowth of fundamental cultural developments, and that it
could be attacked most conveniently at the state level. By the
1940s Oscar Handlin at Harvard was emphasizing ethnic group
dynamics and their relationship to politics, and a number of
students followed his lead, undertaking detailed studies of politics
at the local level. At Cornell University, Paul Wallace Gates,
although primarily interested in institutional economic history,
was asking his graduate students to spend time in other social
science departments. No doubt there were others trying to direct
the interests of their students into new channels.

If the writings or teachings of Malin, Handlin, Gates, Cochran
and others have helped to provide a favourable climate for a more
intensive approach to American political history, I must also
mention an early research project that had considerable influence
upon the profession. During the late 1940s, Merle Curti conceived
the idea of studying a frontier county in Wisconsin intensively
and providing a rigorous test of the suggestion that the frontier was
a significant factor in shaping American political institutions, the
thesis stated so attractively by Frederick Jackson Turner in the
1890s. Professor Curti was a graduate student under Turner at
Harvard and was familiar with his interest in systematic political
analysis. One of the handful of scholars who established American

315

intellectual history on a firm foundation, he became chairman of the committee on historiography of the SSRC, organized in 1942–43, which prepared the Council's *Bulletin 54*, entitled *Theory and Practice in Historical Study: A Report of the Committee on Historiography*, published in 1946. This report clearly brought out the concern over the problems of objectivity and relativism which had perplexed and disturbed thoughtful American historians during the previous couple of decades. Both the work of his committee and the somewhat acrimonious discussion which its report provoked, turned Professor Curti's mind to the problems of objectively validating historical fact and theory. By this time also he had concluded that study of the frontier hypothesis had reached an impasse. Margaret Curti, a psychologist with sound training in statistics, had long maintained that historians should concern themselves to a greater extent with quantitative research and with the application of statistics to historical problems. This was the background of a study of Trempealeau county in western Wisconsin, designed to exploit the quantifiable information in the county records and in the manuscript censuses; *The Making of an American Community: A Case Study of Democracy in a Frontier County* was published in 1959.

Professor Curti's statistical methods were less rigorous than some social scientists demand today and some historians have disputed the study's conclusions, but it is a milestone in American historiography. That a man who had done so much to establish intellectual history should turn his talents to such research gave respectability to quantification, as well as testifying to the versatility and liveliness of Professor Curti's mind.

As in the field of political science, the SSRC has had considerable influence in changing the outlook of historians. It has always aided historians in projects with an inter-disciplinary character. During the last twenty years it has sponsored three monographs concerned with the problems of writing history. *Bulletin 54* looked back to the relativist controversy of the 1930s; in *Bulletin 64, The Social Sciences in Historical Study*, and in the more recent *Generalization in the Writing of History*, we find a real commitment in some of the contributors to both social-science methods and theory.[23] I am not aware that any foundation has been uniquely concerned with promoting behaviouralism among historians, but the action of the Ford Foundation in supporting the Institute for Advanced Study in the Behavioural Sciences has contributed to that end. Since its establishment, the administrators have generously allocated places to historians. Many if not most of the quantifiers among American political historians today have been assisted to some degree either by the SSRC or the Stanford Institute.

There are few more difficult tasks than that of explaining why one man adopts new techniques and another does not. We can point to general conditioning factors and to encouraging elements in the intellectual milieu, and we can discern apparent predispositions in the individuals who innovate, but it is hard to explain in the final analysis why some take the plunge and others do not. If the SSRC has aided many of the behavioural historians it has also assisted dozens of others in the historical profession who have shown no disposition to change their approach. But aid from that agency or from the Stanford Institute must be regarded as one of a number of predisposing or confirming factors.

To some extent the behavioural historians appear to have had a broader training than usual: one was a classics major, another majored in psychology, another had a good training in mathematics, and still another a double major. The prodding of graduate directors in the direction of inter-disciplinary work is remembered by members of the group. It is probably no accident that a number of them were initially interested in economic history, which has always had a body of theory and statistical method to draw upon, and in which far-reaching developments have occurred during the last fifteen years.

One learns in discussing the origins of their interests with the behaviouralists that they experienced recurrent dissatisfaction with conventional political history and searched for concepts or methods that would give them greater confidence in the results of research or provide a more satisfying framework in which to present them. A number of them were particularly impressed by the work of Lazarsfield and Key, and probing produces the names of other social scientists who set the thinking of one or more of them on a new track—Rice, Merton, Duverger, Weber, Michels, Lubell, Hannah Arendt, and Riesman. There was some reaction, too, against the practice of borrowing concepts from the social scientists and applying them without rigorous proof. In *The Age of Reform*, for instance, Richard Hofstadter suggested that declining social status was a major motivating factor among both the Populists and the Progressives. Soon status revolution threatened to become a universal historical solvent, applied unfortunately with little resort to the careful quantification that would either corroborate or disprove the hypothesis.

The most influential of the historical behaviouralists specializing in American history is Lee Benson. Having completed a doctoral dissertation on the economic and political background of the Interstate Commerce Act, he went to Harvard to study location theory; there he was greatly impressed by the rigour and precision with which Walter Isard was attacking the problems of location theory, and by the more systematic approach of social scientists in comparison to historians. Moving to Columbia, he met Paul Lazarsfeld and found him appalled both by the flaccidity of historical analysis and by the ignorance of history among social scientists. Professor Lazarsfeld provided funds and encouraged Benson to investigate more precise approaches to American political history. From Benson's work at the Columbia Bureau of Applied Social Research came his long article 'Research Problems in American Historiography', which provided concrete illustrations of the way in which simple time series of election results might be used to explode generalizations long cherished by historians. A few historians were already stressing quantification in their seminars, but it is with the publication of this article that the behavioural trend becomes clearly evident in American historical writing. Other research which Lee Benson began in the 1950s matured as papers on the causation of the Civil War and *The Concept of Jacksonian Democracy: New York as a Test Case.* Benson was a committed economic determinist when he began his doctoral work but, particularly in his study of Jacksonian democracy in New York, he discovered that his formula was inadequate. Ethno-cultural conditioning seemed to explain more than did economic interest.

Stimulated by a small group of social scientists at the State University of Iowa during the late 1940s, William O. Aydelotte conceived the idea of a massive study of the Corn Laws Parliament in which biographical data were to be gathered for the 800-odd members of this assembly, and these materials related if possible to party affiliation and voting behaviour. The Rockefeller Foundation launched the project with a grant and Professor Aydelotte has pushed it steadily forward, searching first for basic biographical information both here and abroad, working out satisfactory classifications of the class and business backgrounds of the members of parliament, recording the divisions, subjecting data first to correlation analysis (with rather discouraging results), then moving to scaling techniques, and along the way teaching himself social statistics and learning the technology of data processing and computer research. Given his subject matter, one is tempted to look to Namier for Professor Aydelotte's inspiration, but he maintains that his early work owed much more to Lazarsfeld and to *The People's Choice* than to Namier's studies of the British Parliament. Aydelotte has not yet summarized his research in a book-length monograph, but he has delivered a number of important papers at historical meetings, publishing some of them as articles, and he has discussed the problems and rewards of such research in numerous informal contacts with specialists in both American and European history. Once a historian recognizes that he must explain why men behaved as they did in the past, he must turn if he is a thorough scholar to the disciplines that concentrate on the explanation of human behaviour; the quantification movement in American political history is one aspect of this change of direction, but commitment to quantification is not equally strong among the members of the AHA committee; one of them wrote recently:

... I am not an enthusiast for quantification. Quantifiable data make up only a portion of the evidence available to the historian. Moreover, if quantifiable data are to be used intelligently, one must have a vast knowledge of the historical context of the situation; the data are not self-interpreting. Another grave danger with quantification is that it can lead to an extremely imbalanced emphasis on those factors that can be quantified, to the exclusion of others of equal or great significance. Quantification, in other words, is merely one tool in the historian's kit; he must not misuse it or throw the other tools away.

In a series of papers and articles, Samuel P. Hays has tried to articulate and to some extent shape the new trend in American political historiography. He has indicted 'conventional political history' as 'so preoccupied with the outward and formal, the episodic, the unique and the individual, that it has failed to draw attention to some of the most significant developments of our political past'.[24] Historians, he urges, must study political structure in detail: the voters, their socio-economic and ethno-cultural groupings, the pressure groups, the leadership cadres, and the systems of decision-making that operate at every level of the American political system, as well as the inter-relationships of these elements. By studying these components of American politics in action through time, by pushing beyond the mere description of political institutions and by penetrating the fog of rhetoric and ideology we can, he promises, reach the basic facts of political motivation, influence, and power. In particular Hays emphasizes the need for study of politics at the grass roots in contrast to the national scene, and the benefits to be gained by distinguishing between political rhetoric and political reality. Recently he has settled upon the term 'the social analysis of politics' as the most appropriate description of this approach. He emphasizes that quantitative data are important tools in this analysis and has also stressed the usefulness of drawing upon the social sciences for both method and theory. Even 'conventional' historians can argue that much of this prescription describes their current operations. The procedures which Professor Hays recommends differ from normal practice in American political history mainly in the relative emphasis that is placed upon local case studies, quantification, and social science theory. His articles describe what behaviouralists and their students have been doing in varying degree for some time. But if his role so far has been primarily that of publicist and synthesizer, his emphasis on the historian's obligation to set his findings within some sort of conceptual perspective has been salutary. On the other hand, his unfavourable assessment of traditional history seems unnecessary or overdrawn to some behaviouralists.

We can say, quite accurately I believe, that a large proportion of our political historians expend their energies in writing the biographies of individual politicians, and that others pursue their research on political bodies, groups, and movements, almost solely in personal manuscripts, newspapers, and legislative debates. Usually American historians have studied elections as unique expressions of the popular will rather than as parts of a time series, and limited their consideration of roll calls to final votes, and perhaps those on major amendments. We have as historians frequently been more impressed by what our subjects have said than by what they have done. As a group we have been unsystematic in our generalizations and too little interested in comparisons and categorization. We often fail to make our assumptions adequately explicit, and in trying to understand human motivation we often ignore the more sophisticated theorizing of the behavioural sciences. The challenge confronting the behavioural historian is to exploit the body of hard quantitative data that exists in election returns, legislative roll calls, court archives, census data (published and unpublished), state, county, and municipal records, and the great accumulation of biographical facts available in other types of sources. This involves both learning the methods necessary to master and manipulate these intimidating sources of information, and becoming more sophisticated in the techniques of research design which are necessary to set findings in useful and defensible theoretical frameworks.

Behavioural history does not promise short cuts or easy answers. If historians have over-emphasized some types of source materials, these cannot be ignored by the historian who quantifies. The scales or other devices which reveal legislative voting patterns can be interpreted fully only if we read the preceding debates. Tables, graphs, and correlations do not explain themselves; they are the product of a particular research design and are subject to various interpretations. The politician's oratory may be designed to conceal or obfuscate his behaviour no less than to explain it, and the scholar who uses the *Congressional Globe* is rather like the prospector who examines a salted claim. Manuscript collections, some will say, are more reliable; here the politician lays bare his motives. He may indeed, but again he may not, and it is shocking to discover how little some of the manuscript collections, regularly cited as major sources in historical monographs, actually reveal about the men who accumulated them. In addition, any manuscript collection is at best an accidental historical accretion, pointing perhaps to conclusions that are completely different from those we would reach if all the related manuscript collections had been preserved. It is sobering also to remember that whenever a politician evaluates his election chances correctly (few run in anticipation of defeat), there are usually one or more opponents who judge the situation incorrectly. Remembering this, we will treat the explanations of politicians with caution. But the interplay of contemporary observation and explanation with quantitative evidence should allow us to push our understanding further than either type of source can carry us by itself.

In writing of cultural sources and economic change, Thomas C. Cochran points out that no one has yet developed a model in which all the variables can be quantified. 'One cannot', he writes, 'speak of units or doses of personality or values'.[25] We will no doubt become increasingly ingenious in developing ways to measure attitudes or values indirectly; the quantifier may build some dams and breakwaters in what Matthew Arnold unfairly termed 'that huge Mississippi of falsehood called history', but there are rapids he will not tame, tributaries he cannot explore, and quicksands he still cannot plumb by quantification. So American political historians are not all going to become quantifiers, and not only for this reason. Much biography and so-called conventional political history is useful and will continue to attract many in the profession. The fact that quantification calls for extra effort rather than a substitution of effort will discourage some from essaying it.

For those who find the fascination of political history in a smooth and colourful narrative, the injection of numbers, tables, and scales may be jarring and unpleasing. The new political history must make its way by appealing to the intellectual curiosity of the reader; its impact must flow from the ideas and the sense of understanding that it imparts rather than from the colourful incident or well-told anecdote. Even so, behavioural historians need not jettison the idea that history is a literary art. There is no reason why political history should not still employ the well-turned phrase or striking illustration, even though based on a foundation of measurement.

For a time in the testing period ahead the behavioural historians may find editors suspicious and cold; their graduate students will encounter difficulties in obtaining proper training in statistics and the use of computers; both faculty and students may find it difficult to obtain financial aid because the National Science Foundation has not officially recognized historians and granting agencies of humanistic temper are not likely to support behavioural history enthusiastically. These problems may in the end be less disturbing than the limitations of the quantitative data of American history and the inadequacies of the techniques now available for analysing them. Since the behavioural historian cannot interview the dead politician of yester-year, he is forced to place considerable emphasis on the study of aggregate data, particularly in election analysis. Here he encounters the problem of ecological correlations which W. S. Robinson described some fifteen years ago. One cannot, on the basis of correlation analysis, deduce the behaviour of an individual from the behaviour of the aggregate. There is, as Austin Ranney has pointed out, a good deal to be learned from the study of aggregates as aggregates.[26] What is more, it is possible in some instances to produce refined aggregate data. In some states, for instance, poll lists of the nineteenth century and census data can be combined so that we know precisely the voters represented in precinct totals and many of their social characteristics—in contrast to situations in which we know only that voters represent a certain proportion of an electorate that has as a group certain demographic, socio-economic, or ethno-cultural characteristics. Must we stop there, or can we minimize the limits of possible error in moving from aggregate to individual, or work with probabilities rather than correlation analysis? Ferreting out virtually pure ethno-cultural or socio-economic constituencies seems off-hand to be a commonsense solution, which election forecasters have used successfully on occasion; but the very purity of such units may impart bias. Assuming that we can use aggregate data in good conscience, we have fewer of them than we would like. One is hard put to it to find historical measures of some of the variables that survey research has found to be important. The emphasis which behavioural historians are placing on the importance of ethno-cultural groups may in part reflect the fact that the ethno-cultural reference group is the easiest to identify in historical data. Moreover, the statistics of social research are unfortunately much more useful in showing the relationships between variables at a particular moment than in demonstrating change over time. Ideally, the behavioural historian requires a statistics of time series, of lag, of transition matrixes, of growth models, and of indirect relationships where the association of two factors is measured by substituting a third for one or the other. Since most social scientists restrict their research to the findings of survey research, there are few outstanding scholars in the behavioural disciplines who are interested in developing or refining the kind of statistical methods that historians would find particularly useful.[27]

Aggregate election data provide evidence of a single act, although to some extent the preparation for this act can be deduced from examination of other variables. The modern panel survey yields information about the period of preparation and sometimes adds retrospective interpretations by the actors as well. Can content analysis of newspapers or other historical documents be refined to the point where it serves in some measure as a substitute for the questionnaire? Its advocates believe that this technique has been greatly improved during the present generation. Contingency and qualitative content analysis in particular seem to promise results that are more interesting to historians than the rather mechanical exercises that were common some years ago. The imaginative and flexible analyst can indeed deduce political values, class structure,

323

influence and power systems, and key election issues from even the highly partisan newspapers of the nineteenth century, provided he remembers that historical evidence may come in all shapes and sizes. But it seems doubtful that content analysis will soon reach the state where it can be used to detect the exact turning points or the precise importance of the various issues in election campaigns. [28]

If the American political historian faces problems in finding adequate quantifiable data and in discovering appropriate statistical techniques, he runs other dangers in using political theory in planning and interpreting his research. In effect he may allow such theory or its related concepts to dehumanize his work. When he writes in terms of social role or status revolution, for instance, he may produce a deterministic history in which his central characters are denied the power of choice or the freedom to make rational decisions, but seem instead the captives of forces beyond their control. The predatory railroad tycoon who bribes a legislature may appear as the guardian of his stockholders, and the representative of a peer group of railroad executives, rather than as a calculating offender against the ethics or law of the community. The abolitionist or progressive leader becomes a man in unconscious revolt against the societal changes that are depriving him of the position of leadership which his father enjoyed, rather than a public-spirited reformer trying to improve society from rational and philanthropic motives. 'If powerful groups are denied access to formal power in legitimate ways', writes Samuel P. Hays, 'they seek access through procedures which the community considers illegitimate. Corrupt government, therefore, does not reflect the genius of evil men, but rather the lack of acceptable means for those who exercise power in the private community to wield the same influence in governmental affairs'. [29] Such explanations may present old material in a new light, but in careless hands they may fit facts to theory rather than using them to test theory; and certainly such analysis gives little hint of the moral indignation that some historians have found in the progressive period. Once such pitfalls are recognized, however, they can be avoided.

Some historians may consider behavioural history to be 'consensus' history. In the introduction to *The American Political Tradition*, Richard Hofstadter noted in 1949 that 'the common climate of American opinion' had 'been much obscured by the tendency to place political conflict in the foreground of history', and showed, in the essays that followed, the very considerable agreement that had existed among American political leaders irrespective of section or party. A few years later John Higham detected a growing 'cult of "American consensus"' in both the intellectual and political history of America, and argued that 'current scholarship' was 'carrying out a massive grading operation to smooth over America's social convulsions'.[30] It seems inevitable that the rather precise measurements and the detailed case studies of behavioural history will qualify the bold conclusions reached in some older general studies. The result need not be homogenized history, however. To prove consensus in our political history, the historian must define politics, political ideas, and the American political system narrowly. In reality it is as much a political act to exclude a racial or an economic minority from participation in formal political institutions, or to keep a depressed sector of the population in bondage by failing to provide adequate educational and economic opportunities, as it is to share in the task of choosing a presidential candidate. With this understood, American political life becomes once more the scene of fundamental political conflict. And some of the behaviouralists do bring this broad view to their study of American political history.

Critics of quantification are common in the historical profession. Some of them suspect inter-disciplinary research on general principles. Arguing by aphorism and analogy, one of my colleagues points out that the supreme achievement of hybridization in the animal world is the mule—a creature without pride of ancestry or hope of progeny. Recently Professor Aydelotte discussed quantification in history in a temperate and closely-reasoned article in the *American Historical Review* (April 1966). He divides the arguments of the most vociferous critics of quantification into four categories, questioning specifically: (1) the value of the work that has been done; (2) the feasibility of this approach in view of the admittedly limited materials available to historians; (3) the reliability of the results obtained by these techniques; and (4) the usefulness or significance of the results. There can, in the end, be only one convincing answer to such criticisms: the usefulness and intrinsic interest of the publications of the behavioural historians will determine whether quantification flourishes or withers as a historical technique.

Lee Benson was sanguine about the future of the new political history when he wrote recently, 'the prediction does not seem absurd that . . . by 1984 [sic], a significant proportion of American

325

historians will have accepted Buckle's two basic propositions: (1) past human behaviour can be studied scientifically; (2) the main business of historians is to participate in the overall scholarly enterprise of discovering and developing general laws of human behaviour'.[31] The date is ominous and the future perhaps less assured than Benson believes. But the methods and theory of the social science disciplines seem to promise much. If the behaviouralists retain the broad and critical knowledge of sources found among conventional political historians, their keen awareness of the range of cultural and socio-economic differences at different times, and their willingness to search widely for alternative hypotheses, they may indeed contribute to a richer and more vital political history of the United States.

NOTES

[1] Orin Grant Libby, 'A Plea for the Study of Votes in Congress', *American Historical Association Report*, 1896, I (Washington, 1897).

[2] This conference is described in a report prepared by Samuel P. Hays and Murray Murphey, 'Research Conference on Political Data: Historical Analysis of Quantitative Data—26 July–13 August 1965, Ann Arbor, Michigan' (mimeographed, 1965).

[3] Robert A. Dahl defines the term in political science in 'The Behavioral Approach in Political Science: Epitaph for a Monument to a Successful Protest', *American Political Science Review*, December 1961, p. 767.

[4] George Daniels, 'Immigrant Votes in the Election of 1860: The Case of Iowa', *Mid-America*, July 1962; Robert P. Swierenga, 'The Ethnic Voter and the First Lincoln Election', *Civil War History*, March 1965; Stanley Parsons, 'Who Were the Nebraska Populists?', *Nebraska History*, June 1963; Howard W. Allen, 'Studies of Political Loyalties of Two Nationality Groups: Isolationism and German-Americans', *Journal of the Illinois State Historical Society*, Summer 1964; Thomas B. Alexander, Kit C. Carter, Jack R. Lister, Jerry C. Oldshue, and Winfred G. Sandlin, 'Who Were the Alabama Whigs?', *The Alabama Review*, January 1963; Thomas B. Alexander and Peggy J. Duckworth, 'Alabama Black Belt Whigs During Secession: A New Viewpoint', ibid., July 1964; Aida DiPace Donald, 'The Decline of Whiggery and the Formation of the Republican Party in Rochester, 1848–1856', *Rochester History*, July 1958.

[5] Joel H. Silbey, *The Shrine of Party: Congressional Voting Behavior, 1841–1852* (Pittsburgh, 1967); David Donald, *The Politics of Reconstruction 1863–1867* (Baton Rouge, 1965); John L. Shover, 'Populism in the Nineteen-Thirties: The Battle for the AAA', *Agricultural History*, January 1965; Edward L. Gambill, 'Who were the Senate Radicals', *Civil War History*, September 1965; Gerald Wolff, 'The Slavocracy and the Homestead Problem of 1854', *Agricultural History*, April 1966;

Howard W. Allen, 'Geography and Politics: Voting on Reform Issues in the United States Senate, 1911–1916', *Journal of Southern History*, May 1961; Glenn M. Linden, 'Radicals and Economic Policies: The Senate, 1861–1873', ibid., May 1966.

[6] Pioneering work of this type appeared in George Mowry, *The California Progressives* (Berkeley and Los Angeles, 1951), pp. 86–104; Alfred D. Chandler, Jr, 'The Origins of Progressive Leadership', in Elting Morison *et al.* (eds.), *The Letters of Theodore Roosevelt* (Cambridge, 1951–54), VIII, App. III, pp. 1462–65; David Donald, 'Toward a Reconsideration of Abolitionists', *Lincoln Reconsidered* (New York, 1961). See also Grady McWhiney, 'Were the Whigs a Class Party in Alabama ?', *Journal of Southern History*, November 1957; Ralph A. Wooster, 'Notes on the Georgia Legislature of 1860', *Georgia Historical Quarterly*, March 1961; 'Membership in Early Texas Legislatures, 1850–1860', *Southwestern Historical Quarterly*, October 1965; Gerald W. McFarland, 'The New York Mugwumps of 1884: A Profile', *Political Science Quarterly*, March 1963; William T. Kerr, Jr, 'The Progressives of Washington, 1910–12', *Pacific Northwest Quarterly*, January 1964; E. Daniel Potts, 'The Progressive Profile in Iowa', *Mid-America*, October 1965; Herbert J. Doherty, Jr, *The Whigs of Florida, 1845–1854, University of Florida Monographs*: Social Sciences, I, Winter 1959, pp. 63–72. Robert A. Skotheim discusses some of the methodological problems involved in this type of study in 'A Note on Historical Method: David Donald's "Toward a Reconsideration of Abolitionists"', *Journal of Southern History*, August 1959.

[7] Richard P. McCormick, 'Suffrage Classes and Party Alignments: A Study in Voter Behavior', *Mississippi Valley Historical Review*, December 1959; 'New Perspectives on Jacksonian Politics', *American Historical Review*, January 1960; Charles Sellers, 'The Equilibrium Cycle in Two-Party Politics', *Public Opinion Quarterly*, Spring 1965.

[8] Lee Benson, 'Research Problems in American Political Historiography', in Mirra Komarovsky (ed.), *Common Frontiers of the Social Sciences* (Glencoe, 1957); *The Concept of Jacksonian Democracy: New York as a Test Case* (Princeton, 1961).

[9] Lee Benson, *Turner and Beard: American Historical Writing Reconsidered* (Glencoe, 1960); Samuel P. Hays, 'History as Human Behavior', *Iowa Journal of History*, July 1960; 'New Possibilities for American Political History: The Social Analysis of Political Life' (prepared for the American Historical Association meeting, 29 December 1964 and lithoprinted by the Inter-University Consortium for Political Research); very similar to the latter is 'The Social Analysis of American Political History, 1880–1920', *Political Science Quarterly*, September 1965; 'The Politics of Reform in Municipal Government in the Progressive Era', *Pacific Northwest Quarterly*, October 1964.

[10] Unless otherwise stated, the contributions discussed in the next two paragraphs are those appearing under their authors' names in footnotes 4 to 9 inclusive.

[11] Joseph Schafer, 'Who Elected Lincoln', *American Historical Review*, October 1941. Schafer was a student of Turner and much of his work exemplifies the empirical side of the Turner tradition.

[12] Samuel P. Hays, 'The Politics of Reform', and 'Political Parties and the Local-Cosmopolitan Continuum, 1865–1929', prepared for the Conference on American Political Party Development, Washington University, 1966, and cited here by permission of Professor Hays and William Nesbit Chambers.

[13] Joel H. Silbey, 'The Civil War Synthesis in American Political History', *Civil War History*, June 1964.

[14] Stephan Thernstrom, *Poverty and Progress: Social Mobility in a Nineteenth Century City* (Cambridge, 1964); Samuel B. Warner, *Street-Car Suburbs: The Process of Growth in Boston, 1870–1900* (Cambridge, 1962). For those interested in the rural community the work of James C. Malin is still essential; see 'The Turnover of Farm Population in Kansas', *Kansas Historical Quarterly*, November 1935, and *The Grassland of North America: Prolegomena to its History* (Lawrence, 1947), pp. 278–315. Several studies bearing on Iowa are summarized with additional data of my own in Chapter I of *From Prairie to Corn Belt: Farming on the Illinois and Iowa Prairies in the Nineteenth Century* (Chicago, 1963).

[15] Samuel P. Hays speaking on 'Computers and Historical Research', Purdue Conference on the Use of Computers in the Humanities, 29 October 1965.

[16] David Easton, *A Framework for Political Analysis* (Englewood Cliffs, N.J., 1965), p. 7.

[17] Lee Benson, *Turner and Beard*, p. 228.

[18] In the introduction to the paperback edition of *The Concept of Jacksonian Democracy* (New York, 1964), Benson includes a specific description of his methodology.

[19] The following list is not intended to be comprehensive: Walter D. Burnham, 'The Changing Shape of the American Political Universe', *American Political Science Review*, March 1965; William N. Chambers, *Political Parties in a New Nation: The American Experience, 1776–1809* (New York, 1963); Robert A. Dahl, *Who Governs? Democracy and Power in an American City* (New Haven, 1961); Manning J. Dauer, *The Adams Federalists* (Baltimore, 1953); V. O. Key, Jr, 'A Theory of Critical Elections', *Journal of Politics*, February 1955; 'Secular Realignment and the Party System', ibid., May 1959; with Milton C. Cummings, Jr, *The Responsible Electorate: Rationality in Presidential Voting, 1936–1960* (Cambridge, 1966); Theodore J. Lowi, *At the Pleasure of the Mayor: Patronage and Power in New York City, 1898–1958* (Glencoe, 1964); Duncan MacRae, Jr and James Meldrum, 'Critical Elections in Illinois: 1888–1958', *American Political Science Review*, September 1960; John R. Schmidhauser, 'The Justices of the Supreme Court: A Collective Portrait', *Midwest Journal of Political Science*, February 1959; 'Judicial Behavior and the Sectional Crisis of 1837–1850', *Journal of Politics*, November 1961; Ruth C. Silva, *Rum, Religion, and Votes: 1928 Re-Examined* (University Park, Pa., 1962).

[20] The members of this committee are Robert W. Fogel, Lionel W. McKenzie, Frederick Mosteller, William O. Aydelotte, Oscar Handlin, and Allan G. Bogue.

[21] Robert A. Dahl, loc. cit., note 3.

[22] James C. Malin, op. cit., note 14. Professor Malin's position on historiographic problems is developed in *Essays on Historiography* (Lawrence, 1946), and in *On the Nature of History: Essays about History and Dissidence* (Lawrence, 1954).

[23] Social Science Research Council, *Theory and Practice in Historical Study: A Report of the Committee on Historiography, Bulletin 54* (New York, 1946); *The Social Sciences in Historical Study: A Report of the Committee on Historiography, Bulletin 64* (New York, 1954); Louis Gottschalk, ed., *Generalization in the Writing of History: A Report of the Committee on Historical Analysis of the Social Science Research Council* (Chicago, 1963).

[24] Hays 'New Possibilities', loc. cit.

[25] Thomas C. Cochran, *The Inner Revolution: Essays on the Social Sciences in History* (New York, 1964), p. 142.

[26] Austin Ranney, 'The Utility and Limitations of Aggregate Data in the Study of Electoral Behavior', in Austin Ranney, ed., *Essays on the Behavioral Study of Politics* (Urbana, 1962), discusses the problems inherent in the use of aggregate data.

[27] Gösta Carlsson comments on the 'timelessness' of much social theory in 'Time and Continuity in Mass Attitude Change: The Case of Voting', *Public Opinion Quarterly*, Spring 1965.

[28] Ithiel De Sola Pool, *Trends in Content Analysis: Papers, Work Conference on Content Analysis* (Urbana, 1959), is a relatively recent survey of the state of the technique.

[29] Hays, 'Politics of Reform', loc. cit., p. 166.

[30] John Higham, 'The Cult of the "American Consensus": Homogenizing Our History', *Commentary*, February 1959, p. 94.

[31] Lee Benson, 'Quantification, Scientific History, and Scholarly Innovation', *AHA Newsletter*, June 1966, p. 12.

APPENDIX A

Notes on the Organization of Research in Contemporary History

I

IN THE NETHERLANDS
by F. Tichelman

In the Netherlands the study of contemporary history forms part of the activities of a number of institutes whose work either covers a longer or shorter period or a specialized field.

The theory of contemporary history has not yet been studied extensively. Two small publications on this subject are worth mentioning:

Professor Dr J. Presser, *Historia modierna* (Leiden, 1950), an inaugural address delivered in Amsterdam in 1950.

Professor Dr A. E. Cohen, *Problemen van de historiografie van de tweede wereldoorlog* (Problems of the historiography of the Second World War).

The present report contains information on:

1. Institutes chiefly aiming at research.
2. Teaching institutes which assist staff and students of the history departments of several universities.
3. Professorships specifically in contemporary history and dealing with contemporary history in the context of a wider field.
4. Other relevant activities, e.g. institutes dealing with contemporary history as part of their work, societies and committees publishing source material, monographs, and/or periodicals on or related to contemporary history.

No attempt has been made to include all institutes and professorships that may touch upon contemporary history as an aspect influencing their field of studies (economics, political science, social studies).

I. INSTITUTES CHIEFLY AIMING AT RESEARCH

(a) *International Instituut voor Sociale Geschiedenis*
(International Institute of Social History)
This collects material (archives, books, pamphlets, periodicals, etc.) on social history from the beginning of the labour movement. It publishes sources, bibliographies, and monographs mainly based on the material available. It also publishes the *International Review of Social History*, a periodical appearing three times a year. The material is made available to scholars and students and is sometimes used for radio or television broadcasts. Examples of recent publications are:
The Trotsky Papers 1917–1922. Edited and annotated by Jan M. Meijer, vol. I (The Hague, 1964).
Mouvements ouvriers et crise économique 1929–1939. Edited by Mme Denise Fauvel (Assen, 1965).

(b) *Rijksinstituut voor Oorlogsdocumentatie*
(Netherlands State institute for War Documentation)
Established in 1945, this institute collects material about the Second World War (archives, books, pamphlets, periodicals, etc.). It publishes the principal sources and monographs about various aspects of the German occupation of the Netherlands dealing with actions of the occupation forces as well as the activities of the Dutch Resistance. It is preparing a complete history of the Second World War in the Netherlands and her colonies.

The collection is used by students, but also to assist in the prosecution of war criminals and to establish the legal claims of war victims.

The institute plays an important part in providing information for television documentary programmes and in assisting teachers of history. Examples of recent publications are:
Professor Dr J. Presser, *De ondergang. De vervolging en verdelging van het Nederlandse jodendom 1940–1945* (The history of the persecution and destruction of the Dutch Jews 1940–1945) (The Hague, 1965).
B. A. Sijes, *De arbeidsinzet* (The history of conscription of labour 1940–1945) (The Hague, 1966).

2. TEACHING INSTITUTES

(a) *University of Amsterdam*

Documentatiecentrum voor Nieuwste Geschiedenis
(Documentation Centre for Contemporary History)
Collects printed material about contemporary history from about 1900.

Oosteuropa Instituut
(East European Institute)
Collects printed material about Russia from 1900, in particular about the history of the Soviet Union and the other Slavonic countries from 1945. Edits the quarterly East European Series of the *Internationale Spectator* (see under 4, 'Other activities').

Sociologisch-historisch Seminarium voor Zuidoost Azië
(Seminar for the Study of the Sociology and History of South East Asia).
Collects printed material about South and South East Asia, chiefly of the twentieth century.

(b) *University of Nijmegen* (Roman Catholic)
Instituut voor nieuwe Geschiedenis
(Institute of Modern History)
This institute has a department for contemporary history and is building up a library and collecting material on current affairs.

(c) *University of Utrecht*
Instituut voor Geschiedenis
(Historical Institute)
  (i) *Sectie Nieuwste Geschiedenis*
      (Section of Contemporary History)
      Collects printed material from 1870.
  (ii) *Geluidsarchief*
      (Library of recorded sound)
      Collects gramophone and tape-recordings mainly in the field of Dutch political, social, and economic history from about 1930. Contains an extensive section on the Second World War, e.g. the complete recording of the transmissions of 'Radio Oranje', London.

3. PROFESSORSHIPS

(a) *Specifically in contemporary history*

University of Amsterdam
Professorship in the Political, Social, and Economic History of the Twentieth Century.
University of Nijmegen
Professorship in World History of the Twentieth Century.
University of Utrecht
Professorship in General History from 1870.

(b) *Touching upon contemporary history as part of a wider field*
University of Amsterdam
Professorship in General and Dutch History since the Middle Ages.
Professorship in Economic History.
Professorship in Russian History and Russian Studies.
Professorship in Sociology and Modern History of the non-Western Nations.
Vrije Universiteit Amsterdam
(Free University [Reformed])
Professorship in General and Dutch Modern History.
Professorship in Economic and Social History.
University of Groningen
Professorship in Modern History, including Contemporary History.
University of Leiden
Professorship in Modern General History.
Professorship in Modern Dutch History.
Readership in Social History.
Professorship in the History of the Far East.
University of Nijmegen
Professorship in Social and Economic History.
University of Economics Rotterdam
(Nederlandse Economische Hogeschool)
Professorship in Economic and Social History.
University of Economics Tilburg
(Katholieke Economische Hogeschool)
Professorship in Political, Social and Economic History (chiefly from 1870 to 1945).
Agricultural University Wageningen
(Landbouwhogeschool)
Professorship in Agricultural History.

4. OTHER ACTIVITIES

Rijks Geschiedkundige publicatiën, The Hague
(National historical publications)
Publishes sources, including documents concerning Dutch foreign
policy in the nineteenth and twentieth centuries.

*Commissie voor Bronnenpublicatie betreffende de geschiedenis van
Nederlands-Indië 1900–1942* (Commission for the publication of
sources concerning the history of the Dutch East Indies)
Publishes sources, e.g. *Het Onderwijsbeleid in Nederlands Indië
1900–1940* (Education policy in the Dutch East Indies 1900–1940).

Genootschap voor Internationale Zaken, The Hague
(Society for International Affairs)
Publishes fortnightly *De Internationale Spectator* which deals with
current international affairs.

Studie- en Documentatiecentrum voor Latijns Amerika, University
of Amsterdam (Study and Documentation Centre for Latin
America)
Collects printed material and publishes the *Boletino informativo*
containing bibliographical material and information on current
research.

Economisch-Historische Bibliotheek, Amsterdam
(Library for the Study of Economic History)
Collects chiefly printed material on economic history.

Nederlands Economisch Historisch Archief, The Hague
(Dutch Archive for Economic History)
Collects archive material on economic history.

Afrika Studie Centrum, Leiden
(Study Centre for Africa)
Collects printed material on Africa. Publishes *Kroniek van Afrika,*
a quarterly review mainly on contemporary African affairs.

Instituut voor het Moderne Nabije Oosten, University of Amsterdam
(Institute for the study of the Near East in modern times)
Collects printed material.

Polemologisch Instituut Groningen, University of Groningen
(Research Institute on War and Peace)
Publishes the periodical *Nieuwe literatuur over Oorlog en Vrede*

and bibliographical information concerning recent literature on war and peace.

II

IN AUSTRIA

by Ludwig Jedlicka

There are at present in Austria two institutions concerned with research into contemporary history. They co-operate closely to avoid overlapping. They complement each other especially in the field of the contemporary history of Austria, including of course Austro-German relations and, in the widest sense, Austria's connections with its other neighbours. For example, a very promising collaboration with the Prague Institute for Political Science and Contemporary History is under way, as also is one with the Historical Institute of the Hungarian Academy of Sciences. It is planned to prepare joint editions of documents on the history of the inter-war period.

I. THE AUSTRIAN INSTITUTE OF CONTEMPORARY HISTORY

This was founded in 1960 and is staffed at present by only two academicians, a number which it would seem urgently necessary to increase in order to develop the institute. It is financed by annual subsidies from the Federal Ministry of Education, and studies are undertaken for it by holders of research scholarships.

At a conference of experts held from 14–16 December 1960 on the theme 'Austrian contemporary history as a subject of historical teaching', the then Federal Minister, Dr Drimmel, outlined the institute's proposed functions as follows:

The Institute of Contemporary History will not work behind closed doors, but expects to operate in the same manner as this gathering. It will be responsible for carefully collecting materials, classifying documents, and organizing the output of publications. Above all I trust that it will obtain and place on record, while there is still time, using the technique of the modern interview, statements from those eye-witnesses of recent history who have not managed to record their testimony for posterity in book form. The witnesses of this period are always diminishing in number. Perhaps we shall also one day publish a journal, as is already done at Munich.

But the Institute's work must also go hand in hand with what is taught in our schools and universities, and I hope therefore that academic teachers will co-operate in the work of the Institute. Co-operation of this sort is one of the Institute's most important obligations.

The following organization was set up to cover the allocation of work within the institute:

(1) Library,
(2) Research department,
(3) Publications department.

On 1 January 1966 the library contained about 6,000 titles, mainly comprising, as well as works on general history, works dealing with Austrian history since 1914, the basis of a specialized collection. Especial emphasis was laid on party and ideological history, Austrian military organizations, biography, etc. It has already been enriched by donations from Austria and foreign countries, including the German Federal Republic, Czecho-slovakia, France, and the USA. As exchanges take place with other bodies and with the increase in the institute's own publications, the library will very quickly grow still further. Recent acquisitions include a large number of political pamphlets, booklets, and news-papers bearing on the history of the first Austrian Republic: this valuable source material is in course of being classified and utilized. The library is open to the public but is more especially at the disposal of students of the University of Vienna. Space is available to cover the needs of the next two years.

The main task of the research department is, in close collabora-tion with the lectures and seminars given by the director of the institute, to collect material for purposes of historical analysis over and above that contained in the official archives. This consists for the most part of the private papers of political personalities, many of which have been obtained by the institute either permanently or on loan. Since the institute was founded, statements have been taken from such personalities both in writing and by tape-recordings, gramophone records of historical importance are also collected. Annexed to the research department are collections of photographs, pamphlets and posters, and newspapers (the last in course of formation). The department's main purpose is to form an information centre for documents on recent Austrian history and for research projects in this field. These requirements in turn dictate subjects of practical research. By 1 January 1966 seminars had been conducted on 370 subjects recorded in the institute, eighteen theses had been approved, and twenty-six more were in preparation.

In accordance with the peculiar requirements of research into contemporary history it was necessary to spend two years examining German archives stored in the United States and now available on microfilm for material on Austria So far, 326 rolls of film have been purchased from this source and thirty-six more ordered, and four microfilms have been made by the institute itself All this valuable material can now be studied with the aid of the institute's microreaders This extensive and so far unexploited material on recent Austrian history will fill important gaps during the next few years

The institute's publications deal with specific problems of recent history and are also intended to assist the further training of secondary school teachers The authors and subjects to date are:

Gottlieb Ladner:

Seipel's Role in Surmounting the Crisis of the Summer of 1922

Erwin Steinbock:

The Carinthian Home Guard and the Volunteer Units.

Josef Hofmann:

The Pfrimer Putsch and the Trial of the Styrian Heimwehr in 1931.

Grete Klingenstein:

The Lausanne Loan: a Contribution to the History of the First Republic in 1931–1934.

In addition, material brought from Prague by the director of the institute on the subject of Dollfuss's murder was published in 1965 by the Europa-Verlag, Vienna, under the title *The Rising of the Austrian Nazis in July 1934.* Professor Jedlicka's book *The twentieth of July 1944 in Austria* (Vienna, and Munich, 1965) was partly based on the institute's archives.

In 1962 the institute was entrusted with the task of compiling an account of the Austrian resistance movement. By 1964 about 10,000 pages of judicial and police records and other archives had been scrutinized and a large card index compiled.

The institute is intended to include in its purview the whole of the twentieth century, including the political history of the First World War, still much neglected in Austria. Special attention is also paid to the history of parties and ideologies between the wars, and post-war history down to the State Treaty of 1955.

2. THE VIENNA UNIVERSITY INSTITUTE OF CONTEMPORARY HISTORY

In 1966, at the instance of the board of professors of the philosophical faculty of the University of Vienna, a new chair of recent and contemporary history was created, its first incumbent being Professor Jedlicka. On 3 June the University Institute of Contemporary History was founded, with Professor Jedlicka at its head. This has led to close co-operation with the neighbouring Austrian Institute of Contemporary History, which, however, retains its independent status. In practice, the University Institute will take over the organization of lectures and seminars, and will have the task of assigning theses or the diploma studies provided for in the new organization of higher education in Austria. At the same time, a broad initiative will be developed in close co-operation with the other historical institutes of the Austrian universities. The foundation of the University Institute also makes possible the best possible use of documents from the state archives. It is planned in future to bring out the publications of the Austrian Institute of Contemporary History jointly with those of the University Institute. The latter so far has a research assistant and a librarian. Fortunately it was possible during the summer term of 1966 to secure sufficient accommodation for both institutes at Rotenhausgasse 6, Vienna 9.

I

SOME PROBLEMS OF RESEARCH
IN EUROPEAN ARCHIVES

by Leo Kahn

If this paper pays almost exclusive attention to the German records of the period from the end of the First to the end of the Second World War, the reason is simply that they are, with some exceptions, free of any general restrictions on access. Insofar as the study of European history of that time has been using primary sources at all it has had to rely predominantly on German records. They are not, of course, the only primary sources to hand, and as 'closed periods' expire and restrictions are relaxed, their special status will gradually disappear. For the time being, however, they are the best means of illustrating some basic problems with which the study of contemporary history is faced if it aspires to be, in any sense, a scientific discipline.

It was the total defeat of Germany in 1945, and the policy of unconditional surrender, which made a vast amount of official documentary material almost immediately accessible to historians. In theory at least, the student of the 1918 to 1945 period could check his own and his contemporaries' experiences and impressions, and the interpretations suggested by modern political science, sociology, and psychology against the evidence of public records, and vice versa. But it can hardly be said that historical research has been able to make full use of this opportunity. The fact that documents are 'accessible', i.e. not subject to a closed period or other legal restrictions, does not, of course, mean that they are 'available' in the sense that a scholar can find the material relevant to his research without spending much more time and effort than he can afford in practice. The same circumstances which created the opportunity militated against its systematic exploitation. The captured documents, torn away from the orderly process of gradual transfer from originating department to record office, were found to have been dispersed to a great number of provisional repositories all over the world, more often than not taken out of their proper order for extraneous purposes, and not seldom handled by persons with little or no training for the job. There was no co-ordinated effort to preserve and catalogue all this material for historical research.

This is not to say that the challenge of the situation was entirely ignored. Immensely valuable work has been done in respect of a number of individual archives or collections. The Whaddon Hall project on German Foreign Ministry records, the microfilming programme and preparation of guides at Alexandria, Virginia, the cataloguing of the *NSDAP Hauptarchiv* at the Hoover Institution, and the processing of Nuremberg Documents at the Institut für Zeitgeschichte, Munich, and other centres are outstanding instances. But even such large and costly programmes, carried out by experts, did not entirely succeed in making their subject matter sufficiently 'available', even if we agree that it is neither necessary nor desirable to 'coddle the researcher'.

About the German Foreign Ministry records Raymond J. Sontag wrote seven years ago:[1]

For most scholars, the documents that are finally selected for publication will suffice. Those who wish more exhaustive documentation will find a wider selection on the special microfilm prepared for the editors in chief, together with the information needed to secure still further documentation. If the heroic researcher is not exhausted by then, the documents identified on the note card will undoubtedly contain references to still other documents, which the scholar may (or may not) be able to track down in the film collection. But anyone trained to the standards of exact research by the individual scholar is bound, in the end, to admit defeat in face of the overwhelming size of modern official archives. Co-operative research has many defects, but no scholar could, by himself, sift the evidence on any major problem in the history of nazi foreign policy, either from the microfilm or from the documents themselves, as they are now filed.

Although considerable progress[2] has since been made and is continuing, these words are still essentially true and apply *mutatis mutandis* to many other document holdings—not to mention the substantial number of collections to which there are as yet no finding aids at all.

As for the huge miscellaneous material microfilmed in Alexandria, Va., it is recognized that the existing guides are only a first step, albeit a very important and indispensable one.[3] At the moment, a general 'guide to the guides' as well as a detailed index to the guides are in preparation.

Perhaps the most striking example of an unsatisfactory situation despite great individual efforts is provided by the records of the Nuremberg trials. Trials have potentially an especially high value as historical evidence. As a rule, a document is proof only of the fact that a certain statement was made by a certain person at a particular time and place, and possibly that this statement was received by other persons. It is, at best, only *prima facie* evidence of the truth, purpose, and significance of the statement (a truism which is all too often ignored). In legal proceedings, on the other hand, a document is evaluated in the light of corroborating and conflicting evidence of all kinds. Admittedly, the legal rules of evidence are necessarily different from the principles of historical inquiry, and the 'legally established facts' may therefore well differ from 'historical truth', but as long as this is borne in mind there is no doubt that the documents, read together with the transcription of the proceedings in which they were discussed, are an incomparably better source than the documents alone. Yet, whilst we have a fairly adequate index to the proceedings of the Nuremberg International Military Tribunal, those of the twelve 'subsequent trials' are still an almost completely uncharted sea. The records of hundreds of other important trials are not even accessible.

It need hardly be pointed out that these deficiencies were to a large extent inevitable. The cataloguing[4] of such huge collections, each containing a great diversity of subject matter, would have required an apparatus far beyond the means which the organizations concerned had at their disposal. Things were easier where the terms of reference were more limited and clearly defined.

Such institutes as the Rijkinstituut voor Oorlogsdocumentatie, Amsterdam, or the Centre de Documentation Juive Contemporaine, Paris, have achieved, or are in sight of achieving, a cataloguing position which will satisfy all reasonable demands.

The bulk of the original German documents which survived the accidents of war and evacuation and fell into American or British hands has now been returned to the Federal Republic, and most of the records which were left in Germany in places where they did not belong have found their way into the official record offices. A large number of archives and collections were handed over to the East German authorities from the Soviet Union, Poland, and other Eastern European countries, but few details are yet known. Considerable holdings of original German documents still exist in other formerly German-occupied countries. Although, broadly speaking, the majority of German records are now in permanent repositories and will in due course enjoy the advantages of orderly archival administration, the situation is still one of considerable complexity and confusion. The reports of the Foreign Documents Centre of the Imperial War Museum, London,[5] provisional as they are, may indicate this situation clearly enough to make further elaboration at this point unnecessary. There are, however, some general points which should be mentioned.

1. It will take decades before all the millions of documents which were rushed into the German state archives during a comparatively very short period can be properly arranged in *fonds d'archives* and adequately catalogued. On the other hand, these records are legally accessible and their inspection is urgently demanded, not only by historians, but also by economists, political scientists, lawyers, and others with equally legitimate interests. The archivist is therefore constantly confronted with a choice of priorities, and his choice, if it is not to be entirely arbitrary, will be based on what he conceives to be the essential character of contemporary history and the most urgent requirements of research. His decisions will materially affect the research facilities of the academic historian, but although archivists are acutely aware of the problem it has attracted very little attention in academic circles.

2. Similar reflections arise from another aspect of modern archival work. It is now generally recognized that official records are not the only, and in many cases not even the most important, sources on which historical research should be based. This applies particularly in the case of the German record holdings, which are hardly ever complete and require supplementary material in order to satisfy the demands of the researcher. Almost all German state archives are therefore collecting material which is related to the *fonds d'archives* in accordance with the principle of 'pseudo-provenance'. One has tried to find a reasonably narrow definition of the kind of collection which can be brought under this head,[6] but logically the limits can be extended almost at will. On the other hand, the resources of even the largest record offices are limited. Again we have a problem of choice with which the discipline of history as a whole is vitally concerned. The historian of the remote past must reconcile himself to the fact that history consists of the

records which happen to have been preserved. The contemporary historian can and should take an active part in creating the body of documentary material on which he is to exercise his craft. It may be mentioned in passing that, although this broadening of the archivist's activities is on the whole a welcome development, it also tends to blur the distinction between his proper function and that of historical research institutes, and thus on occasion adds to the confusion of the scholar in search of his sources.

3. The inclusion of collections on a fairly large scale gives prominence to another problem of archive administration. It is still the primary function of public record offices to preserve and list the records of the originating offices in the general order in which they were created. Obviously, collections cannot be dealt with in this way. Some system of subject classification is required—an additional, stiff task for offices already over-burdened with work.

In the case of the official records of the nazi regime, the need for subject classification exists even where it is possible to restore the original file order. The reason for this lies in the peculiar character of the regime, in which personal rule and a one-party system were not substituted for but superimposed on the administrative structure of a constitutional federal state, with the result of constant shifts of responsibility. Sontag touches upon this aspect in the article already mentioned:

From 1936 the problem of reconstructing the story of German diplomacy from the Foreign Office Archives becomes unbelievably complex. In the first place, the Archives never contained all the evidence. Policy was determined by Hitler, and he did not always take even the higher officials of the Foreign Office into his confidence. The execution of policy was often entrusted to party representatives, intelligence officers, or the military; evidence of their activity reached the Foreign Office Archives only by accident.

The difficulty is perhaps even more apparent in such contexts as economic affairs, the administration of justice, and police matters. The students cannot rely on finding the documentation of any particular issue in the files of obviously responsible departments, he may need an index in order to find out first which offices or persons may have been responsible. As Martin Broszat aptly comments,[7]

Since there is no conceivable prospect of computers and machines taking over the indexing of historical documents (this being a task that demands

343

both knowledge of the subject and ability to abstract) it will be a long while before the archives are completely opened up. In the meantime the historian will have to go on relying on lucky finds. For modern archives are not only mines of information but also excellent places of concealment.

So far, the attempts to introduce systematic subject classification have not been very successful. This is not surprising in view of the mass of material to be processed. In order to deal adequately with the 'paper explosion' of our times, we shall have to resort to the most modern methods of data storage and retrieval.

For while it is true that modern machinery cannot take over the indexing itself it can efficiently integrate the work done by skilled individual indexers into large, central finding aids. However, the programming and installation of even the smallest system of this kind is such an expensive affair that it should only be undertaken on a national or, preferably, on an international basis. As a preliminary step this would require the devising of an internationally acceptable classification scheme, which in itself is a formidable, though by no means impossible, enterprise. Useful spadework has been done in this direction within the framework of the International Council on Archives and in informal working groups formed by representatives of leading European record offices. The discussions are continuing, and it may well be that they will lead to concrete proposals in the not too distant future, but this seems to be another matter which should not be left entirely to the archival profession.

It is surely evident from all this that as far as research into primary sources is concerned, contemporary history must deal not only with the often debated issue of freer access, but also with other special problems which call for a collective effort and the formation of a body to bridge the existing gulf between academic historians and archivists. Specifically, the possible functions of such a body may be summarized as follows:

(a) to sponsor the preparation of comprehensive guides to documentary sources, in co-operation with offices which are already active in this field;
(b) to sponsor courses and textbooks for the purpose of instructing academically trained but inexperienced researchers in the proper use of modern archive facilities;
(c) to advise public record offices systematically on the question

which *fonds* are most urgently needed for research and should therefore be catalogued with priority;

(*d*) to work out proposals for classification schemes suitable for international central indexes of document holdings.

NOTES

[1] *Guide to the Diplomatic Archives of Western Europe*, edited by Daniel H. Thomas and Lynn M. Chase (Philadelphia, 1959).

[2] e.g., the publication of the first three volumes of *A Catalogue of Files and Microfilms of the German Foreign Ministry Archives* (1920–1945), by George O. Kent (Stanford, California, 1962, 1964, 1966), and the archival work carried out in the Politisches Archiv des Auswärtigen Amtes, Bonn, and the Foreign Office Library, London.

[3] For a balanced assessment of the merits and defects of the Alexandria project see Wilhelm Rohr, 'Mikroverfilmung und Verzeichnung deutscher Akten in Alexandria, USA', *Der Archivar*, vol. 19, No. 3, July 1966.

[4] The term is used in the general sense of the German 'erschliessen'.

[5] So far four reports, on repositories in Great Britain, the German Federal Republic, Italy, and the German Democratic Republic have been issued. A comprehensive register of centres containing German records of the 1918–45 period is being kept at the FDC. It already lists more than 150 centres, and it is far from complete.

[6] cp. Hans Booms, 'Grenzen und Gliederungen zeitgeschichtlicher Dokumentationen, *Der Archivar*, vol. 19, No. 1, February 1966.

[7] Martin Broszat 'New Focus—1: Nazism', *The Times Literary Supplement*, 8 September 1966, p. 829.

II

A MARGINAL NOTE ON SOVIET ARCHIVES

by John Erickson

Since this is nothing but a number of observations on a limited experience of a particular Soviet archive in a particular field—'war history' (by which I mean more than mere military narrative and include both political and social aspects)—then it bears the classification of a mere marginal note. The reason for presenting it lies in the possibility that such experience may be generalized to some degree and may therefore provide items of interest or utility to

CONTEMPORARY HISTORY IN EUROPE

those concerned with the formidable problem of access to Soviet records. Not that the psychological problem is itself so unique: the Soviet addiction to a kind of bureaucratic secrecy is just about the same as the British, so that the ground, whether Muscovy or Whitehall, has a certain familiarity. Yet this disadvantage is offset by genuine and persistent assistance by individual scholars and specialists in the Soviet Union, who will take a great deal of trouble to discuss the form of an investigation and how it might be pursued, both from printed and original sources. At this point I should like to dispense with the institutional formality of 'archive' and speak rather of 'original material', whether privately or publicly lodged, for this has proved in my own case to be a distinction of some relevance.

I. THE PROBLEM OF LOCATION

In the absense of catalogues one has to devise one's own. For that reason, there is no alternative but to work through printed Soviet sources to uncover the type of material and to begin what is, in effect, a catalogue. The study of the archival footnotes in Soviet monographs can yield much useful information. For example, in recent studies of Soviet military policy in the 1920s two reputable works used the same document, quoted *in extenso*, so that comparison was possible, but with quite different citations for archive call numbers. This suggests different collections of the same material, so that if one is closed, the other—for quite arbitrary reasons—may be accessible. The only way to investigate this is to tackle the Soviet scholars concerned and ask them, and the answers are usually forthcoming (even if they are not, there is courtesy enough for one to be handed on to someone who can answer the point). In this instance, the answer lay in the fact that one author was using the party archives, the other the military archives and I have found the military historians on the whole to be very responsive to serious professional exchanges. The reason also for insisting on 'original materials' is that personal interview with an active participant in an event may lead to his presenting papers and records from his 'personal records', for which permission to copy may or may not be forthcoming (as anywhere else). The fact that this material is highly regarded may be supported by the presence in Soviet periodicals of notices asking individuals to send their records for use in particular projects (after which they are returned). Obviously, this has particular application in the field of military history, but it is not always 'military men' *per se* who have these records.

At first sight, this would seem to make the problem of 'access' even more difficult—involving time, space, and distribution. These can nevertheless be compressed by resort to the printed source, then to the specialist, and then to the individual. Speaking personally, I have never found a Russian who would volunteer information 'off the cuff', but once shown that one knew the sources available very well, the result was prompt and extensive co-operation. There is, therefore, one practical suggestion which I would wish to put forward: that journals devote some small section to the type of materials 'liberated' in Soviet writing, so that there is wider (and more comparative) knowledge of what stirs in the undergrowth of Soviet footnotes. In the field of foreign policy studies, this is a particularly good time to embark upon this. Here one has to point to the relevance of estimating what use Soviet historians make of captured enemy materials and how they are distributed—into which collections, whether 'originals' or whether copies obtained from our collections. A good example is L. N. Kutakov's *Istoriya Sovetskoyaponskikh diplomaticheskikh otnoshenii* (Moscow, 1962) on German-Japanese relations, and the use he makes of non-Soviet materials.

2. THE 'SUB-COLLECTIONS'

Although each institution and organ has it archive (Ministry of Foreign Affairs, Defence, etc.), in the interests of Soviet research and Soviet projects 'sub-collections' have been made and centred on institutes. This applies specifically in the field of military-political research—e.g., there are the Ministry of Defence archives, the archives used by the Historical Section of the General Staff under Major-General Grylev, the archives of arms and services (all of which are operational sectors and hence sensitive) but the 'History of the Great Patriotic War' project has in the Marx-Lenin Institute its own giant archive concerned with 'war history 1941–45' in the widest sense. Before discussing this in greater detail, I should like to make some remarks on the work and disposition of the Historical-Scientific Section of the Soviet General Staff, headed, until his death in 1964, by General Platonov and now under Major-General Grylev. Both of these officers worked as historians in the formal sense, and their staff included excellent military historians working in diverse fields—Soviet and non-Soviet. These specialists were never averse to extensive discussion, usually of the highest professional standard, and would willingly discuss sources (the presence and the lack of them) with all the professional candour and command found elsewhere. In addition, the group of military historians associated with *Voenno-istoricheskii Zhurnal*, edited by Major-General Pavlenko, exhibited the same degree of co-operation and candour. (I hesitate to quote from personal experience, but one item was of great importance to my own work: the problem of the Soviet (and German) strategic planning in 1942 is, to say the least, complex and here I was able to go through the Soviet side with a Soviet specialist who made specific comment about, criticism of, and recommendation for source material. The problem in this context was—and presumably is—that certain materials have not been de-classified for general study by *Soviet* historians and thus it is difficult to show a non-Soviet historian what the native scholars have not seen in the original. Even so, in support of one issue, I was shown such material, and, lest the cynic think I was deliberately fed, I was allowed to select and to take whatever notes I wished although under no circumstances might I photo-copy. In this instance I wished to see some specific orders of Marshal Zhukov and I saw them to what was my own satisfaction. There is one 'war history' archive I should like to see (all separately catalogued to judge by the citations) and that is the Academy of Sciences archive, presumably of special materials and studies (collected, I am inclined to think, for the big war history which Soviet scholars thought they were going to write immediately after 1945).

The Marx-Lenin 'Great Patriotic War' collection may well be typical of Soviet 'sub-collections' (by which I mean to distinguish archives attached to their institutions as opposed to specially formed record centres). In organization, it consisted of a major library of printed sources (Soviet and non-Soviet), an impressive newspaper and contemporary print (journals, magazines, regional newspapers, etc.) library, and an archive proper of original documents. The mass of material was enormous, but the control system was simple and efficient: there were two card indexes, for each day of the war, with cards registering each 'item' for a particular day (e.g., meeting of Supreme Soviet, battle report X, Y, Z Fronts, information on the rear) and the cross-reference against the document: thus one could 'scan' the war either by day or by document.

To take an example: under industrial evacuation, there was (a) the decisions of the State Defence Committee (GKO), (b) the organization and activity of the 'Soviet for Evacuation', and (c) the related materials—railways, administrative reports, local reports, military co-operation, etc. This could also be looked at by region—Leningrad, Moscow, the south (or by date, if one wished). Obviously it would take years (as it has taken Soviet historians) to work through this on any systematic scale—and this is the collection which is footnoted in the six-volume history as 'Great Patriotic War Collection'. What I could not discern was how the captured enemy materials were integrated into this collection (though such materials were used): presumably there was a separate index, and in one set of papers I came across large numbers of reports on the German war economy and war industry by Speer (these were photostats and may have come from another Soviet archive, either military (Defence) or Foreign Ministry). Because of this 'redistribution', some of the documents are typewritten copies of originals, attested as such by the officers of the main or parent archive, and even in a main archive (Defence) there are typed copies for actual *handling* (and also what looked like Xerox copies): since the originals are incontestably fragile in many cases (on very thin, almost transparent paper), there is obviously some need for preservation.

3. ACCESS

It was frequently pointed out to me, as it has been to many others, that it was only in 1957 that Soviet scholars really got access to their archives (after the resolution of the Twentieth Party Congress) and that one major task was to sort out the confusion. To judge by the evidence in the 'sub-collections' and from description of the Defence archives, this confusion has now been well and truly overcome, but then there is the ever-present problem of access for Soviet scholars, who, apparently, are not short of complaints on this score. Wider access for Soviet scholars may well mean less inhibition for the non-Soviet researcher. It goes without saying that the choice of theme or area of interest is of crucial importance (to Soviet and non-Soviet researcher alike), though it is quite impossible to draw up any rules of predictability about what might or might not be acceptable. There are many parts of wartime history which are far from palatable for the Russians, yet when it 'comes to the crunch' I found far less reticence than I might have expected. Does this mean that there is in fact a whole sector where the non-Soviet researcher might operate well *inside* Soviet constraints ? The answer would seem, in my estimation, to be in the negative, that the 'rule' (if there is one) is that increased Soviet access is the key, and benevolence to non-Russians is an off-shoot.

At least one major point I proved (with a little persistence) to my own satisfaction: that the Russians respond to the argument that 'verbal evidence' itself is not enough, no matter how distinguished the source. (Conversely, a very senior Soviet diplomatic historian advised me, indeed prompted me, to seek verbal confirmation of written evidence from the participant—and did not let august rank stand at all in the way of his suggestion. It proved to be both feasible and profitable.)

Under this heading, I should like to present a few points which may serve to promote the cause of 'access', though I imagine it to be a long haul, yet one with the prospect of success :

(*a*) a more consistent attention in journals to 'Soviet archives', that is, to covering topics and areas in which original material is being released systematically (and hence in which the problem of Soviet access is at least solved),

(*b*) the approach through institutes (*Institut Istorii* of the Academy) on an individual basis, for although institutional patronage may be slow it is more sure,

(*c*) in connection with (*b*), the development of close contact with individual Soviet specialists, who themselves command the field,

(*d*) exhaustive screening and analysis of printed sources,

(*e*) the exploration of the possibility of 'participant-interview'.

It would be precipitate to do other than to repeat that this is based on limited experience in a limited sector, yet it is legitimate to report upon the results of that experience. It was *always* of the greatest value to be shown the special library collections: it was essential before embarking on discussion of materials to have command of what was extant: it was possible to check 'statement' with 'fact' and to initiate an inquiry which led to the sources: in a number of instances, prime materials were in the hands of individuals who were prepared to produce them. Of things most valuable, I would submit that the detailed discussions with Soviet specialists served me best, and here I was shown every co-operation and courtesy, which professionals best demonstrate amongst themselves. (In the matter of the forensic evidence on Hitler's death, I was shown far more than I wished.)

In the field of contemporary history there is clearly increased scope for co-operative ventures, the terms of which might be more fully explored and here 'exchange' would be at a premium. It may be that the greatest break-through could be contrived here, though from personal experience I am aware of the duration of the negotiations involved, and it is here that a knowledge of Soviet access to Soviet archives (original materials) is of great importance, for one is obliged to make realistic requests. In this context, publications such as *Istochnikovedenie istorii Sovetskovo obshchestva*, Moscow, 1964: Institut Istorii/AN SSSR, proved to be of some significance, not least for its bibliographical note on 'researching on original materials' drawn from discussions in *Novaya i noveishaya istoriya*, *Voprosy istorii KPSS*, *Voprosy istorii*, and a section entitled 'From the experience of working with historical sources' (*Iz opyta raboty s istoricheskimi istochnikami*), with one useful citation of an essay on Soviet dissertations (cf. Professor John Armstrong's previous essay on 'Soviet dissertations as a guide to the political archives'.) This particular set of essays uses the technique of showing the disparity (and concordance) of archival, printed documentary, and secondary sources with respect to several issues of Soviet history (ranging from the strength of the armed forces in 1917 to a study of the preparation of the Central Committee decree of 5 January 1930 on the pace of collectivization). Much of this type of work is apparently done in the Moscow State Historical-Archival Institute, *Moskovskii gosudarstvennyi istoriko-arkhivnyi institut*, a part of Moscow University and a centre which would possibly repay further investigation.

The 'Soviet use of Soviet archives' has by now become almost a subject in itself: much also depends on the quality of the individual scholar, and this can best be learned by first-hand contact. The first step must be the development of this contact, beneficial as it is to both sides (though I submit, with others, that there will be fields—party history, foreign policy, sensitive but unknown 'operational items'—which will be sternly guarded). Much, nevertheless, remains, and the problem is how to work out a 'protocol' to cover it.